LIFE AND LABORS
OF
BISHOP BARAGA

LIFE AND LABORS OF BISHOP BARAGA

First Bishop of Marquette, Michigan

To Which Are Added Short Sketches of the Lives and Labors of Other Indian Missionaries of the Northwest

Fr. Chrysostom Verwyst, OFM

Caritas Publishing

Imprimatur:
F. X. Katzer,
Archiepiscopus Milwauchiensis.

P. Theodorus Arentz, O. F. M.
Minister Provinciales.

First published as *Life and Labors of the Rt. Rev. Frederic Baraga*, in 1900. Republished January 19, 2017, anniversary of the passing of Bishop Baraga.

Special thanks to MJC.

ISBN: Paperback: 978-1-945275-20-3
ISBN: Hardback: 978-1-945275-21-0
Ebook: ⓒ ⓢ Always free! NOT to be sold. Share liberally. Visit caritaspublishing.com for free download. Note the ebook does not have the Chippewa or the styling of the print verson.

LIbrary of Congress Control Number: 2017931948

Rev. Father.

We forgot to ask at Eagle River, whether my <u>Deeds</u> are recorded, or not. Have the kindness to ask when you go there again, and to pay the Recorder; for the amount I could pay. Keep the deeds safe for me until a <u>sure</u> opportunity offers to send them to me. Please be careful, not to lose them.

There is an urgent necessity here to build a church up at the Iron Mines; and I see, that if I don't make a commencement, the church will never be built. So I concluded to sacrifice about $250., in order to have it up this fall. And as this is more urgent and necessary than your gallery, so I will be not able to do anything for your Cliff church this year.

Your affectionate father in Christ
Frederic Baraga

Marquette, Sept. 6. 1860.

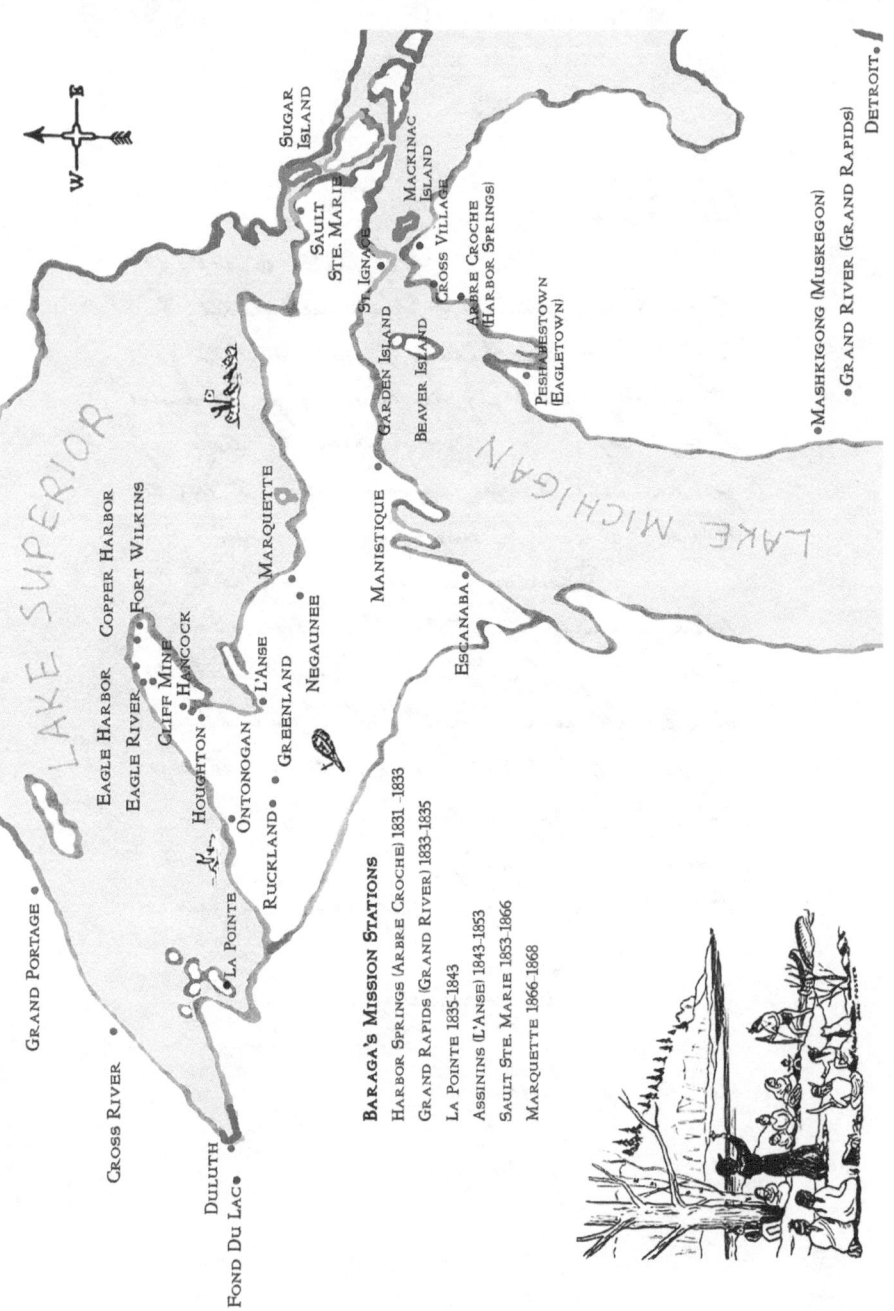

Contents

PREFACE i
CHAPTER I
  Indians of the Northwest; Their Language, Origin, Religious Beliefs and Customs. 1
CHAPTER II
  First Attempts at Evangelizing the Indians of the Northwest.—Jogues and Baymbault at Sault Ste. Marie, Mich.—Gabbeau and Dreuillettes. 9
CHAPTER III
  Father Menard; His Labors Near L'Anse, Michigan, and Death in the Wilds of Wisconsin. 12
CHAPTER IV
  Father Allouez; His Apostolic Labors in the Lake Superior Region and Other Parts of Wisconsin. 18
CHAPTER V
  The Labors of Father Marquette at the Mission of the Holy Ghost on the Shores of Chequamegon (Ashland) Bay and at St. Ignace, Mich. 21
CHAPTER VI
  Father Marquette Discovers the Mississippi; Establishes the Mission of the Immaculate Conception; His Edifying Death. 25
CHAPTER VII
  Father Gabriel Dreuillettes, S. J. ; His Labors in Maine, Canada, and Michigan. 36
CHAPTER VIII
  Missionaries That Labored in the Northwest During the Eighteenth Century. 41

CHAPTER IX
Missionary Labors of Fathers Richard, Badin, and Dejean in the Northwest Prior to the Arrival of F. Baraga. 46

CHAPTER X
State of Catholicity in the United States at the Time of Baraga's Arrival in our Country in 1830.. 56

CHAPTER XI
Description and History of Baraga's Birthplace. 62

CHAPTER XII
Birth and Early Education of Frederic Baraga; Death of His Parents; He Studies at Laibach and Vienna; Resolves to Enter the Priesthood; Studies at the Clerical Seminary at Laibach and is Ordained There.. 67

CHAPTER XIII
Father Baraga's Labors at St. Martin's. 76

CHAPTER XIV
Father Baraga's Labors at Metlika. He Resolves to Devote Himself to the Indian Missions of America; Is Received Into the Diocese of Cincinnati. Scene at His Departure from Metlika. 82

CHAPTER XV
Father Baraga Leaves Europe. Incidents of His Journey. Arrives at Cincinnati. His Labors in That City.. 89

CHAPTER XVI
Father Baraga Sets Out from Cincinnati for His Indian Mission. His Labors Among the Whites Along the Route. He Arrives at Arbre Croche. 95

CHAPTER XVII
Labors of Father Baraga in Arbre Croche. 99

CHAPTER XVIII
Father Baraga's Visit to Beaver Island. 105

CHAPTER XIX
A Letter from Some Indian Chiefs at Arbre Croche to Bishop Fenwick. Last Visit of Bishop Fenwick to Arbre Croche; His Untimely Death from Cholera; Baraga's Account of the Bishop's Death.. 111

CHAPTER XX
Continuation of F. Baraga's Labors During the Year 1832. His First Indian Prayer book Printed at Detroit. What Father Hatscher, C. SS. R., And Others Say of Him and His Work. 115

CHAPTER XXI
Baraga's Labors During 1833. Visits Little Detroit, Manistique and Beaver Island. Baptizes a Great Many Pagans During Pentecost Week at Arbre Croche. 119

CHAPTER XXII
F. Baraga's First Visit to Grand River; He Baptizes Many; Returns to Arbre Croche. Resume of His Missions. He Leaves Arbre Croche and Is Succeeded There by Rev. F. Sanderl, C. SS. R. 124

CHAPTER XXIII
Labors and Hardships of F. Baraga at Grand River.. . . . 130

CHAPTER XXIV
Description of Indian Drunkenness at Grand River; F. Babaga's Life Endangered. Indian Council. F. Baraga Dedicates His New Church. 134

CHAPTER XXV
F. Baraga Leaves Grand River Mission; Winters at St. Claire; Goes to La Pointe Wisconsin. 145

CHAPTER XXVI
F. Baraga Arrives at La Pointe, Wis.—Incidents of the Journey.—He Builds His First Church. 150

CHAPTER XXVII
Father Baraga's First Visit to Fond Du Lac (Minn.). . . 154

CHAPTER XXVIII
Baraga's Labors at La Pointe.—(Continued).. 157
CHAPTER XXIX
F. Baraga Goes to Europe.—He Is Received Everywhere with Great Distinction.—Lectures on Indian Missions.—Returns to La Pointe.— Finishes His Church.—First Confirmation in La Pointe by Bishop Rese in 1838.. 160
CHAPTER XXX
State of La Pointe Mission During 1839 and 1840. Peculiar Indian Customs at Funerals, Mode of Burial. Interesting Letter of Father Pierz. 164
CHAPTER XXXI
Baraga's Personal Appearance and Peculiar Traits of Character.—His Humility, Poverty, Kindness, Burning Zeal and Restless Activity.—La Pointe, Population, Pursuits, Early Settlers. 170
CHAPTER XXXII
Father Baraga Laments the Want of Indian Missionaries. Takes Down His Church and Builds Another Larger One. 176
CHAPTER XXXIII
Father Baraga Leaves La Pointe to Found the Mission at L'Anse, Mich. 180
CHAPTER XXXIV
Father Baraga's Labors in L'Anse Mission During the Years 1843-1844. Bishop Henni's, of Milwaukee, First Visit to La Pointe in 1844.. 184
CHAPTER XXXV
Father Baraga's Labors During 1844-45. His Long Journeys on Foot to Distant Missions.. 188
CHAPTER XXXVI
Wonderful Escape of Father Baraga, When Crossing Lake Superior in a Small Sail-Boat. His Adventure on a Floating Field of Ice. 193

CHAPTER XXXVII
Further Testimony as to F. Baraga's Work at L'Anse. Accident on Lake Huron in 1852................. 197

CHAPTER XXXVIII
Father Baraga in Detroit Superintending the Printing of Some of His Works.—Bishop Lefevre Gives Confirmation for the First Time in L'Anse.— The Indians All Take the Total Abstinence Pledge..................... 201

CHAPTER XXXIX
Opening of the Copper Mines in Northern Michigan.— Baraga Visits His New Mission.—He Labors on His Famous Chippewa Grammar and Dictionary.......... 204

CHAPTER XL
Father Baraga Goes to Fond Du Lac, Baptizes a Very Old and Blind Woman.—Suffers Much Hardship on His Return Journey................... 207

CHAPTER XLI
Continuation of F. Baraga's Labors at L'Anse in 1848 and 1849.—"The New York Observer's" Estimate of His Work.— Hardships and Dangers................. 212

CHAPTER XLII
Letter of Rt. Rev. Peter Paul Lefevre, Bishop Of Detroit. F. Baraga Gets His Grammar and Instruction Book for the Indians Printed in Detroit. New Labors. His Terrible Journey in the Winter of 1850-1851................ 220

CHAPTER XLIII
Baraga's Elevation to the Episcopal Dignity.—Sault Ste. Marie His Episcopal See.—A Short Historical Sketch of the Place and of the Missionaries Who Labored There.. . . 226

CHAPTER XLIV
Bishop Baraga's Pastoral Letter to the Faithful of His Vicariate-Apostolic Announcing His Elevation to the Episcopal Dignity..................... 231

CHAPTER XLV

Bishop Baraga's First Letter to the Leopoldine Society After His Elevation to the Episcopate.—He Goes to Europe to Secure Priests and Funds for His Infant Diocese.. . . . 241

CHAPTER XLVI

B. Baraga Returns Home.—He Goes to La Pointe, Ontonagan, and L'Anse.—First Ordination in Sault Ste. Marie. 247

CHAPTER XLVII

Labors of B. Baraga In 1856; He Visits Fort William, Grand Portage, Superior, La Pointe, and Other Places. 251

CHAPTER XLVIII

Happenings During 1857.—B. Baraga Makes His Annual Visit to the Principal Missions of His Diocese.—Interesting Communication of Hon. C. D. O'Brien. 255

CHAPTER XLIX

B. Baraga Attends the II. Provincial Council of Cincinnati and Has Three of His Indian Works Printed.—His Hardships on the Way.—He Visits the Missions of Lake Michigan and Lake Superior. 261

CHAPTER L

Death of Rev. Lautischar.—B. Baraga Visits His Mission Stations.—Arrival of Father Chebul. Baraga's Opinion in Regard to the Feasibility of Forming Indian Priests and Sisters.—Interesting Reminiscences of Rev. Father Chebul About B. Baraga.. 269

CHAPTER LI

Doings and Happenings of B. Baraga During the Year 1860.—Great Miseries on His Winter Trip to Mackinac and St. Ignace.—He Visits Superior, La Pointe and Bad River Reservation. Interesting Entries from His Journal. . . . 280

CHAPTER LII
Bishop Baraga Attends the III. Provincial Council of Cincinnati.—Hardships Endured on the Way Thither.—His Visit to the Scattered Missions of His Diocese.. 289

CHAPTER LIII
B. Baraga Writes on the Civil War.—Establishes a New Indian Mission at St. Martin's Bay.—Visits the Mission at the "Baye Des Goulais." 296

CHAPTER LIV
Bishop Baraga's Labors During the Year 1863.—Anecdotes About Bishops Baraga and Marty. 301

CHAPTER LV
Labors of B. Baraga in 1864.—Two Letters Dated Sept. 18 and Nov. 29, 1864. 306

CHAPTER LVI
Interesting Account of the Founding of the Sisters' School at L'Anse Mission.—B. Baraga's First and Last Dying Gift to the School.. 311

CHAPTER LVII
Removal of the Episcopal See from Sault Ste. Marie to Marquette.. 316

CHAPTER LVIII
Bishop Baraga's Last Sickness and Death. 321

CHAPTER LIX
Short Resume of the Life and Labors of Bishop Baraga; His Many Virtues and Accomplishments; A Model Student, Priest, Indian Missionary, and Bishop. 327

SHORT BIOGRAPHICAL SKETCHES Of Missionaries Who Have Labored Amongst the Indians of the Northwest.
Rev. Francis Pierz 335
Rev. Otto Skolla, O. S. F., St. Obs. A Short Sketch of His Labors in the Missionary Field. 347

Very Rev. Edward Jacker of the Diocese of Marquette, Mich.
A Short Sketch of His Life and Labors.. 361
Rev. Laurence Lautischar: His Short Missionary Career and
Sad Death. 366
Rev. Father Van Den Broek, O.P.: One of the Pioneer Indian
Missionaries of Wisconsin. Short Sketches of His Life and
Labors. 372

APPENDIX

UNUM EST NECESSARIUM 380
UNUM EST NECESSARIUM (Chippewa) 387
A Few Peculiarities of the Chippewa Language. 396
Historical And Biographical Notes 402
An Interesting Article on the Life and Labors of Bishop
Baraga, Copied by "The L'Anse Sentinel" from the
"Gladstone Delta" 402
A Lake Superior Historical Sketch 406
Massacre of a Dacota Peace Delegation at Sault Ste. Marie,
Upper Michigan, in the Spring of 1674. 406
Notes. 410
Short biographical sketch of Vincent Roy, lately of
Superior, Wis. 420

Novena in Honor of Bishop Baraga. 424

Preface

In presenting this "Life and Labors of Rt. Rev. Frederic Baraga" to the public, we hope that we are doing a service to religion, to the Church in the United States, and to our fellow-citizens in general. The subject of our narrative was a man of uncommon ability, learning, and piety. He distinguished himself as author of many works, written for his countrymen, for his Indian converts, and for linguistic scholars. As Indian missionary he was most wonderfully successful, having converted more Ottawas and Chippewas than any other priest the writer knows of. His converts were of the genuine kind, deeply religious, fervent, and well-behaved. If in the course of time some of them, or of their children, degenerated from their pristine fervor, it was not his fault, but the natural outcome of circumstances and environments, over which he could exercise no control, and which were detrimental to Indian moral advancement.

Bishop Baraga has won the lasting love and respect of the people of the Northwest, among whom he labored so long self-sacrificingly. To perpetuate his memory unto future generations the remembrance of his life of labor, prayer, and suffering, is the object of this work. We are well aware of its many imperfections, but we have endeavored to give the reader a perfectly reliable account of Bishop Baraga's life and labors. We have generally let him tell his own story, as there is a peculiar charm in reading the accounts he gives us of his doings and happenings. Moreover, they give us an insight into the motives and feelings that actuated him in all he did and suffered for God and the spreading of His kingdom on earth. Besides, our object is to edify the reader by the recital of the labors, trials, and success of a truly Apostolic man, a Christian gentleman in the full sense of the word, a model

Indian missionary and bishop. He united in himself the activity of Martha and the contemplativeness of Mary, being wonderful in both.

We have utilized the annual reports of the Leopoldine Society of Vienna, Austria, kindly furnished us by His Grace, Most Rev. Frederic Katzer, of Milwaukee, and Very Rev. Father Rainer, rector for many years of the Salesianum. Baraga usually wrote to the above-named society every year, giving a faithful account of his labors, trials, and success in the Indian missionary field. We have deemed it unnecessary to always designate in what annal and on which page were to be found the extracts taken from Bishop Baraga's letters. However, in most cases, we have given the dates of his letters used in the preparation of this work. As to other sources of information, we have endeavored to always mention the author's name or the social standing of our informant, thus enabling the reader to judge of the reliability of his statements. Truth the reader wants, not exaggeration, or foolish tales. Our work is but a compilation. We have put together and arranged what others personally acquainted with the saintly man have said and written. Although this work has cost us much labor, it has been a labor of love.

We owe a debt of gratitude to all those who have kindly aided us in the compilation of this work. Besides the above-named Most Rev. Archbishop and Very Rev. Rector of the Milwaukee seminary, we are under great obligation to Rt. Rev. John Vertin, Bishop of Marquette, who kindly loaned us two volumes of Baraga's journal or diary, which have been of great service to us; also to his worthy predecessor, Rt. Rev. Bishop Mrak, for information given. Moreover, we wish to give public expression of our thanks to Hon. Richard R. Elliottt, of Detroit; Hon. C. D. O'Brian, attorney-at-law, of St. Paul, Minn.; to Rev. G. Terhorst, the worthy pastor of the L'Anse Indian mission; to Rev. John Chebul, of Newberry, Mich.; Hon. Fr. Jacker and Hon. E. Edgerton, of Jacobsville, Mich., and all friends and helpers.

If we have succeeded in making saintly Bishop Baraga more known and respected, and in so doing have benefited, at least a little, the cause of religion and the well-being of society, we shall consider our labor amply rewarded.

Fr Chrysostomus Verwyst, O.F.M.,
August 15th, 1900.

Chapter I

Indians of the Northwest; Their Language, Origin, Religious Beliefs and Customs.

As the subject of our narrative, Rt. Rev. Frederic Baraga, labored long and successfully as missionary and bishop among the Ottawas of Michigan and the Chippewas of Wisconsin, a short dissertation on the language, origin, religious beliefs and customs of these Indian nations will not be out of place.

There are at present fifty-two Indian nations in the United States, each of which has a dialect of its own. These fifty-two dialects are reducible to eight distinct families of languages, each of which differs as much from the others as the Latin, Slavonic, Germanic and Celtic languages of Europe differ radically from each other. As the Latin nationalities, the Italian, French, Spanish and Portuguese speak cognate tongues, so also do the many Algonquin nations of the St. Lawrence Valley and the Lake Superior country. To the great Algonquin family belong the Algonquins, properly called, the Montagnais, the Abernakis of Maine, the Pequods and Narragansets, the Delawares, the Ottawas, the Chippewas, the Illinois, the Sacs and Foxes or Outagamies, the Pottawotamis, the Menominees, and, to some extent, also the Crees of British America, in whose language many Algonquin words are to be found. These nations— *wrongly called tribes* —once inhabited a tract of country which extended from the Atlantic on the east to the Mississippi and British Columbia on the west, and from the confines of the Esquimoes on the north to the Middle States on the south, a vast territory almost as large as Europe.

The inhabitants of this immense territory spoke *radically* the same language, each nation having a dialect of its own more or less different from the others, but radically the same as to the roots of words and the grammatical structure of the verbs. However, as in Europe, the German, Dutch, Danish and Swedish tongues are radically German, yet are now classified as so many distinct languages, so we can justly call the above-named Indian tongues so many distinct Indian languages, though radically they belong to one family.

A careful study of the Chippewa language has brought the writer to the conviction that the Indians belonging to the Algonquin family of nations must have attained to a high degree of civilization at a remote period of time and that their subsequent lapse into barbarism was due to incessant wars and migrations. Our opinion is based on the following reason: A nation's language is a true and reliable index of the mental capacity and intellectual status of its people. A barbarous, mentally undeveloped race cannot originate a systematic, Philosophically regular, grammatical language. I think this needs no proof. Now, anyone who has a grammatical knowledge of the Chippewa language, will concede that it is wonderfully systematic, regular, euphonic, plastic, and expressive. It must, therefore, have originated with a people mentally well developed. A thorough study of the roots and grammatical structure of the language will show that it is Asiatic in origin and somewhat allied to some European tongues. In a former work of the writer, "Missionary Labors of Fathers Marquette, Allouez and Menard in the Lake Superior Region," the reader will find a list, by no means complete, of Chippewa words, which evidently have a common origin with similar words in European languages. To those who love philological studies we would recommend Baraga's Chippewa Grammar and Dictionary, published by a firm in Montreal.

Rev. Martin Farrar, S.J., now deceased, composed an exhaustive dictionary of the Chippewa language, which, however, is still in manuscript form, as the gifted author died before completing his great work. He intended also to write a glossary to said dictionary, comparing Chippewa roots with similar ones in Sanscrit,

Greek and other ancient and modern languages. Such a work would, indeed, be highly interesting to students of philology.

As to the origin of the Indian races, they are no doubt from Asia. We have seen in missionary periodicals photographic pictures of some Asiatic people, and we can truly say that they so closely resemble our Indians that there is no doubt about their common origin. Father Grellon, who had labored for years amongst the Hurons of Canada and had left that country after the destruction of the Huron Mission in 1648-'49-'50, and went to Asia, relates in the "*Lettres Edifiantes*" that he met, in Central Asia, a Christian Huron woman and heard her confession in the language which neither of them had spoken for years. This poor woman had been sold as a slave from tribe to tribe till she was brought far into the interior of Asia.

There is no doubt that in remote times Asiatic tribes, many of whom are still of a roving, nomadic disposition, crossed Behring's Strait, and, once on American soil, pushed on southward and in other directions. Moreover, the many islands in the Pacific Ocean seem to indicate that at a remote period there was a large continent, perhaps like Australia, between Asia and America. This may have become submerged in the course of time, ages ago, and perhaps many of the islands in said ocean are but portions of this continent. The ruins of Yucatan, Mexico, and Peru point to an Asiatic origin and civilization.

The facial difference between some European and Indian races is not very great. Many of our half-breeds strongly resemble southern European races. They have very much the same complexion, dark, black eyes, black hair, etc. Besides, it is wonderful how easily, by inter marriage, the Indian race merges into the white. At our Indian boarding schools can be found quarter-breed children, that is, the children of half-breeds married to whites, who are perfectly white, as to feature, color, hair, in a word, in every respect. This shows that two or three successive intermarriages with the whites are sufficient to transform the Indian into a white.

Besides, the Algonquin races seem to have far more intellectual features than the southern and western Indian tribes. This would indicate that they are descended from a more intellectual type of Asiatic races. There is about the same difference between the Chippewa Indians and those of the Pacific Coast as there is between the intellectual Hindoo and the nomadic Mongolian of Central Asia. It is our opinion that the different Indian nations of this continent belonged originally to different Asiatic nations. We hold that climatic changes, diet, mode of living, and intermarriage have a great deal to do with the formation of national features, color, intellectual capacity, and other peculiarities. It is noticeable that our Germans, French, Irish and other foreign nationalities gradually undergo considerable change of feature after having been in this country many years. This is especially true of their descendants in the second, third, and further generations.

As to the religious ideas of the Algonquin family of nations, they seem to have undergone a considerable change since the advent of the first European missionaries in the seventeenth century. If we can rely on Allouez, Marquette, Charlevoix, and others, the Indians of their time seem to have had hardly any idea of a Supreme Being. Some tribes appear to have picked up a vague notion of such a being from their intercourse with the French.

Speaking of the Indians on the shores of Chequamegon (Ashland) Bay in 1665, Father Allouez says:

"There is here a false and abominable religion, similar in many things to that of some ancient pagans. *The Indians here do not acknowledge any sovereign master of heaven and earth.* They believe that there are many manitous, some of which are beneficent, as the sun, the moon, the lake, the rivers and woods; others malevolent, as, for instance, snakes, the dragon, cold, storms; and in general all that appears to them useful or injurious they call a manitou, and they render to such objects the worship and veneration which we give to the true God alone. They invoke them when they go to hunt, to fish, to war, or on a voyage. They offer them sacrifices with ceremonies only used by such as offer sacrifice.

"For the rest, as these people are dull, *they do not acknowledge any deity purely spiritual.* They believe that the sun is a man and the moon his wife; that snow and ice are also human beings, who go away in spring and return again in winter; that the devil dwells in snakes, dragons, and other monsters; that crows, hawks and other birds are manitous and talk as well as we do, pretending there are some Indians who understand their language just as some of them understand a little French."

Another fact that goes far to show that in former times the Indians, *with few exceptions*, did not know nor worship a Supreme Being, is that there is no particular word for God in their language. The names they *now* give to God, e.g., Great Master, Kind Manitou, Master of Life, etc., seem to be of *Christian, not pagan*, origin. As we see from Father Allouez, the word a manitou" does not mean a spiritual being or God, but any beneficent or malevolent being, possessed of strange and, to the Indian, mysterious powers. We must then conclude that the Indians of former times, before the advent of the whites, were polytheists and idolators, like the ancient Babylonians, Egyptians, Greeks, and Romans, and that one of their principal gods was the sun. As among the Greeks and Romans were to be found a few more enlightened men, who believed in the one, true, living God, for instance, Socrates, Plato, Cicero, so also we find such men amongst the ancient Indians; the masses, however, were polytheists. But now the reverse is true. The pagan Indians of our day are monotheists; they believe and invoke the Great Spirit. But we strongly believe that this is due to their intercourse during the last two centuries with the French-Canadians, who have constantly traded and freely intermarried with them. Another result of this intercourse seems to have been the well-nigh total abolition of polygamy. Two centuries ago polygamy was universally practiced by the Indians of the Northwest. At present it is very seldom that a pagan Indian has two wives. Two centuries ago the missionaries complain of universal libertinism and horrible immorality among the Indians. Now Father Pierze tells us that, where they are not corrupted by intercourse with the whites, pagan Indians are innocent and moral. The Indians of our times are far superior to their forefathers in knowledge, religion, and morality, where not perverted by bad whites.

Our pagan Indian of the Algonquin family of nations strongly believes in the Great Spirit and shows deep respect to Him. But his greatest concern is to placate and gain the good will of the manitous or demi-gods, with whom his imagination peoples the sky, land and waters. They have countless legends, some droll, some childishly absurd, about Menabosho, or, as some pronounce it, Wenabosho. The universal deluge forms an important point of their belief. This great catastrophe, recorded more or less distinctly in the ancient traditions of most all nations, is related by our Chippewas in true Indian fashion, embellished with a thousand fantastic, ridiculous stories about Menabosho, who, it is claimed, remade the earth after the flood and for that purpose used a muskrat, who dived down and brought up from the depth a little dirt in one of its paws, which Menabosho dried in the palm of his hand, as he was sitting on the top of a high tree with the water up to his chin, and blew around him and where ever the dust fell firm land was formed! By constantly repeating the above proceeding he increased the size of his island till it became the earth as it now.

Besides Menabosho, our pagan Indians have other manitous, whom they invoke at their feasts and incantations. Such are Mishiken and Oshkabewiss, his attendant or servant, who are invoked by the medicine-man at the Indian incantation called Tchissakiwin in order to learn future events or things going on at a distance. Formerly Mishibishi, the god of the waters and storms, was invoked for good luck when going on a voyage or fishing for sturgeon. Their dances have a religious character. They are religious rites by which they mean to propitiate the Great Spirit. Hence they have dances at their meetings or deliberations, when a person is sick, to make him recover, at their funerals in the house of the deceased, when about to go to war, etc. They have the great medicine-dance, the Sioux-dance, the war-dance, the squaw-dance, and the scalp-dance.

Nicholas Perrot relates in his "Memoire" that when an Indian would get up a feast in honor of the manitou he meant to honor, he would address to him the following prayer:

"I adore and invoke thee that thou mayest be favorable to me in the enterprise I have on hand, and that thou mayest have pity on me and my whole family. *I invoke all the bad and good spirits*, all those who are in the air, on the earth, and underneath, that they may preserve me and my party, and that we may be able to return, after a happy voyage, to our country."

As to their customs, our Indians are fast imitating the whites. They build log or frame houses whenever they have the means to do so. The wigwam of former times is fast disappearing, at least among our Chippewas, and will soon be a thing of the past, except when they camp out to make maple sugar, gather wild rice, pick berries, or hunt. They try to get household furniture and live like the whites. A blanket-Indian is seldom to be seen. Face-painting and fantastical, grotesque dressing with feathers, beads, and other Indian paraphernalia is indulged in only by pagan Indians at their religious feasts and dances, also when playing their national game of ball, called La Crosse, or, in Chippewa, Pagaadowewin.

Still they retain some of their peculiar customs. Thus many women still use the Tikinagan or Indian cradle for their little children, which is certainly very convenient for both mother and child, especially when traveling. Moreover the men are fond of wearing mocassins and garters tastefully ornamented with beadwork, in the making of which Indian women are very skillful. They are likewise fond of bright colors, and seem to have little idea of a proper blending or juxtaposition of colors. They often put side by side bright, glaring colors, which produce a grotesque effect.

Our Catholic Indians beautifully decorate their churches for Christmas and Corpus Christi. They will cheerfully devote whole days to this laudable work and spare neither time nor expense to decorate the church nicely. Christmas is preeminently an Indian holyday, on which all, even the most lukewarm, attend the midnight Mass. On New Year's day they go from house to house wishing each other a "Happy New Year." It is the day of universal good will and reconciliation. They all go to the priest and shake hands with him, wishing him, too, a Happy New Year, and kneel down to receive his blessing. In going from house to house, they receive everywhere little presents and occasionally a little "fire water," too. On the eve of All Souls' days, that is, in the evening of the first of November, they go to the church and each time they pray for a deceased parent, child or dear relative, they ring the bell, and this goes on sometimes until midnight or till the priest, tired of the endless dingling, locks the church. This ceremony they call "Nibamadwessing," night ringing, whilst people are sleeping.

Our Indians are open-handed, liberal, and assist each other readily. A miserly, stingy Indian is disliked by all. To be "a big Indian," one must make presents, be kind-hearted and liberal. Hence, at their pagan feasts they give presents to one another, sometimes even of great value, such as a horse, or blanket, or dress. As a rule, they are not thievish or dishonest. A man with money is far safer amongst Indians than amongst whites. To steal is considered very dishonorable, but they are rather slow to pay their debts, which is easily accounted for; because if an Indian owes a dollar he has so many pressing wants for which he needs the dollar he has, that he uses it to buy what he needs and forgets his debt. A merchant doing business with them must do it on a cash basis, for if he begins to sell on credit he will certainly fail, as many of his Indian customers will never pay their debts. Although the Indian has some grave faults, such as sloth, fickle-mindedness, drinking, and playing cards, he has many virtues which offset these faults, such as docility, liberality, hospitality, and others.

Chapter II

First Attempts at Evangelizing the Indians of the Northwest—Jogues and Baymbault at Sault Ste. Marie, Mich.—Gabbeau and Dreuillettes.

As Bishop Baraga was the worthy, though not immediate, successor of the grand old Jesuit Fathers who labored during the seventeenth and eighteenth centuries among the Indians of the Northwest, we deem it proper to devote a few chapters to a brief review of their apostolic labors and sufferings. These saintly men labored at Sault Ste. Marie and Arbre Croche, at L'Anse and La Pointe du Saint Esprit, and in all those missions Father, afterwards Bishop, Baraga worked during thirty-seven years.

The first missionaries that ever visited the Northwest were Fathers Isaac Jogues and Charles Raymbault, of the illustrious Society of Jesus. About the middle of October, 1642, these two intrepid missionaries arrived at Sault Ste. Marie, Mich. Some two thousand Indians from all parts of the Northwest were assembled there to celebrate the feast of the dead. The Fathers were well received and requested to stay there. They told the Indians that they might establish a missionary station at that place, provided the latter were disposed to receive instruction. A council was held, at the conclusion of which the Indians assured the Fathers that they greatly desired the happiness of having them in their midst; that they would embrace them as brothers and profit by their words. However, as the Fathers were needed more pressingly elsewhere, they departed, intending, no doubt, to establish a mission there later on. That same year, 1642, Father Jogues was captured by a roving band of Iroquois, with Rene Goupil and Francois Couture. They were most cruelly tortured and Rene Goupil was shortly afterwards tomahawked by the side of Jogues. Four years later, October 18th, 1646, the latter was treacherously killed at the Indian village of Gandague, now called Auriesville, in New York. Steps have been taken looking to the beatification of Father Jogues, Rene Goupil, and Catharina Tegahkwita, the Iroquois virgin, whose grave has been honored by many miracles.

MARTYRDOM OF FATHERS JOGUES, BREBEUF, LALLEMANT, RASLE, MENARD, RENE GOUPIL

The next attempt to evangelize the Algonquin tribes* of the Northwest was made in 1656 by Fathers Leonard Garreau and Gabriel Dreuillettes. An Ottawa flotilla of fifty canoes, numbering two hundred and fifty men, arrived at Quebec. When about to return to the upper lake country the above-named Fathers embarked with them as they themselves had asked for

---

* The word tribe, although now in general use, is a misnomer when applied to the different Indian nations of America. The Chippewas, Ottawas, Foxes, Illinois, etc., are distinct nations, just as much so as the Germans, Swedes, Dutch, etc., are distinct nationalities. The word tribe might be more fittingly applied to the *different totemic subdivisions* of Indian nations. The northwestern division of the Algonquin family of nations comprised the Chippewas, Ottawas, Outagamies, Pottawatamies, Sacs, Illinois, Menominees and other minor nations. They inhabited Wisconsin, Michigan, and Illinois, and the north shore of Lake Superior.

missionaries to preach the gospel in their country. Unhappily the Ottawas, trusting to their superior numbers, and regardless of danger, fell into an ambuscade near Montreal. At the first discharge of musketry, made by the Iroquois upon the unsuspecting Ottawas, a number of the latter were killed and others dangerously wounded. Among the latter was Garreau, whose spine was broken by a bullet and who was captured and dragged into the Iroquois fort. After suffering for three days intense pains and miseries of every kind, he was finally brought by his captors to Montreal, where he expired, fortified by the holy Sacraments, on the second of September, 1656. Father Dreuillettes urgently requested the Ottawas to take him along, when secretly embarking in the dead of night, but no one would take him in their canoe. Sixteen years later, in 1672, we find the same Father Dreuillettes laboring with apostolic zeal at Sault Ste. Marie.

LA BONNE CATHERINE TEGAHKOUITA

Chapter III

Father Menard; His Labors Near L'Anse, Michigan, and Death in the Wilds of Wisconsin.

The pioneer missionary of the Lake Superior country was Rene Menard, S. J. He arrived in Canada in the beginning of June, 1640, in company with another Father and two lay brothers of his order, together with two Sisters of Mercy and two Ursuline nuns. He labored for many years with great zeal and much fruit in the Huron missions and among the Nipissings and Atontrates. He was the beau-ideal of an Indian missionary, full of burning zeal for the honor of God and full of sympathetic love and compassion for the poor Indians. His exceedingly great kindness won their hearts. After the breaking up of the Huron missions in 1648-9, he was employed among the Indians and French at Three Rivers.

In 1656 an extremely hazardous mission was started amongst the Iroquois at Lake Cayuga. Three Fathers, amongst them Menard, two brothers and fifty-three Frenchmen, left Quebec on the 17th of May of the above-named year for the new mission field. After a long and tedious voyage of about two months they arrived at their destination and were received with great demonstrations of joy by the chiefs and head men of the Iroquois village. The whole affair, however, was nothing but a deep-laid plot to entice the missionaries and French to their country, to hold them as hostages in case that any of the Iroquois should be captured, and to massacre them should they meet with any reverse in their attacks upon the French settlements along the St. Lawrence.

Father Menard soon collected around him at Lake Cayuga a small flock of Christians, composed mostly of captives, brought together from a score of different tribes and kept as slaves in the Iroquois country. Misfortune had softened their hearts and made them accessible to the tidings of salvation. A letter of Menard, written about a year after the opening of the Cayuga mission, to his superior in Quebec, reveals to us the burning zeal of this saintly missionary and the great dangers to which he and his fellow-laborers were exposed. He writes:

"I praise God that your Reverence still takes an interest in our affairs; but I am a little surprised to hear you speak in a tone different from that to which we were accustomed. How long ago is it since you wrote we had nothing to fear, that God continued sending you wherewith to support us in this remote corner of the world? How is it that you now complain of our too great expenses? We are in a place where the cost of living is very much greater than among the Hurons, and where we have no assistance to expect from the country itself, among false traitors, who ill-treat us by right of prescription. There is a crowd of captives here, gathered from all sides, who, after all, are capable of being made children of God. Of these I alone have, since last year, baptized more than four hundred. We walk with our heads lifted up in the midst of dangers, through insults, hootings, calumnies, tomahawks, and knives, with which they often run after us, to put us to death. Almost daily we are on the eve of being massacred, "as dying and behold we live," and you tell us that you are no longer able to support this mission! I prefer, my Rev. Father, to stand by the last words of your letter, where you remark that after all, if we do our part well, God will do His as far as will be needed. Yes, assuredly, He-will succor us, if we seek but His glory, if we expose our lives to have His blood applied to those poor abandoned souls. This very thing all our Fathers here are doing with incredible trouble and labor. Should God, who led us into this land of barbarians, allow us to be slaughtered, praise be to Him forever! Jesus, His Gospel, the salvation of those poor souls, these are the inducements that retain us here and make us tarry, as it were, in the midst of flames. *Men burnt and devoured are sights to which our eyes are accustomed.* Pray you to God that He may make Christians of these cannibals, and that He may strengthen us more and more; and we, we shall beg Him to move the hearts of those who love Him, so that they may enable you to assist us."

The time, however, for the conversion of the Iroquois had not yet come. The tomahawk, treacherously buried for a while, was raised again in the spring of 1658. Only stratagem and secret flight, most skillfully planned and luckily accomplished, could save the lives of the Fathers and Frenchmen secretly condemned to death by the head men of the Iroquois village. With a bleeding heart, Father Menard left with the rest in the silence of the night. Far sooner would he have stayed with his neophytes, and, if necessary, have suffered death at his post. He felt as if his heart had been torn out of his body, or as a mother violently torn away from her children. But obedience called him away, and so he departed with the rest. Two years later we see him going to the Lake Superior country, where he perished in the wilds of Wisconsin, trying to bring the consolations of religion to a few starving Hurons at the headwaters of Black River.

In 1660 an Ottawa flotilla of sixty canoes arrived at Three Rivers. Two Jesuit Fathers attempted to accompany them on their return voyage. One of them, however, only succeeded, namely, Menard. The other Father was unceremoniously set ashore at Montreal. Before starting, Father Menard wrote the following lines to a reverend friend:

"My Rev. Father, — The Peace Of Christ!

"I write to you probably the last word, and I desire it to be the seal of our friendship until eternity. Love him, whom the Lord Jesus does not disdain to love, although the greatest sinner; for He loves him, with whom He deigns to share His cross. May your friendship, my good Father, be useful to me in the desirable fruits of your holy sacrifices. In three or four months you may put me in the memento of the dead, considering the manner of living of these people, and my age and weak constitution. Notwithstanding all this, I have felt such a powerful attraction and have seen so little of nature in this undertaking, that I could not doubt but that I would have had eternal remorse had I missed this opportunity. We were taken a little by surprise, so that we are unable to provide ourselves with clothing and other necessary things. But He who feeds the little birds and clothes the lilies of the fields, will take care of His servants. Should we happen to die of misery, that would be for us a great happiness. I am overwhelmed with business. All I can do is to recommend our voyage to your holy sacrifices and to embrace you with the same heart as I hope to do in eternity.

"My Rev. Father—Your very humble and affectionate servant of Jesus Christ,

"R. Menard.

"Three Rivers, this 27th day of August, at 2 o'clock after midnight, 1660."

The Ottawa flotilla, and with it Father Menard, left Three Rivers on the 28th of August. The journey from Three Rivers to St. Theresa (Keweenaw) Bay, Mich., took over a month and a half. The poor missionary had to endure incredible hardships on the way. He was obliged to paddle all day and to carry very heavy packs on his shoulders at the numerous portages on the Ottawa River. They did not even allow him time to say his office, and threw his breviary into the water, imagining perhaps that the mysterious procedure of passing the eyes over curiously dotted paper was a mighty charm for their destruction. Luckily he found another breviary stowed away in one of his packages. Starvation was his daily companion. He writes:

"But the worst was to come. Having entered Lake Superior after such hardships, there, in place of finding the promised rest and provisions, our canoe was smashed by a falling tree, and that so completely, that no hope of repairing it was left. Everyone abandoned us and we were left—three Indians and myself—without food and canoe. In that state we remained six days, living on filthy offal, which, to keep off starvation, we had to scratch up with our fingernails around an old abandoned lodge. To make soup, we pounded the bones that lay about. We picked up earth saturated with the blood of animals that had been killed there; in a word, we made food of everything. One of us was continually on the lookout at the shore to implore the mercy of those that passed by, and we wrested from them a few slices of dried meat, which saved us from death. At last some, more compassionate, took us up and brought us to our rallying point, destined for our wintering. This is a large bay on the south shore of Lake Superior (Keweenaw Bay), where I arrived on St. Theresa's day (Oct. 15th, 1660), and here I had the consolation of saying Mass, which repaid me bountifully for all my past hardships. Here also I opened a temporary church of Christian Indians, occasional visitors from the neighborhood of our French settlements (on the St. Lawrence), and of such others as the mercy of God has gathered in from this place."

In all probability Father Menard's mission was located at Old Village Point, or Pikwakwewaming, about seven miles north of the present town, L'Anse, Mich. He baptized some fifty adults and many children during the nine months he resided there.

His labors amongst the hardened, polygamous Indians at Keweenaw Bay were attended with little fruit. They were not yet ripe for the Gospel, as in the days of Baraga, who labored ten years and converted nearly all the people there. Menard, hearing finally of a band of Hurons, many of whom were Christians and who resided somewhere at the headwaters of Black River (Wis.), determined to seek them. In the spring of 1661 he employed three of his French companions to visit the Huron settlement and acquaint them with his design. They found the Hurons in a starving condition. Upon their return they tried to dissuade Menard from his intended voyage, representing to him that he would likely perish on the way or die of starvation when there; but all in vain.

"God calls me," said he, "I must go there, should it even cost my life. St. Francis Xavier, who seemed so necessary to the world for the conversion of souls, died well in trying to enter China. And I, who am good for nothing, should I, for fear of dying on the way, refuse to obey the voice of my God, who calls me to the succor of poor Christians and catechumens deprived of a pastor so long a time? No, no; I do not want to let souls perish under pretext of preserving the bodily life of a puny man, such as I am. What! must God be served and our neighbor helped only then when there is nothing to suffer and no risk of one's life? This is the most beautiful occasion to show to angels and men that I love my Creator more than the life I have from Him, and would you wish me to let it escape? Would we ever have been redeemed had not our dear Master preferred to sacrifice His life in obedience to His Father for our salvation?"

So the resolution was taken to go and seek those poor, starving Hurons. A Frenchman accompanied the Father.

All the provisions they had was a bag of dried sturgeon and some smoked meat. His last adieu to the seven French men who had come up with him from Three Rivers, and whom he now was leaving, was in these prophetic words: "Adieu, my dear children. I bid you the great adieu for this world, for you will not see me again. I pray the divine Goodness that we may be reunited in heaven."

So Menard set out on his last journey the 13th of July, 1661, nine months after arriving at Keweenaw Bay. He and his French companion stopped fifteen days near a certain lake—most probably Lac Vieux Desert—expecting the Huron guides, who were to conduct him to their village. As provisions were failing, they determined to push on, having found a small birch canoe in the brush. Finally, while going down river—most probably the Wisconsin—the Father got lost whilst making a portage about two days' journey from the Huron village. But whether he perished from starvation or by the hand of some roving Indian, will never be known with certainty.

It is highly probable that Father Menard was the first priest that ever said Mass on Wisconsin soil, between the 1st and 10th of August, 1661.

Chapter IV

Father Allouez; His Apostolic Labors in the Lake Superior Region and Other Parts of Wisconsin.

The pioneer missionary of Wisconsin was Claude Allouez, S. J. He labored longer on the Indian missions of that state than any other of his illustrious order; that is to say, for almost a quarter of a century. As he labored amongst the same class of people on the shores of Chequamegon Bay, that Father Baraga did a century and a half later, a brief notice of his labors and trials will not be out of place here.

Father Allouez left Three Rivers, Canada, on the 8th of August, in the year 1665, in company with six French men and about four hundred Indians of different tribes, who had come to traffic with the French at Three Rivers and Quebec, and who were then returning to their country. After a long and difficult voyage of almost two months in a poor birch canoe, he arrived at "Chagaouamigong" (Chequamegon Bay) on the first of October, 1665. On the way, the poor Father suffered much from the brutality of his Indian traveling companions. Their head men, especially their medicine-men, did all in their power to prevent his coming to their country; they insulted and ridiculed him on all occasions. Hunger and misery of every kind was his daily lot. Speaking of these hardships he says:

"When, in addition to these hardships, hunger comes, it is a very severe suffering, which soon taught me to take liking to *most bitter roots and rotten meat.* It pleased God to make me endure the greatest hunger on Fridays, for which I most gladly thank Him. I had to accustom myself to eat a certain moss, which grows on rocks. It is a kind of leaf in the shape of a shell, which is always covered with caterpillars and spiders. When boiled, it makes an insipid, black, stickey broth, which serves rather to keep death away than to impart life.

"On a certain morning a deer was found, dead since four or five days. It was a lucky acquisition for poor famished beings. I was offered some, and although the bad smell hindered some of them from eating it, hunger made me take my share. But I had, in consequence, an offensive odor in my mouth until the next day."

Speaking of the location of his mission at the head of Chequamegon Bay, he says:

"On the first day of October, 1665, we arrived at Chagaouamigong, for which place we had sighed so long. It is a beautiful bay, at the head of which is situated the large village of the Indians, who there cultivate fields of Indian corn and do not lead a wandering life. There are at this place men bearing arms and numbering about eight hundred; but these are gathered together from seven different tribes, and live in peaceable community. This great number of people induced us to prefer this place to all others for our ordinary abode, in order to attend more conveniently to the instruction of these heathens, to put up a chapel there and commence the functions of Christianity.

His first baptism was that of a Pottawatami child, whom he named Francis, having likely baptized him on St. Francis day, October the 4th. The child died after two days, "the first fruit of this mission."

At the head of the bay were two large villages, the one inhabited by Hurons, and the other by Ottawas. The mission was called, "The Mission of the Holy Ghost." It was located between those two villages. There were, moreover, scattering villages and hamlets along the western shore of the bay, inhabited by bands of Illinois, Pottawatamies, Sacs, Foxes and other tribes. These poor people had been driven westward by the fierce Iroquois about the middle of the seventeenth century. They lived in peace and security at this western end of Lake Superior for about twenty years. But having foolishly made war on the powerful Sioux, and been defeated, they were obliged to leave in 1670-71. Some of them went to live on Manitoulin Island, in Lake Huron; others at Mackinac; others again at the head and on the shores of Green Bay.

During the three and a half years that Father Allouez spent with them at Chequamegon Bay, he baptized about five hundred adults and children. In the spring of 1669 he went to Quebec and was succeeded by Father James Marquette, who arrived at the same bay on the 13th of September, 1669. This pious missionary, the famed discoverer of the Mississippi, labored there, but not with great success on account of the war excitement, until the spring of 1671, when the war between the Sioux in Minnesota, and the Hurons, Ottawas and other tribes in Wisconsin, broke up the mission. From the above-mentioned date till 1835 there is no account of any Catholic missionary laboring on the shores of Lake Superior. In 1835, Father Baraga founded the mission of St. Joseph on La Pointe Island, and so revived, it may be said, the ancient mission of Allouez and Marquette at the head of Chequamegon Bay.

After Father Allouez's return from Quebec in 1669, he went to Green Bay to found at the head of that bay a new mission. He departed with two Indians in a birch canoe from Sault Ste. Marie on the 3d of November, and after suffering many hardships and much cold, he arrived at the head of Green Bay on the 2d of December, 1669. He said holy Mass on December the 3d, feast of St. Francis Xavier, with all possible solemnity, and dedicated to that great saint the mission he was establishing.

This indefatigable missionary may be justly called the ancient Indian Apostle of Wisconsin, for he was the founder of all the principal missions within its borders. He founded St. Michael's Mission among the Menominees, that of St. Mark among the Foxes on the Wolf River, that of St. James, on the Upper Fox, amongst the Illinois, Miamies, and Kickapoos; besides other stations on the eastern shore of Green Bay, among the Winnebagoes, Pottawatamis, and Sacs. He also labored with great zeal in Illinois and died a holy and edifying death in St. Joseph's Mission, Michigan, about the year 1689.

CHAPTER V

The Labors of Father Marquette at the Mission of the Holy Ghost on the Shores of Chequamegon (Ashland) Bay and at St. Ignace, Mich.

Father Marquette, who had been laboring for about a year among the numerous Indians at Sault Ste. Marie, was sent by his Superior, in 1669, to the Mission of the Holy Ghost, to continue the work so auspiciously begun by his zealous predecessor, Father Allouez. He arrived at "Chagaouamigong" on the 13th of September of the above-named year. In a letter, most probably written from Sault Ste. Marie in the spring of 1670, he speaks of his labors at Chequamegon Bay. We will give a few extracts:

"Divine Providence having destined me to continue the Mission of the Holy Ghost, which Father Allouez had begun, and where he baptized the headmen of the Kiskakonk tribe, I arrived there on the 13th of September. I went to visit the Indians, who were living in clearings divided, as it were, into five villages.* The Hurons, to the number of from four to five hundred souls, are nearly all baptized, and still preserve a little Christianity. Some of the principal men, assembled in council, were much pleased at first to see me. I gave them to understand, however, that I

---

* The location of these five Indian villages on the shores of Chequamegon Bay may have been as follows: 1, at Fish Creek; 2, at Nash; 3, at Van der Venter's Bay; 4, near Pike's Bay; 5, Bayfield.

did not as yet know their language perfectly, and that there was no other Father to come here, partly because they were all gone to the Iroquois, and partly because Father Allouez, who understood them perfectly, did not wish to return here for this winter on account of their not showing enough attachment to religion. They admitted that they well deserved punishment and afterwards during the winter they spoke of it and resolved to do better, which they in reality have shown me by their conduct.

"The Outaouacs (Ottawas) are remarkably superstitious in their feasts and juggleries and seem to harden themselves against the instructions imparted to them. They are, however, well satisfied to have their children baptized. God has this winter permitted a woman to die in her sins. Her sickness had been concealed from me, and I heard nothing about it, except by a report circulated about that she had requested a very bad dance to be performed for her cure. I immediately went into a wigwam, where all the headmen were at a feast, and among them some Christian Kiskakonk. I pointed out to them the wickedness of that woman and of the medicine-man (in getting up such an immodest dance). I instructed them, speaking to all present, and God willed that an aged Outaouac should take the word, saying that my request should be granted, no matter if the woman were to die. An aged Christian also spoke, telling the tribe that the debaucheries of the young people ought to be stopped, and that Christian girls should never be allowed to be present at these dances. To satisfy the woman, the dance was changed into a child's play, but this did not prevent her from dying before daybreak.

"The extreme danger in which a young man lay sick induced the medicine-man to say he would invoke the devil by means of very extraordinary superstitious performances. The Christians made no invocation whatever. Only the medicine-man and the patient did so. The latter was made to walk over large fires, which had been lighted in all the wigwams. They say that he did not feel the heat of those fires, although his body had been anointed with oil for five or six days. Men, women, and children ran from wigwam to wigwam, proposing, as an enigma, anything they had in their minds, and the one who guessed it was very well satisfied to receive whatever he was looking for. I prevented them from practicing the indecencies, in which they are in the habit of indulging at the end of these deviltries. I think they will not return to them again, as the sick man died shortly after.

"The Kiskakonk tribe, which for three years had refused to receive the Gospel announced to them by Father Allouez, finally resolved in the autumn of the year 1668 to obey God. This resolution was taken in a council and made known to the Father, who was obliged to winter with them for the fourth time, in order to instruct and baptize them. The headmen of the tribe declare themselves Christians, and in order to attend to them, the Father (Allouez) having gone to another mission, the charge of this one was given to me, which charge I took up in the month of September of the year 1669.

"All the Christians were in the fields at that time, harvesting their Indian corn. They listened to me with pleasure, when I told them that I had come to La Pointe merely through consideration for them and the Hurons; that they never would be abandoned, but would be cherished above all other tribes, and would henceforth form one nation with the French. I had the consolation of seeing their love for religion, and how much they appreciated their being Christians. I baptized the newly-born children and visited the old men, all of whom I found well disposed. The chief had allowed a dog to be attached to a pole near his wigwam, which is a kind of sacrifice to the sun. I told him that it was not right and he immediately took it down himself.

"A sick man, who had been instructed but not yet baptized, begged me to grant him this grace, or to stay near him, because he did not wish to employ the medicine-man to get cured, and feared the fire of hell. I prepared him for Baptism. I was often in his wigwam and the joy my visit caused him partly restored him to health. He thanked me for the care I had taken of him and shortly after, saying I had restored him to life, he made me a present of a slave, who had been brought to him from the Illinois two or three months before.

"In the evening, being in the wigwam of a Christian, where I used to sleep, I made him say some prayers to the guardian angel, and related some anecdotes to make him understand the assistance the angels give us, especially when in danger of offending God. He told me that now he knew the invisible hand that struck him, when, after his Baptism, he was on the point of committing sin with a woman, and having heard a voice that told him to remember that he was a Christian, he departed without committing this sin. Afterwards he often spoke to me about the devotion to the guardian angels and conversed about it with other Indians"......

These few extracts from Marquette's letter give us an insight into his labors at "La Pointe du Saint Esprit," the name given by the ancient missionaries to Bayfield peninsula. In the spring of 1671 the mission broke up. Some of the poor Indians immigrated to St. Ignace, Mich., on the mainland, about four miles from Mackinac Island, and thither Marquette followed them. The "Relation" of 1672, speaking of this new mission, says:

"Father Marquette, who followed them from La Pointe du Saint Esprit, still has charge of them. But he has not given us any particular memoirs of what took place in this mission (St. Ignace). All that can be said of it is that this tribe (Huron) had been formerly brought up in the Christian religion prior to the destruction of the Huron nation, and that those who have persevered in the faith are at present very fervent. They fill the chapel every day — yes, even often during the day do they visit it. They sing the praises of God with a devotion, which has been communicated in a great measure to the French, who have witnessed it. Adults have been baptized and old men set a good example to the children to go to prayers diligently. In a word, they practice all the exercises of piety that can be expected of Christians converted over twenty years ago, although for the greatest part of that time they were without a church and pastor, having no other teacher than the Holy Ghost."

FATHER MARQUETTE SETS OUT
TO DISCOVER THE MISSISSIPPI RIVER

Chapter VI

Father Marquette Discovers the Mississippi; Establishes the Mission of the Immaculate Conception; His Edifying Death.

In 1672 Louis de Buade, Comte de Frontenac, succeeded M. de Courcelles as governor of Canada. As soon as he had arrived, M. Talon, the intendant, laid before him the plan of exploring the Mississippi. For this great undertaking Sieur Jollyet and Father Marquette were chosen. On the 8th of December, 1672, feast of the Immaculate Conception, Jollyet arrived at St. Ignace and told Father Marquette the joyful news of their appointment to visit and explore the Mississippi. During the winter they perfected their plans for the undertaking, and on the 17th of May, 1673, started from St. Ignace, in company with five Frenchmen, who had volunteered to accompany them on this glorious though hazardous journey.

At the mouth of the Menominee River, where it empties into Green Bay, was a settlement of Menominees, several of whom were Christians. They tried very hard to dissuade Marquette and his companions from the intended exploration. They told him he would meet with savage tribes, who showed no mercy to strangers; that war had broken out between the tribes along the proposed route; that the great river was very dangerous and full of horrible monsters, which devoured both men and boat; that a demon or manitou obstructed the passage and drowned all who dared to come near, and that the heat was insupportable. Father

Marquette, however, made light of all their objections and boldly pushed forward. On the 17th of June, 1673, their canoes glided into the Mississippi. For upwards of a hundred leagues they met not a single human being on the Wisconsin and Mississippi. Finally, on the 25th of June, they discovered a trail leading from the river to an Indian village. This they followed in silence and prayer. It led them to a settlement of Peoria (Illinois) Indians on the banks of Des Moines River, consisting of three villages situated at a short distance from one another.

They were offered the calumet, or pipe of peace, and one of their chiefs thus addressed them: "How beautiful, O Frenchman, is the sun, when thou comest to visit us! All our village waits thee and thou shalt enter all our cabins in peace." He then conducted them into his wigwam, where a great crowd, as Marquette graphically describes it, devoured them with their eyes. Soon an invitation came from the head chief of the tribe to visit his village, as he desired to hold a council with them. On the way thither they were accompanied by the whole village.

When they arrived at the village of the great chief, they saw him standing in front of his cabin in the midst of two old men, with their calumets turned towards the sun. The chief bade them welcome in a neat little speech and offered them his pipe to smoke. Father Marquette then spoke, telling them the object of his visit. He told them that he and his party were traveling in peace to visit the nations that lived along the great river; that he was sent on the part of God to enlighten them with the knowledge of the true God, of whom they had been so long ignorant; that the great chief of the French had subdued the Iroquois and made peace everywhere, and finally he requested them to give him all the information they could about the sea and the nations, whom they would have to pass to get there.

The chief then arose and laying his hand on the head of a little slave, whom he meant to give them as a present, he spoke as follows:

"I thank thee, Black-robe, and thee, Frenchman,"— addressing M. Jollyet,—"for having taken so much trouble to come and visit us. Never was the earth so beautiful nor the sun so bright as today. Never was our river so calm nor so free from rocks, which your canoes have removed in passing by; never had our tobacco so good a flavor, nor did our corn appear so flourishing as we now see it. Behold, here is my son, whom I give to thee, that thou mayest know my heart. I implore thee to have pity on me and all my people. Thou knowest the Great Spirit who made us all; thou speakest to Him and hearest His word. Ask Him to grant me life and health, and do thou come and live with us to make us know him."*

The council was followed by a great banquet, consisting of four dishes. The first consisted of a large wooden plate of sagamity; that is, corn meal boiled in water and seasoned with fat. The master of ceremonies put a spoonful of it into the Father's mouth, as one would feed a little child; he did the same to Jollyet. The second was a plate of fish. The master of ceremonies took some choice pieces, removing the bones, blew them to cool them, and then put some into their mouths. The third dish consisted of a large dog, which had been hastily killed and prepared for the occasion, but learning that their guests did not relish dog meat, it was removed. The fourth was buffalo meat, of which he put the fattest pieces into their mouths. They left these kindhearted Indians the next day and continued their voyage down the Mississippi.

As they were gently floating down the river in their canoes, they suddenly beheld some Indians armed with guns. The Father held up the calumet, the pipe of peace, which he had received at the Illinois village, whilst his companions prepared to defend themselves. He spoke to the Indians in Huron, but they did not answer. Their silence was interpreted at first as a sign of hostility. It seemed, however, these Indians were as much frightened as their French visitors. Finally the latter were given to understand that they should land and eat with the Indians, which they did. They were regaled with buffalo-meat, bear-oil, and plums of an excellent flavor. These Indians had guns, axes, hoes, knives, beads and glass bottles, in which they carried their gun-powder. They informed Marquette that they obtained those articles from Europeans, living eastward from there; that those people had

---

* We doubt whether a white orator could have made a more touching, simple, and beautiful extempore address than this child of the prairies on such an occasion. Many Indian speeches are models of oratory, showing that the gift of true eloquence is not confined to civilized nations.

rosaries and images and played musical instruments, and some of them were clothed like him. Father Marquette instructed them somewhat and gave them some medals.

At about 33 degrees of latitude they saw a village near the river, called Mitchigamea. Perceiving the strangers, the Indians quickly prepared to fight. They were armed with bows and arrows, tomahawks and war-clubs. They jumped into their large wooden canoes. Some of them stationed themselves at the river below, whilst others took position above the party, so as to cut off their retreat. Those on the bank ran back and forward, shouting and animating one another to fight. Some young men even jumped into the river to seize Father Marquette's canoe, but the current being too strong, they were obliged to swim back to the shore. One of them threw his war-club at the party, without, however, hitting any one. In this great danger the Father most fervently invoked the Blessed Virgin Immaculate, while showing continually the calumet. At length it was seen by some of the old men, who then restrained the young. Two of the headmen came into his canoe, throwing down the bows at his feet to give him to understand that no harm would be done to him and his party. They all disembarked, not, however, without some feeling of fear on the part of the Father. He spoke to them by signs, as they did not understand any one of the six Indian languages he knew. Finally an old man was found who could speak a little Illinois. The Father told them that he was on his way to the sea, and he gave them some instruction on God and the affairs of their salvation. All the answer he received was that eight or ten leagues further down the river he would find a large village called Akamsea, where he would get all the information he desired.

Early next morning they embarked, accompanied by an interpreter and ten Indians in a canoe, who rowed a little ahead. Having arrived within half a league of Akamsea, which was located opposite the mouth of the Arkansas River, they saw two canoes coming to meet them. The headman stood up in his canoe and showed them the calumet. He then sang an agreeable song, offered them the pipe of peace to smoke, and served them with sagamity and corn-bread, of which they partook a little. The people in the village in the meanwhile had prepared a suitable place under the scaffold of the chief warrior. They spread out fine mats made of rushes, on which the Father and his companions were invited to sit. Around them sat the chiefs of the tribe, further back the warriors, and behind them the rest of the people.

The Indians told Marquette that they were ten days' journey from the sea (Gulf of Mexico), but the Father thought they could have made it in five. They said they were not acquainted with the tribes that dwelt there, because their enemies hindered them from having intercourse with the Europeans there; that the axes, knives and beads they saw had been sold to them by tribes living towards the east, and partly by a village of Illinois four days' journey towards the west; that the Indians whom they had seen with guns, were their enemies, who cut them off from all intercourse and trade with the Europeans; finally that it would be dangerous to go any further, because their enemies continually sent out war-parties on the river, whom they could not encounter, armed with guns as they were and accustomed to war, without exposing themselves to great danger.

Father Marquette and Jollyet deliberated amongst themselves whether they had better push on further or return home. Knowing they were within a few days' journey of the Gulf of Mexico, and being convinced that the Mississippi emptied into said gulf and not towards Virginia nor California, the main object of their exploration had been realized. Having therefore rested themselves a day at the village of Akamsea, they left on the 17th of July, having spent an entire month in exploring the Mississippi. They returned home by way of the Illinois River, and coasting along the western shore of Lake Michigan, arrived safely at the Mission of St. Francis Xavier, near the present city of De Pere, Wis., towards the end of September. They had made in their small birch-canoes a journey of over 2,700 miles.

Father Marquette had suffered much on his voyage down the Mississippi in consequence of which he was attacked with the dysentery. He remained at St. Francis Xavier Mission for a whole year. Finally, to his great joy, he was ordered by his Superior to proceed to the country of the Illinois to establish there the Mission of the Immaculate Conception. He left on the 25th of October, 1674, and after traveling for upwards of a month by way of Green Bay, Sturgeon Bay, where they made a portage of three miles to Lake Michigan, and the western shore of the last named lake, he and his two faithful companions arrived at the Chicago River. They wintered at the portage between Chicago and Illinois River. Marquette had a new attack of his old ailment, which never left him entirely after that, though he was able to say Mass every day. He had all along a presentiment of his death, for he told his companions plainly that he would die of his ailment, and on that very journey. He made the spiritual retreat of St. Ignatius with great devotion and consolation, said Mass every day, confessed and communicated his two companions twice a week, and spent most of his time in prayer. He made with them a Novena in honor of the Blessed Virgin Immaculate that she might obtain for him the grace not to die till he had founded his intended mission. His prayer was heard.

On the 29th of March, 1675, he departed from his winter encampment and traveled down the Illinois River for eleven days amidst great hardships. Finally, on the 8th of April he arrived at the village of the Kaskaskias, where he was received as an angel from heaven. He went from cabin to cabin to instruct the people. On Holy Thursday he said holy Mass in the open air in the presence of an immense concourse of Indians, having first preached to them a most touching sermon on the death of Jesus Christ on the cross for the redemption of man. On Easter Sunday another great meeting was held, at which he said Mass again and preached with fiery zeal. The good people listened to him with great joy and approbation. Thus Father Marquette was the first priest that offered up the holy Sacrifice on the soil of Illinois in 1674-5. His work was done and he prepared to return in order to die, if possible, amongst his brethren at St. Ignace.

We shall give the particulars of his holy death in the words of the "Relations":

"After the Illinois had taken leave of the Father, he continued his voyage and soon after reached the Illinois Lake (Lake Michigan), on which he had nearly a hundred leagues to make by an unknown route, because he was obliged to take the eastern side of the lake, having gone thither by the western. His strength, however, failed so much that his men despaired of being able to bring him alive to the end of their journey; for, in fact, he became so weak and exhausted that he could no longer help himself, nor even stir, and had to be handled and carried like a child.

"He, nevertheless, maintained in this state an admirable equanimity, joy, and gentleness, consoling his beloved companions and exhorting them to suffer courageously all the hardships of the way, assuring them, moreover, that our Lord would not forsake them when he would be gone. During his navigation he began to prepare more particularly for death, passing his time in colloquies with our Lord, His holy Mother, His angel guardian and all heaven. He was often heard pronouncing these words: 'I believe that my Redeemer liveth' or 'Mary, mother of grace, mother of God, remember me.'' Besides a spiritual reading made for him every day, he, towards the end, asked them to read to him his meditation on the preparation for death, which he carried about him. He recited his breviary every day, and although he was so low that both sight and strength had greatly failed, he did not omit it till the last day of his life, when his companions induced him to cease, as it was shortening his days.

"A week before his death he had the precaution to bless some Holy Water, to serve him during the rest of his illness, in his agony, and at his burial, and he instructed his companions how to use it. On the eve of his death, which was a Friday, he told them, all radiant with joy, that it would take place on the morrow. During the whole day he conversed with them about the manner of his burial, the way in which he should be laid out, the place to be selected for his interment. He told them how to arrange his hands, feet, and face, and directed them to raise a cross over his grave. He even went so far as to enjoin them, only three hours before he expired, to take his chapel-bell, as soon as he would be dead, and ring it while they carried him to the grave. Of all this he spoke so calmly and collectedly, that you would have thought he spoke of the death and burial of another, and not of his own.

"Thus did he speak with them as they sailed along the lake, till perceiving the mouth of a river with an eminence on the bank, which he thought suited to his burial, he told them it was the place of his last repose. They wished, however, to pass on, as the weather permitted and the day was not far advanced. But God raised a contrary wind, which obliged them to return and enter the river pointed out by Father Marquette. They then carried him ashore, kindled a little fire, and raised a wretched bark cabin, where they laid him as comfortably as they could. But they were so overcome by sadness, that, as they afterwards said, they did not know what they were doing.

"The Father being thus stretched on the shore, like St. Francis Xavier, as he had always so ardently desired, and left alone amidst those forests—for his companions were engaged in unloading—he had leisure to repeat all the acts in which he had employed himself during the preceding days. When his dear companions afterwards came up, quite dejected, he consoled them and gave them hopes that God would take care of them after his death, in those new and unknown countries. He gave them his last instructions, thanked them for all the charity they had shown him during the voyage, begged their pardon for the trouble he had given them, and directed them also to ask pardon in his name of all our Fathers and Brothers in the Ottawa country, and then disposed them to receive the Sacrament of Penance, which he administered to them for the last time. He also gave them a paper, on which he had written all his faults since his last confession, to be given to his superior to oblige him to pray more fervently for him.

In fine, he promised not to forget them in heaven, and as he was very kind-hearted, and knew them to be worn out with the toil of the preceding days, he bade them go and take a little rest, assuring them that his hour was not so near, but that he would wake them when it was time, as in fact he did two or three hours after, calling them when about to enter his agony.

"When they came near he embraced them for the last time, while they melted in tears at his feet. He then asked them for the Holy Water and his reliquary, and taking off his crucifix, which he wore around his neck, he placed it in the hands of one, asking him to hold it constantly opposite him, raised before his eyes. Then, feeling that he had but little time to live, he made a last effort, clasped his hands, and with his eyes fixed sweetly on his crucifix, he pronounced aloud his profession of faith and thanked the Divine Majesty for the immense grace He did him in allowing him to die in the Society of Jesus; to die in it as a missionary of Jesus Christ, and, above all, to die in it, as he had always asked, in a wretched cabin, amidst the forests, destitute of all human aid.

"Hereupon he became silent, conversing inwardly with God; yet, from time to time, words escaped him: 'Sustinnit anima mea in verbo ejus—my soul hath relied on His word, 'Mater Dei, memento mei!—Mother of God, remember me!' which were the last words he uttered before entering on his agony, which was very calm and gentle. He had begged his companions to remind him, when they saw him about to expire, to pronounce frequently the names of Jesus and Mary. When he could not do it himself, they did it for him; and when they thought him about to die, one cried aloud: ' Jesus, Maria!' which he repeated several times distinctly, and then, as if at those sacred names something had appeared to him, he suddenly raised his eyes above his crucifix, fixing them apparently on some object, which he seemed to behold with pleasure, and thus, with a countenance all radiant with smiles, he expired without a struggle, as gently as if he had sunk into a quiet sleep, May 18th, 1675.*

"His two poor companions, after shedding many tears over his body, and having laid it out as he had directed, carried it devoutly to the grave, ringing the bell according to his injunction, and raised a large cross near it, to serve as a mark for passers-by. When they talked of embarking, one of them, who for several days had been over whelmed with sadness and so racked in body by acute pains that he could neither eat nor breathe without pain, resolved, whilst his companion was preparing all for embarkation, to go to the grave of his good Father and pray him to intercede for him with the glorious Virgin, as he had promised, not doubting that he was already in heaven. He accordingly knelt down, said a short prayer, and having respectfully taken some earth from the grave, he put it on his breast, whereupon the pain immediately ceased, his sadness was changed into joy, which continued during the rest of the voyage.

"God did not suffer so precious a deposit to remain unhonored and forgotten amid the woods. The Kiskakon Indians, who for the last ten years publicly professed Christianity, in which they were first instructed by Father Marquette at La Pointe du Saint Esprit, at the extremity of Lake Superior (between Ashland

---

* We have given this affecting narrative of Father Marquette's death in full. Well may we pray in the words of Holy Writ: "May my soul die the death of the just and may my end be like unto theirs." It is highly probable that Father Marquette died where the modern town of Ludington now stands, though some claim it was near Charlevoix.

and Washburn), were hunting last winter on the banks of Lake Illinois (Michigan). As they were returning, early in spring, they resolved to pass by the tomb of their good Father, whom they tenderly loved, and God even gave them the thought of taking his remains and bringing them to our church at the Mission of St. Ignatius, at Missilimakinac, where they reside.

"They accordingly repaired to the spot, and after some deliberation they resolved to proceed with their Father, as they usually do with those whom they respect. They opened the grave, divested the body, and though the flesh and intestines were all dried up, they found it whole, the skin being in no way injured. This did not prevent their dissecting it according to their custom. They washed the bones and dried them in the sun. Then putting them neatly in a box of birch bark, they set out to bear them to the house of St. Ignatius.

"The convoy consisted of nearly thirty canoes in excellent order, including even a good number of Iroquois, who had joined our Algonquins, to honor the ceremony. As they approached our house, Father Touvel, who is Superior, went to meet them with Father Pierson, accompanied by all the French and Indians of the place. Having caused the convoy to stop, they made the ordinary interrogations to verify the fact that the body, which they bore, was really that of Father Marquette. Then, before landing, he intoned the 'De Profundis' in sight of the thirty canoes still on the water, and of all the people on the shore. After this the body was carried to the church, observing all that the ritual prescribes for such ceremonies. It remained exposed under a pall, stretched as if over a coffin, all that day, which was Pentecost—Monday, the 8th of June (1677). The next day, when all the funeral honors had been paid it, it was deposited in a little vault in the middle of the church, where he reposed as the guardian angel of our Ottawa Missions. The Indians often come to pray at his tomb."

On September 3d, 1877, Very Rev. Edward Jacker, then stationed at St. Ignace, discovered the grave of Father Marquette. A monument has been erected on the spot, with the following inscription:

IN MEMORIAM:
REV. DI PTRIS J. MARQUETTE, S. J.,
QUI OBIIT

DIE 18 MAII, MDCLXXV.
XXXVIII ANNOS NAT:
ET SEPULTUS EST IN ISTO SEPULCHRO
A.D., MDCLXXVII.
R. I. P.
LAPIS ISTE ERECTUS EST AB INCOLIS OPPIDI
ST. IGNATII
A. D., MDCCCLXXXII.

Chapter VII

Father Gabriel Dreuillettes, S. J. ; His Labors in Maine, Canada, and Michigan.

Another most worthy predecessor of Bishop Baraga in the Northwest was F. Gabriel Dreuillettes, S. J. He arrived at Quebec on August 15th, 1643, accompanied by two Fathers of his Order, namely, Leonard Garreau and Noel Chabanel. These two Fathers died as martyrs in the missionary field; the former was shot by the Iroquois, the latter was most probably assassinated by an apostate Huron. On the same ship also arrived Rev. Chartier, a secular priest, and three nuns.

In 1645 F. Dreuillettes accompanied some Indians on their winter chase. The poor Father endured untold hardships, hunger, and every kind of misery. His ministry, however, was productive of abundant fruit in the hearts of the poor people, who had an opportunity to hear frequently the word of God and receive the Holy Sacraments. The continual smoke in their wigwams made him blind for some time, but through the powerful intercession of the Blessed Virgin Mary, for whom he had always entertained filial devotion, and whom he had invoked most earnestly with his simple, but pious people, he recovered his sight instantly and perfectly, whilst in the act of offering the Mass of the Blessed Virgin, which he knew by heart.

For several years he labored with great zeal amongst the Abenakis of Maine. He was exceedingly kind-hearted and thereby gained the hearts of all who came in contact with him. He nursed the poor, sick Indians with all the love and kindness of a father. By day and by night he would watch at their bedside. He used to bring them food, and if he received any delicacies from others, he would bring them to the sick.

In his travels amongst the Indians of Maine he came to a New England settlement on the Kenebec River, where he was received and treated most kindly. He also visited other white settlements near the sea coast and was everywhere treated with great respect. They had found out that his conduct was most exemplary and that he sought not furs, but souls. Even the Protestant ministers of Plymouth and Boston approved of his apostolic labors amongst the Indians.

At Pentagouet he found a small community of French Capuchins, who overwhelmed the good Father with kind attentions during the few days he stopped with them.

F. Dreuillettes accompanied his Indians everywhere on their chase, doing an immense amount of good by his mortified, apostolic life, his sublime virtues, his incessant labors and his wonderful, if not miraculous, cures. He was truly "a hunter of souls." Noticing day after day the saintly, self-sacrificing life of this holy man, even the pagans were struck with admiration. They contrasted the holy life of the missionary with that of their pagan medicine-men.

"The God, whom this Father preaches," said they, "must be powerful, since He cures so perfectly the greatest and most contagious diseases, which the manitous cannot accomplish, whom our sorcerers invoke. This God must be great and wise, since He makes this stranger speak our language in two or three months, which the Algonquins cannot do after living with us a whole year. This God must be good and powerful, since He takes from this Patriarch (that was the name they gave him) the fear of the most contagious diseases and protects him against the threats of our sorcerers and against the evil of their charms, at which he mocks. This man is different from our medicine-men. They are always begging; he never asks for anything. They are, so to say, never with the sick; he stays with them day and night. They seek but the furs of beavers and other animals; he does not even look at them through a corner of his eye. Our sorcerers make good cheer as long as possible; the Father fasts sometimes fifty days, with only a little corn and without wanting to taste of meat. If we give him some delicacy, he brings it immediately to our sick. He is full of cheer in the dangers and sufferings of a long voyage. He is always busy with us, our children and our sick. He is welcome everywhere. The French at Pentagouet treated him most kindly; and, what is more wonderful, the English, who are not of the same country nor of the same language, respect him; all this shows that his God is good and powerful."

The Iroquois having struck terror into the hearts of all the surrounding country by their great victories over the Hurons in 1648-1649, the Abenakis of Maine deputed F. Dreuillettes to visit the governor of Boston and prevail upon him and his people to aid them against the fearful enemy. He accordingly went to Plymouth and Boston and visited also other New England settlements and was everywhere well received. He did not, however, succeed in stirring up the people of New England against the Iroquois. There was too much jealousy and bad feeling between the two European nations, who contended for the mastery of the great North-American continent.

What helped the cause of religion among the Indians under the Father's charge was his wonderful, if not miraculous, success in healing the sick. He was a very holy man, and hence his prayers very powerful with God. It would be out of place here to dwell at length on the countless cures he performed upon the sick Abenakis, Montagnais, Hurons, and Upper Algonquins. Many of them are recounted in the Jesuit Relations between 1643-72. However, the writer cannot forego the pleasure of giving his own account of one performed on an old man, almost a centenarian, in Maine in 1647. He writes (Relation of 1652, page 27):

"I met an old man of about one hundred years. I had baptized him already in 1647, believing him to be on the brink of the grave. This good neophyte, whom I named Simeon, received the life of the body and of the soul as suddenly after three or four years of languishing sickness in his extreme old age, that he was a subject of astonishment to all his countrymen. 'You know well,' he said to them, 'that I was dead (so to say) before my Baptism. I did not live anymore. I could not move. Two days afterwards I was seen in health. I have killed this winter four moose that I overtook in running. I have slain two bears and killed a number of deer. I continually think of Him who made all. I speak often to Jesus; He fortifies and consoles me. I outlive my family; I have seen die my son, my wife, and my little nephews. At first I felt some grief in losing them, but as soon as I began to pray, my heart was consoled, knowing that those who believe and are baptized go to paradise. I thanked Him, who made all, that they died as Christians. I feel happy in my soul because I shall soon see them in heaven. When my heart wants to wander away in grief, I throw myself down on my knees and prayer makes me find anew my heart.'

"Another old man, still more advanced in years, is so strongly addicted to prayer that he passes a part of the night conversing only with God. Sleeping once in his wigwam, I heard him get up secretly. The darkness withdrew him from my eyes, but not from my ears. He commenced his prayers with those I had taught him. He then added others so well and made such amorous acts of love to God that I was over-delighted."

These extracts, and many other edifying facts that might be added, did we not fear to tire the reader, show that those grand old Jesuit missionaries of Canada formed Christians of the very best kind. They show that the religion of these Indian converts was not, as some of our enemies assert, mere formalism, but that it penetrated deeply into their hearts, purifying, enlightening and ennobling them, making them Christians that would compare favorably with any Christians of Europe, of ancient or modern times.

In 1656 Fathers Dreuillettes and Garreau attempted to go and convert the Upper Algonquins, by which name were designated the Ottawas, Chippewas, Illinois and other tribes belonging to the great Algic family of nations. They embarked on a flotilla of more than sixty canoes of these Upper Algonquins. However, on the 30th of August the party was ambuscaded by a small band of Iroquois, who awaited the flotilla near Montreal at a place where they had to pass by. The enemy firing from behind the trees on the bank, killed several of the Algonquins and also mortally wounded F. Garreau. He died three days later at Montreal. In their hasty departure the Algonquins abandoned Dreuillettes, who was thus obliged to postpone his intended voyage.

Four years later, in 1670, he was sent to Sault Ste. Marie, where, by his apostolic labors, his exceedingly great kindness, and his miraculous cures, he converted a great number of pagans. Of all the ancient Canadian missionaries F. Dreuillettes seems to have been gifted in a particular manner and to a wonderful degree with the "grace of curing—gratia curationum." Wherever we read of him in the Relations we find accounts of his miraculous cures. The "Relation" of 1671 mentions ten of his wonderful cures at Sault Ste. Marie. It was greatly due to these extraordinary cures that the Christian religion was so highly extolled by the Indians and so many of them converted. They brought their children in great numbers to be baptized, declaring themselves ready to embrace the faith as soon as they would be sufficiently instructed. One of their head chiefs, named Ishkouakite, one day seeing Father Dreuillettes summoning by the sound of a little bell the women and children to instruction, remarked as follows:

"The Black-robes are truly our fathers. It is they who take care of us and give life to the Sault by assembling our wives and children at their place (for instruction) and by praying for us to Jesus, the God of war. Yes, even if the Sioux should come to attack us, as we have been informed they intend to do, we put all our confidence in the King of heaven and earth, who is preached to us. He alone can guard us. It is He that heals so often our sick; it is He who preserves our young men from accidents, when they go to traffic or war. How happy are we in dwelling so near the Church! Young people, women and children! Let no one be slothful in attending prayer!"

Father Dreuillettes continued to labor year after year at Sault Ste. Marie. As late as 1675 he is mentioned as laboring at his post with his customary zeal and success. He spent about thirty-five years in the Indian mission field. The writer has not been able to ascertain the year of his death.

For an account of a terrible tragedy, that occurred in 1674 at Sault Ste. Marie, we refer the reader to a note in the appendix.

Chapter VIII

Missionaries That Labored in the Northwest During the Eighteenth Century.

Between the years 1678 and 1800 there is a great dearth of missionary accounts. This is due to several causes. One of the principal reasons was the discontinuance of the Jesuit Relations in 1672. The discontinuation of these edifying and interesting accounts is much to be deplored by all students of Canadian and Northwestern history.

Some fragments of later Relations, condensed and compiled by Father Dablon, bringing the account of Jesuit labors in Canada and the Northwest down to 1678, have been published in our days through the untiring zeal of Father Martin, S. J., and John Gilmary Shea, under the title, "Les Missions du Canada." They contain F. Marquette's Journal, his discovery of the Mississippi, his establishing the Mission of the Immaculate Conception amongst the Illinois, also the labors of Fathers Allouez, Andre, Dreuillettes, etc. Many of these accounts will be of special interest to Catholic historians of Wisconsin. However, as it is our intention to confine ourselves in this work to the territory consecrated by the labors of Baraga, we will speak here only of those missionaries who labored before him in the same field which he afterwards tilled with such great success.

It is a fact patent to all readers of Catholic missionary accounts that the eighteenth century was far less productive of good results than the century preceding it. For this many reasons may be assigned. One was the unsettled state of Canada and the Northwest. For seventy-four years there was almost incessant war between England and France and their American colonies for the mastery of the St. Lawrence Valley. There was:

King William's war, A. D. 1689-1697.
Queen Anne's war, 1702-1713.
King George's war, 1744-1748.
The Old French and Indian war, 1754-1763.
Conspiracy of Pontiac, in 1763.
The American Revolution, 1776-1783.

These wars were very unfavorable to missionary work. The Indian was kept in continual excitement. It is true, there were many wars during the preceding century; but they had, at least for the Christian Hurons and Algonquins, to some extent, the appearance of religious wars, as they viewed the Iroquois not only as enemies of their country, but also of their religion.

Moreover, the Canadian governors, at least several of them, for instance, Comte de Frontenac, were more or less unfriendly to the Jesuits. The latter opposed with all their might the nefarious liquor traffic between the French and Indians, which several governors tolerated from motives of trade. It was principally the Jesuits that labored amongst the Indians. The secular clergy and the Franciscans confined their work chiefly to the French settlements and military posts. It is easy to see that this unfriendly feeling towards the Jesuits could not but be injurious to their work. Finally, the suppression of their Order in 1775 was a fearful blow to Indian missionary work. The once flourishing missions of Sault Ste. Marie, Green Bay, St. Joseph, Mackinac, were almost entirely abandoned until they were revived again in the forepart of the present century, by Fathers Gabriel Richard, Francis Vincent Badin, Baraga, Van den Broek, and others. For a list of the clergymen who officiated at Mackinac and Detroit during the last century we refer the reader to the appendix at the end of this work.

Arbre Croche being near to Mackinac, was attended from time to time from the last-named mission during the seventeenth and eighteenth century. Father Sebastian Kasle, S. J., who labored for some time amongst the Illinois, and finally among the Abenakis of Maine, and who was slain in 1724 by a New England party, states that there were Fathers of his Order in 1691 at Mackinac, Arbre Croche, Bay of the Puants, or Green Bay, and St. Joseph. As to the labors of those devoted men we know next to nothing. Let us hope that future research in Canadian and French archives may bring to light some of their letters. We will give a few items of interest about Father Du Jaunay, S. J., who, though stationed at Mackinac, or Point St. Ignace, resided also for some time at Arbre Croche, where, it is said, the Ottawas gave him a tract of land, some of which he cultivated. John Gilmary Shea asserts that he died at Arbre Croche, whereas others claim that his death occurred at St. Joseph's Mission.

In 1763 Pontiac, the Chippewa chief of St. Clair, plotted the destruction of all the English forts in the Northwest. On the 2d of June of that year a Chippewa party played their national game of lacrosse, or pagaadowewin, near the fort of Mackinaw. This fort was not located on the Island of Mackinac, nor at St. Ignace, but south of the Strait of Mackinaw, at the northern extremity of the southern peninsula of Michigan, where Mackinaw City now stands. During the play the ball was several times thrown designedly over the walls of the fort, when it would be thrown back by those within. Finally, to facilitate matters, the gate of the fort was left open, so that the players could get the ball themselves, if it should happen to be thrown inside the fort. That was just what the Chippewas wanted. The next time the ball was thrown into the fort the players rushed in, seized the arms, which their squaws held concealed under their blankets, rushed upon the few unsuspecting English soldiers and butchered them before the eyes of the French within the fort, who themselves were not molested. Captain George E. Etherington was seized and bound and was about to be burned, but was saved by the timely arrival of Charles Langlade. Whether Father Du Jaunay was in the fort at the time of the massacre does not appear. We are inclined to think that he was not there, but at Arbre Croche at that time. At any rate, he did all he could for the English commander and the remaining soldiers of the fort. We will give a few extracts of Etherington's letter and another contemporary document. Writing to Major Gladwyn, commandant at Detroit, under date of June 12th, 1763, he says:

"I have been very much obliged to Messrs. Langlade and Farli, the interpreter, as likewise to the Jesuit, for the many good offices they have done us on this occasion. The priest seems inclined to go down to your post for a day or two, which I am very glad of, as he is a very good man, and has a great deal to say with the savages hereabouts, who will believe everything he tells on his return, which I hope will be soon. The Cutaways (Ottawas) say they will take Lieut. Lesley, me and the eleven men, which I mentioned before were in their hands, up to their village (Arbre Croche), and there keep us till they hear what is doing at your post. They have sent this canot (canoe) for that purpose. I refer you to the priest for the particulars of this melancholy affair, and am, dear sir,

Yours very sincerely,
GEO. ETHERINGTON.

To Major Gladwyn:

P. S.—The Indians that are to carry the priest to Detroit will not undertake to land him at the fort, but at some Indian village near it; so you must not take it amiss that he does not pay you the first visit. And once more I beg that nothing may stop your sending him back the next day after his arrival, if possible, as we shall be at a great loss for the want of him, and I do not doubt that you will do all in your power to make him return, as you see the situation we are in, and send up provisions as soon as possible, and ammunition, as what we had was pillaged by the savages. Adieu.

GEO. ETHERINGTON"

The priest mentioned in Etherington's letter is Pere Du Jaunay. This courageous missionary, who had already rendered the greatest service to the British prisoners in the hands of the Ottawas, in order to be still more useful to them, did not fear to expose himself to the dangers and fatigues of a long and monotonous canoe-voyage upon Lake Huron. He accomplished his mission with fidelity, had an interview with Major Gladwyn, then left Detroit to return to Michillimackinac on the 20th of June, 1763, as we learn by the following extract from a curious narrative, entitled, "Diary of the Siege of Detroit":

"June 20th, 1763. This morning the commandant gave to the Jesuit a memorandum of what he should say to the Indians and

French at Michillimackinac, as also to Captain Etherington, seeing he did not choose to carry a letter, saying that *if he was asked by the Indians if he had any, he would be obliged to say yes, as he had never told a lie in his life.* He gave him a belt to give to the Ottawas there, desiring him to tell them that he was very well pleased with their not having meddled in an affair which must have brought on their ruin; and that if they would send their prisoners to Montreal, they would convince the general of their good intentions, for which they would probably be well rewarded."

CHAPTER IX

Missionary Labors of Fathers Richard, Badin, and Dejean in the Northwest Prior to the Arrival of F. Baraga.

During the latter half of the eighteenth century very little missionary work was done in the great Northwest. The little that was done during that time was confined almost entirely to Michillimackinac and Detroit. Things, however, changed for the better with the arrival of Rev. Gabriel Richard. He was born in Saintes, France, on the 15th of October, 1767. He was ordained at Issy, near Paris, and became a Sulpician in 1791. The following year he came to America and was sent by Bishop Carroll to Illinois to labor among the French-Canadians, half-breeds, and Indians at Kaskaskia. After six years of apostolic labor he was sent to Detroit, where he arrived in 1798. Here he labored for thirty-four years with great zeal and success, though not without many trials and hardships.

On the 3d of June, 1799, he visited Mackinac Island and remained there three months. He found things in a sad state. In his letter to Bishop Carroll he says:

"The trade here is principally in liquors, and as long as this state of things exists there can be no prospects of making them (the Indians) Christians... God only knows how many evils flow from this traffic. It has been observed that English rum has destroyed more Indians than ever did the Spanish sword. Several

Indian chiefs have requested that the trade in liquors be abolished by law."

In 1812 Detroit was taken by the British and Father Richard taken prisoner and sent to Sandwich. The writer found an interesting item about him and Tecumseh, which he gives without, however, guaranteeing its historical truth, as he has not found it in any historical work. The fact is narrated in the Detroit *Catholic Vindicator*, May 5th, 1855, by a well-educated Indian of Mackinac. He says:

The circumstances mentioned in that article were related to me by a person who had heard Father Richard himself speak of them.

"When Hull surrendered in 1812, the British required the citizens of Detroit, not prisoners of war, to take the oath of allegiance to the king of Great Britain. In return protection to persons and property was promised. With these advantages in view, some took the oath; while others, preferring to stand by their country even in the dark hour of her misfortune, refused to take it. Among the latter was Father Richard. When asked to swear allegiance to the king, he answered: 'I have taken one oath to support the Constitution of the United States, and I cannot take another. Do with me as you please.' Upon this refusal he was seized and hurried away to Maiden and was there placed among the prisoners of war.

"At Maiden, the place of confinement for the prisoners, was a pen or small enclosure of high pickets. On one side of it, near the ground, there was a small opening, through which the prisoners were thrust in, and their daily allowance of food passed to them, when it was not thrown in over the pickets, as was sometimes done. Within this enclosure there was no covering or shelter of any kind as a protection against the hot rays of the noon day sun, or the inclemency of the weather. This was the place into which Father Richard was thrown, after having been denied the use of even his hat. While he was an inmate of this pen the other prisoners paid him the utmost respect, and they would open for him, while reciting the Rosary of the Blessed Virgin, a narrow walk through the middle of it.

"Among the Indian allies of the British in the war of 1812, Tecumseh, as everybody knows, was one of the most distinguished, and was apparently held in high estimation by them. One day, while the above scenes were passing at Maiden, he presented himself before the British commander and, in tones and bearing of one well aware of the importance of his services, said to him in substance as follows:

" 'I have come to tell you that my young men will fight for you no longer, for you hold the Black-robe as a prisoner. I cannot answer for my warriors while you keep him shut up. I demand his liberty.'

"The commander, well acquainted with the character of his red visitor, and being unwilling to lose his friendship at such a time by a refusal, wrote immediately the order discharging Father Richard unconditionally, thus leaving him to pursue his peaceful ministry in the country unmolested. Was Tecumseh a savage?"

Speaking of Father Richard's extensive mission, Hon. Richard R. Elliott says in his "Sketch of the Life and Times of the Rev. Gabriel Richard": "Probably the greatest missionary work accomplished under the direction of any one priest in this country during the first three decades of this century may be claimed for Father Richard."... "The territory included much of the ground occupied by the Jesuits in the seventeenth and eighteenth centuries, and extended from the River Raisin, near Lake Erie, along the American shore of the Straits of Detroit, around Lake St. Clair and tributary streams, Lakes Huron and Michigan, as far as the River St. Joseph on the Indiana border, Green Bay and other parts of Wisconsin, the Island of Mackinac, the islands in Lake Huron, the Georgian Bay, and up the River St. Mary to the mouth of Lake Superior."

In 1832 the Asiatic cholera visited Detroit. Father Richard was day and night busy attending the countless sick-calls of his poor, plague-stricken people. He finally succumbed to the dread disease and died on the 13th of September, 1832. Bishop Fenwick and Fathers Badin and Baraga were at his dying bed. Thus passed away a noble missionary priest after forty years' service in the cause of religion, humanity, literature and patriotism.

In 1823 the Ottawas at Arbre Croche sent the following petition to Congress by hand of Very Rev. Gabriel Richard, a member of that body:

"We, the undersigned, chiefs, headsmen and others belonging to the Ottawa tribe, who reside at Arbre Croche, on the eastern shore of Lake Michigan, use this opportunity to make known our wishes and wants to our Father, the President of the United States. We thank our Father and Congress for all they have done for us to introduce amongst us morality and the knowledge of Jesus, the Saviour of the red and white people. Confiding in your fatherly goodness, we ask for freedom of conscience and for a teacher or preacher of the Gospel, who belongs to that society (church) to which belonged the member of the Catholic Order of St. Ignatius, which was established at Michillimackinac and Arbre Croche by Father Marquette and other missionaries of the Jesuit Order. They lived many years in our midst. They cultivated a field in our land in order to teach us agriculture and Christianity. Since that time we have always longed for such priests. Should you deign to grant us such, we shall ask them to settle again on the shore of Lake Michigan near our village, Arbre Croche, on the same place which Father Du Jaunay possessed.

"If you comply with the humble wish of your faithful sons, they shall be forever thankful to you and pray the Great Spirit to shed his blessings over the whites.

"In witness whereof, we have hereunto signed our names. August 12th, 1823.

   HAWK,   FISH,
   CATERPILLAR,   CRANE,
   EAGLE,   FLYING FISH,
   BEAR,   DEER"

Four months later, Macate Binessi—Black Bird— wrote as follows to the President of the United States:

"My Father! I desire thee now to hear me—me and all thy children in this far-off land. They extend their hands to shake thine. We, the chiefs, fathers of families, and other Ottawas, residing at Arbre Croche, pray thee and earnestly implore thee, Renowned

Father, to obtain for us a Black-robe (priest) like those who instructed the Indians in the neighborhood of Montreal. Thou art our Father. Be charitable to thy children; listen to them. We desire to be instructed in the same principles of religion which our forefathers professed when the Mission of St. Ignatius was in existence.

"We address ourselves to thee, the first and greatest Chief of the United States. We entreat thee to help us build a house of prayer. We will give land for cultivation to the Minister of the Great Spirit whom thou shalt send to instruct us and our children. We shall do our very best to please him and to follow his good advice. We shall feel very happy if thou send us a Man of God of the Catholic religion like those who taught our forefathers. Such is the prayer of thy devoted children. They trust that thou, their Father, wilt kindly hear their prayer. This is all thy children ask of thee now.

"Father, all thy children extend their hand and press thine with all the affection of their hearts.

Macate Binessi."

In 1825 Father Vincent Badin visited Arbre Croche, Mackinac Island, Green Bay and other places, as we learn from a letter to his brother in France, dated Detroit, December 25th, 1825. He left Detroit on the 25th of April of the above-named year on the schooner "Jackson." After a long and tedious voyage he arrived at Mackinac Island, or, as it was formerly called, Michillimackinac. He arrived in the evening and was received with the greatest joy by all the inhabitants, Catholics and Protestants. He was conducted to the court-house, which was lit up and tastefully decorated for the occasion, and held service the same evening he arrived. He spent a few days with the poor people, mostly French-Canadians, preparing them for the Holy Sacraments, which they were to receive at his return from Green Bay.

At Green Bay he stayed two months, teaching and instructing the poor people, who were awfully ignorant, for they had not seen a priest for fifty years, except in 1823, when Father Richard visited them. During the eight days the latter remained with them he baptized one hundred and twenty-eight persons and married twenty-six couples. For two months Father Badin labored undefatigably amongst those rude, ignorant, but well-disposed people. His instructions were well attended by old and young, Indians, half-breeds, and whites. A log church, 40x45, had been begun, it seems, during or shortly after Father Richard's visit in 1823. It was completed under F. Badin's care and supervision and by him blessed on the 26th of June, 1825, in honor of St. Francis Xavier. He baptized a large number of adults and children and admitted seventeen persons, between thirteen and thirty years of age, to their first Holy Communion. He then returned to Mackinac.

His next visit was to Arbre Croche, where he arrived on the 19th of July, 1825. At his first visit to Mackinac he had sent word to the Indians of Arbre Croche to erect a prayer-wigwam in honor of the Great Spirit and in front of it a cross. When he, therefore, arrived at their village he was agreeably surprised to find a log chapel, 25x17 feet, on the summit of the hill. He compares it to the temple of Solomon, for neither iron nor nails had been used in its construction, but only an axe! The poor Indians sang Ottawa hymns during Holy Mass with great devotion. Indian singing is slow, solemn and affecting. It is not art, but the heart that sings. Their singing is more suitable for divine service and more soul-elevating than that we hear in many of our large churches, with their "sharps and flats" and their endless and senseless repetitions. Indian singing inspires and promotes devotion. Would to God that this could be said of all our church singing! As Father Badin had arrived at Arbre Croche on St. Vincent's day, his patron-saint, he dedicated the little chapel to him.

After a short visit to St. Joseph's Mission and Drummond Island, he returned to Mackinac and Arbre Croche. As a specimen of Indian letter-writing we insert the following letter of one of the chiefs of Arbre Croche to Father Richard:

"I salute the Black-robe of Detroit and the chief Black-robe at Rome, as also the highly celebrated Father of the French, the King of France, and I press his hand.

"Now that there are so many hats (white people) in the country, we cannot kill enough game to support our children.

"But, before all things, we want a Black-robe to instruct us. We will listen to his word and fulfill his commands.

"There is too much whiskey here and we are reduced to extremes. We want to have at Arbre Croche a French priest to teach us temperance and the way to salvation. The number of Indians amounts to 650, including women and children.

Makate Binessi."

On the evening before his departure from Arbre Croche F. Badin buried with all possible solemnity a poor Indian child, which he had baptized shortly before. The darkness and stillness of the night, the burning lights, the solemn prayers of the church, the singing, combined to make a deep impression on their minds. In fact, one of the Indians wanted in all earnest to leave wife and children and become a priest! It took all the influence and persuasion Father Badin was capable of to induce this child of nature to return to his wife and children.

The next day, at sunrise, all the poor Indians assembled at the beach to bid farewell to the Father, whom they had learned to love so well. They cast themselves on their knees on the sandy beach to receive his parting blessing, which he gave them with a heart overflowing with emotion at the thought of never seeing them again.

During the voyage to Mackinac, a venerable old man, who accompanied them, spoke continually and with much feeling of the Jesuit Fathers who had formerly been stationed at Mackinac. The names of Frank and Du Jaunay were ever on his lips. They were stationed at Mackinac from 1741 to 1764, perhaps even later. He spoke very warmly about Father Du Jaunay, who had prepared him and given him his first Holy Communion. That must have been at least sixty years before. He had also often served his Mass. He showed Father Badin the place where the good Father used to say his breviary walking up and down. This seems to refer to Arbre Croche, where Du Jaunay resided part of the time. Nothing escaped the good old man's memory and with love he dwelt on the smallest circumstances connected with the Father's actions and labors.

On their way back to Mackinac Father Badin disembarked at St. Ignace, about six miles from the island, on the main land, the seat of the old Jesuit Mission founded by Father Dablon in 1670, of which F. Marquette was the first resident priest from

1671 to 1673. In 1705 the mission was abandoned. The Fathers themselves fired the buildings before departing in order to preserve them from being desecrated by the pagans. Before the church, where in 1877 Father Edward Jacker found some relics of Marquette's body, a large cross was erected, which was renewed from time to time. It was always held in great veneration by both Christians and pagans. With feelings of deep reverence towards the noble missionaries, who had lived and labored there, F. Badin endeavored to find traces of their house and church. The memory of their many virtues and labors, of their zeal, courage and self-sacrifice passed before his mind's eye. They were the red man's truest and best friends, whom they sought to elevate to a nobler mode of thinking and living, striving to make him both a true Christian and a civilized man.

Finally, having spent seven months on his missionary tour in the Northwest, F. Badin returned to Detroit by the middle of November.

In 1829 Father P. S. Dejean, a French secular priest, came to Arbre Croche, as its first resident pastor. During his two years' pastorate he accomplished much good. He built a church, 54x30 feet, with ten large windows, likewise a school and parsonage, 46x20 feet, with three rooms, the largest of which was used for a school room. These buildings were constructed of hewn logs. As the poor Indians had no horses nor oxen, they were obliged to carry the heavy logs out of the woods to the place where the church and school were to be erected. As some of these logs were thirty feet long and very heavy, it took a great number of men and hard work to carry them. At times forty or fifty would work hard at these buildings for a whole week. Certainly those poor Indians deserve great praise for their persevering zeal in erecting two large buildings under such unfavorable circumstances and with such incredible labor. This chapel was dedicated and first Mass said therein on the last Sunday of September, 1829, when many received also for the first time Holy Communion. The school was opened on the 23d of August, 1829, and within a month had thirty-eight scholars, of whom eighteen were girls. Twenty-five children boarded at the school, their parents bringing them some potatoes and corn and the missionary giving them some lard and salt. The boys were made to work at clearing the land to raise vegetables. Mr. L'Etourneau and Miss Williams were the teachers of these children of the forest. Father Dejean, in a letter to F. Richard, praises very much their zeal in instructing the poor children, who suffered considerable from the want of proper clothing.

Luckily we have another witness of those times, we mean E. J. Blackbird, who most probably attended this school himself in his boyhood days. He says:

"In the fall of 1827, my father left his subjects at Arbre Croche proper, now Middle Village, in charge of his brother, Kaw-me-no-te-a, which means Good Heart, as he was persuaded by other chiefs to come and establish himself where the mission was and send his children to school. There were only three Indian log houses at that time in Little Traverse (Harbor Springs), one belonging to my uncle, Au-se-ge-nock, one for Joseph Au-saw-gon, my father's messenger, and another to Peter Sho-min. But we and all other Indians lived in wigwams, and all the Indians were dressed in Indian style. Rev. Mr. Dejan (Dejean) brought with him a Frenchman from Detroit named Joseph Letorenue (L'Etourneau) as school teacher, and two girls from Mackinac Island (Miss Bailie and Miss Williams) as domestic servants, and an old nun, whose real name I never learned and knew only as 'Sister.' She was exceedingly kind to Indian children and we all liked her very much. The log school house was used as a dwelling as well as a school house, as all the boys and girls who attended school were kept there continually, same as boarding school. The larger boys and girls were taught household duties and to cook for the scholars. The children were kept quite clean. The French teacher took very great pains to teach them good manners, and they were taught no other but the French language. In the spring of the year each family of Indians gave one large mocok (a kind of box made of birch-bark) of sugar, which weighed from eighty to one hundred pounds, which Father Dejan would empty into barrels, and then go down to Detroit with it to buy dry goods, returning with cloth with which to clothe his Indian children. Rev. Mr. Dejan did not say Mass on week days, only on Sundays. He visited the Indians a good deal during the week days, purposely to instruct them in the manners and customs of the white man, ordering things generally how to be done and how the women should do their domestic duties, not work out of doors, and take good care of what belonged to their household."

In his letters to F. Richard, three of which are published in the annals of the Leopoldine Society, Rev. Dejean says that he baptized two hundred and twenty-four Indians, many of whom were adults. His health being poor, he left Arbre Croche towards the end of the year 1830 and returned to France.

CHAPTER X

State of Catholicity in the United States at the Time of Baraga's Arrival in our Country in 1830.

In 1783 Great Britain acknowledged the independence of the original thirteen colonies, which then formed the United States of America. They were bounded on the north by Canada, on the south by Florida and the Spanish territory along the Gulf of Mexico, and on the west by the Mississippi River. Later on Spain ceded Florida, and France Louisiana to the United States. At a still later date Texas, New Mexico and the Pacific country were added to her domain.

Before the Revolution of 1776 there were but very few Catholics in the thirteen colonies and these were confined principally to Maryland and Pennsylvania. Bishop England says that in 1783, at the close of the Revolution, there were probably not one hundred Catholics between the Potomac and Florida. Out of a total population of 3,000,000 in the United States at that time there were but 25,000 to 30,000 Catholics, with about forty priests, of whom one-half were Jesuits. The far greater number of these people were poor farmers—in Maryland—and laborers in the principal cities, Irish and German immigrants from Europe. They were a persecuted, despised and barely tolerated class of people. Prior to the Revolution the statute books of almost all the original thirteen colonies contained odious laws against Catholics. After the Revolution these anti-Catholic laws were gradually repealed. This was partly due to the fact that Catholics had fought gallantly side by side with their Protestant fellow-soldiers in the great struggle for liberty and independence. Moreover, it could not be denied that the colonists would never have achieved their independence had not Catholic France helped them in the hour of supreme need. Another circumstance aided this revulsion of feeling towards the Catholic Church. About the middle of the present century thousands upon thousands of Catholic immigrants from Ireland and Germany poured into our country, settling principally in the Eastern, Middle and Western States. The American people gradually became more and-more acquainted with these people, their religious principles, their industrious and law-abiding ways, and so prejudice and bigotry gave place to a more liberal and enlightened attitude towards their Catholic fellow-citizens. At one time, it is true, the Know Nothings, and very recently the American Protective Association, endeavored to rekindle the fire of bigotry and blind hatred against Catholics, but with poor success, for such anti-Catholic movements are too much at variance with the tolerant and enlightened sentiments of the great mass of our American people of today. The attempt to transplant Irish and Canadian Orangeism to American soil was a failure.

Prior to 1790 the Catholics of the original thirteen colonies were subject to the ecclesiastical jurisdiction of the Vicar-Apostolic of London, England. In 1790 the See of Baltimore was erected and Rt. Rev. John Carroll was consecrated first Bishop of the United States in the Chapel of Lulworth-Castle, England. The number of Catholics kept on increasing, and so in 1808 the dioceses of New York, Boston, Philadelphia and Bardstown were erected, and Baltimore made an Archbishopric and the Metropolitan See of the United States. In the South Catholicity made but little progress; in 1796 the total number of Catholics, exclusive of Florida and Louisiana, was about one thousand.

The archdiocese of Baltimore comprised, in 1830, Maryland, Virginia and the District of Columbia. Maryland contained a Catholic population of 70,000. They were, as a rule, poor in earthly goods, but good, practical Catholics. Virginia had 4,000, and the District of Columbia 1,000, making a total of 75,000 for the archdiocese. At Emmetsburg was the mother-house of the

Sisters of Charity, in Georgetown a Convent of the Visitation, and in Baltimore another of Carmelite nuns. It was in St. Mary's County that Lord Baltimore started his Catholic colony in 1632. The Catholics in this and St. Charles County were poor and their land unproductive. Their churches were cheap, wooden structures, attended occasionally by priests from other parts, as the people were unable to support a resident priest. In the District of Columbia there were some Catholics at Washington, Georgetown, and Alexandria. Washington had two churches, one of them large, the other small. In Georgetown were likewise two churches and a Jesuit college.

Out of a total population of 1,211,272 in Virginia in 1832, scarcely 4,000 were Catholics. Most Rev. James Whitfield had charge of the archdiocese, 1828-1834.

One of the foremost dioceses of the United States in 1832 was that of Philadelphia. The Catholic population of the city amounted to 25,000 out of a total of 160,000. It had five churches, four large and one small. The diocese had fifty churches, thirty-eight priests, and a Catholic population of upwards of 100,000. It was under the care of Rt. Rev. H. Conwell, with Rt. Rev. Francis P. Kenrick as Coadjutor, consecrated in 1830 Bishop of Arath. In Pittsburgh was a convent of Poor Clares, and a small clerical seminary in Philadelphia. There were flourishing congregations in Lancaster, Elizabethtown, Clearfield, Shippeville, Pittsburgh, etc.

The diocese of New York, erected in 1808, was under the care of Rt. Rev. John Du Bois, 1826-1842; it embraced the states of New York and New Jersey. In 1832 New York City had 30,000 Catholics out of a total population of 200,000. Many of these Catholics were rich and influential, but the far greater number were poor immigrants from almost every country of Europe. In 1783 there was not a single Catholic Church in the city, nor any Catholic priest anywhere in the state. The oldest church, St. Peter's, built with funds collected in Cuba and South America, was erected sometime between 1784 and 1790. In 1832 there were four large churches in New York City, also one in Brooklyn, dedicated to St. James. There were also some schools in charge of Sisters of Charity and an orphan asylum. In Albany were many Catholics, who had a large church, an orphan asylum and a school. The diocese had about thirty priests, with as many churches. Out of a total population of 2,073,987 in New York and New Jersey there were about 80,000 Catholics.

The diocese of Boston, erected in 1808, was in charge of Rt. Rev. Benedict Jos. Fenwick, consecrated in 1825. At that time there were but four priests in the diocese, which embraced all the New England States. In 1832 the number of priests had increased to twenty. The first Bishop of Boston was Rt. Rev. John Lefevre de Cheverus, afterwards Archbishop of Bordeaux in France and Cardinal. Besides the Cathedral, there was a small chapel in South Boston and a nice church and Ursuline Convent in Charlestown. The latter was soon after destroyed by a fanatical mob. The Catholic Intelligencer was published in Boston and the Catholic Press in Hartford. In Maine were many Catholic Indians, whose forefathers had been converted by Gabriel Dreuillettes, S. J., and other Jesuit missionaries of the seventeenth century. The total population of New England in 1830 was 1,960,015, of whom a little over 15,000 were Catholics.

The diocese of Bardstown was erected by Pope Pius VII. in 1808, and its first Bishop, Rt. Rev. B. Flaget, a Sulpician, consecrated by B. Carroll in 1809. In 1832 Bardstown contained a large Cathedral, a college and a seminary. There was also a Dominican monastery at St. Rose, and nearby a convent of Dominican Sisters, of whom fifteen were professed members of their Order. In Nazareth, about three miles from Bardstown, was a convent with seventy Sisters and one hundred boarding scholars. The community had charge of several Catholic schools throughout the diocese. There was, moreover, a convent of Loretto Sisters at Loretto, Washington County, containing one hundred professed Sisters. The diocese embraced Kentucky and Tennessee; a part of Indiana and Illinois was for a time attached to the diocese as a missionary district. Bishop Flaget had a Coadjutor, Rt. Rev. Bishop David. There were about twenty priests and twenty-five churches in the diocese. Out of a total population of 1,872,923 there were about 25,000 Catholics belonging to Bardstown and 5,000 in Illinois belonging to St. Louis.

The diocese of Cincinnati, erected in 1821, had for ten years Rt. Rev. Edward Fenwick as Bishop. Out of a total population of 30,000 in 1830, Cincinnati had about 6,000 Catholics. The diocese embraced the State of Ohio, with Michigan and the

Northwest attached as a missionary district. There were about eighteen priests and as many churches. In Somerset, Perry County, O., there was a Dominican monastery, St. Joseph's, and a convent of Dominican Sisters, St. Mary's. The Catholic population of Ohio, Michigan and Northwestern Territory in 1830 was a little over 32,000, of whom almost one-half belonged to Michigan and the Northwest. There were large congregations of French, Germans, Irish and Indians at Detroit, Green Bay and other places. In 1833 Detroit was made an Episcopal See, with Rt. Rev. Frederick Rese as its first Bishop.

The diocese of St. Louis, Mo., was erected in 1826. It embraced Missouri and Arkansas, with about one-half of Illinois—the western part along the Mississippi River —attached as a missionary district. Its first Bishop was Rt. Rev. Joseph Rosati, consecrated July 18th, 1826; died at Rome September 25th, 1843. The diocese was immense in extent. On the north it extended on the western side of the Mississippi to British America, on the south to Texas and New Mexico, and on the west to the Pacific Ocean. The far greater part of the Catholic population in 1830 were of French descent, besides some Irish and Germans in Missouri and Illinois, and some Catholic Indians in the far west. The Catholics numbered about 40,000, of whom over 3,000 lived in St. Louis, which had then (1830) a total population of 8,000. About three-fourths of the Catholics in the city spoke French. The diocese contained the following institutions and missions: A convent of Ladies of the Sacred Heart, with about one hundred boarding pupils; a hospital in charge of Sisters of Charity; a Jesuit college with eighty students. The above institutions were in the city of St. Louis. There was a diocesan seminary at Perryville (Barrens), in charge of the Congregation of the Missions, with one hundred students; also a Catholic congregation of 200 families with a resident priest. At Ste. Genevieve there was a French-speaking congregation of 2,000 souls. At St. Michael's there were 200 Catholics with a stationary priest. Carondelet had 140 families of French descent. St. Ferdinand, at Florissant, had eighty families, mostly French, with three Jesuit Fathers. There was likewise a convent with novitiate of the Ladies of the Sacred Heart. At St. Charles were about one hundred families, mostly French, attended by two Jesuit Fathers; also a school in charge of the Ladies of the Sacred

Heart. On the banks of the Mississippi was Portage des Sioux, a French village with forty families, attended from St. Charles. Another small settlement, La Dardenne, containing but eighteen families, was also attended from St. Charles. Cote Sansdessein, another small French mission, ninety miles from St. Louis, had sixty Catholic families. La Vieille Mine (in the lead-mine district) had a church and resident priest.

In Illinois were: La Prairie du Rocher, a French village with forty Catholic families and a church built by Father Murin, the last Jesuit missionary there before the suppression of the Order in 1775. Chare Settlement contained a considerable number of English-speaking Catholics. Kaskaskia was an old French-Indian mission station dating from Father Marquette's time. In 1830 there were but few Catholic Indians left; the French population was about 1,400. Prairie du Chien (Wis.) and La Riviere aux fievres contained about 500 Catholics. Langamo, about one hundred miles from St. Louis, had forty Catholic families.

The diocese of Charleston was erected in 1820, and its first Bishop, Rt. Rev. John England, consecrated September 21st, 1820. The diocese embraced North and South Carolina and Georgia, with about 11,000 Catholics out of a total of 1,836,432 in 1830. There were eleven priests. Charleston had about 5,000 Catholics, many of whom were negro slaves. There were two churches of moderate size, the Cathedral and another, in the city. The oldest Catholic paper in the United States, the *United States Miscellaney*, was published in Charleston. It began to appear about 1820. The Franciscan Fathers in Superior have one small volume of the above-named paper, dated 1824.

Mobile, erected as Vicariate-Apostolic in 1824 and made an Episcopal See in 1829, comprised Alabama and Florida. When Spain ceded Florida to the United States most of the Spanish clergy and people left the country, taking along almost everything of value belonging to the Church. The first Bishop of this diocese was Rt. Rev. Michael Portier, consecrated in 1826. With funds collected in Europe he built a college and seminary, containing, in 1832, about one hundred students and twelve seminarians. There were but six or seven priests in the diocese, which contained about 8,000 Catholics out of a total population of 343,931 in both states.

Chapter XI

Description and History of Baraga's Birthplace.

We enter now upon the life and labors of saintly Bishop Baraga, the man chosen by Divine Providence to take up and bring to a successful issue—after a lapse of almost a century—the glorious work of the grand old Jesuit missionaries of the seventeenth and eighteenth centuries. The latter had labored most zealously and self-sacrificingly among the Indians of the great Northwest but only partial success crowned their efforts. The Indian was not as yet ripe for conversion. Polygamy was one of the great impediments to his conversion. This great evil had gradually and almost entirely disappeared prior to Baraga's arrival in the Indian country. Moreover, the fame of the French "Black-robes" as men, who loved the poor Indian, who deeply sympathized with him in the cruel wrongs he suffered at the hands of his crafty and powerful white brother, and who labored so disinterestedly for his spiritual and temporal good: the memory, I say, of Marquette, Allouez, Du Jaunay, Gabriel Richard, Badin and others; all these memories and traditions, faithfully handed down from father to son, paved the way for Baraga and his noble co-laborers, such as Bishop Mrak and Fathers Pierz, Skolla, Van den Broek and others, to work successfully at the conversion of the Indian nations dwelling near the great lakes.

Before entering, however, upon the life and apostolic labors of B. Baraga, we beg leave to say a few words about his birthplace.

The parish of Döbernig (Slov. Dobernice), in which the illustrious subject of our narrative was born, is situated in the diocese of Laibach, Unterkrain (Carniola), Austria. It lies in a deep, arid valley. The inhabitants often suffer from the want of water, as neither river nor creek flow through it. Hence the whole country, from Treffen to Ribnica, a distance of upwards of thirty miles, is popularly called "Suha Krajina," which signifies in English: Arid Krain. The inhabitants of this waterless district, who are mostly farmers, depend upon rain for their supply of water, which, falling on the roofs of their houses and barns, is gathered and conducted by means of gutters and conduit-pipes into cisterns. In times of great drought they are obliged to haul water in barrels from the River Krika or Temenica. The country is not very beautiful, but the people are staunch Catholics and very pious, as a rule.

The parish of Döbernig is very ancient, as parish priests were stationed there in the fourteenth century. For a time it was in charge of the religious of the Cistercian monastery of Sittich, founded A. D. 1135. This monastery is about six miles from Döbernig. It was secularized in the year 1784. For some time Fathers of the Conventual Branch of the Franciscan Order had charge of the parish. However, most of the time it was attended by secular priests. Döbernig has a population of 2,400 souls, and is in care of a parish priest and his assistant.

The parish Church is dedicated to St. George, Martyr. It has two side altars, one of the Dolorous Mother, and the other of St. Anthony of Padua. In front of the latter there is a subterraneous vault, in which Baraga's maternal relatives, the de Jencic, are buried.

B. BARAGA'S BIRTH PLACE

The parish of Döbernig has eight station chapels (chapels of ease), namely:
1. St. Ann, in Smaver, in the midst of vineyards.
2. Blessed Virgin Mary, in Dobrava.
3. St. Agnes, V. M., in Knezjavas.
4. St. Peter, in Korita.
5. Holy Cross, on Mount Lisee.
6. St. Maurus, M., in Smaver.
7. St. Anthony, the Hermit, in Selca.
8. Holy Ghost, in Tahovee.

For several years a curious report has been circulating among the people of Döbernig and vicinity that as soon as Bishop Baraga would "be made a saint," canonized, his remains would be brought from their present resting place in America and be buried under the high altar of the Holy Cross Church on Mount Lisec. Perhaps so! God knows!

Baraga was born in the castle of Malavas (German: Kleindorf), as before stated, in the parish of Döbernig. As to the history of this castle, Baron Weikhard Valvasor (+1693) relates as follows in his work, "Renown of the Dukedom Krain" (Book XL, pages 308-309):

"In the parish of Döbernig there used to stand on a mountain a very ancient castle, called Kozjek. At present (1683) only a few ruins remain. During the unhappy times caused by the eruption of the Turks in the fourteenth, fifteenth and sixteenth centuries, this castle was often attacked by the Mussulmans, but never captured. Towards the end of the seventeenth century the castle Kozjek was abandoned by its owner, Count Auersperg, and in consequence Count Wolfgang Engelbert von Auersperg built—c. 1670—in the valley a smaller castle in order to live more conveniently. The materials of the ancient castle Kozjek were removed to Malavas (Kleindorf).

"After the death of W. E., Count of Auersperg, his brother, Johann Weikhard, Prince of Auersperg, inherited said castle, and after his death it passed over to his son Ferdinand, Prince of Auersperg."

In the beginning of the eighteenth century the family Morautscher (Slov. Moravcer) bought said castle. After the death of Franz Morautscher, March 3d, 1742, the castle was purchased

by Josef Karl Kern, who a few years later, c. 1750, sold it to Bernard Anton de Jencic, Baraga's maternal grandfather. In this castle were born unto Bernard A. and Katharina de Jencic the following children:
1. Anton Daniel Josef, born May 31, 1756.
2. Maria Theresia, born October 24, 1757.
3. Maria Katharina Josefa, born March 21, 1759. (Mother of Bishop Baraga.)
4. Anton Bernard Josef, born May 22, 1760.
5. Maria Elisabeth, born January 7, 1762.
6. Josef Stanislaus Anton, born May 17, 1763.
7. Ferdinand Josef Michael, born September 24, 1764.
8. Francisca Haveria, born November 6, 1765.
9. Wilhelm Vincenz Ignaz, born March 9, 1768.

In the castle Malavas, in which Baraga was born, was a very beautiful chapel, served by chaplains in the employ of Bernard Anton Jencic, who also acted as tutors to his numerous children. They were: In 1753, Christophorus Tobonneth; in 1763, Georg Zelenec; later on, Valentin Terbar, who died at the age of thirty, in Malavas, and who in the Records of the place is described: "Moribus et vita praeclarus." He was buried under the altar of St. Anthony of Padua in the parish Church of Döbernig. From 1780 to 1783 Anton Bolka was stationed as chaplain in the castle Malavas. He afterwards became parish priest of Döbernig, 1800-1827. The family Jencic were also in constant friendly intercourse with the inmates of the Cistercian Abbey of Sittich. From all this it is easy to be seen that the children of Bernard Jencic were brought up very piously and that they received a thoroughly religious education. Thus young Baraga inherited from his dear able all his lifetime.

After the death of Bernard Anton Jencic, his daughter, Maria Katharine Josefa, mother of Bishop Baraga, inherited the castle Malavas from her father. She was rich, but Johann Nepomuc Baraga, whom she married on the 16th of May, 1792, seems to have been a man of but moderate means, as he was but overseer of the castle of Neudegg. Two years after the birth of Frederic Baraga, they sold the castle Malavas to a man by the name of Santo Treo, whose grandson, Julius Treo, still owns it. Baraga's parents bought in Treffen a larger and more beautiful castle in 1799, situated about two miles from Malavas. After the death of his father, in 1812, young Frederic inherited this castle. Subsequently, when preparing for the priesthood in the clerical seminary at Laibach, he donated freely this grand mansion with adjoining lands to his sister Amalia, not even reserving an annual allowance for himself. He could therefore truly say with the royal prophet: "Dominus pars haereditatis meae et calicis inei: tu es qui restitues haereditatem meam mihi"—The Lord is the portion of my inheritance and of my chalice; it is thou who wilt restore to me my inheritance." (Ps. xv, v. 5.)

Chapter XII

Birth and Early Education of Frederic Baraga; Death of His Parents; He Studies at Laibach and Vienna; Resolves to Enter the Priesthood; Studies at the Clerical Seminary at Laibach and is Ordained There.

In the Register of Marriages in the parish Church of Döbernig we find the following entry:

*"On the 16th of May, 1792, Johann Nepomue Baraga, widower, overseer of the castle of Neudegg, of the parish of Neudegg, was united in marriage to his spouse Katharina, virginal and legitimate daughter of Bernard Jencic, of Kleindorf (Malavas), in the parish of Döbernig , in the presence of Anton Lakner and Joseph Wuzeli, witnesses, by Thomas Zajec, parish priest of Döbernig."

Five children were born of this marriage:
1. Maria, born and died March 13, 1793.
2. Vincenz Johann Nepomue, born January 23, 1794; died February 24, 1794.
3. Amalia, born July 16, 1795.
4. Irenaeus Friedrich, born June 29, 1797.
5. Antonia, born February 4, 1803.

---

* "Die 16 Maii, 1792, D. Joannes Nepomucenus Baraga. viduus, praefectus in arce Neudegg. Parochiae Neudegg, cum sua sponsa Catharina. Dni. Bernardi Jencic, fil. leg. coelibe ex Kleindorf. Parochiae Dobernicensis coram testibus D. Antonio Lakner et D. Josepho Wuzeli copulatus est ab A. R. D. Thoma Zajec. parocho Dobern."

Irenaeus Frederic Baraga, the subject of our narrative, was born, as the above shows, on the 29th of June, A. D. 1797, in the castle of Malavas, or Kleindorf, in the parish of Döbernig, diocese of Laibach, Unterkrain (Lower Carniola), a Slavonic province of the Austrian Empire. The full name of his father was Johann Nepomuc Baraga, and that of his mother Maria Katharina Josefa Jencic. As in the above-cited matrimonial record, the first name of his mother, Maria, was dropped, so also young Baraga never used in after life his first name, Irenaeus, neither did he ever use it in any of his official documents as priest or bishop. Hence we will also drop it and simply call him Frederic, as he always did himself. As the name of his parents indicate, F. Baraga was a Slavonian by birth and not a German, as is stated in some magazines.

In the Baptismal Record of Döbernig we find the following entry:

*"On the 29th of June, 1797, was baptized Irenaeus Frederic Baraga, legitimate son of Johann Nepomuc Baraga and Katharina Jencic (pron. Jentschitsch). The sponsors were Andreas Zurbi and Juliana Abulver, by Anton Herman, assistant priest."

Young Frederic had the inestimable blessing of having deeply pious and God-fearing parents. His early education was in the hands of pious house-chaplains, who instructed him in the first rudiments of learning and religion. His mother being very pious, instilled into the hearts of her children from their earliest years the love of God, a loathing of sin, and great compassion for the poor and suffering. Young Frederic was thus brought up under most favorable circumstances, under the vigilant eyes of pious parents and tutors, away from the seductions of the world and from contact with bad children.

In the year 1806, at the age of nine, Frederic was sent by his parents to Laibach. There, under a private tutor engaged for him, he studied the main branches that were taught at the high school of that city. This no doubt was done to shield the innocence of the pious child, to keep him from coming into contact with bad children, who might easily sow the seeds of sin in his pure,

---

* "Die 29 Junii, 1797, baptizatus est Irenaeus Fridericus Baraga, filius legitimus Dni. Joannis Nepomuceni Baraga et D. Catharinae Jencic. Patrini D. Andreas Zurbi et D. Juliana Abulner, per cooperatorem Antonium Herman."

innocent heart. Under this private teacher he made rapid progress in all his studies.

After having spent two years at Laibach, his pious mother died. Although deprived at the early age of eleven years of his dear mother, her memory never faded from his mind. Her piety and love were a source of most happy recollections to his tender heart, and her motherly admonitions and pious examples guided him safely through the dangers of his childhood days. Bodily taken away by death, she lived in his memory and her loving spirit accompanied him upon all the ways of his afterlife.

In the year 1809 he entered the gymnasium at Laibach. That same year Napoleon Bonaparte took possession of Carniola, Frederic's native land, and established the "Kingdom of Illyricum." It remained under French rule till 1813. After Napoleon's disastrous Russian campaign and his retreat from Moscow, during which he lost almost half a million of men, Austria shook off the galling yoke of the Corsican usurper and with the help of other continental nations drove him from his throne and landed him in Elba.

During the French occupation young Frederic commenced to study French, to which he took such a delight that he continued it even after the French had been driven from his native country. The knowledge of this language was of great service to him during his long missionary career in America. As he was the only son of the family, neither he nor anyone else could think otherwise but that he would be in future the sole heir of the domain of Treffen, especially as his father, who died in 1812, transferred them to him. Hence his prospects for a life of worldly happiness were all that could be wished for. He was unusually bright, intelligent, gifted with great talents, had many friends, a large domain, good health, and the prospect of a long and happy life. Yet he renounced all these worldly advantages to devote himself to the service of God as priest and missionary.

After the death of his father, in 1812, young Frederic went to live with George Dolinar,* professor of canon-law and ecclesiasti-

---

* He died October 21st, 1858, at the ripe age of ninety-four years. Though but a layman, he was professor of Canon Law and Church history at the diocesan clerical seminary in Laibach. He was a very learned and pious man, and wrote, in 1837, a

cal history in the theological department of the Laibach Lyceum. He lived with this pious man for four years, until 1816, and found there a truly Christian home. The same order, the same Christian virtues, which he had seen constantly practiced at the house of his dear parents, were also prevalent in the house of his dear friend and protector. With great delight did young Baraga often write in his letters to his sister Amalia, of the wisdom, learning, and deep piety of this good man. It was certainly through a special and loving arrangement of Divine Providence that Baraga's youthful days were spent under the best possible surroundings. It is, after all, true that man is to a great extent a creature of circumstances. A child brought up, as Baraga was, will in mostly all cases be good and virtuous, whereas another living in bad surroundings will generally turn out to be bad. Baraga had saintly parents and tutors and he became a saintly man himself.

Whilst pursuing his classic studies at Laibach he applied himself likewise to other useful branches of knowledge, such as music, painting, and languages. He once painted a picture of the Good Shepherd and sent it to his sister Amalia, writing at the same time: "The picture shows the Good Shepherd who gave his life for his sheep and who, when one of the hundred is lost, leaves the ninety-nine and seeks the lost one until he finds it. Do you recognize the Good Shepherd, dear Amalia'?" Surely his beloved sister, who received this letter and looked often at this picture, of which her brother so frequently spoke in his subsequent letters, must have felt then that he would sooner or later become a living and true image of the Good Shepherd.

After Frederic Baraga had finished his course of classics at Laibach he entered the University of Vienna in the year 1816, being then nineteen years of age. In the Austrian metropolis he was surrounded by dangers on all sides, but, thanks to his early training and the nobility of his soul, he escaped the contagion of vice and, in the words of St. James, "preserved himself unspotted from the world." Moreover, his tender, strong, and pure love for his sister Amalia had an ennobling and purifying effect on his young and sensitive heart. In a letter written to her from Vienna, and dated May 6th, 1819, he says:

book entitled, "The Life of Our Lord Jesus Christ."

"You are and continue to be the consoling source of my thoughts. Although my soul is sometimes engaged in other thoughts and finds pleasure in them, yet my spiritual joy is but imperfect and weak and my heart endures it only for a short time. Sometimes there is in my heart such a desolation and emptiness that it can only be filled by raising my thoughts to God and His eternal love and with thinking for your dear, sisterly love, your affection for me."

Here Baraga shows his great affection for his sister, but he guards this feeling by directing it towards God. He says in one of his letters to her, "More and more do I understand that the eternal love gave me a heart craving for love, and I also see what a great favor God has bestowed upon me by giving to my heart another heart to which it is given to appreciate the sentiments of my heart and to return them a hundred fold. Indeed, my dearest Amalia, if my heart were not filled with the purest love to you, it would be impossible to attain to that high degree of holy love, with which a Christian soul loves the eternal Love (God), for the ways are unknown to us, by which God's love draws us to Himself. God Himself gave you to me as a gift, that by this gift He might remind me of His infinite love to us. Never have I felt love so strongly as I do since I have loved you more than anything else on earth. In this manner has earthly affection, my love to you, in the designs of the Almighty and All-wise God, become the means by which He prepares our hearts for the joys of heaven and draws us more and more to Himself."

Young Baraga was a great lover of drawing and painting. He sometimes spent from six to eight hours at landscape painting. From Vienna he sent two beautifully bound books with drawings of his own, executed with paint-brush and pen, and also in colors. In the first and larger book he wrote the following dedicatory words:

"Dir, geliebte Amalia, zum Andenken von deinem Friedrich."

On the next page he wrote:

> "Nimm es hin, O liebe, Theure Schwester,
> Dieses Denkmal nimm aus meiner Hand,
> Es knüpft inniger und enger, fester
> Unser schönes, zartes Liebesband."

This book contains fifty-two drawings, all executed by himself, some of them miniatures, representing rustic scenes. At the conclusion a flower is painted with the following inscription:

"Zärtlich brüderliche Liebe
Weihet diese Blumen dir."

On the next to the last leaf a wreath is drawn with symbols of the four seasons, and below are the following words:

"Jede der vier Jahrzeiten
Möge Freude dir bereiten."

On the last leaf are the following words in German:

"Gezeichnet und gemahlt
von
Friedrich Baraga
Hörer der Rechte
An der hohen Schule zo Wien
im Jahre des Heils
1818.

The second book of his drawings has the following title:

"Kleinigkeiten aus dem Lanschaftsfache, gezeichnet v. F. G. B."

It contains a beautiful poem of his own composition, which we give in full, as many of our readers may be conversant with the German language:

1. Bist du ewig fort-geschwommen,
Himmlische Vergangenheit?
Wirst du nimmer wieder kommen,
Nimmer wieder, schöne Zeit?

2. Durch die buntgeschmückten Fluren,
Folgend selbstgewählten Spuren,
Sang der Hirt der Herde nach.

3. Unschuld alles, was er dachte,
Unschuld alles, was er machte,
Unschuld alles, was er sprach.

4. Wo er immer hingekommen,
War er freundlich aufgenommen,
War er unter Freundes Dach.

5. Alle liebt 'er ja wie Brüder,
Die geliebten liebten wieder,
Denn die Herzen waren eins.

6. Doeh der nachtumflorten Räume
Fürst zerknickt die zarten Keime
Dieses göttlichen Vereins.

7. Tückisch führte er den Milden
Aus den duftenden Gefilden
Seines blumenreichen Hains.

8. Lehrte ihn nach Schatzen trachten,
Zeigte ihm des Berges Schachten,
Wo versteckt der Demant glüht;

9. Liess ihn Gold und Perlen schauen,
Lehrte ihm Paläste bauen,
Und sieh da—die Unschuld flieht!

10. Nach der Flur zu ihren Lieben,
Die allein noch treu geblieben,
Sie aus Marmorsäulen zieht.

11. Und in ihrer reinen Mitte,
In der anspruchslosen Hütte.
Wohnt sie, selber anspruchslos.

12. In der Städte Dunstrevieren
Lässt sie Sünden triumphieren,
Ruht in der Gefilde Schoss.

13. Den sie rein und würdig findet,
Sie mit reinster Lust umwindet,
Die aus ihrem Füllhorn floss.

14. Und auch dich, hat sie umschlungen,
Dir auch ist ihr Ruf erklungen,
Dich auch sie im Arme hält.

15. D'rum hab' ich die Heimath-Scenen
Dieser Hehren, dieser Schönen,
Dir zum Denkmal auserwählt.

16. Nimm sie hin die Heimath-Scenen
Dieser Hehren, dieser Schönen,
Die dich fest im Arme hält.

At Vienna, Baraga studied law, rhetoric, aesthetics, English, French, and Italian, all of which were of great use to him in afterlife. He also took good care of his health by shunning all youthful excesses, abstaining from wine and alcoholic liquors, and by undertaking long journeys on foot during the seasons of vacation. Thus he walked on foot all the way from Vienna to Pesth, walking through Moravia, Bohemia, and Bavaria. It was thus he prepared himself for his future apostolate in the wilds of America. Both body and soul were trained for the great work in store for him.

The thought of embracing the sacerdotal state entered his mind gradually during the time when he was pursuing his studies at the University of Vienna, and seems to date from the year 1819, after he had spent three years in the study of law and other useful sciences. How it originated, we have no means of ascertaining, as he kept it a secret. He had painted the Good Shepherd some years previous and spoke of it repeatedly in his letters to his beloved sister Amalia. As he was filled with the love of God, may we not suppose that the frequent thought of the Good Shepherd seeking the lost sheep may have gradually awakened in his pious and loving heart the desire to imitate Him by devoting himself to the priestly state?

Baraga's spiritual guide and confessor at Vienna was Blessed Clemens Maria Hofbauer, that illustrious member of the congregation of the Most Holy Redeemer, who died on the 15th of March, 1820, and was beatified in 1888. It was most likely this holy man that awakened in the heart of Baraga the desire of devoting himself to the ecclesiastical state. Baraga visited him frequently at Vienna, and the sight and conversation of Blessed Clemens Hofbauer must have made a deep, lasting, and salutary influence on the pious and sensitive youth. Although Baraga never said anything about how, or when, or by whom he was induced to study for the priesthood, we may safely conclude that, after God, it was due to the counsels and prayers of his holy confessor. The burning zeal of St. Alphonsus was infused into the heart of his worthy disciple, Blessed Clemens Maria Hofbauer, and he again communicated it to his spiritual child, Baraga.

In order not to do anything hastily, he continued the study of law until he had finished his course in 1821.

He then applied for admission into the archdiocese of Vienna, and his petition was readily granted. However, when he returned to Laibach and told his bishop, Rt. Rev. Augustine Gruber, the latter prevailed upon him to enter the diocese of Laibach, to which he belonged by right, and he accordingly entered the Seminary of Laibach in the month of November, 1821. He was an exemplary theologian, most fervent in prayer, a close and earnest student, observing conscientiously all the rules of the house, performing all his duties with punctuality and fidelity, whether the eyes of his superiors were upon him or not. With what untiring zeal and happy results he applied himself to his theological studies is shown by the fact that he completed certain branches of study within a year, which others could scarcely accomplish in two. So at the end of two years he was duly prepared and received Holy Orders on the 21st of September, A. D. 1823, at Laibach, and the next day he said his first Mass in the Cathedral of that city.

We will not attempt to describe the feelings of joy and happiness which flooded his pure soul on that grand day, when he consecrated himself unreservedly for his whole life to the service of his Divine Master. Having conveyed all his rights and title to his paternal domain of Treffen to his sister Amalia, he refused even to accept an annuity of 600 fl., which she wished him to reserve.

Chapter XIII

Father Baraga's Labors at St. Martin's.

After his ordination, F. Baraga continued his theological studies for another year, during which he preached the word of God with great fervor and unction from time to time. Speaking of the feelings that animated him at that time, he writes to his sister:

"I am now without an inheritance in this world. When He shall come, whose name is Love, to call His faithful servant, He will say, 'Come! I will give thee what is right!' Here I am, Lord; give me now what is mine; give me my crown, as thou didst give it the Apostle St. Paul."

In the autumn of the year 1824 he was sent to the parish of St. Martin, as assistant to its reverend pastor. There he had abundant opportunities to show his great zeal and administrative talents. The one great thought ever uppermost in his mind was the salvation of the immortal souls entrusted to his care. This solicitude for their spiritual welfare made him become "all to all" in order to gain all. He labored with all the energy of his loving heart to convert sinners, to reclaim them from the ways of sin and vice, and lead them back to the path of virtue. The better everything that he undertook for the good of his people succeeded, the more favorable was the judgment they passed upon his priestly labors and the higher rose the burning flames of his fatherly love for them. He gave himself neither rest nor peace, so that his sister was obliged, even in the first month of his pastoral labors, to implore him to take a little care of himself and not to ruin his health. His answer was characteristic of the man:

"Without work I cannot live. In labor I find my sweetest consolation. I want to labor and I must do so as long as it shall please God to keep me in good health. At present my strength for work is at its best. God's harvest-field is immeasurable; the grain is high and ripe. The servant, whom the Master has called to work in the harvest-field, should not stand by and look on idly whilst the wild birds are devouring the ripe grain. No, this I cannot do; it was not given me to act thus, even if I should have to give up my life right here."

No, it was not given him to be idle. His whole life might be described in these few words: sanctity in action. He sought no reaction here below, no rest before the final rest of death, the rest of the grave. As a true pastor of souls, he labored "in season and out of season" for their salvation. With fiery zeal he announced the truths of salvation, taught the little ones entrusted to his care the rudiments of faith in plain catechetical instructions, heard confessions day after day—for people flocked to his confessional from far and near—and visited, consoled, and helped the sick and poor.

As he himself knew and felt the sweetness and happiness which are the fruits of a thorough knowledge and understanding of the consoling truths of the holy Catholic religion, he had also the peculiar gift of teaching and explaining those truths with that convincing power and burning zeal that even the most hardened sinners were moved to repentance and yielded to the sweet and powerful workings of divine grace in their hearts. And when those poor, repentant sinners came to him to open to him their hearts, it was his greatest joy to receive them, to pour the oil and wine of consolation into their lacerated hearts, to bind their wounds and bring them back to the Good Father from whom they had strayed. He knew how to inspire them with a salutary fear of the justice of God and unite the same to the consoling confidence in His infinite mercy. While engaged in the study of civil law in Vienna, he gave expression to this double sentiment of fear and confidence, which should animate the repentant sinner, in a letter to his sister Amalia, written in 1819. He says:

"Great and fearful are the offenses committed by men. But the greatest and most awful offense is the sin of despairing in the infinite mercy of our eternal Father. O that I could imprint with angelic words upon the heart of the miserable sinner who with a contrite heart wishes to return to his offended Father, but who, under the sense of the immense outrage committed against God, cannot imagine how the eternal, just God can forgive him; O that I could impress upon his heart these words: My friend! In the everlasting justice of God is also at the same time the love of an infinite mercy, though we cannot understand this with our poor, limited intellect. By your offense you indeed outraged the divine justice so much that all mankind combined could not sufficiently atone for this outrage, but the eternal Son of God gave Himself for you, sinner, as a just reconciliation. He reconciled you with the Eternal Justice and made it possible for you to be re-united again with the Eternal Love through love. See, God demands nothing else from you but your good will."

With F. Baraga's coming to St. Martin, new life came to the parish. Before that but few frequented the Sacraments; many did not comply with their Easter-duty. Moved by his soul-stirring discourses in the pulpit and his boundless love and compassion towards poor sinners in the confessional, numbers came to him from all quarters; sinners, to be led back to God; just to be conducted by his pious and prudent counsels on the road of Christian perfection. Being thoroughly convinced of the truth that the spiritual life of a congregation will flourish in proportion as it is nourished by the frequent reception of the Holy Sacraments, it was his first and chief endeavor to induce his people to approach the Sacraments worthily and frequently. And the people, seeing how it made him happy to go to the confessional, and how he was ever ready, at a moment's notice, to be at their disposal, needed no long sermons and exhortations to bring them to confession in large numbers.

Moreover, on Sunday afternoons and on holy days he taught catechism, and the instruction proved so attractive and popular that the church used to be filled as at High Mass, many people from the country remaining in town after the morning services in order to attend the same.

Would to God that all priests having the care of souls would imitate this saintly priest. The children are the choice portion of the flock of Christ. Upon their training depends the future of the family, Church and State.

F. Baraga took special pains to instruct such poor children as could not be sent to school on account of the poverty of their parents. He gathered them around him, and that with such results that he could write in the very first month of his arrival at Metlika, to send him sixty A-B-C books, as those he had brought along were not sufficient for even one-half of the children that frequented his school.

His inborn kindness as well as supernatural love to souls made him assiduous in attending the sick. He consoled them in their sorrows and relieved their wants as far as was in his power. Kind-heartedness and charity to the poor and destitute he had imbibed, so to say, with his mother's milk. He learned the practice of these virtues at the side of his mother when visiting with her the sick and needy. Greed or covetousness he knew not. The more he had the more he gave. He had a beautiful saying: "Whatever you give to the poor, that you shall have; what you do not give, that someone else will have." He frequently used the words of our Lord: "As long as you did it to one of these My least brethren, you did it to Me."

People tell of him how one day he came home barefooted, because he had given his shoes to a shoeless beggar whom he had met on a sick-call. Another time he found a sick beggar lying on the street, unable to help himself. F. Baraga took the poor man in his arms, carried him to the priest's house and nursed him until he recovered. If at times he expressed a wish to have something, it was only that he might be able to give to the poor and sick, or to do good with it. His usual saying was: "I do not want riches, but to have a penny (to give away) I would like well enough."

In the year 1826 F. Baraga published a Slavonian prayer book with the title, "Spiritual Food." The editor of the Slavonian Life of Baraga, Dr. Voncina, speaks of this prayer book in terms of the highest praise. He says:

"Of all the prayer books that were ever edited there is none which was so suitable to the needs and wants of the Slavonian people, none to which they were so accustomed, as to this prayer book of Baraga, 'Dusna pasa;' very many editions of it have already appeared; it remains even to this day the most popular prayer book in Krain (Carniola). This book is a dear souvenir, by which Baraga lives and shall continue to live in the grateful memory of the pious Slavonian people, wherever they reside."

In the year 1830 F. Baraga published a work called, "The Veneration and Invocation of the Blessed Virgin, Mother of God." He translated this work from the German into Slavonian at the request of his reverend friend and benefactor, Very Rev. Augustin Sluga.

At the parsonage in St. Martin's parish there was an aged servant by the name of Mica (Mary). F. Baraga used to say to her: "Mica, please go and see whether any one is waiting at my confessional; I shall be very thankful to you for so doing." The good old woman would go into the church at two or three o'clock Sunday mornings, because generally at that early hour there would be people in the church preparing for confession, to whom Baraga would attend immediately. His confessional used to be besieged with crowds of penitents, for people from other parishes, ten or twelve miles away, would flock to his confessional. Hence it was a common saying with the people of St. Martin: "With us it is *always* Portiuncula."

This great zeal of Baraga met with disapproval from his colleagues. Many of the Austrian priests of that period had received their clerical training in seminaries infected with Febronianism and Jansenism. The clergy educated at such institutions were destitute of the true, Catholic spirit of piety and discountenanced the frequent reception of the Sacraments. The result may easily be imagined; a universal stagnation of Catholic life and devotion. Baraga had imbibed a different spirit. His constant aim was to enkindle everywhere true piety and promote the frequentation of the Sacraments. On this account he was disliked, belittled, and ill-spoken of by many of his luke-warm, Josephinistically-educated colleagues. The people, however, held to Baraga. They loved and venerated him as a saint. Even at the present day, after a lapse of seventy years, his memory is still fresh with them, and in almost every house in St. Martin's parish a picture of Baraga may be seen. Many a pious legend they tell of their former curate. On a certain occasion, they say, he was taking the Blessed Sacrament to a sick person, his sacristan accompanying him. They came to the River Save, which had to be crossed. As there was no bridge anywhere nearby, the sacristan took Baraga on his shoulders and carried him across the river *without feeling any weight.*

The only priest in the whole neighborhood, who befriended Baraga and who was heart and soul with him, was Rev. Augustin Sluga, the last member of the suppressed Cistercian Abbey of Landstrass in Unterkrain. He was at the time parish priest of Krainburg (Slov. Kranz), and also dean of that district. Baraga found in him a true friend and protector. The latter invited him to preach, during three consecutive days before Ash Wednesday, 1827, in the parish church of Krainburg on the Holy Eucharist, which he did before an immense concourse of people, to the great mortification of his envious colleagues in the ministry. They wrongly accused him to his Bishop, Rt. Rev. Anton Aloys Wolf, who removed him from St. Martin and sent him to Metlika, near the boundary of Croatia, in June, 1828. His friend, Rev. Augustin Sluga, died at the ripe age of eighty-nine, on the 19th of July, 1842, being at the time honorary Canon of the Cathedral Chapter at Laibach.

As to Baraga's personal wants in those days, they were few and easily supplied. His meals were extremely frugal; he seldom ate meat, and then but little; he never drank wine. He generally slept on hard boards, and had very little furniture in his room. He gave all he had to the poor and for beautifying the House of God. He was remarkably kind to children, especially to those who were poor. On great feast days his sister Amalia used to send him from Treffen all kinds of confectionary, not a bit of which he would put in his own mouth, but would divide these sweetmeats among the children, the poor and the sick. The latter he visited very often and consoled and helped them in every way possible.

Chapter XIV

Father Baraga's Labors at Metlika. He Resolves to Devote Himself to the Indian Missions of America; Is Received Into the Diocese of Cincinnati. Scene at His Departure from Metlika.

In Baraga's time the parish of Metlika was large, with more than 6,000 souls and twenty or more stations with chapels. The people were very kindhearted, but sadly neglected and very ignorant as to their religion.

In this place Baraga labored with his customary zeal and forgetfulness of self. God visibly blessed his labors. One of his first cares was to procure a beautiful set of stations or Way of the Cross for the parish church of that city, to promote devotion to the Passion of our Lord. In due season they arrived and were carried in solemn procession through the streets of Metlika from the parsonage to the church. They were solemnly blessed and erected in the month of October, only four months after his arrival in that city. F. Baraga himself describes vividly this celebration in a letter to Amalia:

"When we arrived at the church, the men, who carried the pictures, placed themselves, two and two at the places where the pictures were to be hung. Then I ascended the ladder and it was a real joy for me to hang up the pictures with my own hands. Oh, dearest Amalia! I cannot tell you how the hearts of my people beat with joy at this unusual solemnity. I have often shed tears, but our people never shed tears so readily and so abundantly as on that Sunday. Now let me tell you how we finished this solemnity. In my inexpressible delight I ascended the pulpit and out of devotion for the Way of the Cross, I spoke with such fervor that very soon all my hearers were in tears, and many have declared afterwards that this day would remain for all time in the memory of the people of Metlika. Everlasting praise to the Heavenly Father, whose hand was opened with such fatherly mercy at this celebration, for it is He that effected all this. Our country people cannot control themselves, so great is their delight at the sight of the holy stations, and they often ask when the priest will pray the stations with them."

Scarcely had this one wish of Baraga's been fulfilled, namely, to see the Way of the Cross erected in the parish church of Metlika, when he turned his attention to other needs of the church. The high altar, as well as the side altars of the parish church were in need of renovation, new vestments, and other church utensils had to be bought for the churches under his care. All these things were procured in a short time, mostly at his own expense. At the same time he found time to publish a work, entitled: "Visits to Jesus Christ in the Most Holy Sacrament," a translation of a similar work of St. Alphonsus Liguori. All this shows how much a zealous servant of God can undertake and accomplish, who has God's interests and the salvation of souls at heart.

Whilst F. Baraga was thus laboring with all the earnestness and energy of his noble soul for the salvation of his countrymen, the thought of so many poor pagans living in the darkness of heathenism, in ignorance and sin, awakened gradually in his heart an earnest desire to devote himself to their conversion. It cannot with certainty be said when and where this thought of going to the pagans first originated in his mind. Certain it is that it was dormant several years before he finally revealed it to others. The author of the Slavonian Life of Baraga remarks:

"Taking into consideration that already at St. Martin's he usually slept on *bare straw or on a board*; that he would not shrink neither from great cold nor excessive heat; that he not only abstained entirely from wine, but that very often his *breakfast and supper consisted only of bread and water*; from these and many other such fasts and mortifications in eating and drinking, we must conclude that this resolution must have been growing for several years even if he had not so declared in a letter to his sister. For this reason he kept silent and did not reveal this his heart's desire to anyone, until from various indications he had been fully convinced that his wish in this matter perfectly agreed with the will of God, and that it was God who was calling him thither where his own heart's longing was directed."

In the year 1829 a society was organized in Vienna, Austria, which had for its avowed object the supporting of the North American missions. This society was called "Die Leopoldinen-Stiftnng" (Leopoldine Society). It was approved by Pope Leo XII., who, eleven days before his death, issued in its favor an Apostolic Brief and granted certain indulgences to its members. His Imperial Highness, Archduke Rudolph, Cardinal Prince Archbishop of Ollmutz deigned to act as its supreme head and superintendent, and he appointed the Prince Archbishop of Vienna as his representative. The rules and regulations of the society were published at Vienna on the 13th of May, 1829. This society has done immense good to the struggling church of our country. Year after year large contributions were sent to the poor bishops, missionaries, and religious societies. In the appendix of this work the reader will find a detailed statement of the contributions sent to this country between 1829 and 1868.

Father Baraga looked upon the establishment of this society in his country as one of the many indications of his vocation to the Indian missionary field. He, therefore, made known the secret wish of his heart, namely, to go to the Indians, to his bishop and to the managers of the Leopoldine Society, all of whom highly approved of his design. Full of joy at the successful outcome of his request, he immediately wrote from Metlika to his sister Amalia, under date of November 4th, 1829:

"You say the truth when you write that the will of God is seen plainly in my choice to go on the mission. Therefore I most firmly hope and I am immensely rejoiced that God has looked upon me with a truly great love and *that He has heard my most fervent prayers and supplications, which are of several years' duration!* From all that has happened in such an extraordinarily short time, I hope to foresee that it will be through the will of God that I go to the mission. I prayed to God, especially when going to Laibach, and later until I received my answer from Vienna and the bishop's representative, to so guide and dispose my spiritual and temporal superiors, whose hearts are in His hands, that by their decision His most holy will might be made known to me, which I could not know in any other way. And see, without any hesitation, both my spiritual and temporal superiors grant me their permission to go to those missions, on condition that I obtain from the corresponding bishop the assurance that he will receive me into his diocese."

Having thus obtained the necessary permission to leave his diocese, he wrote to Rt. Rev. Edward Fenwick, Bishop of Cincinnati, for admission into his diocese. This letter was lost. In vain F. Baraga waited and waited for an answer. No answer came. However, during the long months of anxious suspense he had ample opportunity to examine and consider any doubts that might have arisen in his mind as to the true nature of his vocation to the missionary life. But as in all things, so also in this important affair, he sought nothing but the fulfillment of the most holy will of God. *Fiat voluntas Dei* —may the will of God, not mine, be done—was his daily and hourly prayer. These sentiments of entire resignation to the will of God are beautifully expressed in a letter to Amalia, his sister, dated January 22d, 1830. He writes:

"You now think that after all it may be that I will need those books myself. To be sure, with God everything is possible. God could allow my letter to the Bishop of Cincinnati, or his to me, to be lost on its long and unsafe transit. I will certainly write another letter if I receive no answer by March the 19th, feast of St. Joseph. Almighty God can permit my second letter to be lost, like the first, if it should be His holy will that I am not to go there. But He has at His disposal a thousand other means of turning me away from my design. He is the Lord— His holy will be done!"

Having waited in vain until the 5th of April, he wrote a second letter to Cincinnati. The answer came on September 22d, 1830, and filled him with great joy, to which he gives expression in a letter to his sister:

"Now at length I hear from afar the voice, which invites me to come to the holy mission. On the 22d of September, just on the seventh anniversary of my first holy Mass, I received a letter from

North America, from the Bishop of Cincinnati, in which his representative, that is, the Vicar-general, entreats me most pressingly to come as soon as possible to that so much neglected part of the Lord's vineyard. Now I dare hope that all obstacles have been removed; now I shall soon reach the goal for which I have so long aspired."

In another letter, written to that same sister he loved with such a strong and pure love, shortly before his departure from Metlika he says amongst other things:

"I must scold you a little for giving yourself so much unnecessary trouble and care, that you are so much afraid on my account of the cold winters, of the hardships, hunger and thirst, and all kinds of dangers, which may overtake me on my travels. Do not, my dear sister, do not, I beseech you, let these trifles worry you. If the missionaries troubled themselves about cold, heat, hunger and thirst, fatigues, dangers and other hardships, they would not bring many heathens into the Christian fold. As merchants do not shrink from perils and hardships in order to increase their possessions which they can enjoy only to the end of their short life, why should these difficulties frighten me who have no other object in view than to gain immortal souls for heaven? Banish, then, all these vain cares from your mind, which oppress you so much as you write in your letter, and give me up perfectly and completely to the Lord."

After Baraga had arranged all his affairs and received all things necessary for his long journey, it was his only care to start as soon as possible. Great was the grief of the good people of Metlika when the day of his departure was come. He had labored among them for two years and had endeared himself to them by his many acts of kindness and fatherly goodness. He had been a true father and friend to them all. His departure from Metlika was indeed sad. Towards the end of October, 1830, on a Sunday after catechism, he spoke a few words of farewell to his people. Cries and lamentations broke forth on all sides. Baraga himself could not restrain his tears. He left the pulpit and kindly requested one of his reverend colleagues to pray the Litany in his stead. But when the people noticed that he was not kneeling as usually before the altar, they ran out of the church after him and kissed his hands and garment, crying piteously at the same time.

The next day the wagon that was to take him away was waiting in front of the priest's house. Hundreds of people had come from all sides to see him once more and receive his parting blessing. When Baraga came out of the house all crowded around him to kiss his hands or garment. All wept bitterly.

After Baraga had taken his seat on the wagon, someone attracted his attention by tapping on his arm. It was the parish priest, who was also dean, Rev. Marcus Derganc. He had entertained for a long time a great dislike to Father Baraga on account of the latter's great popularity. "Father Frederic," says he, addressing Baraga, "you have rummaged a great deal in our churches and wanted to make yourself important by getting things for them. But all is not paid for yet. Who will pay for them when you are gone?"

Baraga arose from his seat and looked sadly at the dean. Tears glistened in his eyes. He said: "Very Rev. Dean, you know very well that I have no property and that my pockets are empty. I willingly give you my coat that you may pay with it the remaining debts." He then began to pull off his coat, which he had lately got made to cover with it his shabby clothes. At this, loud murmurs of discontent were heard. The people were highly incensed at the dean's unreasonable display of ill-will against Baraga. The dean hastily withdrew, full of confusion and without taking Baraga's coat. The debts, which the latter had contracted in repairing and ornamenting the churches under his care, were afterwards paid mostly by his sister Amalia and partly by the voluntary contributions of pious people.

After the dean's departure, Baraga wanted to drive away. But the people seized the wheels of the wagon on which he was sitting, and forcibly held back the horse and wagon. He could not stir. He consoled them and begged to let him depart, but in vain. It was only after a long delay that they finally let him go. Once more he gave them his blessing, and the wagon began to move. Many ran after him. All cried so loud that their cries and lamentations could be heard at a great distance. We are reminded here of St. Paul's departure from Miletus (Acts Ap., ch. xx). "Magnus autem fletus factus est omnium."

Great, also, was the grief of his dear sister Amalia. when, on the 29th of October, at half-past nine in the evening, she accompanied him to the stage coach which was to carry him away. But this we must mention: that Baraga himself, though very tender-hearted and easily moved to tears, left everything that was dear to him—sister, fatherland, all—with a cheerful heart. All was forgotten in the happy thought of becoming now a missionary in America.

After a journey of two days and three nights, he arrived at Vienna on the 1st of November. There he was received with great joy and much kindness everywhere, especially by the directors of the Leopoldine Society, who gave him 400 florins to pay his traveling expenses, as he was their first candidate for the Indian mission. Others presented him with various articles for his mission.

Chapter XV

Father Baraga Leaves Europe. Incidents of His Journey. Arrives at Cincinnati. His Labors in That City.

Having obtained his "Exeat" from the Rt. Rev. Bishop of Laibach and his admittance into the diocese of Cincinnati, Father Baraga departed from Vienna on the 12th of November, 1830. Traveling by way of Linz, Passau, and Landshut, he arrived at Munich, Bavaria, on the 15th of said month. He stayed there two days, and went, on the 19th, to Strassburg. Being on French territory, he feared trouble on account of the excited state of the country. He was not molested, however, in the least. On November 23d he arrived at Paris and remained there three days to see the most celebrated sights of the great French metropolis.

On the 27th of November he arrived at Havre de Grace, where he was obliged to wait until the first of December, on which day he embarked for New York. It is an indication of F. Baraga's humility and frugality that he traveled as deck-passenger. The fare from Havre de Grace to New York was but 52 florins. The weather was, on the whole, very favorable. On the second Sunday and Monday of Advent, however, they had a fearful storm, which filled the passengers with terror, as the mountain-high waves threatened to submerge the ship. During the voyage F. Baraga suffered much from sea-sickness, but no sooner had he landed than he recovered and enjoyed better health than he formerly had in his own native land.

He landed in New York on December 31st, 1830. With feelings of deep gratitude to Divine Providence, who had brought him safely across the stormy Atlantic, he stepped on the soil of the New World, where he was to labor so long and faithfully for the conversion of innumerable souls.

Although New York contained then one hundred and sixty churches of all possible denominations, he found only four Catholic places of worship, and that in a city which then had a population of 200,000. On the 4th of January, 1831, F. Baraga left New York, and landed the same day in Philadelphia, where he stopped five days. At the urgent request of the priest, who had kindly received him, he preached with a heart full of emotion, in German, on Sunday, the ninth of January.

On the following day he set out from Philadelphia, and arrived late that same day in Baltimore. The next day he paid a visit to Most Rev. James Whitfield, Archbishop of that city. The good Prelate received the young priest most kindly and praised his good intention of devoting himself to the Indian mission. He left Baltimore on the 12th of January. A short distance from Columbus, O., an accident occurred, which might have cost him his life and which shows the loving care of God for the young missionary. As he was traveling on a stage, he arrived, sometime after midnight, at a hotel not far from Columbus. The passengers got out to warm themselves. Scarcely had they done so when the horses became frightened and ran away. At a considerable distance the stage was found in a ravine all smashed to pieces. The passengers thanked God for their wonderful escape, for had the accident occurred a few moments sooner, while they were on the stage, some of them would probably have lost their lives. At the next house another conveyance was hired, and so they arrived safely at Columbus, whence a stage brought them to Cincinnati, where Baraga arrived on the 18th of January. The whole cost of the journey from Vienna to Cincinnati was 365 florins. Bishop Fenwick received F. Baraga most cordially. It pleased him highly that Baraga had arrived so soon, for he had not expected him before May. He was particularly delighted when F. Baraga told him that he had come, not to stay in the city, but that he wanted to go to the Indians to labor for their conversion. The good Bishop told him to remain over winter in Cincinnati and that he would take him along on his next Episcopal visitation and station him at a suitable place.

F. Baraga was enthusiastic with praise of Bishop Fenwick. He says one cannot imagine a more humble, kind, pious, and zealous Prelate than the Bishop. He compares him to St. Francis de Sales on account of his affable and saintly disposition. As to his labors during his stay in Cincinnati, F. Baraga writes as follows to his sister Amalia, under date of March 19th, 1831:

"We have here in Cincinnati two congregations—the one English-speaking, the other German. In a former letter I have informed you that the number of German Catholics here is quite considerable, and I have to hold divine service for them until I leave for the Indian mission. Now, during Lent, I preach three times a week, as the Bishop has enjoined me to do, namely, on Sundays, Wednesdays, and Fridays, in the afternoon, besides which I have another sermon at the 10 o'clock Mass on Sundays. In addition to this I have catechism for the German children three times a week—on Tuesdays, Thursdays, and Saturdays. Moreover, I attend sick-calls and have other pastoral duties to perform.

"Whatever spare time I have I bestow upon improving my knowledge of the English language. What I have learned of this language in Vienna is of such service to me now that I can understand almost all I read in English and express myself in conversation. It is not difficult to learn English in our residence here, as almost all our conversation is carried on in that language.

"Not long ago I had to perform a missionary duty in English. The case was this: A negro, who could speak but English, was in danger of losing his life through a contusion that happened to him on board a steamboat. This negro had often entertained the wish to be baptized, but had never executed this good resolution and had not belonged hitherto to any religious denomination. But when this misfortune brought him to his death-bed, the desire to be baptized and become a Catholic revived in him lively. A woman, therefore, came to our house to bring an English-speaking priest to this negro, but there was none just then at hand. As the woman declared that the sick man was in danger of death, I went immediately with her. When I arrived at the house and found the negro really very sick, I asked him whether he earnestly desired to be baptized and become a Catholic. He declared expressly that such was his wish, whereupon I baptized him after some preliminary instruction and preparation. He was afterwards more fully instructed by another priest.

"A missionary in North America should know almost all languages that are spoken in Europe, for people of all European nations are to be met with here. During the short time that I have been here, I have used in the performance of my pastoral duties all the languages I know except the Slavonian. I have heard several confessions in Italian and French, and God gives me the grace not to find it as difficult to hear French and Italian confessions and give instructions in these languages as it was in Slavonian during the first year of my priestly career.

"I have also not omitted to learn the language of the Indians a little. An Indian youth, who is being educated in our house, occasionally gives me instructions in that language, which, however, is not easy to be learned. It has long and queer-sounding words, but I hear it is poor in words and very simple. Here are a few:

God means in Ottawa—Kitschemanito.
Heaven—Wakwing.
Hell—Anamakamegong.
Earth—Aki.
Sun—Kisis.
Moon—Tibikikisis.
Day—Kischigak.
Night—Tibikot.
Water—Nibisch.
Fire—Skote.
Soul—Ninschibam.
Father—Nosse.
Priest—Makateokonoje.

Mary, mother of grace, means in Ottawa—Maria, quenatsch ningwinam.

Mary, our protectress, pray for us, means in Ottawa-Maria, genawenimiiang! gaganotamawischinam.

"Today, that I am writing, is the feast of St. Joseph. Here it is not a feast of obligation; otherwise I would not have had time to write to you. All day I am thinking of my dear relatives and acquaintances in Europe. I love you all as dearly as I did when yet in Europe, and even at this great distance I think daily of you. We live, it is true, in different parts of the world, and the immense ocean rolls between us, still we can always be united in sentiment and prayer and remain united until the divine love unites us still more intimately hereafter in the kingdom of everlasting love."

As we have seen above, there was as yet no separate German Church in Cincinnati, although the Germans were even at that time numerous enough to form a large congregation (in 1831). The ground, however, had been bought for a German Church, but the people were very poor, having come but lately to Ohio, and being mostly laborers and farmers. There was thus but one Catholic Church in Cincinnati in 1831, which was Bishop Fenwick's cathedral.

Father Baraga enumerates, in a letter dated January 22d, 1831, the churches built in Ohio during Bishop Fenwick's administration, prior to 1831: The cathedral in Cincinnati, a church at Lancaster, Somerset, Canton, Zanesville, New Lisbon, one in Guernsey County, two churches and a monastery in Perry County, and a church in Brown Co.; in all, ten churches. In the following places churches were soon to be erected: A German Church in Cincinnati, another church in Tiffin, Clinton, a German Church in Huron County, and others.

Bishop Fenwick (Edward), who was himself a Dominican, led with his priests and ecclesiastical students a real monastic life in a poor, dilapidated building, dignified with the name of seminary. At five in the morning the bell would ring and all would rise. Before and after meals prayers were said aloud, as is customary in monastic houses; after meals followed a short adoration of the Blessed Sacrament. There were five priests and four ecclesiastical students, one of them a full-blood Ottawa Indian from Arbre Croche, Mich., with the name of William Maccatebinessi (Blackbird), a youth of eighteen years, who could speak English and Ottawa, and was to be sent back, after his ordination, to his people in the wilds of Michigan to work at their conversion. He was subsequently sent to Rome by Bishop Rese, and studied with marked distinction in the Urban college of the Propaganda Fide, where he died on the 25th of June, 1833.*

The residence of Bishop Fenwick and his priests was very poor indeed. With the money received from the Leopoldine Society, Vienna, he had erected, prior to Baraga's arrival, a three-story college, at a cost of $7,500, and Baraga estimated that it would take about $4,000 more to finish and furnish it. At the special request of his beloved Bishop, F. Baraga wrote a letter of thanks to the above-named society for their generous donations to the Cincinnati diocese. The very first donations of the Leopoldine Society were for the diocese of Cincinnati. In April, 1830, they sent 22,220 florins, and in August of the same year again 12,200 florins; in all, 34,420 florins. We shall show hereafter how much the Catholic Church in the United States owes to Austria, to the generosity of her ruler, of her nobility, clergy and people.

---

* In his work: "History of the Ottawa and Chippewa Indians of Michigan," the author, A. J. Blackbird, asserts that William Macatebinessi was assassinated at college. For a full refutation of this groundless assertion see note in appendix.

Chapter XVI

Father Baraga Sets Out from Cincinnati for His Indian Mission. His Labors Among the Whites Along the Route. He Arrives at Arbre Croche.

As we have before remarked, Bishop Fenwick told F. Baraga, upon his arrival in Cincinnati, that he would take him along in the spring, when visiting the Indian missions of his diocese, and duly install him amongst his future spiritual children. The burning zeal of the saintly Father manifested itself, as might be expected, everywhere on this journey. Wherever there was an occasion to preach the word of God, to baptize poor children, to hear confessions and bring back sinners to God, or to visit the sick, Father Baraga was there. He gave himself no rest seeking the poor "lost sheep of the house of Israel." Of him it may be truly said as it was of our Lord: "Pertransiit benefaciendo"—he went about doing good. We will give to the kind reader the particulars of this journey in Baraga's own words:

"On the 21st of April, this year"—his letter was dated Arbre Croche, August 22d, 1831—"I set out from Cincinnati to betake myself to the mission station assigned to me. To complete my narrative, I must mention here what the humility of my Rev. Bishop passed over in silence in his former communications to the Leopoldine Society regarding his indefatigable zeal for the cause of God. It is this: In order to further the cause of the Indian mission, the Bishop resolved to make the entire journey from Cincinnati to Arbre Croche with me. The Indians of that place are acquainted with him; he had been there once before. They call him the Great Black-robe or High Priest and have great respect and unbounded confidence in him. It was therefore very good that he came here with me and installed me in their midst. The distance from Cincinnati is at least as great as that from Vienna to Naples.

"Bishop Fenwick desired me to leave Cincinnati a couple of weeks before him in order to hunt up, on the way, Catholic families and give them an opportunity to perform their Easter duty. In a small town called Miamisburg, thirty-five miles from Cincinnati, I found the first Catholics, and they were Germans. I stayed there a few days, said Mass, preached three times, and heard confessions. I learnt here that there was another Catholic family twelve miles from Miamisburg. I went thither and found a good man and his equally worthy wife and six children. These good people were highly rejoiced at my coming. They prepared themselves for their Easter confession, and the next day both of them and their two oldest children received Holy Communion. I preached there likewise in a large room of his house. In the neighborhood there are many Germans, who, it is true, are all Protestants, but who gladly hear the word of God, even when announced by a Catholic priest. This man had informed his neighbors that a Catholic priest had arrived —as I was informed, I am the first Catholic priest that ever came to that part of the country—and thus many assembled to hear the sermon. They were satisfied with the doctrine announced, but no tree falls with one blow!

"Next day this man conducted me three miles further into the woods to a venerable old Irishman. I had been informed that this poor old man of eighty-one years had been living a long time in the wilderness, that he was half blind and deaf, and that for many years he had had no chance to receive the Holy Sacraments. The evening before my intended visit I sent a boy to tell him that a priest would come the next morning in order to hear his confession and give him the Holy Sacraments, at which the good old man was very much rejoiced. I accordingly went and found him in a very miserable hut. In this shanty resided the old man, his wife, and three other women with five small children. The poor old man, who had not seen a priest for upwards of *fifty years*, received the Holy Sacraments, of which he had stood in want for so long a time.

"The other inhabitants of this hut were not Catholics. I was heartily glad to have been able to give spiritual help to this poor old man, who stands at the door of eternity. But God gave me, in addition, another ineffable missionary joy. As above remarked, there were five small children of different mothers in this hut, and I learnt that not one of those children had yet been baptized. Their mothers are unhappy creatures, who profess no religion, and, consequently, did not trouble themselves about having their children baptized, as there are many such in this wild and too free country. Besides, no priest had ever before penetrated this wilderness. When I proposed to them to baptize their children, two of the mothers immediately consented, but the third did not. However, she soon acquiesced, and the holy baptismal function proceeded. I thanked God most heartily and begged Him at the same time that, if it were His holy will, He might take to Himself all or some of these poor creatures, who had now become His children, or, that He might let them become more fortunately situated (for their religious good) than they are at present.

"I then returned to Miamisburg and journeyed on further to another pretty large city named Dayton. Here I awaited Rt. Rev. Bishop Fenwick. In the meanwhile I performed missionary duties in this city. There are but few Catholics there and they are very lukewarm, with the exception of a few.

"On the first of May I said Mass in the house of the Catholic with whom I was stopping. In the afternoon I preached in a Protestant Church. There are many Germans here of all sects. It appeared to me very singular to preach in a Protestant Church and before a Protestant congregation. Besides, the sermon was preached in my secular clothes, without surplice and stole. Alas! It is really a misery the way religion fares in this country. In addition to the many sects that are found here, there are everywhere a great number of atheists. They are neither baptized, nor have they any kind of faith or religion. There are many good-natured people to be found amongst them, who have grown up in this sad state solely through neglect on the part of their parents and through want of priests. And now they remain in their infidelity because they know nothing better. Many of these unhappy creatures might easily be gained for God and the Church, if there were but more priests to preach the Gospel to them. *I intended to ask my Bishop for permission to let me always travel around in the country to seek such lost souls* and stay with each one until he would be thoroughly instructed, baptized, and strengthened in his holy faith, and then go on further. How many souls might I not gain for God! When in Cincinnati I deliberated about this matter with Very Rev. Vicar-General Rese, but he told me it would be more useful and better for me to go to the wild Indians; that the prospects there were brighter still. Hence in this regard all I can do is to pray God to send soon several laborers into this abandoned part of His vineyard, that so many immortal souls, redeemed with His precious Blood, may not perish."

The above reflections show the heart of a true pastor. Not ease and comfort, not money or honors, souls, immortal souls, redeemed with the precious Blood of Jesus, these were all that F. Baraga sought. To the true pastor the soul of the poorest Indian or negro child is as precious as that of the greatest king or millionaire.

Father Baraga continues: "From Dayton I set out, in company with my Bishop, for Detroit, where we arrived on the 15th of May, and where we remained five days. There are many German and French Catholics in this city. I spent my time in preaching and hearing confessions.

"From Detroit we traveled by water to Michilimackinac, where I did not delay long. On the 28th of May (1831), I arrived at Arbre Croche, and shortly after came also my Bishop. Happy day which placed me among the Indians, with whom I will now remain uninterruptedly to the last breath of my life, if such be the most holy will of God!"

Chapter XVII

Labors of Father Baraga in Arbre Croche.

The good Indians of Arbre Croche were highly pleased at the arrival of their new pastor. They were filled with unbounded joy when, at Baraga's first Mass in their rude chapel, Bishop Fenwick told them that he would leave him with them and that their new Father would always remain with them.

The newly converted Indians gave their new pastor great consolation. In his report to the Leopoldine Society of 1831 he praises their docility, humble and ready obedience, piety and child-like attachment to him. They always called him with the endearing name of Father and behaved towards him like good children do towards their father. Whatever he told them to do was immediately done and the order of divine service punctually observed.

At five in the morning the Angelus bell was rung and the whole village assembled at the church for morning prayers, which were read aloud by one of the head-chiefs. Then followed Holy Mass, at which a great number assisted every day. Every evening the bell was rung again and all assembled for night prayers, at which they sang pious hymns in their native tongue. After devotions, he gave them a short catechetical instruction, which, of course, the poor, ignorant, but well-meaning, Indians needed very much. On Sundays and holy days of obligation they had divine service *four times*, namely, early morning prayers in common, then High Mass at 10 A. M. At 3 o'clock in the afternoon were Vespers and catechism, and night prayers at sunset. Truly this was a model Christian community.

INDIANS LOGGING NEAR HARBOR SPRINGS (ANCIENT ARBRE CROCHE)

In the beginning F. Baraga, like all missionaries, employed the service of an interpreter. Luckily, he had an Indian who could speak French fluently. When preaching, F. Baraga would say a few sentences in French and stop; then his dusky interpreter would tell his countrymen what the Father had said. He likewise heard confessions in the same way. The people were satisfied at this, as they knew that their beloved Father could not as yet speak their language and that the interpreter was a good Christian and well instructed. The writer had to do the same thing when he preached and heard confessions among the Menominees at Keshena in the winter of 1865-1866. Although confessing through an interpreter is highly disagreeable to white people, it does not seem to be so repugnant to the Indian, provided the interpreter be a person of great virtue and discretion. F. Baraga praised his people for going often and willingly to confession. Scarcely a day passed without someone going to confession. Between Christmas and New Year all the communicants, to the number of one hundred and thirty-seven, approached the Holy Sacraments. This filled the heart of the pious pastor with sweet joy and consolation. He also kept up the school, started by his predecessor, Rev. F. Dejean. He had at first forty children, boys and girls, whom he and his interpreter instructed in reading, writing, and the catechism.

Speaking of his labors at Arbre Croche during the fall and winter of 1831, he says:

"It is unspeakably consoling and joyful to me to be here. The conversions of pagan Indians, who live around here, are so numerous that in the short space of two months and a half that I have been here, seventy-two Indians, children and adults, have been baptized; among them are venerable old men of sixty and seventy years. I make, from time to time, excursions into the country with my interpreter, and when I find a wigwam I enter. In some wigwams I find only Christians, in many they are all pagans, and in some they are mixed. Where I find pagans I try to show them the utility and necessity of the Christian religion, which God Himself has taught us. I have often the joyful consolation of seeing how deep the word of God penetrates into the hearts of these poor savages and how they resolve to embrace a religion which can make them happy for time and eternity. I then take care to have these catechumens instructed in the first rudiments of the Christian faith by others who are already Christians and live near them, and then they are solemnly received into the Church. I cannot express with what heartfelt joy and grateful feelings I baptize newly converted pagans, especially when there are several to be baptized together. On one day I had seven, and on the 12th of July—O happy, never to be forgotten day!—I baptized at one time eleven pagans.

"The inhabitants of this part of the country are real heathens and idolators. They adore not only the sun and the moon, but have, moreover, their household gods, to whom they offer solemn sacrifice, at the conclusion of which they have their sacrificial banquet. They are full of idolatrous superstitions and have bags full of all kinds of superstitious objects, of which they make use at their sacrifices and other pagan ceremonies. Now, when a pagan having such a bag is converted, he brings this devil's bag to the missionary to be burnt. Not long ago such a bag, full of superstitious articles, was brought to be burnt in front of our church. I hope that the Lord of hosts, who alone should be adored, receives with great satisfaction such burnt offerings. The pagan who brought me this sack to be burnt is one of the chiefs of the Ottawa nation. I hope that his conversion, which caused quite a commotion, will bring about that of a great many others.

"God, the sole cause and perfecter of all good, be a thousand times praised for all the good He allows to be accomplished here."

Father Baraga's church, school and house were no architectural beauties. They were the work of Indian carpenters, whose *principal*, if not *only*, tool, was their axe or hatchet. The roofs of these buildings were covered with birch-bark, and when it rained the water came in through many a hole. On such occasions he would spread his cloak over the table, on which he kept his books and papers, and open his umbrella and put it above his bed to keep it dry; he himself would sit down in that part of the room where it rained the least. Truly his was a poor, hard life; a life full of privations, yet he says he felt happier in his little room, notwithstanding all hardships and miseries, than many others in their gilt palaces. "Superabundo gaudio in omni tribulatione nostra"—I exceedingly abound with joy in all our tribulation.

Baraga's church was comparatively large and could seat about four hundred persons. It was a very poor building, built of logs and covered with bark. He had nearby two small missions, which he often visited. In one of these places not only the roof, but the whole church was made of birch-bark, like the common Indian wigwam; it was, in Indian parlance, a birch-bark prayer-wigwam.

He found the Ottawa language at first very difficult, not having any books to aid him in the study of the language. His interpreter, however, was of great help to him, and with his assistance he worked at composing an Ottawa dictionary and grammar. He also intended to compose an Indian catechism with prayers and hymns, which Bishop Fenwick promised to have printed in Cincinnati.

During the summer and fall of 1831 the number of conversions was so great that nearly all the people of that place were now either Christians or catechumens under instruction, and soon to be baptized. By the 4th of January, 1832, that is, in less than six months, he had 131 converts, mostly adults. It was his intention to leave Arbre Croche as soon as most of the pagans were converted, and go north, where, as he was told, there were a great many pagans who had never heard or seen a missionary. Of course, there were some pagans at Arbre Croche and in the neighborhood who were hardened in paganism and sin. No missionary can convert all. Even our Lord, the great model of all true missionaries, did not convert the hardened pharisees and scribes. Faith is a gift freely offered to all, but it is not forced upon anybody. Of the Apostle's ministry it is said: "brediderunt quoti quot praeordinati erant ad vitam aeternam," "As many as were ordained to life everlasting believed."

"I cannot thank the love of God enough," he says, "that He called me to a country where there are still so many pagans and so few preachers of the holy faith, There is but one priest in the neighborhood, who is about fifty miles away from me, at Mackinac. The other missionaries are 400 to 500 miles away, and the further north one goes, the fewer missionaries does he find, and the more pagans. Oh, how glad I am and how thankful to God that I have left a country which has a superabundance of priests and have come here where I can count my fellow-priests, who are hundreds of miles away! If some of my younger fellow-priests would know what happiness Indian missionaries experience, and how many occasions they find to work at the salvation of their fellow-men, certainly some of them would resolve to brave all the hardships and dangers and come to this country in order to preach the word of life to the heathens, and make them Catholics, and thus bring them to eternal life. It is true, many hardships are connected with the missions in this country, but they are far outweighed by the consolations and spiritual joys which are enjoyed here."

May these saintly words of Baraga find a responsive echo in the hearts of many a young, noble-hearted priest! "The harvest is great, but the laborers are few." There are about 300,000 Indians in the United States and Alaska. Of this number a great many are still pagans. The Jesuits, Benedictines, Franciscans and some secular priests are doing noble work among them; still much remains to be done.

Although Father Baraga had such great success, this did not elate him nor make him proud. He was little in his own eyes. All our Indians praise his great humility. We see this beautiful virtue shine forth in all his letters. They breathe humility, gratitude to God and his benefactors, ardent zeal for the salvation of souls and great love and kindness towards the poor Indians. He was truly a man of God, a man of prayer, gifted with apostolic virtues; hence God's blessings attended his work everywhere.

Speaking of his labors during the winter of 1831-1832, he says: "Indescribable is the goodness of our God, which reveals itself here so much. I am infinitely thankful that He has deigned to use a poor man as an instrument for manifesting to these poor heathens His merciful love and grace. Conversions continue steadily and those converted are very good Christians. They live in peace and brotherly love and have an extraordinary fear of committing sin. They like very much to go to confession and keep going oftener and oftener. Some days I have from twenty to thirty confessions."

"I await with great longing the near arrival of spring, for then I will again have more numerous conversions and baptisms. There are many pagan Indians in this neighborhood who promised me, last summer and autumn, when I went to seek them in their wigwams and forests and spoke to them about the Christian religion, that they would embrace it and be baptized next spring. Many of them are being instructed during this winter in the principles of our holy faith by such of their fellow Indians as are already converted, in order to receive Baptism immediately this spring."

Chapter XVIII

Father Baraga's Visit to Beaver Island.

In the early part of spring, 1832, a Christian Indian of another part of the country came to tell Baraga that he had conversed with many of his pagan countrymen about the Christian religion, and that they had assured him that they, too, would become Christians as soon as a priest would come and instruct them. This made our good Indian so happy that he made a journey of three days to tell the Father the joyful news. He invited the missionary to visit that section during the coming spring and assured him that he could establish quite a mission there. F. Baraga praised his zeal for taking such an interest in the eternal welfare of his countrymen, gave him some pictures, and bade him return home and strive to keep his people in their good disposition. From two other Indian villages came the same joyful tidings. The good Father's expectations were not disappointed. Between Easter Sunday, April 22d, and June 24th, that is, in two months, he baptized one hundred and nine pagans, mostly adults. Several of these converts were venerable old men, who, at the brink of the grave, so to say, received the grace of spiritual birth in Jesus Christ and with it eternal life.

He writes: " Since the conversion of the pagans was the only motive I had in leaving my dear fatherland and coming to this wild country, I feel great satisfaction and experience unspeakable spiritual delights at the great success the Lord of the harvest gives to my labors. I cannot sufficiently thank God for coming here, where so much good can be done. Even if I would have nothing else to do for the rest of my life than to keep and confirm in the faith the Indians thus far converted, I would be perfectly satisfied. I hope, however, that God will give me the grace to convert many more pagans to the true faith, and bring them through the saving teachings of Christianity to civilization."

During the past winter F. Baraga had often made enquiries whether there were any other Indian villages nearby. He was informed that there was one a day's journey distant, another a day and a half, and a third a distance of three days. As soon as his Indian parishioners at Arbre Croche had performed their Easter duty, he made a trip to Beaver Island, a beautiful island in Lake Michigan. The island is of considerable size and named Beaver Island from the many beavers that used to be found there. There was a small Indian village on this island, consisting of eighteen wigwams. The principal source of support was fishing and making maple sugar.

During the past winter one of these poor Indians had imbibed some knowledge of Christianity by conversing with some of his Christian countrymen. He came afterwards to Arbre Croche and was baptized. He proved to be a very good Christian. When about to return to his island-home, F. Baraga requested him to tell his people that he, Baraga, would visit them the next spring and preach to them the word of God. So in due time the zealous missionary embarked in a small sail-boat with some Christian Indians of Arbre Croche. We will give his own account of the journey:

"My heart beat sensibly when we approached the island. I have a white flag with a red cross in the middle, which I unfurl to the winds when going to a mission, so as to make the boat of the missionary recognizable. We had a favorable wind when sailing toward the island. Lovely floated in the wind the friendly banner of the cross and announced the coming of the minister of the Crucified. As soon as the island dwellers—who, as all savages, have remarkably sharp eyes—saw and recognized my banner far in the distance, the head-chief caused his flag to be immediately hoisted over his wigwam. My Indians of Arbre Croche immediately noticed the flag of the head-chief and interpreted this as a very good sign, which made me feel at ease.

"Finally, when we approached Beaver Island, I saw a number of these pagans hasten to the shore to bid us welcome. The men fired a double salute with their guns to show how much they rejoiced at the coming of the missionary. Scarcely had I stepped ashore, when all the men came and shook hands with me to bid me welcome. They then conducted me to their village, composed of poor birch-bark wigwams. I first entered the wigwam of the head-chief, where a number of these poor savages assembled and could not satisfy their eyes gazing at the Black-robe, for they had never seen a priest before.

"When a person has any business to transact with the Indians of this country he must observe certain formalities. Hence I did not tell them immediately what I had to say to them, but conversed on other different subjects. At last I requested the head-chief to convene next day a grand council."

An Indian council is called in Chippewa: Sagasswaidiwin, a smoking together, because at such public deliberations every Indian smokes whilst listening to the speeches made by the tribal orator and other speakers. Women are excluded from such public assemblies.

The Father continues: "I told him"—the head-chief of the island—"that I would speak to the people about important matters. So next day they all assembled and I made them a speech, in which I briefly and clearly showed them the necessity and benefits of the Christian religion, and finally requested the chief to answer. The latter did so through his orator, assuring me that they were very much pleased and reckoned themselves happy at seeing a priest on their island and that they desired most earnestly to embrace the Christian faith. You can imagine what a heartfelt joy this answer caused to the missionary. I remained some time with them, instructed them, and the 11th of May was the happy day on which I baptized twenty-two of these Indians.

"From there I went to another small village, which is two days' journey from Beaver Island, on the other side of Lake Michigan, in the territory of the Northwest. As I have remarked above, I had last winter an opportunity to send word to the Indians of that village that I would visit them during spring. Hence when I arrived there they received me in the most friendly manner and rejoiced exceedingly at the coming of the missionary. The good feeling of these poor savages, who had remained pagans so long solely because no preacher of the faith had ever before come to them, filled my heart with inexpressible sadness and joy. I was deeply moved and surprised when I saw that these good people, in whose hearts the anticipating grace of vocation to the holy faith worked so mightily, had begun to build a little church, Indian-fashion, of logs and bark, even before I had come to them! They had not thought that I would so soon fulfill my promise of coming and seeing them, and that was the reason why they had not as yet completed their church. When I saw them working so diligently at their church, I, too, began to work, and my companions, nine in number, encouraged by my example, aided in the good work, and we finished the church that very day. The next day I called them all together and, having first blessed the church, I said Holy Mass in it and preached. I cannot describe with what deep emotion and gratitude towards God I performed the ceremonies of the church. The thought: In this wild place, in this primeval forest, where but lately only the cry of savages was heard and idolatrous sacrifices offered to the wicked spirits, now in this same place stands a temple of the living God, in which the immaculate Lamb of God is offered to the heavenly Father—this thought affected me so strongly that I wept tears of the deepest emotion and I could not find words with which to thank God. Happy are we that He needs not the expression of words! He sees our hearts! This little church is built but of logs and bark and is in want of all that can please the eye or express artistic taste; yet it appears to me to be a more precious temple than so many churches in Europe, richly decorated with gold and works of art, and which are often desecrated by the lukewarmness and misbehavior of those that visit them.

"I dedicated this little church to the honor of God under the name and patronage of His Virginal Mother Mary. When I made—in Europe—the resolution to consecrate my life to the (Indian) mission, I promised our dear heavenly Mother that I would dedicate the first church, which I would bless amongst the Indians, to her protective Name, for I am convinced that she continually prays to her divine Son for the success of our mission.

"I remained quite a long time with these good Indians, instructing them in the doctrines of religion, and said Mass every day. All the Indians of this place, large and small, old and young, embraced the Christian religion with one solitary exception, namely, an old man, to whom God seems to have denied the grace of faith on account of his pride. He is unwilling to believe anybody except his own very weak reason. He maintains stubbornly that he lived once before on earth, that this is his second life, and after ending this life he wants to go where his pagan forefathers are." This last remark is a common saying with pagan Indians.

"The 25th of May was for these Indians the happy day, on which they were regenerated by water and the Holy Ghost unto eternal life. I baptized on that day nineteen pagans. Thanks be to the good Shepherd, who has so mercifully led these poor lost sheep to His fold. Thanks be also to Mary the loving Mother of grace, who continually prays for the conversion of pagans.

"After Baptism they brought to me all their idolatrous articles, which they had hitherto used in their pagan sacrifices. I had a fire made and burnt all these abominations of paganism as a holocaust to Him, the Almighty, the Eternal, to whom alone sacrifice is due and to whom be praise and glory forever! Before leaving these good and happy people I distributed among them a great many religious pictures and promised to visit them from time to time in order to preserve and strengthen them in the faith, which promise consoled them very much.*

"From there I returned to Beaver Island, where they also brought me all objects used in their idolatrous sacrifices, which I likewise burnt. The newly converted Indians determined to erect a small chapel. At the present time they had constructed a kind of chapel of logs, birch-bark and mats, in which I daily said Mass with grateful feelings and gave religious instructions three times every day. Six more pagans were converted and baptized. However, there are yet many pagans in this island who refuse to be converted. One day a number of them came to my tent; some of them were quite naked with the exception of a piece of mat tied around their waist; this was all their clothing. One of them spoke, and in a shrill, monotonous tone made a very

---

* This mission was located at Manistique, as is evident from F. Baraga's description, not Manistee.

foolish speech, in which he declared to me, in the name of all those who had come with him, that they did not want to embrace the Christian religion, but would live and die in the religion of their forefathers. I answered him mildly and forcibly, and I hope that in the course of time also these will be converted to the truth. I then returned home. The Christians of Arbre Croche were very much rejoiced when they heard that so many of their countrymen had now embraced the Christian religion. I did not remain long at home, but went to the third village, spoken of before, about a day and a half journey distant, in the opposite direction. I went there, although I had heard that those Indians were outspoken enemies of the Christian religion. The reason is this: These Indians are incited to and kept in a hostile disposition against religion through wicked fur-traders, who visit them often and bring them rum for their peltries. For these godless traders know very well that Indians, when they embrace Christianity, must give up entirely the use of intoxicating liquors, and especially drunkeness, a vice to which pagan Indians are much addicted. Now in order to make a profitable trade with the Indians, they endeavor in every possible way to make them averse to Christianity and keep them in paganism. However, I went there and spoke to them of the Christian religion, but I found little hearing. Still God gave me the consolation of not having gone there entirely in vain. There were five pagans who took God's call to heart. They were instructed and baptized on the 3d of June. I stayed some days longer with them and gave them additional instruction in religion and read Mass. After promising to visit them again in the near future, I returned to Arbre Croche.

"Here in Arbre Croche the infinitely merciful God gives me unspeakable consolation. Almost every day, especially on feast days, Indians come to me asking for holy Baptism. On Pentecost Sunday I baptized five and on Pentecost Monday, fifteen. God be praised and thanked for all!"

Chapter XIX

A Letter from Some Indian Chiefs at Arbre Croche to Bishop Fenwick. Last Visit of Bishop Fenwick to Arbre Croche; His Untimely Death from Cholera; Baraga's Account of the Bishop's Death.

We insert here a letter of some Indian chiefs and head men of Arbre Croche to Bishop Fenwick, of Cincinnati, when sending him some of their children to learn useful trades. The letter is not dated, but we think it was written in 1832. It gives an insight into the great love and attachment which Indians have for their children.

"Our Father! You desire to have some boys of our nation for Cincinnati in order to place them in apprenticeship with some tradesmen. We are very much pleased with your proposal and we send you four of our children from Old and New Arbre Croche, namely, Joseph Boyd and Michael Shawanibinessi (Southern Bird) to learn the blacksmith and locksmith trade; Michael Fenwick and Michael Medoayandagashe to learn the carpenter and cabinetmaker's trade. We also wish that these children learn to read and write your language.

"Our Father! We pray you to get a good place for our children and to take fatherly care of them, for they are also your children in Jesus Christ.

"We beg of you also to send the married man you promised us. We will give him and his family some land, so that he can live with us.

"We recommend ourselves to your prayers and give you our hand.

"+Joseph Nawimashkote, head-chief of Old Arbre Croche and father of Medoayandagashe.

+Weshimaweto, father of Michael Shawanibinessi.

+Joseph Kiwekwaam, father of Michael Fenwick.

+Wabisagime (White Mosquito), father of Joseph Boyd.

+Leon Pakusikan, Alexander Missawakwat, head-chiefs of Arbre Croche."

HARBOR SPRINGS—THE ANCIENT ARBRE CROCHE—MICH.

During the month of July F. Baraga had not much to do in Arbre Croche, as his people were gone to Canada to get the presents which the Canadian government annually distributed among the Indians of the Northwest. These presents were valuable and a great help to the poor people. Hence their missionary had no objection to their making this trip to secure them. He had intended to go in the meanwhile to Detroit to get his new Ottawa prayer book printed; but, learning that Bishop Fenwick was to come to Arbre Croche to give Confirmation, he postponed his intended trip to Detroit till September. This gave him, moreover, time to prepare his people for Confirmation. The good Bishop arrived on the 2d of August (1832), and on the 5th he conferred that holy Sacrament on one hundred and forty Indians. Baraga had taken great pains to prepare them well, and so they received it with great solemnity, decorum, and edification.

Speaking of this last visit of saintly Bishop Fenwick to Arbre Croche, F. Baraga says:

"It is impossible to describe the heartfelt joy which our good Indians showed when they saw their 'great Father' approach their village. They all assembled at the lake shore, forming a long, double file. In the one row were the men, and in the other the women and children. The men fired three salutes with their guns. The unfeigned manifestations of joy on the part of these, his best children, touched the pious Bishop very much. He gave us his apostolic benediction and then had the kindness to shake hands with each one of them, a thing the Indians regard as a great sign of friendship. We conducted him in procession to the church, where, after making his adoration to the Blessed Sacrament, he made a touching address to the Indians, which deeply penetrated their hearts. On the 5th of August, after Confirmation had been given, the Bishop convened all the chiefs and headmen of my mission and made known to them some civil regulations which he had made for the Ottawas. The Indians accepted these rules with great satisfaction and solemnly promised to keep them. The missionary and four head-chiefs are the executors of these laws."

Little did Bishop Fenwick think, perhaps, that his days were so soon to come to an end, and that one of his last official acts would be giving Confirmation to his poor, but good-hearted and fervent Indian children. Yet so it was to be. F. Baraga, in a letter dated Detroit, October 10th, 1832, thus writes about the death of his dear Bishop to the Directors of the Leopoldine Society at Vienna:

"With most profound sorrow I inform your Reverend Board of Directors that our Rt. Rev. and dear Bishop, Edward Fenwick, died of the cholera on the 26th of September (1832), at noon. He always lived as a zealous missionary in holy poverty, and he also died on a mission-tour, like St. Francis Xavier, poor and abandoned. He was just on his way returning from a mission and visitation-tour, such as he used to undertake annually to the great spiritual benefit of his diocese, when all of a sudden he was seized with terrible cramps. He was obliged to get out of the wagon and entered the house of a Catholic family. The nearest priest was immediately sent for, but he lived thirty miles away. When the priest arrived, our dear Bishop was already dead and buried. Thus this apostolic man departed this life without the help of a priest; for, in order not to deprive a congregation of its pastor, he generally traveled alone, without a priest accompanying him. However, the angels and the Queen of the angels, towards whom he had all his lifetime cherished a very fervent and tender devotion, no doubt assisted him in his dying hour. And, although his mortal remains were buried without a priest being present to bless them, his beautiful soul was no doubt conducted by the angels before the face of our Lord, to whom he had devoted his whole life. No grand monument tells posterity that here rest the mortal remains of the Apostle of Ohio, but he erected to himself thousands of standing monuments in the hearts of all those whom he brought to the knowledge of God through his wonderful zeal and pious prayers. May he rest in peace and light eternal shine upon him!" He died at Wooster, Ohio.

Chapter XX

Continuation of F. Baraga's Labors During the Year 1832. His First Indian Prayer book Printed at Detroit. What Father Hatscher, C. SS. R., And Others Say of Him and His Work.

After Bishop Fenwick's departure from Arbre Croche, F. Baraga visited his new missions, begun in the spring. In one of them, called Manistique, he stayed five days, being all that time occupied in hearing confessions and giving instructions. He felt great consolation in finding his neophytes steadfast in their holy religion. He baptized there an Indian family of five persons. From Manistique he went to Beaver Island, where many Indians had prepared themselves for Baptism. He examined them and on Assumption Day baptized fifteen persons.

Shortly afterwards he went to Detroit to get his Indian prayer book printed. The prayer book of F. Dejean was not in Ottawa, but in Algonquin, which language, though it strongly resembles the Ottawa, still has many words unintelligible to the Ottawas. Hence the necessity of a prayer book in their own language. This book is the "Anamiemasinaigan" of Baraga, which contains not only the prayers usually found in prayer books, but also a great number of hymns for different festivals of the year, in honor of our Lord, the Blessed Virgin, Holy Eucharist, etc., which our Indians delight to sing. It contains, moreover, a complete catechism of the Christian doctrine. It is the best Indian prayer book we have and is most highly prized by our Indians, both Ottawas, Chippewas, and Menominees. Bishop Fenwick had given F. Baraga two hundred and twelve dollars, which sufficed to pay for one thousand copies. F. Baraga felt much rejoiced that he could give this so necessary and useful prayer book to his dear Indians, many of whom could read.

Before continuing our narrative of Baraga's labors in the extensive mission of Arbre Croche, we will give the opinions of different parties as to the man and his labors.

In a letter of Father Francis Xavier Hatscher, C. SS. R., to his Superior, Rev. Simon Sanderl, dated Detroit, the 17th of September, 1832, he writes thus of F. Baraga:

"Rev. Father Baraga has come here from Arbre Croche to get his Indian reading and prayer book printed. He works with me like a brother and helps me very much, but he will be obliged to return soon to his dear Ottawas, *amongst whom he works miracles of salvation. He is very poor and lives like a Trappist, but with all that he prizes himself over-happy.* I understand this well and desire to be made a partaker in the hardships and consolations of this noble man. Rev. Baraga wishes to take along my companion, Brother Alois, to Arbre Croche, in order that the latter may teach some of his Indians the locksmith and blacksmith trade. This will be a great benefit to the good Indians, in order that they will not be obliged to come to the city (Detroit), which is several days journey distant, the visiting of which is injurious to their morality."

Speaking of F. Baraga and his flourishing mission at Arbre Croche, Rt. Rev. Rese, first Bishop of Detroit, says: "The mission of Arbre Croche is one of the most flourishing amongst the Indians, since it numbers over one thousand converts, who can be regarded as models of true piety."

To the above we beg leave to add Father Bonduel's account of the religious, moral and temporal condition of the Arbre Croche Indians under F. Baraga's successor, Rev. Simon Sanderl, C. SS. R., in the early part of 1835. He says:

"... It is but a few years ago that the beneficent voice of religion reached the Indians of Arbre Croche. But since the day that the word of God preached by Catholic missionaries penetrated their dense forests and the cross of Christ was planted on the shores of their little bay, the progress of these people in morals, religion, and civilization has been wonderful... At present there is no Indian tribe that can compare with them in patience, meekness, and spiritual resignation. This change is but the happy result of our holy religion. The interesting account, which our Rt. Rev. Bishop made known to the public in the *Catholic Telegraph*, of his Episcopal visit to Arbre Croche, I found entirely verified when I visited that Indian mission for the first time. *They are the jewels of his diocese, the crown of his apostolic labors.*

"Some days after my arrival there, I preached to a large congregation morning and evening. Nothing can compare with the attention which they gave to my simple sermons. The pose of their bodies, the expression of their countenances, their outward propriety, and their veneration for the word of God—all gave testimony of the inward piety and religious feelings which were expressed in their outward conduct. The extraordinary and unbroken silence during the whole sermon filled me with respect for the congregation and with reverence towards Father Sanderl, their pastor, who had led them so far on the narrow path of Christian perfection. The devotion of these good people penetrated my soul and tears filled my eyes whilst surrendering myself to the emotions it awakened in me."

On page 45, Leopoldine Society Report for the year 1833, we find an Indian's comparative estimate of Catholic and Protestant missionaries. We give this queer piece of Indian philosophical observation in full.

"Our forefathers had men with black-robes as leaders. They had neither wives nor children. They devoted themselves entirely to prayer and to the service of the red men.

When these men ate, they were satiated, for they had but one mouth to fill, and when one of them died, he did not need anything more, for he had all he needed in heaven, and when we buried him we had only to pray for his spirit (soul). Now they give us men like ourselves as chiefs of prayer. These men have women, and they love them. They have children, and they love them. The women and children have many mouths and many backs. The children grow larger every day, and the poor man of prayer has great fear because he loves (wife and children). He fears that these mouths will not all be filled and these backs will not all be clothed. He fears very much to die, for then those he loves will suffer hunger, if we do not support them. As long as he lives he takes care of his wife and children, and when he does this he says to the red skin: 'I do my duty;' and the red-skin goes away and thinks what his father said that the Black-robe was a man not like one of us and that he loved the red-skin very much because he had but the Great Spirit and his people to love. He had no wife and no child. He had but one mouth and one back, and when he died this mouth was shut and this back cold, and he feared not when the time came to die, and he looked only on the red-skin, whom he loved."

Sound Indian philosophy!

Chapter XXI

Baraga's Labors During 1833. Visits Little Detroit, Manistique and Beaver Island. Baptizes a Great Many Pagans During Pentecost Week at Arbre Croche.

During the winter of 1832-1833 F. Baraga's labors were confined principally to the Indians of Arbre Croche and two small villages not far distant. Most all the inhabitants of these three places were now Christians, full of fervent piety and morally well-behaved.

During that same winter the zealous missionary was under the necessity of making a journey of thirty or forty miles on snowshoes to Mackinac and back. The entire distance both ways, taking into consideration the turnings and windings of the road or trail, would probably be not much less than one hundred miles. The Indian snow-shoe is made of a wooden frame-work about forty-eight to sixty inches long and twelve inches broad or more, interlaced with buckskin strings. They are very useful for traveling in winter, when the snow is deep and there are no beaten roads or trails. They are, however, pretty heavy, and to one not accustomed to walk with them it is a very difficult and painful task to travel a considerable distance. F. Baraga not being as yet accustomed to walk with snowshoes, found it very hard to go with them all the way to Mackinac. The journey took him two days. Often he sank down in the snow quite exhausted. The return trip was still more painful. Many a time he thought he would be unable to go further. His kind Indian guides had great pity for their poor Father and would wait for him whenever he would be obliged to stop and rest. Many such journeys did he make later on, as we shall see hereafter.

His first mission-trip in the spring of 1833 was to an island in Lake Michigan, called Little Detroit. The inhabitants had never seen the face of a priest, but they had heard from some Christian Indians who had visited their island about the Black-robe and his religion, and expressed a desire to see and hear him.

As soon as F. Baraga heard of it he embarked on the journey. The wind was unfavorable and the weather very disagreeable. Besides, the boat was unsafe and they were in constant danger of being engulfed by the waves. Baraga, however, was calm and fearless. He knew that the good Shepherd was leading him to some of His sheep, whom he was to bring to the fold. Finally, after a thousand miseries and dangers, he landed at the island. The poor Indians were very much pleased to see a priest at their village. He remained with them eight days and instructed them thoroughly, as he noticed their good disposition towards Christianity. The 14th of May was a happy day for both Indians and priest. On that day twenty-two of them were made children of God by the holy Sacrament of Baptism.

The others were not opposed to religion. They gave him hopes that they, too, would become Christians upon his next visit to their island. He promised to see them again in the course of the summer, and they agreed to build in the meanwhile a log chapel at a place designated by him.

On the home journey the party were in great want of provisions. It is true the good people of Little Detroit had given them some potatoes and fish; these were soon consumed and they were without anything to eat. But divine Providence did not forget them. Sailing by a rocky islet, they saw a great number of seabirds, gulls, fly up. They concluded that they must have their nests on the islet. They therefore landed and found one hundred and thirty eggs as large as goose eggs and of an excellent taste. Having made a hearty meal of these eggs with many thanks to God, they continued their voyage.

On this journey he also visited Manistique, where, to his great joy, F. Baraga found all his converts true to their holy faith. They had made great progress in their knowledge of religion, thanks to the untiring zeal of a well-instructed Christian from Arbre Croche, who had wintered with them. They were likewise busy building a new and better church than the one hastily erected the previous year, and were in hopes of finishing it during that summer. As all had been baptized at his visit except one old headstrong pagan, F. Baraga had only two children to baptize.

He says he cannot sufficiently praise these good Indians, especially on account of their extraordinary love of prayer. They faithfully said long prayers every morning and evening. They likewise said the Holy Rosary every day very devoutly; some of them did so even twice or three times. Whatever time they could spare from their work they devoted to reading their Indian prayer books, praying, singing spiritual hymns, and learning the catechism. Most of them knew how to read; the rest were trying hard to learn.

When reading this account, penned by F. Baraga himself, who does not think of the words of Jesus: "I confess to Thee, Father of heaven and earth, that Thou hast concealed these things from the wise and prudent and revealed them to the little ones." We see a number of poor, ignorant Indians embrace the religion of One who was poor and despised like themselves, whereas millions of whites, puffed up with pride and learning, are left in heresy and infidelity to perish in their sins.

From Manistique F. Baraga sailed to Beaver Island, where the number of Christians was greater than either in Little Detroit or Manistique; still the majority of the inhabitants were yet pagans and bitter enemies of the Christian religion. They despised and mocked their Christian countrymen and tried in every way to avert them from the faith. They likewise prevented them from building a church, as the latter had intended, and threatened to burn it down should they erect one. To gain their good will F. Baraga bought them presents—cloth, little scissors, needles, thread, etc., and much tobacco, of which they are passionately fond. The pagans then promised to no longer molest the Christians, but would not allow a church to be built on their island. Baraga visited them from time to time and continued giving them all sorts of little presents. At the same time he complained to them that, notwithstanding all his kindness to them, they were so unfriendly to him and his children and would not allow a house of prayer to be erected on their island to the Great Spirit. Finally they relented a little. Meeting, before his tent, their spokesman said that they were no longer opposed to the building of a church, but it should not be put up in their village, but far away in the woods. They then showed him the spot where he might build his church. F. Baraga thanked God for this concession and felt glad that they could now worship God far away from those stubborn, hard-hearted pagans. He remained a few days on the island and baptized three pagans.

On the 24th of May he returned to Arbre Croche, where great labors, but also great consolations, were in store for him. He had a very great number of confessions to hear for Pentecost Sunday. That day, as he says, was the happiest of his life, for he then baptized in his church at Arbre Croche *thirty-eight pagans*, all of them adults except six small children. The heart of the saintly missionary overflowed with joy and gratitude to God, who had deigned to shower down such abundant blessings on his labors. The next day he baptized six adults; on the 1st of June three, and on the 3d two more. Besides, twelve more were to be baptized that week; in all sixty-one persons, almost all adults.

"Thanks be to God forever for all this," he exclaims; "I feel unspeakably happy that the most holy Providence has placed me in the happy situation of an Indian missionary and I thank Him for it from the bottom of my heart. Would to God that I could fulfill truly, worthily and zealously the duties of the holy ministry which He has entrusted to me! God grant that I may gain very many souls and bring back many lost sheep to the fold! I thank the Reverend Directors of the Leopoldine Society and my former Rt. Rev. Bishop, who have so kindly received my petition for permission to go to the (Indian) mission and who have aided its execution. I also thank all benefactors of the Leopoldine Society for all the gifts in money and other useful articles received from them. All these presents are very useful to my churches and my neophytes. Many of them, such as church ornaments, holy pictures, and rosaries cannot be obtained here even for money. The Indian converts are so much attached to and entertain such a veneration for these objects of devotion that they all ask for them, and if anyone loses his rosary or little cross, he comes immediately to the missionary to get another; hence I need an enormous number of them."

On the 5th of June F. Baraga baptized fifteen pagans, mostly adults, at Old Arbre Croche, a village about twenty-one miles distant from New Arbre Croche, afterwards called Little Traverse, now Harbor Springs. It was at New Arbre Croche where the parish church of the whole mission was built. Many a time before had F. Baraga visited Old Arbre Croche* and baptized there, but never so many at a time.

---

* It was at Old Arbre Croche, as we learn from the author of the "History of the Ottawas and Chippewas in Michigan," that Father Vincent Badin had Mass in a small, rude chapel erected by the Indians in 1825. It was also there that Father du Jaunay labored among the Ottawas in the middle of the last century.

Chapter XXII

F. Baraga's First Visit to Grand River; He Baptizes Many; Returns to Arbre Croche. Resume of His Missions. He Leaves Arbre Croche and Is Succeeded There by Rev. F. Sanderl, C. SS. R.

When Bishop Fenwick installed F. Baraga as pastor of Arbre Croche in 1831, he told him to do his best to seek out and convert all the Ottawas to the true faith. Having learned that there were many of them at Grand River, he most earnestly urged F. Baraga to visit and try to convert them. However, during the first two years the zealous missionary was too much occupied with the conversion of the Indians in and near Arbre Croche to think of going to Grand River. Now the time of visitation, the time of grace was come for these poor Indians who had been living so long "in the region and shadow of death."

During the winter of 1832-1833 Baraga founded a forerunner, a John the Baptist, in the person of a pious and well-instructed Indian of Arbre Croche, who intended to winter at Grand River. The good Father commissioned this pious man to visit from time to time the various scattered villages of his countrymen at the above-named river, to speak to them about the Christian religion and tell them about the Black-robe, who was living with their countrymen at Arbre Croche and assure them that he would visit them without fail the next summer. This new John the Baptist, as

F. Baraga styles him, fulfilled his commission most faithfully and effectually prepared the way for the zealous missionary. So well did our Indian labor that many of his countrymen at Grand River promised to embrace the religion of which he spoke so highly, as soon as they would have the happiness of seeing and hearing the ambassador of the Great Spirit.

With great longing did F. Baraga await the return of his Indian precursor. At length he arrived. Grasping the hand of his dear Father he said, smiling: "Happy news, my Father, happy news!" Then he told him all he had done in the cause of religion and how bright the prospects were at Grand River, if there were but a missionary there, for whom many of the people longed most eagerly. The nearest mission to it was that of St. Joseph amongst the Pottawatamies, which was about 160 miles distant. Fathers Francis Vincent Badin and Deseilles labored there at the time.

F. Baraga immediately made preparations for the long journey to Grand River, which was some 200 miles from Arbre Croche and where there were about 900 Indians, all pagans, excepting a few Protestants. He left Arbre Croche on the 7th of June (1833) and after incredible hardships and fatigue, arrived at Grand River on the 15th of the month. He was the first Catholic priest that set his foot on Grand River soil, the first to offer up there the Holy Sacrifice of the Mass.

At that time the above-named river formed the boundary between the unceded Ottawa country and that belonging to Michigan. The country north of said river belonged as yet to the Ottawas, the country south of it belonged to Michigan. The largest Indian village was located a day's journey up the river and it was there F. Baraga established the seat of his new mission. He described the surrounding country as wonderfully beautiful. Opposite the village, on the other side of the river, a rich French-Canadian family had settled. This family was very numerous, as is frequently the case with Canadian French, who in this respect are very different from their "cousins" across the broad Atlantic. They were also good, practical Catholics and were exceedingly glad at the arrival of the pious missionary in that country, for they had not seen a priest for a long time. F. Baraga had to stop with this good family, the members of which overwhelmed him with kind attentions. They converted their new house, but lately erected, into a temporary church, in which the missionary daily said holy Mass with great fervor and grateful emotion. Here, likewise, did he preach mornings and evenings to great numbers of Indians, who came over from the other side of the river to hear the Black-robe, the first one many of them had ever seen, preach in their dear native tongue the truths of Christianity. He remained there twenty-three days, busily employed in the holy work of the mission. On the day before he left he baptized with all possible solemnity forty-six pagans.

"I baptized," he writes, "on this day forty-six pagans at one time, the first fruits of this new flourishing mission, in which, as I hope, with God's saving grace, many souls will be rescued from perdition and brought to eternal salvation. O what an unspeakable consoling prospect for me, who have come only for this into the wild country to seek for lost sheep and to rescue them, with God's help, from eternal ruin!"

In addition to the forty-six Indians baptized at the principal village of Grand River, he baptized many others in other smaller hamlets. In one of these he baptized six, in another twenty-one, and in a third thirteen; in all, eighty-six. Truly, God was with this saintly missionary.

F. Baraga's wonderful success at Grand River determined Bishop Rese, the first Bishop of Detroit, Mich., to establish there a permanent mission or congregation, consisting partly of Indian converts and partly of French-Canadians, many of whom lived there and needed a priest very much.

A minister had preceded Baraga in that place; but, although he had been there nine years and had had abundant pecuniary assistance, he had converted in all that length of time but ten Indians. The same is also noticeable elsewhere.

To have the necessary means for building a cheap church and parsonage, F. Baraga wrote for help to the Leopoldine Society, which was granted, as we shall see hereafter.

It was intended at that time—July 26th, 1833—to get two Redemptorist Fathers to make an establishment of their congregation in Arbre Croche, in which case Father Baraga was to remove to Grand River; and certainly religious orders are best adapted for missionary work. The Superiors can select the men best suited for the work. Should one become sick or be removed, his place can be supplied by some other member of the community. Moreover, they have more means at their disposal than individual priests. If the latter becomes sick or otherwise incapacitated, his Indian mission may be left without a priest for years, perhaps even entirely abandoned. Witness the poor Winnebagoes of Wisconsin, many of whom were formerly baptized by Father Van den Broeck and others, and who are now left in their paganism.

After his return to Arbre Croche, F. Baraga received from the Leopoldine Society a box full of religious articles and 1,100 florins, a present of some kind benefactors of the diocese of Laibach, Austria. These things and this money were to be used for the new mission of Grand River. With a heart overflowing with gratitude, he promised not only to remember his benefactors at every holy Mass, but also to offer up the Holy Sacrifice for them from time to time.

With this end his labors in Arbre Croche. Within two years and four months he had baptized four hundred and sixty-one Indians, besides eighty-six at Grand River; in all, five hundred and forty-seven.

After his return from Grand River, he made a last and short visit to his different missions before leaving for good.

Towards the end of July he visited an Indian village not far from Arbre Croche. The inhabitants were all now Christians. They had built a neat little church, which F. Baraga blessed on the first of August, dedicating it to St. Ignatius of Loyola. Then he visited Manistique, where he found everything in the best of order, the Indians all fervent in prayer and of good morals. Shortly before, a young Indian woman had come to said village with the resolution to leave her pagan parents and her home to live in Manistique for the rest of her days and become a Christian. From there Baraga went to Little Detroit, where the Indians had built a chapel of birch bark, which he blessed in honor of St. Vincent de Paul. He baptized there on the 12th of August three Indian women. Before leaving he gave to the islanders a letter to the priest at Green Bay, asking him to take charge hereafter of this small island, as it was nearer to Green Bay than to Arbre Croche. He also landed at Beaver Island, but found most of the Indians gone to Canada to get their usual gifts from the Canadian government. The church could not be finished on account of the hatred of the pagans against Christianity. F. Baraga advised the Christian Indians to leave the island and settle at Arbre Croche. Finally he returned to the last-named place, where he found his successor, Rev. F. Sanderl, Superior of the Redemptorists in the United States, with three lay brothers of the same congregation.

F. Baraga gives the following list of his missions:
1. The Arbre Croche, the church of which was dedicated by Father Dejean to St. Peter.
2. Old Arbre Croche.
3. Mission of St. Mary, with a church dedicated by F. Dejean.
4. Mission of St. Paul, also a church dedicated by the above Father.
5. Mission of St. Ignatius, founded by F. Baraga.
6. La Grande Traverse, with nineteen Christians.
7. Beaver Island, with fifty-five Christians.
8. Manistique, with thirty-three Christians.
9. Little Detroit, with twenty-six Christians.

Speaking of the happy conditions of his people at Arbre Croche in those primitive days, A. J. Blackbird (Mackadebenessy), son of Mackadebenessy, says in his work, entitled, "History of the Ottawa and Chippewa Indians of Michigan," p. 49-50:

"The Indians were very strict in their religion at this time. They did not allow any drunkenness in their village, nor allow anyone to bring intoxicating liquors within the Harbor (formerly New Arbre Croche). If any person, white or Indian, brought any liquor into the Harbor, by the barrel or in small quantities, and it came to the knowledge of the old chief, Awpawkosigan, who was the war-chief, but was acting as principal chief at Little Traverse, he would call out his men to go and search for the liquor, and if found he would order his men to spill the whisky on the ground by knocking in the head of the barrel with an axe, telling them not to bring any more whisky into the Harbor, or wherever the Ottawas were, along the coast of Arbre Croche. This was the end of it, there being no law-suit for the whisky.

"They used to observe many holidays, particularly Christmas, New Year, and Corpus Christi. At New Year's eve every one of the Indians used to go around visiting the principal men of the tribe, shooting their guns close to their doors, after screaming three times, "Happy New Year!" then bang, bang, altogether, blowing their tin horns, beating their drums, etc. Early on New Year's morning they would go around among their neighbors expressly to shake hands one with another, with the word of salutation, "Bozhoo," children and all. This practice was kept up for a long time, or until the white people came and intermingled with the tribes.

"I thought my people were very happy in those days, when they were all by themselves and possessed a wide spread of land, and no one to quarrel with them as to where they should make their gardens, or take timber, or make sugar. Fish of all kinds were so plentiful in the harbor that a hook anywhere in the bay, and at any time of the year, would catch Mackinaw trout, and if a net were set in the harbor in shallow water, in the morning it would be loaded with fish of all kinds. Truly it was a beautiful location for the mission. Every big council of the Indians was convened in the village of Little Traverse.

"I will mention one or two more things which it might be interesting to my readers to know. Up to 1835, and some time afterwards, there was a very large double cedar tree, which appeared to have been stuck together while growing, but which in reality were two separate trees of the same size and height, growing close together, standing very near the edge of the water, and leaning outward almost like a staircase projecting far into the bay. Under the roots of these trees issued a perpetual spring of water, which is now called McCarlow's Spring, near the present depot. In the fall of 1835 I was clear at the top of those trees, with my little playmates, watching our people as they were about going off in a long bark canoe, and we understood they were going to Washington to see the Great Father, the President of the United States, to tell him to have mercy on the Ottawa and Chippewa Indians in Michigan, not to take all the land away from them. I saw some of our old Indian women weeping as they watched our principal men going off in the canoe. * * * After they all got in the canoe, just as they were going to start, they all took off their hats, crossed themselves and repeated the Lord's prayer. At the end of the prayer they crossed themselves again, and then away they went towards Harbor Point. We watched them until they disappeared in rounding the point."

Chapter XXIII

Labors and Hardships of F. Baraga at Grand River.

Father Baraga left Arbre Croche on or about the 8th of September, 1833. After a long and painful journey, he arrived at the mouth of Grand River on the 21st of the month, and here he rested a day. Finally, on the 23d, he reached his new mission, St. Mary, on Grand River.

The first thing he did was to convoke the Indians to a council. When all were assembled, he informed them that he had come, not to pay them a mere passing visit, but to remain with them for good, in order to instruct them and their children in the holy faith and in all that is good and useful.

The Catholics among them were exceedingly well pleased at this joyful news. The pagans were quite unconcerned. The few Protestants, however, were bitterly opposed to the project of a Catholic mission in the village. This was due to their minister, who excited them against the Catholic missionary.

After some talking had been done for and against the intended mission, F. Baraga harangued the assembled multitude, showing them the many advantages of the mission for all parties. The spokesman of the dissenting Indians did not know what to answer. Finally he declared that he was altogether opposed to the founding of a Catholic mission at the village. He was, however, unable to assign any valid reason for his opposition. This displeased his countrymen, for they saw that it was nothing but bigotry that actuated him. Finally he proposed to F. Baraga to establish his mission further up the river, where, he said, there were other Indian villages. Thereupon F. Baraga told him plainly that he had no right whatever to prevent the establishment of a Catholic mission in their village, as there were already there a great many Catholics, and that the latter had as good a right to have their priest build a church, school, and house in the village as his co-religionists had to allow their preacher to do the same. This silenced his opponent and the debate ended. Baraga then went to the place he had selected for the church and designated the amount of ground to belong to the mission.

As it would take some time before the new church could be built, he fixed up a log house belonging to an Indian and said Mass in it every day. He also kept school in the same building, and on the very first day he had twenty-five scholars, boys and girls, besides four white children, who, with their parents, were not baptized.

Although there were some settlers on the south side of the river, and among them a few Catholics, still, as F. Baraga was first and foremost Indian missioner, he concluded to build his church on the north side amongst the Indians, in order to more readily gain their good will and thus labor with greater effect at their conversion. Such was also the wish of Bishop Rese.

To procure carpenters for his intended church, school, and parsonage, he was obliged to go all the way to Detroit, a distance of two hundred miles, on horseback. The road was bad and muddy, so that it took him seven days to get there, during which journey he suffered much, as he was not used to riding. He succeeded in hiring two men and returned with them to Grand River. The return journey was a great deal harder than the one going to Detroit. There was but the one horse for the three men, on which each one rode by turns, whilst the other two walked. At times they would sink knee-deep into the mud. For the last two days not a single house was to be seen. At the last house they bought as much bread as they could get, but it was not enough, and so the last day they had nothing at all to eat.

Work was begun on the 14th of October, but as there were only two men, the work progressed slowly. He finally secured another man to help, but complains of the high wages and dear materials. His dwelling for some time was wretched. He says it resembled more an open milk-house than a human habitation.

By December 1st he had one hundred converts, and many others promised to become Christians. The number of his scholars had increased to thirty-eight. However, he felt continually uneasy as to the fate of this new mission, partly on account of the great outlays connected with it, partly, also, on account of the great prevalence of drunkenness amongst the Indians.

One old man, the oldest head-chief of the village, was formerly a terrible drunkard. He had been the greatest brave of his band and many a scalp had he taken in his time. When intoxicated he would imagine himself on the warpath, and in his drunken frenzy he was a terror to his wife and children, who were often in danger of their lives. He was converted and baptized and gave up liquor altogether. Not another drop passed over his lips. The pagan wolf became a meek Christian lamb. He used to come to church covered with a poor blanket, and, taking his rosary, which he always wore around his neck, in his hands, would kneel down in a corner of the church and pray most devoutly. He spent his time in working and praying and exhorting his pagan countrymen to embrace the Christian religion.

We see here the soul-renovating and civilizing effects of religion. Futile are all government attempts to civilize the Indian without religion. He will take the money and rations given him, feast as long as provisions last, and then return to pagan starvation and misery. The Catholic Church alone can truly Christianize and civilize the Indian. Look at Paraguay under the Jesuits and California under the Franciscans.

Speaking of his new mission, he writes to the Leopoldine Society as follows:

"O how much do I wish to soon have a becoming church and a commodious, properly-fitted up school! The founding of a new mission in such a wild and distant country costs much, very much indeed. But, considered in the light of faith, all these expenses are nothing when compared to the great good that is thereby realized. How many souls are saved from eternal ruin through the creation of a new mission, who otherwise would have perished eternally! And is not the salvation of a single immortal soul worth more than all the things of this world? Would not

Jesus Christ be ready to be crucified anew to save even one single soul, if it could not be saved otherwise. O that the want of temporal support might never hinder my progress in the conversion of the poor Indians! I begin to fear this when I reflect on the great outlays which are absolutely necessary in the establishing of my new missions. In this, my anxiety and fear, I appear before you, my dear benefactors in my dear fatherland, as intercessor in behalf of my poor Indians so deserving of pity. I stretch out my arms imploringly to you and beg you to have compassion on your unhappy brethren in this part of the world, who are walking in the ways of blind paganism towards perdition. You have the great happiness of being Christians, of knowing God, and of being on the way that leads to life. Procure, as far as it is in your power, this same inestimable blessing for your poor brethren in this country."

Besides the uneasiness arising from pecuniary embarrassments, F. Baraga felt keenly the painful situation of being obliged to live in the midst of pagan wickedness, drunkenness, and superstition. There is something peculiar about such pagan places. Everything is repulsive to Christian feelings. On all sides pagan objects meet the eye; the ear is offended by the sound of pagan drums and revelry. The very air seems infected with pagan diabolism. The missionary feels again and again the truth of the Psalmist's words: "Oii antem gentium daemonia," "the gods of the gentiles are the devils." He feels that pagan worship is truly devil-worship. Everything in such a pagan village jars on his Christian feelings. He seems to feel the demoniacal influence pervading the place. He feels a strange, invisible power fighting him, resisting him, repelling him at every step. He has entered the devil's domains and whole armies of wicked spirits seem to be working against him. The writer owns he always felt this strange sensation whenever he went to such a pagan village or entered a thoroughly pagan house. The very atmosphere breathed paganism. With a feeling of relief he would leave such places, to which he would never go did not duty impel him. Perhaps other missionaries may not have been so impressed; but most likely his experience is also theirs.

Chapter XXIV

Description of Indian Drunkenness at Grand River; F. Babaga's Life Endangered. Indian Council. F. Baraga Dedicates His New Church.

We will let F. Baraga describe the state of things at Grand River. He says:

"Indians are, as a rule, very much addicted to drunkenness. However, they have not always an opportunity of indulging in this vice because they cannot everywhere find intoxicating liquor. But here at Grand River there are so many fur-traders, who follow the Indians whithersoever they go and give them liquor in order to get their furs, that the Indians of this neighborhood and even in this place are almost continually drunk. I have spoken about this matter with several of these traders, who sell their own souls and the souls of the poor Indians to the hellish enemy. But I receive nothing but insults and threats in answer. They hearken to my words even less than the rudest and wildest Indian. To revenge themselves on me, they bring much more liquor to the Indians and advise them strongly not to listen or believe me and also slander me as much as possible.

"Under such circumstances it is evidently hard to hold mission and convert these pagans. However, 'against God there is no counsel.' Notwithstanding all this opposition, many are converted to our holy faith and through Baptism received into our holy church.

"It is a terrible sight to see an Indian in the state of drunkenness, especially the women. They are then real furies. Many Indian women here have no nose. When I came here the first time I did not know how to account for this. I made inquiries and learnt that Indian women, when drunk, attack one another like raging wolves and bite off one another's noses. Others, again, have lost one or more fingers in these bacchanalian fights. The men attack each other with their large knives, which they always carry. Often do we hear of murders perpetrated in drunkenness.

"*My life is here in danger.* At night I am obliged to carefully and securely lock my door in order to preserve myself from the visits of these monsters.

"A few days ago there were many drunken Indians in our village. A fur-trader had brought them such a quantity of whisky that they kept on drinking four days and nights without stopping. Our Christian Indians felt very bad at this and were in danger. One of my best Christians came near losing his life during those unhappy days. One of these drunken wretches came to this man's house and spoke terribly against religion. Finally he tried to stab him with his knife. It was only with the greatest difficulty that the Christian Indian averted this calamity.

"During these same unhappy days I myself had a nightly visit from drunken Indians. Whilst they were yet a great distance from my house their terrible shouts aroused me from sleep. When they came to my door they tried to enter, shouting terribly at the same time. I could not understand a word they said. I remained quiet trusting in divine Providence. When they saw that they could not get in, they went away howling. Whenever I notice that there are drunken Indians in the village I lock my door immediately when evening arrives.

"In Arbre Croche I did not have to undergo such troubles and dangers, for the Indians there are for the most part converted and the few remaining pagans can do no harm. Nevertheless, I have never repented of having come here, as Arbre Croche is far better provided for under the care of my successor, the enlightened and zealous Father Sänderl, than it was when under my charge. Besides, I have the consolation of seeing that many here who heretofore had no knowledge of Christianity, through God's grace and help have been converted to the Christian religion and now live like exemplary Christians."

In the January number of the American Catholic Review is a most interesting article from the pen of Hon. Richard R. Elliott, of Detroit, Mich., entitled: "Frederick Baraga among the Ottawas." The gifted writer gives a detailed account of the nocturnal attack made by a crowd of drunken pagan Ottawas on F. Baraga's house at Grand River Mission. The facts, as recorded, are taken from a manuscript account of Rev. Walter Elliott, the celebrated Paulist Missionary, brother of the above-named writer, and were communicated to him by Very Rev. Edward Jacker, who, no doubt, received them from a perfectly reliable source. Hon. Richard R. Elliott writes:

"There were at the time a number of Ottawa villages in the Grand River Valley. At the chief canton a Baptist missionary had been established for some years, but he had secured only a small number of followers. Here was the seat of the United States Indian agency for southern Michigan; Indian traders and their white followers were numerous, with the result that the Ottawas in these cantons, who were nearly all unbelievers, had become very demoralized. Raw Ohio whisky could be had for twenty-five cents per gallon.

"Debauchery had taken a strong hold to the great pecuniary advantage of the Indian traders. But Father Baraga built his cabin where the city of Grand Rapids now stands, and he began to preach in the Ottawa dialect. This enraged the Baptist missionary's followers, who found active allies among the traders. They instigated a drunken crowd one night to attack Father Baraga's cabin. He had been timely warned of their coming and had strongly barred the doors and windows. Fortunately, they were too drunk to effect an entrance. Had they succeeded he would have been murdered. For hours this drunken mob besieged his cabin. Their yells were frightful. He expected every moment to see the bark roof ablaze and contemplated his death by fire. Word, however, was sent to the acting United States marshal, of the riot, and he came and dispersed the rioters.

"All during this infernal uproar Father Baraga remained on his knees in prayer. Convinced of the evil brought upon his people by the abuse of liquor, he came to the conclusion to offer himself as an example. There in that cabin, but unawed by his assailants, he solemnly vowed to abstain from intoxicating drink during the whole course of his life. He kept that pledge faithfully to the last. But many a time, when overcome with exhaustion, when his stomach was nauseated by unpalatable food, when shivering in his wet clothing, or partly frozen during Lake Superior winters, he sadly needed a glass of wine or brandy to revive both body and mind, he may have been tempted, but the night scene in his cabin on the Grand River would recur to his mind and he offered his privation to his Redeemer whenever experienced."

Baraga's combination church, school and house was 50x30 feet and 12 feet high, a wooden structure, most probably of hewn logs. He estimates the cost at a little over $800. During sugar-making time the Indians were in their sugar-camps, but on Sundays they used to come to the village to assist at Holy Mass.

A day's journey from the mission there were many Arbre Croche Indians, who were accustomed to winter there to hunt and trap and make maple-sugar. The good Father complains of the rapacity of the fur-traders, who cheated the Indians and demoralized them by bringing whisky. On the 26th of February some Indians from Arbre Croche came to the mission and asked F. Baraga to make them a missionary visit. After a long and painful journey through trackless forests and swamps, over bridge-less brooks and rivers, he arrived at their camping ground. They received their dear Father with every mark of sincere joy and attachment. They had twelve sugar-camps. Sometimes two or three families live in such an encampment, working together harmoniously. Although they had intended to stay there but a few months, they had erected a temporary church, in which they would meet twice on Sundays and at other times to offer up their prayers in common. F. Baraga remained with his fervent neophytes three days and said Holy Mass with feelings of gratitude to God. All of them went to confession and many of them also received then their Easter holy communion. They had been preparing themselves for the reception of the Blessed Sacrament and so they received it with due appreciation of its greatness and holiness. They would come to him one after another and say, in child-like simplicity: "Father, examine me; perhaps you will find me fit to receive holy communion." On this trip he baptized three adult Indians.

From there he went almost a day's journey farther, to some Indian wigwams. The name of the place was Mashkigong (Muskegon swamp). The preceding summer, on his way to Grand River, he had baptized there twenty-one Indians. Now there were over thirty converts. They promised to build a chapel and he designated the place for it, a beautiful eminence overlooking the river and Lake Mashkigong. They intended to build it pretty large, as almost all the pagans of the settlement were determined to embrace Christianity.

On the 20th of April, 1834, the third Sunday after Easter, F. Baraga had the consolation of blessing his new church. He describes the joyful solemnity as follows:

"The serenity of the firmament accorded beautifully with the joyful celebration. When the usual hour for divine service had arrived we walked with solemn but happy feelings in procession to the church. An Indian carried the peaceful banner of the cross ahead of us and planted it in front of the church. Quite a number of pagan Indians and Americans, of whom the greater part do not profess any religion, followed the procession in order to view the dedication ceremonies—a thing never before witnessed here.

"The gifts in pictures and church articles, which my pious benefactors had sent me from Europe, did me good service at this solemnity. They are still of great use to me for adorning the altar and church and for performing divine service with due solemnity." The church was dedicated to the Blessed Virgin.

Since his last report to the Leopoldine Society, dated March 7th, 1834, up to the 24th of May, F. Baraga baptized twenty-six Indians. One great reason why converts were less numerous at Grand River than elsewhere was because many of them lived so far away in the woods— several days' journey apart—which made it very difficult for the zealous missionary to visit them. The number of his Indian scholars was thirty-three, all of whom he himself had baptized. Besides these he had many French and English-speaking pupils.

On the 13th of June he went to Mashkigong, where he was eagerly expected, and where there were still many pagans. They worked industriously at their new church, which was dedicated to St. Joseph. While awaiting the completion of the church he said Mass every day in the house of an Indian, and baptized ten Indians, mostly adults.

Baraga describes an Indian council that took place at Grand River in the summer of 1834. Reports were freely circulating that the Ottawas were to be transported to some western country, a thing they dreaded very much. They were entirely opposed to ceding their lands to the United States government. The public press declared, it is true, that the government would not take the Indian country by force, but would buy it.

These government transactions have always appeared to the writer as the veriest humbug in the world. The Indian does not want to sell, but he is urged and, so to say, forced to acquiesce in the demands of the government commissioners. Moreover, the Indian does not receive a thousandth part of the real value of the land he cedes. Then comes the Indian trader with a long account against him. The claim is allowed and the poor Indian goes away minus land and money, or at least he has very little to show for extensive domains bartered away, so to speak, for a song, and which equal in size a European empire.

To give the reader some idea of the wretched condition of the poor Indians, which made them give away for trifling annuities, large tracts of the most valuable agricultural, pine and mineral lands, the value of which they never knew or realized, but which was well comprehended by the grasping "Kitchi Mokoman"—"Big Knife"—American. We append here the concluding remarks of two of their chiefs, Esh-ke-bug-e-coshe and Nay-naw-ong-gay-bee. (Wis. Hist. Coll., vol. II., pp. 343, 344.)

At a treaty made at the Mississippi, in 1855, the chief, Esh-ke-bug-e-coshe, "Wide Mouth," made the following remarks, when the government agents refused to accept a proposition of the chiefs, to sell their lands at a price double that offered them by the agent. He said:

"My Father, I live away north on the headwaters of the Mississippi. My children (band) are poor and destitute and, as it were, almost naked, while you, my Father, are rich and well clothed. When I left my home to come to this treaty to sell my lands—for we know that we must sell for what we can get—the whites must have them—my braves, young men, women and children, held a council and begged of me to do the best I could in selling their homes. And now, my Father, I beg of you to accept of the proposition I have made you, and tomorrow I will start for home; and then you count the days which you know it will take me to reach there, and on the day of my arrival look north, and as you see the northern lights stream up in the sky, imagine to yourself that it is the congratulation of joy of my children ascending to God, that you have accepted of the proposition I have offered you."

At the treaty made in La Pointe, Wis., in 1854, Nay-naw-ong-gay-hee, the "Dressing Bird," one of the head chiefs of the Courtes-Oreilles band of Chippewas, made a speech expatiating on the destitute condition of his people, who were abjectly poor, many of the children being perfectly naked. We will insert only his concluding remarks:

"My Father, look around you, upon the faces of my poor people. Sickness and hunger, whisky and war are killing us fast, We are dying and fading away. We drop to the ground like the trees before the axe of the white man; we are weak, you are strong. We are but foolish Indians; you have wisdom and knowledge in your head. We want your help and protection. We have no homes, no cattle, no lands, *and we will not need them long.* The winds shall soon moan around the last lodge of your red children. I grieve, but cannot turn our fate away. The sun, the moon, the rivers, the forests, we love so well, we must leave. We shall soon sleep in the ground—we will not awake again. I have no more to say to you, my Father."

The reader will please to excuse this digression. We shall now continue our narrative.

On this occasion a large delegation of Arbre Croche Indians came to Grand River to deliberate on what was to be done to avert the threatening calamity, the loss of their homes and lands. They assembled in the open air in a small round valley, in the midst of which several fires were made. At convenient places tobacco and fire were placed; also a large kettle with water, sweetened with maple sugar, to drink. At the entrance of the valley they planted a large United States flag.

After all necessary preparations had been made, a sign was given and the Indians came walking gravely and silently. They squatted down on the ground in true Indian fashion, sitting in a circle. Then everyone lighted his pipe and began to smoke. For a long time not a word was said. At length one of them arose and said: "Now, brothers, why have you come here? What is your intention? Come, speak!" Then the orator of Arbre Croche, a venerable old man and an exemplary Christian, arose. He went around the circle, shaking hands with each man as a token of friendship and good will. After some preliminary remarks he declared that all the Indians of Arbre Croche were firmly resolved never to cede their land to the United States, and not to make themselves and their children unhappy.

After concluding his speech, he handed to the head chief of the Grand River band a string of glass beads strung on a green piece of tape or ribbon, as a mark of their union. Another pause. The head chief then passed the string of beads to his next neighbor, and so it went from hand to hand around the circle. After another long pause, one after another of the Grand River Indians went to their speaker and told him secretly their sentiments as to the matter under discussion. The latter then arose and went to the Indians of Arbre Croche and shook hands with each of them. He then declared in the name of his people that they, too, were determined never to cede their lands. Other speeches followed, and so they spent the whole day in council.

This reminds the writer of a similar council held some 200 years ago at Sault Ste. Marie, to deliberate on the fate of a couple of bad Indians, who had been guilty of murdering some Frenchmen. "They wasted lots of good tobacco, smoking for two days, and—that was all they accomplished. Finally the French took the matter in hand themselves and made short work of it by summarily executing the guilty parties, although they (the French) were vastly in the minority.

During the summer and fall of 1834 F. Baraga frequently visited his scattered missions. The roads, if any, were very poor. Often nothing but Indian trails led through forests and miry swamps. Clouds of mosquitoes afflicted the poor Father on these apostolic journeys. During the cold nights of autumn he often slept in the open air, with perhaps only a single blanket to cover him. This gives us some idea of the many hardships the saintly missionary endured in quest of souls.

"But," says he, "when a person notices the holy longing with which the distant living Indians await the coming of the missionary, and how they implore him with child like importunity at his departure to come soon again, when he notices all this he thinks no more of the hardships, but as soon as the time of the missionary visit comes he sets out on his journey. From now (November 3) till February I will not undertake any mission journeys, for at Christmas all Indians living at a distance come here (to Grand River church) to perform their devotions. In February, if God keeps me alive, I will visit them in their sugar-camps."

In September F. Baraga visited an Indian hamlet two days' journey up the river. As was his custom, he had sent a precursor during the summer to said village "to prepare the way before him." When the missionary arrived he found some well-disposed Indians, whom he instructed and baptized. Others, however, hardened their hearts against the call of grace. They said that they had already a religion, the Indian religion, which they preferred to all others and which they would always keep. In vain did the missionary tell them that a religion, which the Great Spirit himself had made, must certainly be better than the superstitious inventions and dreams of their Indian forefathers. But all his reasoning was of no avail. "As many believed as were foreordained to eternal life." The Gospel makes its tour during the centuries of time through the world. Many receive it and are saved; more reject it and are forever lost. Four entire families were baptized in this hamlet.

Towards the beginning of November he visited the mission of St. Joseph at Mashkigong, where his soul was refreshed with abundant consolation and joy. Although some of the neophytes were from four to six days' journey in the woods hunting, they came to the church of St. Joseph on the day appointed in order to assist at all the devotions to be held during the priest's stay and to receive the holy Sacraments.

What an example for so many lukewarm Catholics, who will scarcely walk a few blocks to go to Mass on Sundays! On the great day of reckoning these poor Indians will arise and condemn them, for they walked 100 to 200 miles through forests and swamps to go to Mass.

F. Baraga had the consolation of again baptizing five Indians at Mashkigong (Muskegon). One case, particularly, deserves mention. A girl of seventeen years desired very much to be baptized. Her father, however, was a hardened pagan, full of bitter hatred against Christianity. When the girl asked her father for permission to go to Mashkigong, the latter surmised the reason and refused her point blank. She, however, persevered in her request. Finally he said, angrily, to her: "Go, then, but don't be so foolish as to become a Christian. But if in spite of my prohibition you do become a Christian, you have nothing to expect of me but that I will cut off both your ears." Hearing this, F. Baraga asked her very carefully and earnestly whether she still wished to receive holy Baptism.

She answered with a firm voice that she was unchangeably resolved to become a Christian. She was baptized. This reminds one of the Christians of the first centuries. Whether her father carried out his brutal threat could not be learned. On her part, she declared that she was willing to suffer all for her holy religion.

At Christmas mostly all his Indians attended church, although some of them were hunting at a distance of three or four days' journey from Grand River mission. What a spectacle to see a number of poor, famishing Indians walking on heavy snowshoes for three or four days consecutively to attend Christmas Mass and receive the holy Sacraments! Baraga remarks that some of them were venerable old men and women, weak and sickly, and others mere children from ten to twelve years of age! Yes, F. Baraga made not only Christians, but heroes of these poor savages of the forest. In this respect he was like all the great missionaries of ancient and modern times, a St. Patrick, St. Boniface, St. Francis Xavier, and a host of others. He was a man of God, imbued with God's spirit, and God was with him wherever he went, confirming his words, if not "with signs," at least with proofs no less convincing, for to change brutal savages into fervent Christians is a greater miracle in the order of grace than raising the dead to life.

Before leaving the Michigan missions to accompany F. Baraga to La Pointe, Wisconsin, we wish to make a few remarks as to the state of those missions at the time of his departure.

Bishop Rese, in a letter to the Leopoldine Society, dated October 12th, 1834, estimates the number of Indian converts in his diocese at three thousand, with twelve churches or chapels. At Arbre Croche he found twelve hundred exemplary Catholic Indians, of whom one hundred and twenty received from him confirmation. He says most of them could read and write and lived like civilized people in houses. He says Father Sanderl learned Ottawa in nine months to such an extent that he was going to publish a grammar and dictionary of that language. We think the good Father's zeal was rather ahead of his ability. No man could learn Ottawa in so short a time to any great degree of proficiency.

In 1834 the Catholic church at Sault Ste. Marie was plundered, the windows smashed, the altar utensils thrown out doors and destroyed, the missal torn to shreds, and the church itself set on fire. Father Hätscher, C. SS. R, was stationed there at that time. It was the work of a fanatical mob.

Chapter XXV

F. Baraga Leaves Grand River
Mission; Winters at St. Claire;
Goes to La Pointe Wisconsin.

In February, 1835, Father Andrew Viszoczky, a Hungarian missionary, who had been stationed at St. Claire's mission, not far from Detroit, near Lake St. Claire, came to Grand River with the secret wish to remain there, if Bishop Rese would consent. F. Baraga was agreeably surprised when Father Viszoczky told him his plan. F. Baraga, who had intended to go to Detroit on some business, told him that he would speak to the bishop about the matter, and that he would do whatever the bishop would tell him.

Father Baraga went to Detroit and told his bishop about the arrival of Father Viszoczky in Grand River and the latter's desire to remain there. The good bishop was perfectly satisfied with this plan and told Baraga that he would take him along to the north the next spring to found there a new mission.

Father Baraga, in his letter to the Leopoldine Society, is entirely silent as to the reason of his departure from Grand River mission, except that he was desirous of carrying the light of the Gospel to other Indian tribes immerged as yet in paganism. He simply says that Rev. Andrew Viszoczky, a Hungarian priest, came to see him and expressed a desire to remain in Grand River mission; that he (Baraga) went to see his bishop about the matter and that the latter approved of Father Viszoczk's plan. Hon. Richard R. Elliott, however, in his above-cited able article gives the real reason of F.

Baraga's going, and that was: the opposition of the Indian agent at Grand River and of his party. He writes:

"Father Baraga had converted and baptized about two hundred Ottawas on the Grand River. He had reformed the habits of these neophytes before baptism, having won them over from their propensity to get drunk, and they gradually fell into the practice of industry and thrift.

"Their example had had its good effect on others; but there were opposing influences at work of such strength as he had never encountered before in his missionary experience.

"The situation was this: All that part of the Grand River valley, where at the time the Ottawa cantons were located and which embraced the field of Father Baraga's missionary labors, was an Indian reservation under the United States government.

"Within the limits of this reservation the potency of the United States Indian agent was supreme; he had for his assistance, in case of need, a small force of United States soldiers; while on any extraordinary occasion he could have a full regiment sent from Fort Dearborn, now Chicago, to the reservation. But the fate of the Ottawas had already been decided.

"The outbreak of the Black Hawk war had demonstrated the danger menacing the western frontier settlements from the vicinity of such Indian nations as the Ottawas, Pottawotomis, Miamis, Illinois, and the Sacs and Foxes.

"During this outbreak, by adroit and prompt measures, the Pottawotomis and Prairie tribes were all assembled at Fort Dearborn, placed under guard, and regularly rationed until Black Hawk had been captured, and his revolt had collapsed; then they were permitted to return to their cantons placated with presents of blankets, kettles and silver trinkets for the squaws. The following summer the Miamis, Ottawas and Pottawotomis were assembled in council at Fort Dearborn, and by the usual methods these nations were induced to sign a treaty by which they ceded their reservations in Michigan, Indiana, Ohio, Illinois and Wisconsin for reservations of five million acres of lands west of the Mississippi to each of the nations entering into treaty obligations.

"But there remained the matter of form process of obtaining the assent of the separate tribes (bands) of each nation to their immigration to the West. With the Christian tribes this assent was not so easy to obtain. This duty devolved upon the Indian agent resident with each nation.

"The Pottawotomis, who were mostly Christians, were reluctant to leave their homes and the vicinity of the graves of their ancestors where for centuries this nation had occupied the soil of the fairest regions of Michigan and of Indiana, and were not unanimous; but speculators wanted their lands, and means were found by the United States Indian agent to obtain the signature of a sufficient number of chiefs to make a majority in favor of removal, which being in opposition to the wishes of the minority, the latter refused to leave their homes. A regiment of United States troops was sent from Fort Dearborn to drive these Christian men, women and children from their own homes by the bayonet and to escort them like wild cattle to the place assigned them in the far distant West.

"Hence the painful scenes accompanying this outrage to which we have already referred. The process of obtaining the assent of the separate bands of the Ottawas to immigration in accordance with the national treaty was then in progress. Hence the tribal councils to which all came; hence the presence of so many Indian traders on the Grand River reservation and the debauchery prevalent while Father Baraga was there. It is certain he would not advise his converts to leave their homes. The United States government did not want a repetition of the disgraceful scenes, which had blackened its reputation in the Pottawotomi removal. But the Ottawas were more efficient warriors; should there be any trouble, another general Indian war might ensue, and the development of the Western states, then in fair progress, would be retarded; Michigan, which at the time was rapidly filling with settlers, would be the theatre of this war. The Indian agent was instructed to effect the removal of the Ottawas peaceably, and to avoid the violent methods resorted to with the Pottawotomis. The government had acquired the title to the Indian lands by treaty, while the less important details could be managed by well known methods. Besides, there was not at the time the same sharp crowd of land sharks and speculators eager to acquire lands in Michigan as there had been in Indiana and Ohio, to rush the Indian agent to rid the territory of the original owners of the soil.

"While Father Baraga was so successful in his apostolic work, this success was creating an opposition he probably was not at first aware of.

"The reform in the morals of the Ottawas seriously lessened the quantity of whisky which the Indian traders had been selling; while the probability that the converted Ottawa bands would object to remove to the unknown country west of the Mississippi would bring the Indian agent into trouble with the government at Washington for inefficiency in effecting their removal.

"That Father Baraga was considered a serious obstacle to the personal interests and to the official task of the United States Indian agent, however, is beyond any question, for it is proved by the edict of the latter functionary, that the Catholic missionary should leave the reservation for the alleged reason that he was disturbing the peaceful status of its Indians, and that he would thwart in all probability, to some extent at least, the plans of the government for their removal. Father Baraga opposed this edict. Notwithstanding the efforts of Bishops Rese and Purcell, and the intervention of Stevens T. Mason, the youthful governor of the Territory of Michigan, the Indian Department at Washington sustained the action of the Indian agent at the Grand River reservation, and Father Baraga was forced to leave the scene of his successful missionary works. The agent then accomplished the conditions of the treaty of Fort Dearborn, and the Ottawas were removed to the new reservation west of the Mississippi."

During the rest of the winter of 1834-35 F. Baraga labored in a small French mission not far from Detroit. While there he received from his kind friends and well-wishers in Austria a box of church articles and devotionals. This timely gift pleased him very much, as he could use them in the establishment of his new mission, La Pointe, where such things were much needed. He mentions some of the articles received: Four large beautiful candlesticks, a very beautiful missal and nice vestments, etc. He remarks that the cathedral in Detroit did not have as beautiful candlesticks nor missal as he had received for his intended mission.

In a letter dated Detroit, March 13th, 1835, he gives expression to his longing desire to go to his new field of labor. He writes:

"It appears strange to me to be in a congregation of whites. I there live in peace and am much more comfortable than among my Indians. But I feel like a fish thrown on dry land. The Indian mission is my life. Now, having learned the language tolerably well, and being in hopes that I will perfect myself in it still more, I am firmly resolved to spend the remainder of my life in the Indian mission, if it is the will of God. I am longing for the moment of my departure for Lake Superior. Many, I hope, will be converted there to the religion of Christ, and find in it their eternal salvation. Oh, how the thought elevates me! Would that I had wings to fly over our ice-bound lakes, so as to be sooner among the pagans! But what did I say? Many will be converted! Oh, no! If only one or two were converted and saved, it would be worth the while to go there and preach the Gospel! But God in His infinite goodness gives us more than we expect. Certainly, my dear benefactors, the newly converted Indians will thank you on the day of judgment for having contributed so much towards their conversion and salvation. In conclusion, I recommend myself and my future mission to the fervent prayers of all the pious members and benefactors of the Leopoldine Society."

Chapter XXVI

F. Baraga Arrives at La Pointe, Wis.—Incidents of the Journey.— He Builds His First Church.

We will let our zealous missioner himself relate the particulars of his journey to his new mission towards the western end of Lake Superior. His letter is dated La Pointe, August 9th, 1835.

"After a long journey, often interrupted through want of opportunity, I finally arrived, on the 27th of July (1835), at the place where I intend, with the help of God, to establish a new mission. This place is an Indian village, in which, from time to time, also Canadian traders reside, who traffic with the Indians. It is situated on a very beautiful island, near the southern shore of the immense, large lake, Superior. This lake is the largest in land sea of the world, with the exception of the Caspian Sea. It is four hundred and twenty American miles long and one hundred and seventy miles wide, and lies six hundred and thirty feet above the Atlantic Ocean. Its depth is in many places literally unfathomable. English engineers have attempted to measure its depth, but in many places they could find no bottom.

"The place, where I now reside, is called La Pointe. It is 740 miles from Detroit and is situated considerably towards the north. I traveled on this lake in the month of July, the hottest month, and yet some mornings it was so cold on the water that I was obliged to put on my coat over my cassock and envelope myself in my cloak, not to take cold. On the 7th of July ice of the thickness of the back of a knife was found along the shore at the mouth of Lake Superior. Now, however, in August we have very hot days; but the winter is said to be very severe and long here.

"I left Detroit about noon the 8th of June, and at four o'clock in the morning of the 10th I arrived at Mackinac, although these two places are over 300 miles apart; so quick do steamers sail in this country. In Mackinac I remained several days and used the opportunity to pay a visit to the Indians at Arbre Croche. They were very much pleased to see me again. They wished very much to keep me in their mission, for Rev. Father Simon Sanderl had left Arbre Croche in the beginning of June, and is now in Ohio, where these Fathers intend to establish a house of their Order. I represented to the good Indians that their brethren at Lake Superior, who had never yet seen a priest, were in greater need of spiritual help than they, and that certainly another missionary would soon come to Arbre Croche. This quieted them a little.

"I returned then to Mackinac and waited there for Bishop Rese. He was so busy at Detroit that he could not come. He wrote that he could not come to Mackinac before the beginning of August. So I continued my journey, and arrived at Sault Ste. Marie on the 4th of July. It is there that the saintly and zealous missionary, Father Francis Hatscher, of the Congregation of the Most Holy Redeemer, is stationed. But the very day I arrived at Sault Ste. Marie he departed to go to Ohio. He did not know whether or not he would return to the Sault. On the 10th of July I left the Sault on a trading vessel, and after a tedious voyage of *eighteen* days arrived at La Pointe, where the good people received me with exceeding great joy. For many years they had longed for a priest and had urgently requested that one might be sent to them. However, on account of the sad want of priests in our poor diocese, nothing thus far could be done in the matter. Their joy, therefore, was unspeakable when they saw a priest coming to their place.

"Truly the want of priests in our diocese is sad. Would that zealous priests in my fatherland resolve to come to this wilderness to rescue from eternal ruin the poor pagans who live scattered in this country, all of whom it is impossible for one priest to attend. Would it not pay to work and suffer much in order to save even but one soul and make it forever happy! But here souls are saved not by one or two, but by hundreds. Every priest that would come here would infallibly, with the help of God, save hundreds, were he to have even but a little persevering missionary zeal.

"From the Sault to La Pointe is considered to be 330 American miles, and my nearest neighbor priest is now so far distant. When I came here and noticed the good feeling of my people I immediately began to encourage them to commence the building of a church. They started in with such zeal that in seven days they had finished it so far that I could bless it on the 9th of August (1835), and say Mass in it. I dedicated this little church to God under the patronage of St. Joseph, this powerful intercessor with God. The building is strong and durable, although constructed of hewn logs according to the American style of building. It is large enough for the people here, being 50x20 feet and 18 feet high, with a pretty high steeple, wherein a small bell hangs, which was cast in Detroit.

"The number of my catechumens is quite considerable. All ardently long for Baptism, which they will receive as soon as they shall have been more fully instructed. On the 2d of August I baptized twenty-five Indians of those more fully instructed, and who had previously gained some knowledge of religion; I likewise baptized some children. Between the 3d and 9th of August twenty-five others received holy Baptism.

"This week they will begin the building of my house, in which a large room will be partitioned off for a school. I am very contented and cannot sufficiently thank God that everything goes so unexpectedly well in the establishing of this mission, though I am now wholly in want of all earthly resources. After defraying the expenses of my journey hither, I have but three dollars left. Our Rev. Bishop could not give me more, for he is so heavily in debt for the cathedral-church in Detroit and for the church in Green Bay, and has to make so many new outlays to properly equip his school and provide for other necessary institutions in Detroit with what they need, that he expends all the money he gets for these purposes. Had I not found the people so good here I would not have been able to begin anything. However, I see that this cannot continue so on the long run. The soil here is poor. The climate is not favorable to agriculture. The necessary clothing, which they procure from Canadian traders in bartering their peltries, is exceedingly dear, for it has to be brought hither from such a great distance.

"It grieves my heart to see their children running around naked. Their parents would gladly clothe them, if they had the means. How much would it not recommend the missionary and his religion, could he but clothe these poor creatures a little! O how gladly would I do it if I could! At Grand River I have done so, and likewise at Arbre Croche, because I was supplied with sufficient means, but now I have nothing.

"Ninety miles from here is another Indian village, called Fond du Lac, where there are also many Indians, who desire to embrace the Catholic religion. They heard from a pious fur-trader of the religion and the priest. They wish very much to see one in their place. As soon as I shall have transacted the more urgent mission affairs here, I will go there, please God, and spend a couple of weeks with those good Indians in order to receive them by faith and Baptism into the number of the faithful sheep of Christ. I am told that in the neighborhood of Fond du Lac there are many other Indians, who have often made the remark that they, too, would embrace the Christian religion when a priest would be stationed in Fond du Lac to teach religion to them and their children. Moreover, in the interior towards the northwest there are other large lakes, where there are a great many Indians, who are still walking on the road to eternal perdition. Alas, is it not awfully sad to see so many souls go to eternal perdition through want of priests! Ah, why do not some Austrian priests make up their minds to come to the assistance of, these poor pagans! Would to God that some would come to me; I would certainly get them good places. The want of linguistic knowledge should not deter them from coming here. They would soon learn the languages. Let us pray the Lord of the harvest that He may send laborers into His vineyard!"

Chapter XXVII

Father Baraga's First Visit to Fond Du Lac (Minn.)

In his second letter to the Leopoldine Society, dated La Pointe, September 28th, 1835, he remarks that since his arrival he had experienced great consolation and much joy, but also many hardships and adversities. The latter are unavoidable in the establishment of new missions in distant and wild countries. Still, the consolations and spiritual joys of the true missionary far outweigh the hardships he endures. These difficulties are due partly to the nature of the country in which he labors—heat, cold, bad roads, unhealthiness of climate, etc. They are also due in part to the opposition he is sure to meet with on the part of evil-minded people, such as are found everywhere. However, the conversion of a single pagan inspires so much consolation that the missionary readily forgets all his trials and hardships. Baraga remarks: "Truly this is a dreary country. As early as the 22d of September we saw the snow-flakes falling and for several weeks past rooms are being heated."

Since the 9th of August Father Baraga had a great number of Baptisms, mostly of adults. In order to make those holy acts more solemn and impressive, the missionary generally baptized only on Sundays. Hence he had quite a number of Baptisms. During the month of August, the first month he spent in La Pointe, he christened *eighty-six Indians*, and during September, *sixty-two*.

As the good Indians of Fond du Lac were eagerly asking for a priest, F. Baraga went there in September. As soon as he arrived at the village he was most agreeably surprised to find a large number of Indians assembled at the trader's house. As soon as he entered, they all knelt down and asked for the priestly blessing, which the pious and tender-hearted missionary gave them with a heart full of emotion and joy. He thanked repeatedly the good fur-trader for the great interest he had taken in the conversion of those poor pagans. The name of this trader, who was a French-Canadian, was Pierre Cotte. He had been trading with the Indians for upwards of thirty years, and could speak their language fluently.

Through a merciful arrangement of Divine Providence a copy of Baraga's Ottawa prayer book, published in 1832, had fallen into his hands. He began now to invite the Indians of his place to come to his house and then he used to sing for them various Indian hymns to be found in the prayer book. A great number of these hymns are composed according to well-known French airs. The Indians found the singing so nice and pleasant that they used to come to his house every evening. They would often stay till midnight, nay, at times even till daybreak, singing with Mr. Cotté. When he noticed their great zeal he did not confine himself to singing spiritual hymns, but also instructed them in the catechism. He also read to them the morning and evening prayers, which the Indians soon learned by heart. When F. Baraga came, he found many of the Indians very much inclined to religion and well prepared for Baptism. He baptized twenty-one at Fond du Lac on the 6th of September, and thirty at La Pointe on the 9th of the same month. Baraga says:

"God be thanked a thousand times! A considerable number of pagans have already been received into the bosom of the church, namely, one hundred and forty-eight. God grant that all, or at least the greater number of these new converts, may go to heaven! What a consolation for me on the day of judgment!"

Rev. Joseph Prost, Redemptorist, under date of the 12th of November, 1835, wrote to the Leopoldine Society about F. Baraga:

"I have read a letter of Father Baraga to Rt. Rev. Bishop Rese, in which he complains that his winter clothes which had been sent him had not arrived, and that he was exposed to all the rigors of a northern winter in his light summer clothes. This indefatigable apostle now teaches the Indians without an interpreter. It is truly edifying to read his letters to the Rt. Rev. Bishop, for they characterize a man of the strictest obedience to his superior."

Truly this humble, self-sacrificing, obedient priest can serve as a model to all members of religious orders engaged in the Indian mission-field. It was in La Pointe that he began the practice, and ever afterwards kept up, of rising at three in the morning during summer, and at four during winter, and *spend three consecutive hours in meditation and prayer*. This we learn from a casual entry in his journal kept when Bishop. No wonder that a man so highly gifted with the gift of prayer and of such heroic virtues should become the instrument of God for the conversion and salvation of innumerable souls.

Chapter XXVIII

Baraga's Labors at La Pointe.—(Continued).

Between September 28th and December 28th, F. Baraga baptized thirty-three in La Pointe, mostly adults. One of his converts was a venerable old woman of one hundred years. From an old French-Canadian, who had been on the island fifty-three years, her age could approximately be inferred, as she remembered things that had occurred about a century before. The poor old woman felt exceedingly happy when she was baptized. Three of her grand children were baptized with her. Her youngest grandchild, a man of forty years, was baptized on Christmas day. On that great holy day Baraga baptized twenty adult pagans and two children. Several entire families were baptized that day.

Every evening, for a whole month, during the cold winter weather, he walked a distance of three miles to where they lived, to prepare these good Indians for the grace of Baptism, for in the day time they were away fishing or trapping. These instructions used to last a long time till late at night, so that it was always very late before he returned to his modest dwelling. God rewarded His zealous servant. On Christmas day he baptized a large number of adults, as above mentioned. From July 27th, the day of his arrival, up to Dec. 28th—that is, within five months, he baptized one hundred and eighty-four persons.

During the five months that had elapsed since the founding of the mission, only one had "died—a child of two years. This seemingly unimportant circumstance may have aided him greatly in his work of converting. Had many died soon after Baptism, the people, who are naturally superstitious, would have most likely attributed it to that holy Sacrament, as they did in former times, when the Jesuits were laboring in the Northwest.

In a letter written about that time he says:

"I feel grieved that I must continue this mission entirely alone, and that, moreover, I have not a cent of my own. A school would be very useful in this mission, but it is simply impossible for me to do the two things—that is, keep school and properly perform my numerous missionary duties and visit the sick. For often I am in the huts of the Indians all day, where I always find something useful to do. I must necessarily omit one or the other. In this case I rather omit keeping school than attending the mission, for, properly speaking, I am a missionary and not a schoolmaster. Of course, I would gladly do both, if possible. That I have no money at all is also very hard, for I would gladly clothe, at least a little, the poor Indian children, who even now run about half-naked in winter, but I cannot give them a stitch of clothing. That is hard; but in the name of God let it be so for the first year. I hope hereafter to get a teacher and also some assistance."

The winter of 1835-36 was very long and severe. As late as June 7th large blocks of ice were to be seen along the lake shore. Time, however, slipped by pleasantly, partly in instructing his new converts, partly in composing literary works for the press. In a letter, dated La Pointe, June 17th, 1836, he mentions the following works, on which he had been laboring during his first year's stay on the island, namely:

1. A work in the Slavonian language.

2. A German work, entitled, "History, Character, Life and Manners of the North American Indians." (This work was intended for his generous benefactors of the Leopoldine Society.)

3. A prayer book in the Chippewa language.

4. The life of Jesus, also in Chippewa.

On the 26th of May, 1836, he again went by boat to Fond du Lac and remained there two weeks. He found his converts in the very best disposition. He was in hopes they would obtain a resident priest, for Rev. Francis Pierz, who had intended to come to La Pointe the previous fall, but had been prevented from doing so, and had wintered at Arbre Croche, was intended for Fond du Lac. The Indians there had heard of this arrangement and awaited F. Pierz with great desire. This, however, was never to be, for "man proposes, but God disposes."

Through the zealous labors of good Pierre Cotté fourteen pagans were prepared for Baptism. This pious trader assembled them at his house every Sunday during the past winter and instructed them. F. Baraga completed their instruction and baptized them. One of the converts was a head-chief, who, with his whole family, embraced our holy faith. The day before Baraga's departure the head-chief of the Fond du Lac band of Indians came to him with several men and begged of him not to leave, but to stay with them and let some other priest take charge of La Pointe. He answered that it would please him very much to do as they requested, but that he had often promised the good people of La Pointe to live and die with them, if such should be the will of God. Hence it was not optional with him to leave them and go to another mission. At the same time he promised to do his best to procure them a resident priest. At this all were very much rejoiced. They showed the place where they intended to build a church and house for the priest.

Alas, the hopes of these fervent neophytes were never to be realized. Fond du Lac has ever remained a mere mission. During the last fifty years it has been attended by Indian missionaries from La Pointe, Superior, Bayfield, and now, Duluth. There are but a handful of Indian half-breeds there now. Most of them have removed to Papashkominitigong and other places.

At La Pointe the good work kept going on. Twenty-eight converts were received into the church, among them a head-chief, whose conversion made a deep impression on his pagan countrymen. He became a model of virtue and was zealous in the cause of religion. In the early part of June F. Baraga received a box of vestments and other church articles, as also a great quantity of rosaries, medals, pictures, scapulars, etc., for his new church and his dear Indians, from the Leopoldine Society.

Chapter XXIX

F. Baraga Goes to Europe.—He Is Received Everywhere with Great Distinction.—Lectures on Indian Missions.—Returns to La Pointe.—Finishes His Church.—First Confirmation in La Pointe by Bishop Rese in 1838.

The number of converts in La Pointe kept increasing. During the first year of his stay he baptized 255 persons, the far greater number being adults. The little church hastily erected within a week after his arrival, and which was dedicated to St. Joseph, was now too small to hold the congregation, and many were obliged to stand outside during divine service. Then he resolved to enlarge it by building an addition. To accomplish this he determined to go to Europe to collect the necessary funds and get his Chippewa prayer book printed.

He left La Pointe on the 29th of September, 1836. He first went to Paris and remained there for some weeks to superintend the printing of his prayer book. This was the first edition of the Chippewa "Anamie Masinaigan Prayer book," which has since been reprinted a number of times. But his zeal for the salvation of souls gave him no rest. During Lent he preached in German to his countrymen in Paris, a great number residing in the French capital. There he also found his widowed sister, Antonia de Hoeffern, who had gone to Paris to acquire the necessary proficiency in French, as she intended to devote herself to the service of God in

America by teaching school. She came with her saintly brother to La Pointe, but after spending two years there her health failed and she was obliged to return to her fatherland.*

F. Baraga then visited his native land† and preached at Laibach and other places to great numbers of people who flocked together from all parts of the country to see and hear him. He preached in both Slavonian and German, giving an account of his missionary life among the Indians and their ways and customs. He then went to Vienna and gave to the directors of the Leopoldine Society an account of his labors and of the necessities of his mission. He received the necessary funds to complete his church and pastoral residence. On the 8th of October, 1837, he returned to La Pointe and after many labors and trials he finished the church and annexed priests' house in the month of August, 1838. On the 2d of September of the last named year the church was dedicated to God under the name of St. Joseph. On the 7th of the same month Bishop Rese came to this mission for the first time, and on the 9th of September, 1838, confirmed one hundred and twelve converts and Canadians.

Speaking of his countryman, F. Baraga, Rev. Fr. Pierz says:

"Much good has already been done for the Catholic religion, and there is good reason to hope for more, since several zealous missionaries have learned the Indian language and thus they can work upon the Indian directly, without interpreter, and lay the foundation of an Indian literature.

"Herein F. Baraga distinguishes himself before all others, of whom I can justly testify to the honor of Austria and his fatherland, Krain, that Providence has chosen him as a perfect model for all missionaries. For in this man of God shine forth profound and multifarious learning, apostolic piety, united to an insatiable zeal for the conversion of souls, and such wisdom that not only all Catholics, but even Protestants and pagans give him merited

---

* See appendix.
† F. Baraga preached at Laibach in the Cathedral on the second Sunday after Easter, April 10th, 1837. He then went to Döbernig, his native town, and knelt almost a whole hour at the baptismal font in the Church of St. George, where he had been baptized, renewing with the greatest fervor his baptismal vows in the very place where forty years before he had received the Sacrament of regeneration. Would that all Christians appreciated in like manner the great grace of Baptism!

praise. The Lord's blessing accompanied his untiring labors so visibly in Arbre Croche, Grand River, St. Glair, and La Pointe, that his numerous converts are the best Christians in America.

"In consideration of his great merits, our Rt. Rev. Bishop has appointed him his Secretary and Vicar-general. For promoting the cause of virtue and religion he deserves to be placed on the 'candelabrum to serve as a light unto many others.'"

The enlarging of his church, as he himself declares in the Baptismal Record, now in Bayfield, cost him a vast amount of care and labor. He was obliged to superintend the work personally. This took a great deal of his precious time. He had to show his carpenters what to do and how to do it. It is a well-known fact that Indians, when left to themselves, soon grow weary and leave. They want someone to stand by them, so to say, all day long, to show them their work, how it is to be done, and to animate them to exertion, for they are naturally indolent and disinclined to steady work. Every Indian missionary will realize what labor, care and expense good Father Baraga must have had to undergo in order to enlarge and complete his church. In addition to this he had a large congregation of Indians, half-breeds, and whites to attend, to hear the numerous Confessions of his fervent neophytes and others, to instruct those ignorant, though good people in the rudiments of faith, to prepare his sermons in Chippewa and French, to teach catechism, attend sick-calls, visit the pagans in their wigwams, near and far, to attend his distant missions; and besides all this to personally superintend the work being done on the church. All this took up all his time during the day and often a great part of the night.

The interior was decorated with eighteen beautiful oil-paintings, some of which are yet to be seen in the present La Pointe church and one in Bayfield. The beautiful and large oil-painting over the high altar in La Pointe church, representing the Holy Family at work, was painted in Laibach in 1837, and was intended to remind the Indians of the great precept of their Maker: "In the sweat of thy brow thou shalt eat thy bread." Speaking of this beautiful painting, executed by Langus, in Laibach, Father Baraga writes:

"The altar-picture is large and beautiful, painted by Langus in Laibach. It represents St. Joseph working in his shop. The Blessed

Virgin sits at his side and sews, and the Child Jesus is looking at His foster father working. This picture is very appropriate for an Indian mission church, for Indians are by nature inclined to idleness. Missionaries have to admonish them very often to work, and no sublimer pattern of industriousness can be presented before their eyes than the Holy Family."

Speaking of the founding of the Grand Portage Mission F. Baraga says:

"Furthermore I have to report that the intended mission at Grand Portage (Minnesota), on the northern shore of Lake Superior, is now in its beginning. It makes very agreeable progress. I have mentioned in a former letter that on my return from Europe (in 1837) I received a very friendly letter from the head chief there. He declared in the name of his countrymen that they most earnestly desired to hear the Word of God. I then told F. Pierz to go this summer to Grand Portage, which he did. He found the Indians in the very best disposition. They had already constructed a small bark chapel, for they confidently awaited the coming of a priest this summer, because I had promised them *last fall, when I was there*, that I would procure them a priest, who would stay with them and announce to them the word of God. He has already baptized many, who are all very zealous in performing their religious duties. He has also made a missionary visit to another place not far from Grand Portage, called Fort William, where he found the Indians in the very best disposition towards religion."

Chapter XXX

State of La Pointe Mission During 1839 and 1840. Peculiar Indian Customs at Funerals, Mode of Burial. Interesting Letter of Father Pierz.

In his letter to the Leopoldine Society, dated Jan. 25th, 1839, Baraga complains that he has nothing interesting to write, as mostly all pagans, who had any leaning to Christianity, had been converted, and the others seemed determined to close their hearts against the call of divine grace and to persevere in their pagan superstition. "Crediderunt quotquot praeordinati erant ad vitam aeternam," all those believed who were ordained to eternal life."

St. Joseph's Mission at La Pointe was fast assuming the form of a well-regulated parish. The church, still located at Middlefort, near the large Indian cemetery, was finished both inside and out. It had a nice altar, pulpit, pews, and a regular choir, composed of Canadian and Chippewa singers. For many years Theophile Remillard, still alive at this writing (1896), aged 83 years, was head singer in St. Joseph's church; he was assisted by Antoine and Jean Baptiste Gaudin (Gordon) both still alive. Antoine Gaudin resides at present in Gordon, Wis., and is a very good practical Catholic and main-stay of the little mission at his place. His brother, Jean Baptiste, resides at Bayfield, Wis., and is also a very good Catholic, as are also Joseph and Angeligue Gaudin, twins, brother and sister of the above-named men.

We will mention some of the old settlers in La Pointe (1835-43). Besides the above-named singers there were at that time on the island: Alexie Neveu, Gros Cadotte, Michel Cadotte, Alexie Charpentier, Charette, grandfather of Charles Charette, of Odanah; Antoine Charette, Ignace Rabidoux, Jean Baptiste Denommé, Francis Lamoreux, Baptiste Gosselin, Francis Bellanger, Basile Beaulieu, John Bell, generally called Squire Bell; Louis Dufault, Baptiste Beriault, Louis Dufault, Joseph Dufault, Charles Belle Isle, Legault (Lego), John B. Brisette, Vincent Roy-Sr., Vincent Roy, who died last year in Superior, Seraphin Lacomb, Capt. Angus, Michel Boucher, Brobaut, Antoine Perinier, Michael Bassinet, Hilaire Généreau, Megalise, Jean Baptiste Lassard, Robert Morin, Antoine Cournoyer.

There were also three ushers or church-policemen to keep order in church and assist their pastor. F. Baraga had also two grown-up boys to serve Mass and a sexton, everything in true church style. All these men were Canadian Frenchmen, married to Indian women. Many of the parishioners, in fact, by far the greatest number, were very good men and deserving of great praise for their fervor and piety. F. Baraga had also a neat, well-built house, built, of course, of hewn logs, for frames were very rare in those days as being too expensive.

Adjoining the church was the cemetery, that "city of the dead," covered even at present with many little houses built Indian-fashion over the graves of their dead. We see in this mode of burial much that shows their belief in the immortality of the soul and their tender love and regard for the dead. Even Christian Indians adhere tenaciously to their Indian mode of sepulture, unless hindered by their pastor. They hate to bury their dead deep in the ground, preferring to have them buried but slightly below the surface. They generally put something over the coffin, usually a mat, or nice quilt, to keep it from getting wet. After the grave is filled they will immediately spread over it a large piece of birch-bark, as a kind of temporary cover to keep the rain from wetting the grave. If not too poor, they will get a neat little house, or at least a nice roof, built over the grave at considerable expense. To this, then, the Christians attach a cross to distinguish their graves from those of the pagans. The pagan usually plants a United States flag or some superstitiously marked banner on the grave of his dead. On the whole, it can be truly said that they have more regard for the dead than many whites have. The pagans used to bury various articles used by the deceased during life, also place tobacco or sugar on the grave, or in the drawer made for that purpose in the little house built over the grave. But these customs are falling into disuse more and more. A peculiar feeling of sadness and pity seizes one in passing a pagan graveyard. They do not seem to have that aversion to grave-yards so common to whites, for they often build their wigwams or houses close to the graves of their dead. In Bayfield their graves formerly lay on all sides, in front of the church, under the priest's window, at the rear of the house, in short, everywhere. Well does the writer remember the lonely, queer, ghostly feeling that crept over him when, during the first week of his stay in Bayfield, in June, 1878, he had to sleep literally among the dead, without a human soul in the house. However, his slumbers were not disturbed by any nocturnal visitors from the spirit world.

BOARDING SCHOOL OF ODANAH

During the winter of 1838-39 F. Baraga composed his "Gagikwe-Masinaigan"—"Sermon-book," which contains the epistles and gospels of all the Sundays and holydays of the year, besides a short bible-history of the old Testament and instructive extracts from the four gospels, Acts of the Apostles, epistles of St. Paul and other Apostles. This book he intended to have printed at Green Bay, this being the nearest place where it could be done. However the estimated cost of printing and binding was three hundred dollars. It was no doubt for that reason that he wrote to the Leopoldine Society to procure the necessary funds. The "Gagikwe-Masinaigan" now used by our Indian missionaries was printed by Joseph A. Hemann, Cincinnati, O., in 1858.

F. Pierz in a letter dated La Pointe, Wis., July 21st, 1838, writes as follows of Baraga's labors on that island:

"La Pointe is a large island, where fish are plentiful, at the western end of great Lake Superior, 480 miles (?) from Sault Ste. Marie, my former station. A large trading company has a branch store on this island and it is therefore the rendezvous of many Indians and French-Canadians, all of whom lived like pagans before Father Baraga's arrival.

"At first this pious missionary had to contend with many difficulties and hardships, but with his customary, persevering energy and apostolic zeal he soon formed out of these rude, wild barbarians a very large Christian congregation, which continues to grow daily through new conversions. To his great joy he has completed his beautiful new church and a suitable priest's house with the money he brought with him from Europe.

"He teaches daily in the church and in the wigwams of the Indians. On Sunday he preaches *five times* in three or four languages. He is very much beloved and lives with his happy flock like a father with his dear children, in peaceful contentment and the enjoyment of the beautiful fruits of his labors to his great consolation. He has peculiar success and God's visible blessing in converting pagans. In Arbre Croche he formed out of very wild savages several hundreds of such good Christians, that one might propose them to all Christians as models of piety. At Grand River, in a short time, he made out of blind idolators a truly pious, Christian congregation. Here in La Pointe a person is deeply moved, when he hears the newly made converts singing the praises of God with their priest, in their beautifully decorated church, and sees them devoutly adoring their Creator and Lord. As to his personal virtues and rigorous mode of life I will not expatiate upon them in order not to wound his humility. My prayer is that the Lord may preserve him for a long time to labor for the salvation of the Indians and to serve as a noble example to all missionaries, and that He may bless all his undertakings.

"I also mention with pleasure the excellent Indian prayer book which F. Baraga composed and had printed last year at Paris. This interesting work was distributed gratuitously in all the Indian missions and was everywhere received with much joy. It stirred up religious life and laid the foundation for Indian schools. The great benefit and wonderful success of this work for confirming the Christians and converting the pagans is certainly highly consoling for the present and future of the Indians, who are so desirous of instruction.

"In the German work: 'On the manners and customs of the Indians' printed at Laibach, F. Baraga describes only wild savages and their way of living. He relates their horrible cruelties, as gleaned from the earliest historical accounts, without, however, disclosing the traits of goodness in the Indian character. The author, however, admits that he intended to speak in his work only of the manners and customs of Indian pagans and idolaters, and that the description of the manners and customs of newly converted Christian Indians was to be the subject of his report to the Rev. Directors of the Leopoldine Society.

"As regards my own personal experience, having had many opportunities during my three years' stay among the Indians of several places to watch them, pagans as well as Christians, I can justly assert that they are, as a rule, phlegmatic, good-natured, exceedingly patient and docile, and well disposed to lead a good life. Even in their wild, aboriginal state, when they are removed from bad, scandalous people, they do not live at all wickedly and viciously. They listen eagerly to the priest who comes to them, readily embrace the faith and allow themselves to be soon transformed into good, steadfast Christians.

"But where the poor Indians have been scandalized by the great vices of white Christians, or have been spoiled by intoxicating liquor, and have been seduced by the enemies of religion and prejudiced against our holy faith, they naturally become far harder to convert and civilize. Thievery, injustice, or perfidy are found among no nation so seldom as among the Indians. Murders also are very rare. Only when provoked to reprisals, or driven thereto through the instinct of self-preservation, e. g., in case of a deadly famine do they take human life. A Catholic missionary nowadays need have no fear of endangering life amongst the most savage tribes of these people, because owing to ancient traditions about the pious French Jesuit Fathers, who accomplished so much good in this country, they always show great respect to priests and call them reverently: 'Mekatewikwanaie Black Robe' Hence they adopt only that religion as being genuinely Catholic, which is brought to them under the Jesuit soutain and which they call: "Wemitigojianamiewin"—French religion. Whoever preaches to them a different religion is a 'Jaganash'—an Englishman—and his religion is not held in respect by them."

Chapter XXXI

Baraga's Personal Appearance and Peculiar Traits of Character.—His Humility, Poverty, Kindness, Burning Zeal and Restless Activity.—La Pointe, Population, Pursuits, Early Settlers.

As most of the pagans in La Pointe who had any leaning to Christianity had been converted, F. Baraga had but few baptisms in that place after the year 1840. During 1839-40 he baptized only twenty-two pagan adults. He was, however, not idle. He labored hard and successfully in order to ground his converts in the knowledge and love of God and of their holy religion. He was untiring in catechizing both children and adults, preaching with fervor and unction the word of God on Sundays and holy days. His sermons were very plain, adapted to the capacity of his unlearned hearers, and generally short. He was deeply emotional, as the following anecdote, related by Hon. Vincent Roy, of Superior, lately deceased, shows. He says:

"I recollect very distinctly on two or three different occasions while he (F. Baraga) was reading the gospel from the pulpit for the first or midnight Mass at Christmas, in the Chippewa language, that the passage: 'And wrapped Him up in swaddling clothes' would bring him to tears and three or four minutes would elapse before he could control himself, so as to be able to proceed. In fact, I remember one time that after reading those words he was so much affected that his sobs could be distinctly heard all over the church; he could not recover himself and was compelled to descend from the pulpit without completing the gospel."

As to his personal appearance Mr. Roy says: "I remember him as a man of medium height, about 5 feet 4 inches, and weight about 150 pounds. He was stoutly built; his legs were very disproportionately short in comparison to his body. His hair was dark brown and he always wore it long and in curls, as his picture will show. His speech was slow, cool and powerful, and he possessed a well modulated voice and distinct enunciation. His movements were very deliberate and dignified."

Mr. Roy also related to the writer an incident that shows that F. Baraga was naturally very sensitive. For a year or two he used to dine at Mrs. Lacomb's, an aunt of Mr. Roy. The dinner was very simple. It consisted of corn, the shell of which had been removed by soaking the corn in lye or something similar. On one occasion Mrs. Lacomb being almost out of provisions told Baraga, as well as she could, that although she was still willing to keep him - she had hardly anything for him to eat - that he should try to find

another place. Father Baraga became excited and exclaimed: "Do you want to drive me away?" She tried to explain, but he was too excited to listen and left the house. The poor woman felt very bad. She wept bitterly and immediately followed him to the church. After some explanation, F. Baraga was mollified and Mrs. Lacomb left consoled and pleased. He continued taking his poor meals at her house as heretofore. He made her a present of a particle of the Holy Cross, which she took with her when she removed to Courtes-Oreilles, where she was married to A. Corbin. This precious relic was placed with the "authentica" in a neat reliquary by Rev. Casimir Vogt, O. S. F., and is still kept with religious care in the neat, though humble, church of the above-named place. So the poor Indian church of Courtes Oreilles has a treasure, for which many a stately cathedral might justly envy it.

The above incident shows that our saintly missionary was human and as a holy Father says of the Apostles: "Eos vitia non nescisse sed emendasse," so he, too, had to acquire virtue by the constant practice of self-restraint and self-denial.

"From four to five in the morning," said Father Jacker in his funeral sermon at the burial of Bishop Baraga, "or sometimes from three to five you would find him kneeling, wrapped in his cloak, in sweet conversation with his Lord, and this under any and all circumstances. We have seen him thus giving the first hour to God in the dark forest and on the shores of lakes, amidst the roaring storms as well as in his private chapel or in some hidden corner of the crowded stopping places while on his journeys. We have had occasion to observe how he persisted in following this rule even when he had been traveling the whole preceding day under great hardships, by water and by land; sometimes even when he had not been able to go to rest until after midnight. I know some may say: This was over doing things; was unnecessary. This was the way of the saints who knew that a thing torn a little will tear further and further, if not mended in time. They knew when a man begins to grow careless about his exercises of devotion he very soon begins to neglect his duties."

Speaking of how he acquitted himself of his pastoral duties whilst at La Pointe, the above-mentioned Hon. Vincent Roy, who came to La Pointe in 1839, when about fourteen years old, and who, with his brother Francis, received instruction in catechism from F. Baraga in 1840-41 says:

"He said but one Mass on Sundays. I do not recollect his teaching catechism on Sundays. Several times during the week he taught catechism regularly in the afternoon, In his visits he would hastily gather the adults and children of the neighborhood and teach his impromptu class the truths of faith. Vespers on Sundays without sermon.

No stations on Fridays, but during Lent (he had stations), on Fridays and other days of the week. Benediction was given, I think, only on the first Sunday of each month; not oftener than once a month. The singing for Mass was in Gregorian chant, vocal only, only male voices allowed. Vespers were sung in Chippewa, vocal only. Christmas singing was vocal, accompanied by violins and flutes. The choir was composed as follows: Alexis Charpentier, Antoine Gaudin and a Mr. McGillis. On Christmas day the instrumentalists were: violin, Mr. Agnew, a clerk of the American Fur Company; flute, Charles La Rose, government interpreter.

"He made at least one visit to Fond du Lac every year, during the summer, by boat. I remember he and Louis Gaudin made a trip to Fond du Lac on snowshoes. I do not know with whom he stopped when there. There never was a completed church nor chapel there. Father Pierz in 1842 or 1843, started to build one of hewed logs, but it was never completed. About 1840-45 I remember, Francis Roussain, Joseph Charette, J. B. Bellanger, were residents of Fond du Lac, besides the employees of the American Fur Company and other transient visitors. There were no whites nor Indians on the present town site of Superior, but Indians always lived near the entry opposite during the summer and some few further up the Minnesota-Point near Duluth."

Speaking of the make-up of La Pointe's population in Baraga's time, the above-mentioned gentleman says:

"There were no pure European families in La Pointe at that time. European males married into mixed-blood families, with the exception of the families of the Presbyterian mission—Rev. Sherman Hale and Teacher Sprote (two families). The population varied very much according to the season. In the winter they would number about thirty or forty mixed-blood families, besides a very few pagan Indian families. In the summer the population would about double in all shades. It must be borne in mind that La Pointe was preeminently the Indian depot for the distribution of goods to the different minor posts; and it was necessarily the headquarters for all engaged in the fur traffic. Fishing was also carried on very extensively. Those who were engaged in this occupation were those who remained at home during the winter, mending nets and making preparations for the next season's work. Fishing was also a branch of the American Fur Company's business.

"There was but one store and that was the fur company's. They carried in stock everything that was necessary—groceries, dry goods, hardware, etc. The grocery department occupied a two-story building about the same size as the dry goods department building, one standing on each side of a street leading from a dock about the same place where the present dock now is. There was also a baking department, which was situated about 200 feet east of the other buildings. *There was no saloon.* There were two carpenter shops, one operated by Mr. Perinier and the other by Dufault; also one large cooper shop maintained by the company, one blacksmith shop, etc. There was also one very large warehouse for repacking fish; it was about 200 feet long and was situated on the dock. In the rear of these buildings the company also maintained a very extensive garden and orchard, in which were raised all kinds of garden vegetables, grapes, cherries, crab-apples, currants, strawberries, etc. This was enclosed by a high board fence and was in charge of Old Man Oakes, father of Charles H. Oakes, lately of St. Paul, who was an expert gardener. Antoine Gaudin assisted him one or two years, 'Squire' Bell was at La Pointe upon my arrival in 1839. Roubidoux, Charpentiers, Dufaults, Denome, were there before me. Remillard came two or three years after me, Stahls and O'Malley came during Father Chebul's time, about 1860-61.

"Borup and Oakes were headmen for the fur company (John Jacob Astor). All voyageurs, 'runners' as they were called, were employed by said company. They would leave La Pointe about the beginning of September, stay away all fall and winter among the Indians in their respective districts, collect furs, and return about the beginning of June. They would take along blankets, clothes, guns, etc., to trade with the Indians for their furs. They took along very little provisions, as they depended mostly on hunting, fishing, wild rice, and trade with the Indians for their support. There were several depots for depositing goods and collecting furs; for instance, at Fond du Lac, Minn., Sand Lake, Courtes Oreilles, Lac du Flambeau, mouth of Yellow River, etc. The vessels used on Lake Superior for the fur trade were the 'John Jacob

Astor' a three-mast schooner; the 'Brewster' and the 'Siskowit' built by old man Perinier.

"The Presbyterian school was then in full operation under Rev. Sherman Hall; number of scholars at this school, which was a day school, was about forty. The Hon. Vincent Roy went to said school two winters."

SCHOOL CHILDREN FROM BAD RIVER RESERVATION, WIS.

Chapter XXXII

Father Baraga Laments the Want of Indian Missionaries. Takes Down His Church and Builds Another Larger One.

F. Baraga would have gladly brought the light of the gospel to more distant pagan Indians, but he could not find any priest to take charge of those already converted. To abandon them in order to go after pagans would never do, under the circumstances. Hence his letter to the Leopoldine Society from La Pointe, dated October 7, 1840, breathes a feeling of justifiable bitterness. His remarks may justly be applied to more than one of our reverend confreres, who might work with fruit amongst our poor Indians, negroes and others. He writes:

"Our means, moreover, are far too insufficient. I do not mean exactly our pecuniary means, but there are too few apostolic laborers among the Indians. No one wants to work in this truly desolate vineyard of the Lord. The missionaries who come over from Europe prefer to stay with the Germans or with other civilized inhabitants of this country. Hence this part of the vineyard of the Lord remains desolate and wild, with the exception of some small places. In this territory, which extends from Lake Superior north, west and south, and which in size is far greater than the whole Austrian empire, lives the Chippewa nation, whose language I now speak fluently, and for this whole country, so vast in extent, I am the only missionary! And I am stationed at a place which is pretty populous, with enough people in it to need even for itself exclusively all the work of a weak man. A person can imagine, therefore, what progress our holy faith can make under such circumstances in this abandoned country.

"For several years I have been working to get a couple of other missionaries to come here, to place them in different places; but nobody comes! Repeatedly have I had promises and assurances,, but when they were to be carried out those making them preferred living among civilized rather than with wild people, which, of course, is more comfortable; but the poor pagans continue to be thereby the prey of that infernal 'lion, who goes about and seeks whom he may devour'; who never rests and does much more for the eternal ruin of souls than those priests do for their salvation! My heart bleeds when I think of this misery. I purposely abstain from these sad reflections, not to lapse into discouraging sadness.

"On this occasion I must mention that I am on the point of building here a new large church, for the present one was poorly built, and is, besides, too small, for this place grows year after year; since there is a church and resident priest here, many French from Canada, who are all Catholics and who used to live heretofore scattered among the Indians, have now settled here, and every year more are coming. The French-Canadians are married to Indian women and some of them have large families. Their women and children become converted to the Christian religion as soon as they come here and receive baptism after sufficient instruction. Besides, many Indians of this place have been converted and every year some more embrace Christianity. All this increases my congregation and so our church has become too small. Next spring, if God spares my life, the new church will be erected. The contract for building it has been made with the trading company here (American Fur Co.) The building will be constructed of wood, and plastered inside, as is generally done in this country. All the lumber in the present church will be used for the new one, for the boards are perfectly sound yet. Hence the building will cost but one thousand dollars; otherwise the cost in this country, where everything is awfully dear, would certainly be more than fourteen hundred dollars.

"There is a Canadian here, who is considered a pretty good sculptor. Moreover, in order to give a more audible call to those more distant from the church, I have procured a bell from New

York, weighing 477 pounds, and costing in New York one hundred and seventy-eight dollars. On the 2d of this month the bell arrived and the Indians were astonished when they saw it and heard its peals of thunder.

"But now I come to the real cause of writing this letter. I received on the 2d of this month a letter with a check of one hundred florins, with the information that this mild gift came from G. A. G., a pious lady of Salzburg. I hereby return most heartfelt thanks to the pious giver. I also make use of the present occasion to thank most earnestly all our benefactors for their generous gifts. God grant to all of them the never-ending goods of heaven in reward for their temporal benefactions."

As there are some interested parties who, year after year, try to palm off on tourists the ridiculous fable that the present Catholic church in La Pointe was built by Pere Marquette some two hundred or more years ago, we will produce the statement of two perfectly reliable men, Hon. Vincent Roy, of Superior, Wis., lately deceased, and of Bishop Baraga, who superintended the building of the first church erected in 1835, and of the second one, the present, now standing on La Pointe Island, completed in 1841. Mr. Roy says:

"Lego and Belle Isle were both at La Pointe, when I was first there in 1839. I do not know whether they helped to build the first church in 1835. I understood that Joseph Dufauld, the grandfather of Peter Dufauld here, was the builder of the first church at Middle Fort. This church was taken down and removed about 1842 (should be 1841) to where it now stands by Joseph Dufauld (the same as above), who had the whole charge, besides thirty or forty assistants, all volunteers, those who could spare any time. I do not know where the material was obtained for the first building, but no doubt it was right on the ground. Material for the second building was all taken from the first, as above stated in the fore part of this paragraph, with the exception of the shingles and laths and mud and sand for plastering."

Father Baraga made the following entry in the Baptismal Records, at the end of the book:

"In the year 1841 the undersigned missionary caused a new church to be constructed (the old one being destroyed by him, which had been too badly constructed), and at the same time he placed it there where it was nearer to the greater part of the Catholic congregation. In the month of July of the same year this church was finished, and on the first Sunday of August the undersigned missionary dedicated it to God under the name of the same St. Joseph."

(Signed)   FREDERIC BARAGA, Missionary.

The building and completing of his new church involved F. Baraga considerably in debt. He owed the American Fur Company four hundred dollars. As his church had been finished already in July, 1841, it is not to be wondered that after waiting over a whole year for the money due them they "dunned" him for it. Hence his urgent letter to the Prince Archbishop of Vienna, manager of the Leopoldine Society, for help. This letter is dated October 12th, 1842. His appeal was not in vain. The society sent him six hundred and fifty florins, as is seen from his letter of thanks, dated La Pointe, September 12th, 1843.

CATTLE ON MISSION FARM, ODANAH, WIS.

Chapter XXXIII

Father Baraga Leaves La Pointe to Found the Mission at L'Anse, Mich.

In the letter spoken of in the foregoing chapter, Father Baraga says:

"Moreover, I have now a plan to start this fall a new mission at Lake Superior in a place one hundred and eighty miles from here, which, I hope, will be for the salvation of many souls, according to the promises and assurances made to me by pagans living there.

"Here in La Pointe conversions of pagans are now rare. Hence I desire to preach elsewhere the gospel to the poor pagan Indians. I am certain of gaining more of them there where I intend to start the new mission than here. Ah, what a consolation, what unspeakable joy to gain immortal souls for Jesus Christ!

"For establishing new missions a little assistance is always needed. A chapel has to be built, a mission-house, and a school. It is true these buildings are constructed only of wood, but the builders have to be fed and paid. If Your Grace would send me again next spring a little pecuniary assistance, it certainly would be a seasonable benefit unto the eternal salvation of many precious souls. *Ah, the salvation of a single immortal soul is infinitely more worth than all the money of the world!*

"I pray Your Grace to forward again the money intended for my mission through Ramsay Crooks, president of the American Fur Company. This company indeed has failed, but it has recovered again so far that it can resume its business. Moreover, Ramsay

Crooks is my special friend and benefactor, who in case of danger would have special regard for me. This way of sending money is the safest and shortest."

As to the first impulse given to our missionary to found the L'Anse Mission, it seems to have come from Mr. Pierre Crebassa, as we read in his letter, published in the L'Anse Sentinel. He writes:

"I will now give a few facts regarding Rev. Father Baraga, the second priest who came to L'Anse. (The first was Rene Menard, S. J., in 1660.) I came to L'Anse in 1837, and was employed by the American Fur Company. An old chief named Penanshi came to see me every Sunday. I had an old Bible printed in the French language in the year 1815, and the old chief used to request me to read to him from the book and explain it, which I did to the best of my ability. He desired to know if I could get a priest to come here, and I replied that I would write to Father Baraga, who was then at La Pointe, Wis., and was the only priest in this portion of the country. Accordingly I wrote to Father Baraga explaining matters and invited him to come. That was in 1840. He replied that he could not leave La Pointe, as he had a church and a large congregation there. Each year I wrote to him, and at last, in 1843, I received the following letter, written in French, which is correctly translated in English:

"*Mr. Pierre Crebassa, My Dear Friend*—I received your letter on the 6th of the month with great pleasure, and I think I am obliged to accept the invitation you make me. There's now three years' resistance to the invitation to go to L'Anse, for I don't like to leave my children, and now I cannot resist any more, for I think it is the will of God that I must go. It's for that reason I promise you I shall go to L'Anse, if God will let me live. I think I shall go in the schooner of Mr. Mendenhall, the 'Algonquin' in the beginning of May, and I shall go to the 'Soo' for the schooner will not go to L'Anse, and from the 'Soo' I shall get some opportunity to go to your place.

"Dear sir, I pray you tell your Indians if I see they will join the Catholic religion I will stay with them the forepart of the summer, and I will go back with you in the month of July to La Pointe, and you can also tell your Indians if I see that they convert to the Catholic religion in great numbers, I shall try and stay with them if I can, and get another in my place at La Pointe, if our Superior, the Bishop, gives his consent. I am, dear sir, your sincere friend,

"Frederic Baraga, Missionary Priest."

La Pointe, March 13th, 1843.

Through the kindness of Mr. Carl Edgerton, of Jacobsville, Mich., the writer was furnished the following interesting item in regard to the founding of the L'Anse Mission. The article is from the pen of Hon. P. Crebassa, above spoken of. We give his account in full.

Regarding Father Baraga.

"In my last letter I gave a detailed account of Father Baraga's arrival at L'Anse in 1843. He came in June, 1843; shortly after writing me his letter of acceptance, he commenced his labor. I had arranged everything and had a number of Indians camping in wigwams on my place. I gave Father Baraga half of my house to use as a chapel, and for the purpose of teaching the Indians. At the expiration of one week he baptized thirty people, men, women and children. He remained another week and when he left he promised the Indians that he would move to L'Anse in the fall of that year and remain with them for a time. He then returned to La Pointe, and for the journey I furnished him with a canoe and sent two of my men to accompany him. Upon his arrival I received the following letter from him, written in English:

"*Mr. P. Crebassa, L'Anse, Mich., Dear Sir*—I write you only a few lines to thank you for all your charity and goodness to me. I am unable to recompense you for all your goodness and services. I pray God that He may do what I cannot and that He may bless you in this world and in the next.

"I hope you do on Sundays as I requested of you before I left your place for the good work. Also that Almighty God will recompense you. I beg you to continue as long as you remain there.

"Our voyage has been somewhat disagreeable, but short. We arrived here on Friday at six o'clock in the afternoon. Your men intended to start immediately the following day, but Isidore felt a little (wanting in) energy, and they intend to start tomorrow morning. You will please give these little incidents to Marimann.

"With much respect, your sincere friend,

"Frederic Baraga.

"The beads you will give to Nancy, together with my friend's salutation."

La Pointe, June 18th, 1843.

Chapter XXXIV

Father Baraga's Labors in L'Anse Mission During the Years 1843-1844. Bishop Henni's, of Milwaukee, First Visit to La Pointe in 1844.

Having labored at La Pointe for eight years in apostolic poverty, but also with apostolic zeal and success, F. Baraga left the mission on the 4th of October, St. Francis Day, 1843, and arrived at L'Anse on the 24th of the same month. The poor Indians were exceedingly glad that a missionary had come to their place. They came and shook hands with him in a friendly manner. He at once began his labors, which were fruitful in conversions. In about two months he converted and baptized twenty-nine pagans. Within four months fifty-six had been "regenerated of water and the Holy Ghost" and become children of God and members of His holy church. He says: "Among them were some who soon after they had received the grace of baptism entered eternity, clothed in the white garment of baptismal innocence, with which they were immediately admitted to the nuptial-banquet of the Lamb."

Soon after his arrival F. Baraga opened an Indian school, which he himself conducted conjointly with some pious and able persons whom he had brought from La Pointe for that purpose. The number of his scholars was fifty-one, of whom twenty were boys, three men, nineteen girls, and nine women. These scholars were first instructed in reading and Christian doctrine, thereafter also in writing and arithmetic. Most of them easily learned to read, because they had a great liking for it. Several of them were able to read in two months.

Seeing how well-inclined his good neophytes were, he determined to establish a permanent mission in the place. Hence, after his arrival, he commenced to make preparations for building a small church with a room for the priest, a school house and some small log houses for the newly converted Indians. It was his firm conviction that as long as the latter lived scattered in the forests, in their wigwams, they could not be civilized and become accustomed to industry and cleanliness. His plan, therefore, was to make a small Christian "Reduction" or settlement, after the example of the good old Jesuits in Paraguay, and collect the Indians all in one village near the church. This plan pleased them very much. They all promised to live hereafter in houses and to adopt the ways of the whites.

The same plan was carried out, as far as practicable, by the Jesuits in Canada during the seventeenth, and by the Franciscans during the latter part of the eighteenth century in California. To anyone acquainted with Indian ways and the strange, fascinating influence which pagan dances, feasts, incantations, and other species of jugglery exert upon them, it is a foregone conclusion that, if we want to establish Christianity among them on a permanent basis, we must endeavor to get our Christian Indians as much as possible away from their pagan surroundings. Where Indians form exclusively Christian communities they make good, exemplary Christians. We see this exemplified in La Pointe, Bayfield, Buffalo Bay, Baraga, Papashkominitigong, Harbor Springs and elsewhere. But where Indians live among pagans, as in Bad River Reservation, Courtes Oreilles, Pakwewang, etc., they are easily induced to attend, and sometimes even to take part in pagan dances and feasts. In case of sickness, they sometimes send for that species of Indian humbug and trickery, the medicine-man, and have him perform his diabolical incantations. Living with pagans, they readily inter-marry with them. Although such marriages may at times be the human means of bringing the pagan to adopt Christianity, it often results, as in mixed marriages, in perverting the Catholic party, especially if the pagan be a person strongly wedded to his superstitions and possessing a resolute character. The writer speaks from personal knowledge and twenty years' observation. Could we but establish such exclusively Catholic Indian colonies *far enough away from the evil influence of bad whites and pagans*, there would be some hope for the future of the Indian race; as it is, we are working for "a lost cause."

Moreover, the idea that the Indian must first be induced to become a farmer in order to make of him a civilized man is absurd. All his Indian instincts revolt against it. He is quite willing to cultivate a small patch of land to raise some potatoes, cabbage, onions, etc., but to farm on a large scale, as his white brother does, is disagreeable to him. The writer does not know of five Indians in all northern Wisconsin who have as much as forty acres under cultivation. They are born hunters, fishermen, and, to a considerable extent, mechanics. The Indian is imitative, a sort of natural mechanic. Give him tools and, with very little instruction, he will do mechanical work as well as the average white man; he will build houses, barns, make boats, etc., better than a great many whites, unless the latter be trained mechanics. If, instead of letting his pine be logged by thieving corporations, who will cheat him whenever they can, the government had erected cheap saw mills and other factories for working up his timber into lumber, shingles, laths, staves, tubs, barrels, chairs, tables, etc., under the supervision of a few skilled and conscientious white mechanics, his large forests would have supported him for many a year. As it now is, his pine is fast disappearing, and then misery and starvation will be his lot.

F. Baraga wrote on the 12th of February as follows:

"I promised to have fifteen houses built for the newly converted Indians this year. Next year, if God keeps me alive and I get assistance, I shall have several more built. This undertaking will cost considerable money. Our buildings, of course, are constructed merely of logs, which cost nothing here. But the carpenters must be paid and the boards for the floor have to be sawed with whip-saws, as we have no saw-mills here. But what a gain if once this mission be established! How many poor, barbarian savages, who live in huts, which are to be compared to bear-lairs, and whose habits correspond to their surroundings, will become civilized and be transformed into good, God-serving Christians! According to a rough estimate made by me, this Indian settlement will cost between four and five hundred dollars. I respectfully pray Your Princely Highness to do for this 'Reduction' as much as you think proper."

Although all that spoke to F. Baraga about his projects told him they were impracticable, still he succeeded in accomplishing all he had intended. He says in his letter of the 27th of August, 1844, written at La Pointe:

"With the help of the Good Shepherd, whom it pleases to call us to seek, after His example, the lost sheep in the desert in order to lead it back to Him; and with great effort and exertion, I myself working with them during all that time—'ministraverunt manus istae'—I finally succeeded in accomplishing all, unto the honor of God and the salvation of souls, for which be special thanks to God!

"Since I am still, alas, the only missionary in this extensive Lake Superior country, I cannot remain always in one place. Hence I have been now here in La Pointe for a month on a missionary visit. Next Monday, September 2d, I expect to leave for L'Anse.

"The mission of La Pointe belongs now to the new diocese of Milwaukee. On the 14th of this month (August, 1844), we had the honor of seeing here the first bishop of this new diocese. This pious, venerable and zealous bishop John Martin Henni, a German, did much good during the short time he stayed here. His instructions, full of unction and very appropriate, which he gave to this Indian congregation, I acting as interpreter, have made a deep and, as I hope, lasting impression on the minds of these simple-hearted Christians. He confirmed one hundred and twenty-two persons, among others a grown-up sick girl, who died some days after, very well prepared.

"This worthy prelate intends to make next winter a journey to Europe for the good of his new, but very poor, diocese. When he comes to Vienna, I beg Your Princely Highness to lend him as much assistance as possible, for you can imagine that a new diocese, bordering on the Indian country and taking in a part of it, must be very poor. *When he saw our mission-church he said that it was better than his cathedral!* This expresses sufficiently the poverty of his diocese."

Chapter XXXV

Father Baraga's Labors During 1844-45. His Long Journeys on Foot to Distant Missions.

Speaking of a new Indian work, the "Gagikwe-Masinaigan"—"Sermon-book"—he writes:

"I also mention on this occasion that I have now received my third Indian-mission work. It consists of extracts taken from the Bible history of the Old and New Testament, Sunday and holy day Gospels and Epistles. Some years ago I intended to have it printed in Green Bay, but, through want of funds, I sent it to Laibach (Austria) to be printed. The edition contains eight hundred copies, is neatly printed, and so correct that I cannot sufficiently admire the extreme care of the proof-readers, who, after all, do not understand a single word of the Indian language. Great was the joy of my good Indians at this new book in their language. I trust it will produce good fruits in many hearts."

In a letter, dated L'Anse, October 4th, 1844, he states that he had received from the Leopoldine Society 650 florins, and that he would receive in due time the 265 florins sent for him to Bishop Henni, of Milwaukee. He mentions that, contrary to all expectation, he had completed last summer his entire mission establishment. Speaking of his privations there, he says:

"L'Anse is an unpleasant, sad, sterile place, in no comparison with La Pointe. Solely the wish to help these poor Indians attain eternal happiness keeps me here. I have here, it is true, no comforts, *oftentimes barely the necessaries of life*; but what consolation, what grand reward, what unspeakable joy will it be for me when, on the Day of Judgment, some of these, my good children in Christ, or, rather, all of them, as I hope, will surround me and give their testimony before the rigorous Judge: 'He was the first to announce to us Thy divine word; he has told us of Thy mercies, shown by Thee to man through Thy Son, and filled our hearts with faith and love towards Thee! O, how I thank my God for calling me to the laborious, indeed, but at the same time, highly consoling missionary state!

L'ANSE MISSION, BOARDING SCHOOL, CHURCH AND PRIEST'S HOUSE

"I also mention that the 29th of September, the very day I received Your Grace's letter, was one of the holiest days for my new mission, for on that Sunday we celebrated with all possible solemnity the dedication of our mission-church. With joyful and grateful heart I dedicated this church to The Most Holy Name of Jesus. The thought: 'my Jesus, I have built this house to Thy name,' filled my heart with unutterable joy. It is but a small wooden building, yet it is holier than the temple of Solomon, that wonder of architecture, for it is sanctified by the real presence of Him, whom heaven and earth, and the heaven of heavens cannot contain. He does not disdain to dwell in it, whose first abode on earth was a manger."

From his letter of the 24th of October, 1845, we see that he was not forgotten by the Leopoldine Society and that they seconded by liberal donations his efforts in behalf of his new mission. Thus they sent him again two thousand florins to enable him to meet his obligations towards the American Fur Company, who supplied him with all the necessaries for his mission-buildings, etc. As to his personal wants, they were few and easily supplied. What money he received he used for the furtherance of his work, but not for himself. He intended also to apply a part of the money towards building two small churches, one at Fond du Lac and the other at Grand Portage, both in Minnesota. Speaking of the last named mission, he says:

"F. Pierz began a mission at Grand Portage and baptized there very many Indians. But he soon left them and went to reside at Arbre Croche, and so there is no mission-church yet at Grand Portage. I shall build one there and will dedicate it to 'The Most Sacred Heart of Jesus' next fall. I thank my Jesus that He has sent me through my benefactors the funds for building that little church. It is very useful to have churches in all mission-stations, even where a missionary priest does not reside continually; for from time to time a missionary comes to such places, even in winter; moreover, those little churches built of bark cannot always be used. Besides, where Indians have a decent church, they meet regularly on all Sundays and holy days to sing, pray, and read their prayer book, the same as if the missionary were with them continually. So they do here, when I go anywhere, and so they do in La Pointe. O, how happy I am in advance that they will do so also in Fond du Lac and Grand Portage, to the honor of God and the salvation of immortal souls!"

In the winter of 1845-46 a pagan Indian came to see F. Baraga. He came from an Indian village, five days' journey from L'Anse. The Indian informed the Father that the head-chief of that place had a great desire to see and hear him. This was enough. He immediately set out for that place to ascertain the feelings of said chief and his people in regard to religion. The evening of his arrival he requested all the men to meet in the large wigwam of the head-chief. In a long discourse, among other things, he proposed to them to come and settle down at L'Anse, as in their present place of abode the traders were accustomed to bring them the destructive "fire-water," whereas at L'Anse, where all were Christians, the importation of that ruinous poison had ceased. His appeal seems to have met with little success. Some promised to immigrate to L'Anse the next summer and become Christians.

Others, however, were undecided. They told the Father that, by next spring, they would make up their minds whether to remove to his village or remain where they were. It seems that the most of them turned their hearts against the summons of God's anointed minister and remained in their pagan village, where their descendants still reside. Lac Vieux Deserts and Lac du Flambeau are yet strongholds of paganism to this day. As F. Baraga made that long journey on snowshoes, he gives in his letter of January 24th, 1846, a description of the hardships to be endured in that mode of traveling. He says:

"In this connection I will explain how a missionary has to travel during winter in this Indian country. In winter a person cannot travel otherwise than on foot. As the snow is generally deep and there are no traveled roads, the only way to travel is on snowshoes. These snowshoes are from four to five feet long and one foot wide and are tied to one's feet. With them a man can travel even in the deepest snow without sinking in very much. But this style of walking is very tiresome, especially for Europeans, who are not accustomed to it. When a person must walk upon such snowshoes all day long, and that for many days in succession, especially in these trackless North American forests, he cannot travel without extreme fatigue and almost total exhaustion.

"Another hardship is the sleeping in the open air in a northern winter, for there are no huts in which to stay overnight. Generally speaking, a man may travel four or five days in this extensive and thinly settled country before coming to another Indian settlement. It is true, a large fire is made, but this soon goes out, for the Indian guide, who accompanies us, sleeps the whole night as if he were in a feather-bed, and then a person suffers much from the cold. It is hard, especially, to pass the night in such a way, when it storms and snows all night and in the morning a person is covered all over with snow. But all these hardships the missionary joyfully endures if thereby he can, through God's help and grace, save even but one soul.

"I have to make this winter a far longer journey, that is, from L'Anse to La Pointe and Fond du Lac and return, *a distance of about six hundred and ninety miles!* I will begin this journey, please God, on the 4th of February, and hope to be back here again before the end of March. I am going to Fond du Lac, Minn., to make arrangements for the building of a church there, I think, thereafter, I will not go there any more, as now a missionary has arrived for my assistance, namely, Rev. Father Otto Skolla, who spends this winter at La Pointe, where I have been for eight years.

"I take the liberty to ask Your Grace to kindly send me a small box with the following mission requisites: One thousand small colored pictures for children, some large colored pictures, rosaries, medium sized copper crucifixes, 2x3 inches long, two sets of vestments, linen altar cloths, a chalice, a small monstrance, a censer with boat, a ciborium, some tin water cruets, a holy water font, etc.

Chapter XXXVI

Wonderful Escape of Father Baraga, When Crossing Lake Superior in a Small Sail-Boat. His Adventure on a Floating Field of Ice.

We learn from F. Baraga's letter, written in October, 1845, that he intended to go to Grand Portage, Minn., the next fall to build a church there. It is, therefore, highly probable that he made that trip in the fall of 1846. He first went to La Pointe, where, no doubt, he spent some time attending to the spiritual wants of the good people. He then engaged a half-breed Indian, named Louis Gaudin, to go with him to Grand Portage. They had but a small fishing boat with a mast and sail, without keel or centre-board. Such a boat might do on a river or small lake, but would be very unsafe on a large lake, where it would easily founder or be driven like a cork before the wind. The boat was but eighteen feet long. When they started from La Pointe the people laughed at them for attempting to make the journey. They said it would take them a month to make the voyage, as they would have to keep close to the shore all the way, going first west some seventy miles to the end of the lake and then, doubling, turn northwestward, coasting along the northern shore of Lake Superior. This would make the distance about two hundred miles, perhaps even more.

However, Father Baraga and his guide set out on their perilous journey. At Sand Island they awaited a favorable wind to cross the lake, which is about forty miles wide at that place. By so doing they would save from eighty to one hundred miles, but would expose themselves to great danger, as a high wind might arise, whilst they were out on the open lake, and engulf their frail bark.

They set sail on an unusually calm day. Father Baraga steered and Louis rowed the boat. Before they got midway a heavy west wind arose and the lake grew very rough. They were constantly driven leeward and when they finally reached the north shore they were at least thirty miles east of their intended landing place, having made a very perilous sail of seventy miles during that day.

While in the height of the storm, in mid-ocean, it might be said, Louis became frightened and exclaimed in Chippewa to the Father, who was lying on his back in the boat, reciting his office in an unconcerned manner: "Nosse, ki ga-nibomin, ganabatch"— Father, perhaps we are going to perish!" The Father answered quietly: "Kego segisiken, Wizon" (Chippewa for Louis)—"Don't be afraid, Wizon; the priest will not die in the water. If he died here in the water the people on the other shore, whither we are going, would be unfortunate."

When nearing the north shore the danger was even greater than out on the deep water, for there were huge breakers ahead. Louis asked the Father whither to steer, and, as if following a certain inspiration, F. Baraga told him to steer straight ahead for the land. Through a special disposition of Divine Providence watching over the precious life of the saintly missionary, they passed through the breakers unharmed and ran their boat into the mouth of a small river, heretofore unnamed, but now called Cross River.

Full of gratitude for their miraculous escape, they at once proceeded to erect a cross. Hewing a tree in a rough manner, they cut off the top as far up as they could reach, and taking a shorter piece, they nailed it cross-wise to the tree, "Wizon," said the Father, "let us make a cross here that the Christian Indians may know that the priest coming from La Pointe landed here. The cross was, it is true, unartistic, but it was an emblem of their holy faith and it gave the name, Tchibaiatigo-Sibi, "Cross River," to the little stream where they landed.

They arrived none too soon. Ascending an eminence and looking out on the immense lake they saw that the storm was increasing every moment; high waves with white caps, which would surely have engulfed their little bark. They landed about six o'clock in the evening. Having spent the night there, they continued their journey next day, and in two days arrived at Grand Portage, having made the whole journey in three days. May we not think with Louis Gaudin that their safe passage across the stormy lake, and their deliverance from a watery grave, was due to a special intervention of Divine Providence in favor of the saintly missionary?

In 1667 Father Claude Allouez, S. J., then stationed at the mission of the Holy Ghost at the head of Chequamegon Bay, made the voyage across the lake from Sand Island. He made the voyage in a birch-canoe with three Indians. He remarks that they paddled their canoe all day as hard as they could without intermission, for fear of losing any of the beautiful calm weather they had. It took them twelve hours to make the trip across. The Father was then on his way to visit some Christian Indians residing at Lake Nipigon—"Animibigong" in Chippewa. For the particulars of this journey we refer the reader to "Missionary Labors of Fathers Marquette, Allouez, and Menard in the Lake Superior Region."

The following narrative is not to be found in any of Baraga's published letters, but the writer has it from the mouth of trustworthy persons, among whom is Father Chebul, a countryman of F. Baraga, who was stationed at Bayfield for many years. We will give the account, as we have it from Rev. F. Chebul.

One time F. Baraga was going to Ontonogan in company with an Indian half-breed in the month of March or April. At that season of the year the ice, though thick, becomes honey-combed and rotten. Some say that Baraga's companion was a man named Newagon. They went on the ice at La Pointe Island. As the walking on the sandy beach would have been very fatiguing and long, they determined to make straight for Ontonogan over the ice. By so doing they would not only have better walking, but also shorten their way a great deal.

A strong southwest wind was blowing at the time, and the ice, becoming detached from the shore, began drifting lake ward. After they had traveled for some time, they became aware of what had happened, for they could see the blue waters between them and the shore. Newagon became greatly alarmed, for almost certain death stared them in the face. Had the wind continued blowing in the same direction, the ice would have been driven far out into the lake and broken up into small fragments. They would surely have perished.

To encourage the drooping spirit of his companion, F. Baraga kept telling him that they would escape all right and that they must trust in God, their loving Father and Protector. He also sang Chippewa hymns to divert Newagon's attention and calm his excitement. Finally the wind shifted and blew the field of ice back towards the shore.

They landed near Cadotte Point, near Union Bay, a short distance from Ontonagan, which they reached that same day. "See," said the missionary to his companion, "we have traveled a great distance and have worked little." The distance from La Pointe to Ontonagan is about sixty or seventy miles by an air line. Had they been obliged to walk the whole distance around the bend of the lake, it would probably have taken them two or three days of very hard and fatiguing traveling. So what at first seemed to threaten certain death was used by God's fatherly providence to shorten and facilitate the saintly priest's journey.

Chapter XXXVII

Further Testimony as to F. Baraga's Work at L'Anse. Accident on Lake Huron in 1852.

In reading Hon. Richard R. Elliott's very able and interesting article in the "American Catholic Quarterly Review" July, 1896, entitled, "Father Baraga Among the Chippewas," we found a letter of Hon. Peter White, president of the First National Bank of Marquette, which speaks very highly of Father Baraga's work at L'Anse. His testimony is all the more valuable because it is that of a man in high social standing, who knew F. Baraga personally. Moreover, he is a prominent member of the Protestant Episcopal church of Marquette, and being senior warden of that church, his testimony cannot be suspected of partiality. He writes (page 605 et seq.):

"I first knew Bishop Baraga (at the time Father Baraga) at L'Anse in 1850. His residence was a few miles distant from the location of the present town of Baraga.

"There was a population at the Roman Catholic mission of about 800 Chippewas, 100 or more half-breeds, and from twenty to thirty Frenchmen, who had inter-married with Chippewa women.

"Father Baraga was the devoted friend of these people; they all loved him and almost worshipped him.

"He purchased from the government for the families of his mission a tract of land which he divided into large lots, on which he built houses for each family; he partly furnished these dwellings, and gave the heads of each a cooking stove, furniture, clothing and a supply of provisions to commence housekeeping in a civilized manner.

"He taught them to read, write, and to sing, and how to lead Christian lives. He instructed them as to the cultivation of the soil, providing them with seed and other requisites.

"He translated portions of the Bible into their language, prayers, and hymns, and compiled a grammar, speller, and reader for them, and had these separate works in the Chippewa language printed at his own expense.

"He provided and paid a teacher to instruct the Indians and their children.

"They gathered around him like a band of children and listened to the words of wisdom he always had ready for them. Should any of them become sick, he provided a physician and medicine.

"He had probably lived among these Chippewas during twenty years, ministering to their spiritual and temporal welfare, before he was created Bishop of Sault de Ste. Marie.

"Occasionally a 'sick-call' would come to him from Houghton, Eagle River, Eagle Harbor, the Cliff Mine, the Old Albion Mine, or some other mining location on Keweenaw Point.

"I have known him to respond to these 'sick-calls' in the dead of winter, alone and on snowshoes; very laborious journeys they were, full of peril and unlimited hardship, and undertaken to administer the last rites to a dying Christian.

"For years there was no other priest in all that region.

"The houses Father Baraga caused to be built for the people of his mission were not large, but were adequate to their condition and wants; most of them had been accustomed to live in wigwams. They were mostly one story or one and a half stories high, with good windows and doors, but enclosed with plain boards; each had a brick or stone chimney, and probably cost from $500 to $700, while the furniture cost did not exceed $200 for each.

"I cannot give you the size of the lots, but they were from 200 to 300 feet square, and the grantees or their descendants still occupy them. The place is still called the "Roman Catholic Mission," but its population has dwindled down to about a third of its former number.

"On the opposite shore of the bay, where, at a corresponding period, there was a Methodist Mission, comprising many souls, not more than 150 remain. I have one of Bishop Baraga's grammars. The title reads:

> "A Theoretical and Practical Grammar
> of the Otchipwe Language.
> Spoken by the Chippewa Indians; Also
> by the Algonquin, and Pottawotomie
> Indians, with but Little Difference, etc.
> By Frederick Baraga, Missionary
> at L'Anse, Lake Superior.
> Detroit:
> Jabez Fox, Printer.
> 1850."

"It is a great pleasure to me to be, even in a small way, of any assistance to you in such a noble task as you have undertaken, and I regret not being able to give you something better."

The following interesting item we have from the veteran editor of the "Aurora," Hon. Chr. Wieckmann:

"In the winter of 1852 Father Baraga went all the way from Mackinac Island to Detroit on Lake Huron in a sleigh drawn by two Indian ponies. He had been working at his Chippewa dictionary for almost ten years and was anxious to get it printed in Detroit at the printing office of the "Aurora," which was then still small. He accordingly sent for Mr. Wieckmann, requesting him to come to Bishop Lefevre's residence. Arriving there, he found Father Baraga spreading out sheet after sheet of his manuscript-dictionary to dry. He told Mr. Wieckmann that after having traveled for several days on Lake Huron with his Indian companions they had broken through the ice and the entire party came near drowning. As often as the ponies tried to climb onto the ice with their fore-feet, the ice would break off. Finally, after hard working for half an hour, they succeeded in getting onto strong ice again. But as a great part of the journey was still to be made, and that in wet clothes, his feet were frozen. Father Baraga told him that he had been more solicitous for saving his manuscript-dictionary than for his life. It was, indeed, most fortunate that both the author and his manuscript were saved. No wonder that he was so anxious about saving his work. It had cost him ten years of hard labor. Had it been lost, he probably would never again have had the time and leisure to compose another.

Chapter XXXVIII

Father Baraga in Detroit Superintending the Printing of Some of His Works.—Bishop Lefevre Gives Confirmation for the First Time in L'Anse.— The Indians All Take the Total Abstinence Pledge.

Under date of September 18, 1846, F. Baraga writes to the Leopoldine Society:

"With much pleasure and with a grateful heart I received your Grace's communication of the 2d of June of this year. I most humbly thank your Grace for the 500 florins sent me, which in American coin amount to $242.50. At present I am in Detroit and have been here for the last two months. The reason of this is as follows: The Indian mission books, which I got printed in Paris in 1837, have about been disposed of. Hence the necessity of getting a new edition printed, for our numerous Indian missions cannot well be provided for without these little books, as many Indians can now read and love their books of devotion very much and make good use of them. The missionaries, who labor in the Indian missions, all declare that the Christian Indians cannot well do without them and that they derive great benefit from them. So says especially Father Pierz, who, with Father Mrak, has charge of the most populous and best Indian missions of our diocese. I have caused 2,000 copies of the prayer book and 1,200 of the gospel-book to be printed. I had 400 catechisms printed, besides the prayer books, for the use of Indian children. I have enlarged the prayer book very much in this *third* edition and have greatly improved it.

"As regards my mission at L'Anse I have good and consoling news to write. These good Indians have taken hold of our holy religion with all their energy and live up to it faithfully. A few days before my departure this mission had the happiness and honor of an episcopal visitation for the first time. The Rt. Rev. Administrator of the diocese of Detroit, Bishop Lefevre, was there in July. During the few days he spent there he did a great deal of good to my mission. He confirmed a great number of Indians in the real literal sense of the word. His presence, his exceeding great kindness and love, and his edifying exhortations made an indelible impression on the minds of these new Christians.

"Moreover, he organized a temperance society in my mission, to which all who by reason of their age could do so, gave their names. He did this in a solemn manner, after divine service. It was an edifying and consoling sight. The bishop stood in his pontifical robes at the communion railing and held in his hand the temperance-pledge leaflets, which had been printed in the Indian language. Every Indian who wished to become a member of the society, came forward, knelt before the bishop, received his blessing and received the leaflet from his hands. The following words were printed in Indian on the leaflets: I, N. N., renounce entirely and forever the use of intoxicating liquors, and I pray God that He may give me His grace to keep this promise. All Indians of my mission joyfully made this promise, and they kept it faithfully.

"Rt. Rev. Bishop Lefevre also baptized five grown pagans in L'Anse. They were the last baptized Indians of this mission. Yet there are frequent baptisms of adults and the mission keeps growing continually, for from time to time pagans come from the inland forests and settle down near their relatives at L'Anse and become Christians.

"This mission gives me very great consolation, for which I thank God daily. Especially does it please me that this mission is in every way an imitation of the 'Reductions,' which the good ancient Jesuits, these masters in missionary affairs, made in Paraguay.

"*I long to be among my dear children again.* Tomorrow is the day of my departure from Detroit. How glad these good children will be to again see their father, whom they have not seen for the last two months.

"It is very agreeable that the Reverend and pious Father Otto Skolla, who now takes my place in La Pointe has developed into an excellent Indian missionary. He is very much beloved in his mission and devotes himself with great zeal and energy to the study of the Indian language. I hope he will never leave the Indian mission."

Chapter XXXIX

Opening of the Copper Mines in Northern Michigan.—Baraga Visits His New Mission.—He Labors on His Famous Chippewa Grammar and Dictionary.

The mission of the Most Holy Name of Jesus at L'Anse (now Baraga, Assinins P. O., Baraga Co.) kept growing continually, though slowly, by fresh conversions of pagans coming from the interior and settling down at the mission.

Since 1845 F. Baraga's missionary field had begun to widen. At Portage Lake and elsewhere on Keweenaw Point rich copper deposits had been discovered and were being worked. This brought a great many whites to that formerly wild and desolate country, a great number of whom, perhaps the majority, were Catholic Irish, Germans and French.

On the 11th of January, 1847, F. Baraga made a missionary trip to the mines and spent three weeks there. He was astonished at the rapid growth of civilization in the Lake Superior country. Instead of poor Indian wigwams he found beautiful frame houses supplied with all the luxuries of civilization. On this first trip to the mining country he saw about two hundred and fifty Catholics and he says there were many more elsewhere, whom he had not yet visited. In going from one place to another the missionary was obliged to travel on snowshoes and carry all things necessary for divine service. He baptized a number of children, heard confessions almost every day, and administered Holy Communion to a great majority of the people. He went from mine to mine and preached almost every evening after the miners had finished their day's work. He spoke in English at times or in German, according to the nationality of his hearers. The Germans especially were highly pleased to find a priest with a knowledge of their own language in that distant country. On the 10th of May he made another missionary trip to the mines, which took about three weeks, during which he performed all the duties of the ministry with great fruit. He promised to attend these scattering missions three times a year until the people would obtain a resident priest.

Speaking of a new literary work he had taken in hand, he writes from L'Anse June 19th, 1847, to the Leopoldine Society:

"I desire to state that, in accordance with the wish of my Rt. Rev. Bishop and my fellow-missionaries, I have composed a complete grammar of the Chippewa language, which is the language of our Indians here. It has cost me a great deal of labor, as I had to open the way everywhere since no grammar of this language has hitherto appeared. However, as I have been studying that language for the past seventeen years, I was able to finish the work, with the help of God.

"I am also composing a dictionary of the language *Otchipwe-French* and *French-Otchipwe*.* I have collected several thousands of words, and I shall continue at the work during the summer and autumn, and a part of next winter. Next spring I intend to get both works printed and hope by so doing to procure a great and lasting benefit for our missions, which are scattered over three dioceses. For with the help of a complete and systematic grammar illustrating all the rules with numerous examples, and with a copious dictionary in hand, our present and future missionaries, who do not understand much Chippewa, and that not grammatically, will be enabled to learn this curious, very *peculiar, yet systematic and beautiful language*, in a short time, a very important

---

* We think there is a mistake here. Instead of Otchipwe-*French* and *French*-Otchipwe, the reading ought to be: Otchipwe-*English* and *English*-Otchipwe. Baraga wrote his Chippewa grammar in English, and it is natural to suppose that his dictionary was also intended for English-speaking readers.

thing, for it is something quite different if a missionary can speak with the Indians personally, or to be obliged to have his words interpreted by another.

"Now these works of permanent utility to our Indian missions will certainly be ready for the press by next spring, if the Lord prolongs my life. But there is a certain impediment in the way, which, after God, only the generosity of your Lordship can remove. The printing of these works will cost at least four hundred dollars, which I cannot expect from anybody else than your Lordship. If, therefore, it is your wish and that of the Leopoldine Society to have these works of mine published for the good of our Indian missions I most humbly pray you to let me have the above sum by next spring, through the hands of our Rt. Rev. Bishop of Detroit, under whose eyes I will get these books printed."

"The Catholic Almanac," of 1848, published in Baltimore says (page 162, Diocese of Detroit):

"Frederic Baraga, Vicar-general of the Diocese of Detroit, and a most worthy missionary priest, opened a mission at L'Anse, about three years ago amid incredible labor and hardships. He has built a church and school house and has the consolation of having charge of more than thirty-three Chippewa families, which he himself has converted to the Catholic faith, and he has the assured hope that his new flock will be increased by new conversions. The quick advancement in civilization and prosperity of these Indians, whose missions have been lately founded, has become a subject of wonder to all those who have known L'Anse these last two years, for the Indians have entirely abandoned their savage customs, ways, and irregular mode of life, and have become a good, industrious, self-supporting, honest and sober class of people. They now live in decent houses and work their land industriously. Each owns about thirty acres of land in the woods, which he clears, that is, cuts down the trees, plants it and surrounds it with a fence in common and in this common property every head of a family has a lot, which is plowed, planted and cultivated according to each one's needs."

Chapter XL

Father Baraga Goes to Fond Du Lac, Baptizes a Very Old and Blind Woman.— Suffers Much Hardship on His Return Journey.

In a letter, dated Copper Harbor, Mich., October 18, 1847, F. Baraga makes the following reflections, which we give in full as they give us an insight into the boundless charity of this holy man toward the poor, abandoned Indians, and his burning zeal for their conversion and eternal salvation:

"... And now some news about my missionary undertakings. I am on the way to Fond du Lac. This is a mission station in the interior, about 350 miles from here, I have been there before as appears from my former reports. I never remained there longer than eight or ten days, sometimes only three or four. But now I intend to stay in that mission over two months, in order to instruct more fully in religion the newly converted, and, with God's help, to bring some pagans to the way of salvation.

"Next January I hope to return to my mission at L'Anse on snowshoes. It was with difficulty and a heavy heart that I could tear myself away from my dear children at L'Anse. Solely the spiritual commiseration with the Indians at Fond du Lac, who complain so touchingly of the abandonment in which they live, could move me to this resolution.

"How sad it is to have so few missionaries at Lake Superior, where so many of them could find a very salutary occupation unto the honor of God and the salvation of souls, if they would come here and put their hands to work...

"I entreat most earnestly all our dear mission benefactors to pray often, yes, very often, in the Name of Jesus to the Lord of the vineyard that He may send some laborers into this so abandoned part of his vineyard. I have the assured hope that such a universal prayer will have a good effect."

In October, 1847, F. Baraga went from Copper Harbor to Fond du Lac, most probably by boat. The good people of Fond du Lac felt exceedingly happy to again meet their missionary. During his stay there many received the grace of holy Baptism. It was a particular joy to him to have admitted an entire pagan family through the door of Baptism into the fold of the Good Shepherd.

He was especially consoled by the conversion of a very old pagan woman who was perhaps ninety years of age. When he arrived at Fond du Lac he heard that this poor old woman was very weak and sick. He went, therefore, to her wigwam in which she was lying quite alone. She had been abandoned by her pagan relatives, who went far into the woods to winter there. She was alone and helpless until at last a Christian family took pity on her, cared for her, nourished her, and kept her fire burning day and night.

It is thus pagan Indians at times acted toward their aged parents or grandparents when the latter became so old and feeble that they could no longer help themselves— they simply abandoned them. Should this happen in an Indian village, there was always someone to take them and care for them until they died. This was generally done by Christian families. Baraga says that it often happened that such poor old creatures were abandoned in the midst of the forest by their own children and grand-children, in which case they would perish miserably from starvation and cold.

So, also, this poor old woman had been forsaken, but had now been taken in and cared for by a Christian family. When Baraga learned that she had been long sick, he determined to go and visit her and try to save this poor soul.

After having crawled with difficulty into her very small and miserable wigwam, he saluted her. The Christian Indian woman, who had the care of her and who had accompanied the Father, told the poor old creature that the Blackrobe had come to visit her. She could not see the priest, for she was blind, but she stretched out her hands towards him and when he reached his hand she seized it with both her hands and exclaimed: "Nosse, nosse, jawenimishin!" "My father, my father, have pity on me!" Baraga compassionated her abandoned condition and then spoke to her about religion, trying to make her understand how happy she would be in the other world, if she would but receive and believe the word of the Great Spirit and receive holy Baptism. He explained to her the principal doctrines of our holy religion and asked her from time to time whether she understood and believed what he told her. As he was satisfied from her answers that she was well disposed he intended to baptize her immediately. But then again, believing there was no immediate danger he thought it might perhaps be better to come back the next day and instruct her a little more, before administering Baptism. On leaving the wigwam, however, his first thought came again, namely, to baptize her immediately, which he did. When he came home it was late. He felt very happy and satisfied that he had baptized the poor old creature. Early the next morning the head of the Christian family, that had taken care of her, came to tell Baraga that during the night the good old woman had quietly "fallen asleep in the Lord." Only a Christian heart can imagine the unspeakable joy, which the pious missionary felt at this news. He thanked God most fervently for having inspired him with the thought not to postpone holy Baptism till next day, as he had first intended. It was a mysterious disposition of eternal love, whose weak instrument he considered himself to be, which wanted to take directly this poor soul to the eternal joys of heaven. "Parcet pauperi et inopi et animas pauperum salvas faciet." "He shall spare the poor and needy and He shall save the souls of the poor." (Ps. 71, v. 13). He also had the great joy of admitting to their first Holy Communion thirteen poor Indians, whom he had diligently prepared for that holy Sacrament.

Having thus consoled, instructed, and confirmed the poor Indians of Fond du Lac in their faith, F. Baraga prepared to return to L'Anse. This return trip was full of hardships and misery for the pious missionary, especially between Fond du Lac and La Pointe.

He remarks that he had made many hard missionary journeys, but that this was the hardest of them all. At other times he made the trip from Fond du Lac to La Point on foot in four days, but this time it took him seven days. His traveling companion and guide through the pathless forest was Louis Gaudin (Gordon).

They set out from Fond du Lac about the 5th of December, 1847. The first day they reached a point on Lake Superior, between Superior and Bayfield, called in Chippewa, Ga-Pakweiagak. The snow was then but six inches deep. They camped on the sandy beach. During the night it snowed very hard and in the morning they were covered with a thick layer of snow, for about one foot of snow had fallen that night. Hence they resolved to go straight from Ga-Pakweiagak to the mouth of the Sioux River. No trail could be seen through the thick forest.

The next night was very cold and Louis, Baraga's guide, caught a very severe cold and became very sick. He could not sleep all night and kept saying all the time that he would not be able to go a mile further. It was indeed a sad night!. They were far away from any human habitation, in a dense forest, on a high hill or ridge, without any trail. They could not afford to stay there long as their provisions were very scarce. Often during that long, cold night F. Baraga thought that the end of his earthly career was perhaps at hand, which certainly would have been the case had his trusty guide died.

Such, however, was not the will of the Good Shepherd who still wished to preserve the life of this zealous missionary for the salvation of many a soul. Louis partly recruited his strength so that he could rise next morning and walk slowly, but he was unable to carry anything. Hence Baraga was obliged to take the whole pack on his back and carry it for several days in succession through the deep snow over high hills and through low valleys, a thing very painful to one not accustomed to such work. But Baraga was satisfied, if only his guide, upon whom all depended, could come along.

After such days of hardships and fatigue, Baraga was obliged to prepare everything for the night's camping in the open air with no other covering overhead than the starry canopy of heaven. He was obliged to chop enough wood to keep up a good fire during the long night, which, at that time of the year, lasts about sixteen hours in the Lake Superior region. Baraga had never chopped wood before, and hence this exercise must have been very painful to him especially after a fatiguing march all day through the deep snow, carrying a heavy pack upon his shoulders. Their journey was slow, for Louis was very weak. Finally they arrived at the mouth of the Sioux River where they made three large fires to attract the notice of the people of La Pointe Island who then came for them in a boat. They had been a whole week in making the journey from Fond du Lac (Minn.) to La Pointe.

At the last named place he employed another man to go with him to L'Anse, as Louis was too sick and feeble to go any further. The distance still to be made was about one hundred and fifty miles, which Baraga made in four days, although he had to carry his own luggage.

One of the hardships of a priest on these long winter journeys was, as Baraga remarks, the saying of the office or breviary. This could not be done during the day-time, As the days are very short, a person tries to travel as far as possible. Hence the missionary has to say his breviary early in the morning before day break and in the evening after the day's journey is ended, when he has no other light than that of the camp fire.

What a noble example for all priests! We see here a poor Indian missionary traveling all day through snow and cold and ice, fatigued and tired with walking and carrying a heavy pack all day, and yet saying his office out in the cold, open air before a camp fire, shivering with cold. Yes, truly Father Baraga was made of the material that saints are made of! Baraga concludes:

"Having returned to my mission here, I found everything in the best of order, although I had been absent three months. During my absence the Indians assembled on all Sundays and holy days in the church, both in the morning and afternoon, and performed their prayers and singing in common as I had recommended them to do. I live here satisfied and grateful, loving and beloved as a father amongst his children, for which I thank God in the Name of Jesus."

Chapter XLI

Continuation of F. Baraga's Labors at L'Anse in 1848 and 1849.—"The New York Observer's" Estimate of His Work.—Hardships and Dangers.

Scarcely had F. Baraga returned from Fond du Lac, as related in the foregoing chapter, when his restless zeal for the good of souls urged him to visit the scattered Catholics of the mining country. Great was the joy of the good people when they again beheld their common father and pastor. It was seldom he could visit them for his territory was large. For several years Fathers Skolla, Baraga, and Mrak were the only priests in Northern Wisconsin, Eastern Minnesota, and the Northern peninsula of Michigan. The white settlers at the mines wished very much to have a priest of their own, whom they could well support and they asked F. Baraga to request Rt. Rev. Bishop Lefevre to send them one, but the latter answered that with the best will he could not give them a priest, as he had none to spare. The foremen at the mines, although for the most part non-Catholics, being generally men of no particular religion, were also desirous of having a priest stationed at the mines, knowing from experience the immense influence for good which a worthy priest wields amongst his people. As to the public esteem in which F. Baraga was held by all classes of people, Protestants as well as Catholics, and of the great influence exerted by him and other Indian missionaries, we will give an extract taken from a political paper of that time called "*The New York Observer*." The writer remarks:

"To the most common observer it is not difficult to assign the reasons why Catholics have such good success. The number of Catholic whites married to Indian women is greater than that of Protestant. Through this kind of influence the confidence of the Indians is more easily gained than through any other. The children of such marriages are a sure gain. The way to gain a ready hearing on the part of the relatives is thus also facilitated.

"Another reason is this, that it is more apparent in a Catholic missionary that he devotes himself wholly and entirely to the cause which he promotes, since he labors continually for others, since he fearlessly exposes his health to danger in the service of the sick and dying, and since he is more willing at all times to suffer privation.

"An example of this kind is told of Father Baraga at Keweenaw Point, a man almost* sixty years old, who devotes the whole of his large income,† as also his personal services to the cause, he has taken upon himself and receives no compensation for the same. Last winter he went on snowshoes from L'Anse to Copper Harbor, a distance of fifty-seven miles,‡ through an uninhabited region, solely to baptize a child, of whom he had heard that it would probably die. Such proofs of self-sacrifice are not without influence on the observant mind of the Indian.

"The Catholic missionary is everywhere at home, wherever he happens to be. Neither wife nor children are placed in a disagreeable position, when the night overtakes him in an Indian wigwam. He partakes with gratitude of their homely meals and seeks nothing better. He lies down on their mat to rest and thanks his Savior that he is so well provided for. He does not waste a full

---

* "I am fifty-one years old, but my almost eighteen years of missionary service, and especially my difficult winter-trips, have used me up considerably, so that many people, when they saw me for the first time, took me for a man of sixty years. All for the greater honor of God."
† "The kind contributions for my support, which the Leopoldine Society sends me from time to time."
‡ "I perform also other missionary duties. It is, however, certain that I myself, and every Catholic missionary, would be willing to travel, not only fifty-seven miles, but also 570, solely to procure eternal happiness through Holy Baptism for one single immortal, infinitely precious soul."

half of his precious time in enjoying the pleasures of life, nor in the fulfillment of household duties, or in the care of an ever-increasing family, but through his simple and self-sacrificing mode of life, he gains entrance into the hearts of the savages and then their obedience is easily gained to the requirements of the Roman Church. Doctrines, which are taught by visible signs, are easier understood by simple people than moral explanations, no matter in what form of words they may be clothed."

In regard to publishing his Chippewa grammar and dictionary, F. Baraga felt some uneasiness, as he had no funds of his own wherewith to defray the printing expenses. He, therefore, wrote as follows to his old standby, the Leopoldine Society:

"I now take the liberty of speaking again of an affair that may be of some importance to our Indian missions. I wrote in one of my reports to your Princely Highness, (L'Anse, June 19th, 1847) to kindly send me some pecuniary assistance for printing an Indian grammar and dictionary, as I intend to publish both these works in Detroit, for the benefit of future missionaries. I mentioned to Your Grace that I thought four hundred dollars would suffice for printing both works. But I now perceive that the dictionary alone, at which I am still working, will be so large, that after the printing expenses are paid, not much will be left of the above named sum. I therefore, most respectfully ask of the most Rev. Directors to allow me six hundred dollars for the printing of both works, and to forward the same through the hands of my Rt. Rev. Bishop."

The above named Society sent him a thousand florins and two boxes of church ornaments and goods for his missions.

In August, 1849, we find F. Baraga again superintending the printing of a new and large edition of the Chippewa prayer book. He received one thousand florins (about $480.00) from the Leopoldine Society, and this amount, along with some private donations, enabled him to pay for this new edition. These most useful prayer books were, of course, gratuitously distributed all over the Indian country in the Northwest, not only in the States bordering on our great lakes, but also in Canada amongst the many Indians converted by the zealous Jesuit and Oblate Fathers.

Father Baraga writes, L'Anse, August 25th, 1849: "Indians love their prayer books very much and wherever they go the prayer book must go along, that evenings when they have camped they may read in them and sing. I have seen Indians who on their death bed requested, as a particular favor, that after their death, their prayer book might be put on their breast in the coffin, that on the day of judgment they might appear before the judgment seat of Jesus with their prayer books as it were in their hands."

Speaking of the state of his missions he says in the same letter:

"My mission at L'Anse prospers and increases as time goes on. The converts are steadfast and faithful in the fulfillment of all Christian duties. I admire, especially the resoluteness with which they resist all temptations and occasions of relapsing into the vice of drunkenness, to which they were so much addicted before their conversion. They are admired universally by the whites, who are aware of this fact. Many of these Indians were tempted to drunkenness by the offer of considerable presents, but they would rather relinquish all presents than take a single glass of intoxicating liquor. Others were threatened by mean, unscrupulous whites with blows, if they would not drink, but they would rather expose themselves to the danger of being maltreated by these miscreants than to that of relapsing into the vice of drunkenness. They now hate drunkenness just as much as they loved this vice before their conversion. Thanks be to God!

"In regard to industriousness a great and salutary change has been effected amongst these poor children of nature by the holy religion of Jesus, a religion which commands us to *work* and *pray*. Before their conversion they were lazy, as all wild Indians are. The poor women had to do all the work, chop wood and carry it home (on their backs), raise potatoes and dig them, etc. The men did nothing but hunt and spend often whole days lying in their miserable wigwams (smoking). But now these men have become industrious laborers. They work industriously on their ever increasing patches of land and live in good houses, keep poultry and already some have cows and oxen. They continually make considerable progress in industry and economy.

"How true it is that the Christian religion is capable of civilizing barbarous nations and of making them temporally and eternally happy. How often has not our government tried with truly well-meant human, but often mistaken, means to civilize these Indians and make them happy, but in vain. They sought to build without the Lord and they labored in vain. But as soon as the missionaries came among these Indians, and that they had submitted their free, wild necks to the sweet yoke of Jesus, then all good followed of itself. The holy, Christian religion had here as everywhere else all temporal blessings in her train. Americans belonging to no particular religion are beginning to understand and appreciate this fact and give to the Catholic missionary, before all others, the prize in cultivating, civilizing, and making happy the Indian. They give expression to this their conviction on every occasion, both orally and in writing to the honor of our holy Catholic religion, which through this very fact reveals her divine origin and truth."

In the same letter the zealous missionary says that he made again some arduous, but consoling mission trips, These winter journeys were both fatiguing and dangerous on account of the intense cold and deep snow. In February, 1849, he made a missionary journey, which did much good, but on which he was twice in danger of losing his life.

As he knew the road well, he went quite alone, carrying on his back his satchel with all things necessary for divine service at the different missions he intended to visit. At first everything went well. The snow was somewhat trodden down and his snowshoes were light. He visited several small mining towns, preaching, baptizing, and performing all other priestly functions. One day he started to go to a place about ten miles distant. The day before it had snowed heavily, making traveling exceedingly difficult. Oftentimes the road was so deeply covered that it could hardly be made out. The good Father soon perceived that it would be a terrible undertaking to proceed on his way to the settlement, but as he had already traveled some distance, he was unwilling to turn back. The settlement was situated on a high hill and the way to it led over high hills and through deep valleys. The snow before him was getting deeper and deeper. As it was yet fresh, it was so soft that at each step he sank in and could only with great difficulty pull his foot out of the hole made in the snow at each step he took. As everyone knows, nothing is more fatiguing than wading through deep snow. When the good Father had thus been toiling along for three hours his strength began to give way. But his courage and confidence in the help of the Good Shepherd, after whose lost sheep he was going, animated him to pursue his journey. Every little while he would rest a few moments and then continue his wearisome journey. But soon his weakness increased to such an extent that he could no longer carry his pack. He hung it, therefore, on a tree and waded on, but every moment slower and slower. Nature could hardly hold out much longer. At last he could scarcely pull his foot out of the deep snow whenever he made a step. Especially was it hard for the poor priest when the road went uphill. Often he thought he would sink down in the snow and perish. Had he lain down, he certainly would have frozen to death in a short time, for it was exceedingly cold and he was too weak and exhausted to gather wood and make a fire. So he kept on dragging himself along, resting every few steps he made. At last he had arrived within two miles of the place to which he was going. *But he was so weak now that it took him almost three hours to walk that short distance.*

When he left in the morning he had expected to arrive at the end of his journey by eleven o'clock in the morning. But he did not arrive till about five in the afternoon. The kind inhabitants of the place wondered and pitied him very much when they saw him so weak and exhausted. Next morning they immediately sent a young man for his pack, which he had left hanging on a tree. Although this journey had nearly cost his life, yet he felt amply rewarded through the good use the poor people made of his visit.

The second time F. Baraga was in great danger of losing his life was when he returned homeward after having visited the various missions at the mines. He was again traveling entirely alone, and was obliged to walk *thirty miles* to get to the first house on his way. However, he preferred to walk that whole distance in one day than spend the night in the open air sleeping on the snow, a thing that he greatly dreaded. But this journey, this walk of thirty miles, was again connected with fearful hardships. Early in the morning, the moon yet shining, he set out on his journey. At first things went well, for his way lay through the woods, where he was sheltered from the cold wind. But when he came out of the woods his way was over large frozen lakes, and the wind, which blew straight into his face, became stronger and stronger, till it became a perfect storm. It blew so hard that at times he could hardly make a step forward. The wind was so in tensely cold that it threatened to freeze the very blood in his veins—these are his own words. He could make but slow headway against the strong, cutting, icy wind. At times he lost the trail. As to a road, there was none, every foot of the ground was covered with snow. All he could do was to walk on. But it was difficult to keep the straight direction, for many a time he could not see ten paces ahead. The strong wind raised the light snow in clouds around him. It was indeed a fearful walk.

Through this storm, against this icy, cutting wind he had to make his way seventeen miles, on snowshoes! He remarks that if a weakness had come upon him, so that he would have been obliged to rest, even but for half an hour, he would have frozen to death. He tells how some French-Canadians had their ears and noses frozen on that awful day. Thanks be to God, no misfortune of that kind happened to the Father, but after he arrived home, the skin of his face peeled off. He remarks:

"These mission journeys are indeed very hard, but also very fruitful for the honor of God and the salvation of souls. It is this consideration that consoles and upholds the missionary. In the very midst of the storm I sometimes laughed at myself when the wind blew very strong and almost threw me down. Thanks be to God for all! May all result to His divine honor and to our salvation!" In a later letter, dated September 30th, 1849, F. Baraga mentions that he had completed the fourth (enlarged) edition of his Indian prayer book and his Indian dictionary. He had *3,500 copies* of said prayer book printed. The cost of printing and binding amounted to six hundred dollars. He received from the Leopoldine Society three hundred and ninety-one dollars, and the balance of the expenses was covered by donations from generous benefactors. He mentions that at his departure from Detroit his life was saved only through a special protection of God.

"On the 25th of this month (September, 1849) I set out from Detroit to return to my mission. But on the second day of our voyage on Lake Huron such a great storm came upon us that our steamer was almost in danger of foundering. The boat crew said that they had never seen such a storm on that lake. They cast about one-half of the freight overboard, and only by so doing could we be saved. We then sailed for land in order to save our lives. When throwing the lading overboard, they reserved about twenty barrels of fresh pork. They opened barrel after barrel and threw the pork into the fire to make the steam boat go faster. When at length we landed at a good harbor, the sailors noticed that the boiler had a large hole in the bottom. They could not proceed further with the boat. I, therefore, left them and got aboard another steamboat, which was sailing by, and came back to Detroit, from which place I hope to start in a few days and return, with the help of God, to my mission."

Chapter XLII

Letter of Rt. Rev. Peter Paul Lefevre, Bishop Of Detroit. F. Baraga Gets His Grammar and Instruction Book for the Indians Printed in Detroit. New Labors. His Terrible Journey in the Winter of 1850-1851.

We give the following letter of the Rt. Rev. Peter Paul Lefevre, Coadjutor-Bishop and Administrator of the Diocese of Detroit, in full, as it contains his opinion as to the state of Baraga's missions. The Bishop writes as follows to the Leopoldine Society:

Detroit, June 20, 1850.

"*Your Princely Highness*—I duly received, before my departure to the Indian missions, Your Lordship's letter of the 15th of March of this year. Sincerely and from the bottom of my heart do I thank Your Princely Highness and all the mission benefactors in the Austrian empire for the great and numerous benefits with which Your Highness comes to our assistance. It is a pleasure to me to be able to inform you that the amount which Your Lordship procured for us was of far greater utility to us than that of the last years. For the two thousand florins C. M., or one hundred and seventy-four pound sterling, I received $854.52. I have not as yet taken the money, but as soon as I shall have done so I shall give one-half of it, as Your Lordship wishes, to Rev. Frederic Baraga. He is just now here, busy with the publishing of some of his mission works. He will stay here for a considerable time, for he is having two works printed, each of which, as he says, will contain over six hundred pages. His Indian grammar will be very welcome to our Indian missionaries. It will be very useful to them to aid them in learning the Indian language, a thing absolutely necessary to them.

"It is only a few days ago since I returned from the Indian missions, in which I spent six weeks. I have also visited the mission of Rev. Baraga at L'Anse and have administered the sacrament of confirmation to many Indians of his flourishing and steadily increasing mission. I have always much consolation and spiritual joy whenever I go to the Indian missions. It is, indeed, consoling to see how these poor children of the forest, who until recently lived in the most horrible vices of paganism, are now God-fearing Christians *and far surpass the whites in devotion, in faith, and in the fulfillment of their Christian duties.* As often as I visit these missions I think that the life of a missionary is at times really hard and disagreeable, but at the same time very consoling and full of reward, since he sees immediately the fruit of his labors, and after the toil of planting comes immediately the joyful time of reaping. "Seminant missionarii flentes et gementes, sed statim laetantes veniunt portantes manipulossuos—the missionaries sow weeping and sighing, but immediately they come bearing their sheaves."

During his two and a half months' stay in Detroit, in the summer of 1850, F. Baraga worked, as it were, day and night at superintending the printing of two of his works, each of which shows his profound erudition and exalted piety. His Indian grammar is a masterly work of linguistic learning. When we consider that nine-tenths of all Chippewa words are either verbs or reducible to verbs, and that these verbs have thousands of terminations expressive of every shade of meaning, and that Baraga was obliged to learn all these countless terminations by patient inquiries from people who have no more idea of grammar "than the man in the moon," we are struck with astonishment and wonder at the genius, learning, and herculean labor of the man. As Indian linguist he occupies the first place amongst all scholars of Indian languages. We do not, of course, mean to assert that no white man could speak Chippewa better than Baraga. There may be such. But we confidently assert that no known writer had such a full, scientific, systematic knowledge of the language as he had.

Of that his grammar and dictionary are the best proofs. In the appendix we will note a few of the many peculiarities and difficulties of the Chippewa language.

As to the second work, spoken of above, it also shows the wonderful ability of its author. It is written with clearness and perspicuity. The language is simple, the range of words very limited, only those being employed which are in frequent use. The sentences are short, hardly any causal clauses being used. It is just as if a mother would first chew the food and then put it in the mouth of her child, just beginning to eat.

The book opens with a beautiful explanation of Christmas, the feast the poor Indians love so much. Then follow instructions, most simple and appropriate, on New Year's day and Epiphany. About one hundred pages are devoted to the Passion of Our Lord. Then follows an instruction on Easter and Ascension, all beautifully adapted to the limited capacity of his Indian readers. He treats most beautifully of prayer, explaining separately and touchingly each of the seven petitions of the "Our Father," as also the "Hail Mary." He explains in a masterly way each of the commandments of God and the Church. His instructions on the Sacraments are models of Indian composition, clear, logical, simple. At the end of the work are articles on the four last things and certain Indian vices, drinking, gambling, dancing. We have no hesitation in pronouncing this the ablest and best work of Father Baraga. It passed through two editions during Baraga's lifetime, and is now out of print and becoming very scarce. Would to God it could be reprinted and thus be made again accessible to our Indians! But our Indian missionaries are poor and can do nothing.

Speaking of these two works, he writes to the Archbishop of Vienna, one of the directors of the Leopoldine Society, as follows:

"I had two works printed here (in Detroit, in 1850), of which I made mention in my last letter. Now they are finished. One of them is a theoretic-practical grammar of the Indian language, and the other an Indian meditation and instruction book on all the truths of our holy religion (Nanagatawendamo-Masinaigan). I take the liberty of sending to Your Princely Highness two copies of the grammar and one copy of the Indian work (the above-spoken of Chippewa meditation and instruction book). The latter is in the form of a pocket manual, because Indians like to take along their books wherever they go. The dictionary could not be printed at present. There is too much work connected with it. I will immediately send the little box with the books from here, but it will be perhaps late in the season before it gets to Vienna. I pray Your Highness to excuse me for asking you to forward the books in the enclosed package early and safely to Laibach.

"During the whole time of my stay here I was very busy, for I was having both works printed at the same time, and had much to do in correcting the proof sheets. The days were always too short for me and they went by so quickly that it seemed to me as if it was always Sunday. On four Sundays I preached in the French church, on three Sundays in the English, and on the remaining Sundays in the German church.

"Day after tomorrow I shall depart for home and take along to my mission a young, exemplary priest. The Rt. Rev. Bishop sends him with me to learn the Indian language and then labor in the missions. That is a very good, ancient Jesuit plan. For it is really much better that a missionary first learn the Indian language before he begins to work in the missions. It is a very disagreeable and difficult thing if a missionary is obliged to use an interpreter. As a matter of course, this plan must be followed first. But now that we have a grammar and books in the Indian language, young missionaries will easily and soon learn the language. I am glad that this priest is going with me. He is a saintly man and has the firm resolution to spend his whole life in the Indian missions. He is a Belgian and his name is Charles Van Paemel" (should be Angelus Van Paemel).

From a letter of Bishop Lefevre, dated September 15th, 1852, we learn that Father Pierz left his diocese in the spring of that same year and that he went to Minnesota to establish a new Indian mission there.

During the winter of 1850-1851 Father Baraga visited again his mission stations at the different copper mines of Keweenaw Point, Northern Michigan. There were quite a large number of Irish, French, and Germans among the mining population, and to tend to them all meant a great increase of labor and hardships to the zealous missionary. The weather was very cold that winter. He had to go from one place to another on snowshoes and carry his heavy pack, containing all things necessary for divine service. On one of these apostolic journeys he was in the greatest danger of losing his life.

It was towards the end of January, during the coldest days and nights of that month. He was on his way homeward, after having visited the mining settlements. He stayed overnight in a certain house. From this place to the nearest human habitation on his way were thirty miles. Generally he used to walk that distance in ten or twelve hours; but this time it came otherwise. During the entire preceding day and during the whole night it snowed fearfully, so that the snow, which even before was very deep, became a great deal deeper and the walking so much more fatiguing and difficult. And through this deep snow he had to travel entirely alone over thirty miles. It was only through a special protection of God that he escaped with his life.

He left the house, in which he had remained overnight, about seven o'clock in the morning and then he began to make his way. He soon felt very tired, but kept on walking slowly all day long, making but little progress. About five in the evening he had made but half the way. It was truly horrible. It was evening, night was at hand, and he was fifteen long miles away from the nearest human dwelling, all alone. The night was dark and intensely cold. No fire, nothing but a piece of cake to eat, and he ready to sink down in the snow at any moment from exhaustion and weakness! What was the poor priest to do? He had either to walk on or freeze to death. With a fervent prayer he recommended himself to Divine Providence, which had so often before wonderfully protected him, and walked on and on during all that long, dark, and bitterly cold night. At last, at seven in the morning, he arrived at the house and sank down totally exhausted. Nature could stand the strain no longer. The people of the house were astonished beyond measure at his coming. *He had walked twenty-four hours, without resting, through the deep snow, with his snowshoes on and carrying his heavy pack, with nothing to eat but a piece of dry, frozen cake!* He says:

"I could not thank God enough, when I arrived at the house. Many a time I thought during the night, which was bitterly cold, that I would sink down and freeze before I would get to the house. And it was really only through the special protection of my loving, heavenly Father that I could hold out in such great hardship. My trust in the help of God under all circumstances of life was even before that very great; but this occurrence has heightened it a great deal more."

Chapter XLIII

Baraga's Elevation to the Episcopal Dignity.—Sault Ste. Marie His Episcopal See.—A Short Historical Sketch of the Place and of the Missionaries Who Labored There.

We are now to enter upon a new era in the life of saintly Baraga. We have endeavored to give the reader a true picture of his life as child, student, priest and Indian missionary. We are now to narrate his holy, self-sacrificing life as bishop of a large, extensive diocese.

July 29th, 1853, the Northern Peninsula of Michigan was detached from the diocese of Detroit and erected into a Vicariate-Apostolic. On the 1st of November of that same year Very Rev. Frederic Baraga was consecrated in the cathedral of Cincinnati by Archbishop Purcell, Bishops Lefevre of Detroit and Henni of Milwaukee acting as assistant consecrators. It is much to be regretted that no particulars of this important event have anywhere been recorded.

Bishop Lefevre ceded to the newly consecrated bishop the Indian missions of his diocese in lower Michigan, and Bishop Henni did the same in regard to those of Northern Wisconsin; the like was done by the bishop of Hamilton in regard to the Indians of the north shore of Lake Superior. B. Baraga had thus a very large territory confided to his care. It extended from Fond du Lac, fifteen miles beyond the western extremity of Lake Superior, to Arbre Croche and the adjacent islands and missions, thus taking in all the country around Lake Superior, the entire Northern Peninsula, and a considerable part also of the Southern Peninsula of Michigan. From a letter of his we learn that at the time of his consecration there were but two priests in Northern Michigan.

From time immemorial the falls of Sault Ste. Marie were a common camping ground for Indians of the whole surrounding country on account of the abundance of white-fish and lake trout found there. However, the Saulteurs or Bawiting daji-ininiwag were the regular settlers of the place. They formed a branch of the great Chippewa nation who inhabited both the northern and southern shores of Lake Superior.

The first white man to visit Sault Ste. Marie and gaze on the limpid waters of our great inland sea was most probably the Franciscan Father Joseph Le Caron, in 1615 or thereabouts. It seems that Etienne Brulé, a French trader, was there at an early day, too. In 1634— or, as some assert, 1639—Jean Nicollet visited the Winnebagoes near Green Bay, but whether he saw Lake Superior is uncertain. In 1642 Jogues and Raymbault, two Jesuit Fathers, visited the Sault and were well received by the 2,000 Indians assembled there to celebrate the great feast of the dead. Father Marquette spent a year there, 1668-1669, and found the people well inclined to Christianity. Father Dablon was there for some years and may be justly called the founder of said mission. On the 14th of June, 1671, Sieur Lusson, acting in the name of the Intendant Talon and of his Majesty Louis XIV, of France, took formal possession of Sault Ste. Marie and of all the country represented by the ambassadors of fourteen different Indian tribes assembled for that purpose. All the Fathers and Frenchmen in that vicinity, as well as a great number of Indians, were present, and Father Allouez addressed the multitude as follows:

"Behold, a noble affair presents itself to us, my brethren; grand and important is the affair, which is the object of this council. Look up to the Cross, elevated so high above your heads. To such a Cross it "was that Jesus Christ, the Son of God, having become man for the love of man, allowed himself to be fastened and to die, in order to render satisfaction to the eternal Father for our sins. He is the master of our lives, of heaven and earth and hell.

It is of Him I always speak to you and His name and word I have carried into all these countries.

"But look also at this other pole, to which are attached the arms of the great chief of France, whom we call the king. He lives beyond the sea. He is the chief of the greatest chiefs; he has not his equal on earth! All the chiefs you have ever seen or heard of are but children in comparison to him. He is like a great tree and they—they are only like small plants, which are trampled underfoot in walking. You know Onontio, the celebrated chief (governor) of Quebec; you know and experience how he is the terror of the Iroquois, and his mere name makes them tremble, since he ravished their country and carried fire into their villages. There are beyond the sea ten thousand Onontios like him, who are but the soldiers of this grand chief, our great king, of whom I am speaking. When he says the words, "I am going to war," every one obeys him and those ten thousand chiefs raise companies each of one hundred soldiers, both on land and sea. Some embark in ships, one to two hundred in number, such as you have seen at Quebec. Your canoes carry four or five men; at the highest, from ten to twelve. Our French ships carry four, five hundred and even as many as a thousand. Others go to war on land, but in numbers so great that, ranged in double file, they would reach from here to Mississaquenk although we count more than twenty leagues till there. When he attacks, it is more terrible than thunder; the earth trembles, the air and sea are on fire with the discharge of his cannons. He has been seen in the midst of his troops, covered all over with the blood of his enemies, of whom so many have been put to the sword by him, that he does not count the scalps, but only the streams of blood which he has caused to flow! He carries off so great a number of prisoners of war that he makes no account of them, but lets them go wherever they like, to show that he does not fear them. At present no one dares to make war on him. All those living beyond the sea have sued him for peace with the greatest submission. From all parts of the world people go to see him, to hear and admire him! It is he alone that decides all the affairs of the world! What shall I say of his riches? You esteem yourselves rich when you have ten or twelve sacks of corn, some hatchets, beads, kettles, or some other things similar. He has more cities belonging to him than there are men among you in all these countries in five hundred leagues around! In each city there are stores in which enough axes could be found to cut down all your forests; enough kettles to boil all your moose, and enough glass beads to fill all your wigwams! His house (palace) is longer than from here to the head of the Sault—that is, more than half a league; it is higher than the highest of your trees, and it holds more families than the largest of your villages can contain."

No wonder the Indians were filled with wonder and astonishment that there was a man on earth so great, so rich and so powerful! Good Father Allouez indulged in hyperbolic language, to impress his dusky hearers with a great idea of the grandeur of the "Grand Monarch," Louis XIV.

In 1674, three years after the above narrated solemn act, a delegation of Sioux came to the Sault to take part in a general Indian council of the northwestern tribes. During one of the deliberations a sanguinary affray occurred between them and the assembled Crees and Chippewas. All the Sioux were killed, but also many of their enemies, and the mission building was set on fire and burned to the ground. Father Dreuillettes labored long and successfully at the Sault. After his departure or death the mission seems to have been abandoned, the Fathers concentrating their forces at St. Ignace in Michigan, St. Francis Xavier, at De Pere, Wis., and Kaskaskia, Ill.

In 1834 the Redemptorist Father Hatscher labored with great zeal and much fruit at the Sault. Bishop Rese visited the mission that year, baptized many Winnebagoes and confirmed more than one hundred of them. A small Catholic church had been built there. It was, however, soon after destroyed by a fanatical mob, that smashed the windows, threw the vestments, chalice and other utensils outdoors and destroyed them. They tore the missals into shreds. When Father Hatscher attempted to decorate his church for All Saints' day they fired the building. It is a remarkable coincidence that the same blind hatred against the church impelled a mob to destroy that very year, on the 11th of August, the Ursuline Convent at Charlestown, Mass., founded in 1820 by Bishop—afterwards Archbishop and Cardinal—Cheverus. Father Hatscher, however, continued to labor at the Sault until the 4th of July, 1835, when he was moved by his superior, F. Sanderl, to Ohio.

In the fall of 1836 Father Pierz took charge of the Sault and commenced to build another church. He also visited the Island of St. Joseph and Kitchimitigong (Large Tree). In the last named place he converted many pagans. We find him still at the Sault in 1838, during which year he visited Michipicoton, where almost all the pagans received holy baptism. He then went to Okwanikissong, where he baptized many Indians. After having spent nearly a whole year at Grand Portage, Pigeon River, and Fort William, he returned to the Sault in 1839. Thereafter he made his home in Arbre Croche, whence he visited, from time to time, the Sault and other stations until 1852, when he went to Minnesota, residing most of the time in Crow Wing.

In 1846 the Jesuit Fathers came to reside in the Sault, namely, F. Menet and another Father. In 1847 F. Kohler of the same order came to take charge of the mission of the Canadian Sault across the river with F. Hamipaux as itinerant missionary among the Indians. Father Menet remained at the Sault until 1860, when he was withdrawn. During this period there was but one regular residence for the missionaries, namely, at the village of Sault Ste. Marie. After Father Menet's return in 1864 a residence of Jesuit Fathers was opened at the Canadian Sault and later on at Garden River, about twelve miles below on the Canadian side. Both those residences, however, till about a decade ago, remained dependent on the American Sault. The Fathers of the last named residence have charge of the following missions: Bay Mills, Donaldson, Indian Point, Ishkonigan, Pickford, Sugar Island, Waiskey Bay and White Fish Point.

Chapter XLIV

Bishop Baraga's Pastoral Letter to the Faithful of His Vicariate-Apostolic Announcing His Elevation to the Episcopal Dignity.

Shortly after his elevation to the episcopal dignity Bishop Baraga addressed two distinct letters to his people, the one in English, the other in Chippewa. Both are well worthy of perusal. The tone of the English encyclical is different from most documents of this kind. It breathes throughout the feelings of a loving, fatherly heart.

He does not use the words, "Beloved brethren," he addresses them with the affectionate name of children, saying, "My dear children." He speaks more like a father than a dignitary.

In the appendix we shall give the Chippewa document with accompanying translation. We do this the more willingly as B. Baraga's pastoral letter to his Indian children, whom he loved most warmly, is an unicum of its kind. As far as the writer knows, no such official document was ever issued in any Indian language. It is, therefore, well worth preserving, as well for its intrinsic as also for its historic value.

"FREDERIC BARAGA,
BY THE GRACE OF GOD AND THE FAVOR
OF THE APOSTOLIC SEE,

BISHOP OF AMYZONIA, VICAR APOSTOLIC OF THE UPPER PENINSULA OF MICHIGAN.
TO THE FAITHFUL OF HIS DIOCESE, HEALTH AND BENEDICTION.
VENERABLE BRETHREN OF THE CLERGY, AND DEARLY BELOVED CHILDREN IN CHRIST JESUS.

Grace be unto you and peace from God the Father, and from our Lord Jesus Christ, who gave himself for our sins, that he might deliver us from this present wicked world, according to the will of God our Father.

And the will of God, our heavenly Father, is our sanctification, our eternal happiness; that we should love him and serve him in this world, and be happy with him forever in the next. And there is no true happiness but with him and in him. God Almighty has created us for happiness; and he could not create us for anything else, because he is Charity, and all his designs and ways are charity and mercy. He has created all things for us, but he has created us for himself. And if we, nevertheless, see how much misery and unhappiness there is among us in this world, and are taught that innumerable souls are in eternal sufferings in the next world, we must acknowledge that the cause of all that, is not the will of God, but our own wickedness, our want of obedient submission to the most holy and merciful will of God Almighty. Our Savior and our God is infinitely faithful to his promises. He promised us solemnly that whosoever shall fulfill the will of his Father, and our Father, that is in heaven, shall enter the kingdom of heaven, and be there eternally happy with God. We see then plainly before us the way to happiness; it is: The fulfilling of the will of God, the fulfilling of our duties towards him.

Dearly beloved, as I wish your eternal happiness with the same heartfelt desire as I do my own, I entreat you with all my heart, be faithful in the fulfilling of your duties toward God, and God will reward you for it in his heavenly kingdom.

I will now explain to you our principal and most sacred duties towards God, that you may mind them, and with the help of God fulfill them faithfully. Read these instructions with attention; not only once and then throw them away and forget them, but read them repeatedly, and endeavor to practice them. This is the first time I speak to you, through these lines, as your principal Pastor and Bishop. Let these words enter into your hearts as they come out of my heart. This heart has ever loved you, my dear children, but never so paternally as now.

I. Our first essential duty towards God is the duty of *Faith*, which consists in the believing of every word that God has revealed to us, without rejecting a single point of revealed faith. Some truths of our religion are so sublime that we cannot comprehend them with our feeble and limited reason. These truths we also must believe on the authority of God who never can err, never deceive nor be deceived. That there are in our holy religion some truths so sublime that we cannot comprehend them shows the divine character of it and admonishes us of the necessity, of the absolute submission of our limited reason to the infallible authority of God. To reject a single point would be to destroy the whole; because if God could err or deceive only in one point, his authority would be no better than human.

This duty of faith is essential and the fulfilling of it necessary for salvation, because without faith it is impossible to please God. And Christ said very expressly: "He that believes and is baptized, shall be saved; but he that believes not, shall be condemned." But we must not think that faith alone will save us, as many believe who do not belong to the true church of God. We have the infallible authority of the word of God for it, that faith without good works is dead; and a dead faith will certainly not procure us life everlasting. The devils also believe and tremble, but they remain devils, because their faith is fruitless, and ever was so. Our faith must be a living faith; and a living faith only will give us life everlasting in heaven. In order to have a living faith, we must show it in our life and behavior; we must live by our faith according to the principles of our holy religion; we must make it our *rule of life*. If we have, and preserve until death, the true faith, and do not live according to its precepts, we shall be cast out into exterior darkness on the day of judgment, like that slothful servant, who received a precious talent at the hands of his master, and merely preserved it, but made no profit on it. Our holy Catholic faith is a most precious and immense treasure, infinitely more precious than all the gold and silver of the universe.

This is that precious talent which our heavenly Lord and Master entrusted to us, His servants, that we may deal in it, and make all possible profit by it, against the day of account. He that merely preserves this talent, and makes no profit of it, will certainly be cast out into that horrid darkness of eternal damnation.

Examine yourselves, beloved children, whether your faith is living and profitable, or dead and fruitless. How unhappy is the negligent Catholic who possesses that previous talent, the true faith, revealed by the Son of God, and does not profit by it! Oh, how those unfortunate victims of the justice of God regret that they did not make a better use of their religion when it was time! Would they be allowed to return to this world, oh! how faithful would they be in fulfilling all Christian duties! They will never more be allowed to return to this world; but you, my dearest children, are yet in this world. But your time will soon pass away forever. Profit by it; it will be for your everlasting happiness. You have an immense treasure in your hands, you can buy heaven with it. How unfortunate would you be if you profit not by such an opportunity!

II. Another great duty of a Christian towards his God is the duty of *Adoration.* As soon as we believe in God and believe in His revealed word, we will easily understand how great our duty is to adore Him and Him alone, "The Lord thy God thou shalt adore and serve Him alone." We are often accused by our adversaries of adoring creatures equally with the Creator. Let them say what they please. Every Catholic child knows that we adore only God Almighty, and no other being. But we pray to the saints in heaven that they may pray with us and for us to God Almighty.

The duty of praying is a great and holy duty. We are expressly commanded to pray continually and never to cease. Not only the word of our Savior, but also His holy example teaches us the duty of praying; He was continually praying and spent whole nights in prayer.

Never neglect your prayers, beloved children. A Christian without prayer is like a soldier without arms; exposed to every attack of his enemies, and easily overcome. We are soldiers of Christ; our whole life is a kind of warfare against our enemies, visible and invisible; and our strongest weapon is prayer. If you throw away that weapon, how will you be able to withstand the violent and repeated attacks of your enemies? Remember the warning of our Savior, that we must watch and pray; or else the enemy will soon overcome us.

Although we have always to pray and never to cease, still there are some periods of time in which we are more strictly obliged to pray. These are especially the beginning and the end of every day; therefore every faithful Christian ought, invariably, to perform his morning and evening prayer. And if he does not, he neglects a decided and sacred duty towards God, and deprives himself of many graces; because prayer is the principal channel through which the grace of God flows into our hearts.

Dearly beloved children, be faithful in the fulfilling of this holy duty; and never say, I have no time to pray. Consider how ungrateful this is. God Almighty gives you twenty-four hours every day for your works and wants. And out of these twenty-four hours you cannot give a few minutes to God for the fulfilling of a great duty? Fear the reproaches of God on the day of judgment! It requires only a good will and a firm resolution to fulfill this duty, and you will find means and time to do it. And don't think, my dear children, that in remote places you are not very strictly obliged to perform your prayers. This is a pernicious illusion. God is everywhere, and must be served everywhere. Our Savior says plainly that the true adorers and servants of God will adore Him everywhere in spirit and in truth.

Be especially faithful in fulfilling the duty of praying on the day of Our Lord, on Sunday, which is set apart by God Almighty for His special service. We read in Holy Scripture how severely God has punished Sabbath-breakers in ancient times. If He does not punish them always now in this world, He certainly will in the next. It is a melancholy fact (but, nevertheless, very true, and it came a thousand times within my experience) that many Christians living in remote places neglect more their duty of praying and commit more sins on Sunday than on any other day in the week. How horrid this is! And what a responsibility on the day of judgment! Be careful, dear children, and fear the judgment of God. It may fall upon you on a sudden and unexpectedly. Watch and pray. Perform your prayers every morning and every evening, and during the day frequently remember God; and so you will fulfill that precept of our Savior: "Pray continually and never cease."

III. The third of our principal and most essential duties towards God is the duty of *Respect*; that we ought to respect God more than any person on earth. This duty seems to be plainly understood, and it seems to be a matter of course that God be more respected than any person on earth, because He is the most Perfect Being. And still there is hardly any other duty towards God that is so often transgressed, especially by many classes of people, than this very duty of respect.

To fulfill this duty, we ought never to forget the presence of God, but continually to remember, as we are taught by our faith, that God Almighty is everywhere present, that He knows our thoughts, hears our words, and sees our actions; and then to behave as it becomes the awful presence of God. When a believing Christian (as they commonly are) is in the presence of a respected and worthy clergyman, he behaves decently; not a single word will escape his lips that could offend the respected person; not a single action or gesture will take place that could hurt the feelings of the person of that respectable character. But consider the same Christian when he is in his ordinary common society, amongst persons whom he does not particularly respect. He will behave quite differently, he will use bad language, he will curse, swear, blaspheme, and pronounce impure, obscene words. And all this in the very presence of God, the Most Holy, the Most High. What a want of respect! And what a perversity! He respects the presence of a man, and does not respect the awful presence of his God! And transgresses horribly the sacred duty of respect towards God. If God Almighty would require of us only as much respect for His Most Holy Majesty as we use towards respectable persons on earth, every believing Christian would say that this would not be enough. And indeed it would not be enough, because there is no comparison between the respectability of the highest person in this world and the Most Holy Majesty of God! And still—to the shame of the majority of Christians we must acknowledge it—there is less respect among Christians for God Almighty than for respectable persons in this world.

Consider this, dearly beloved children, and reflect seriously how often you have transgressed this sacred duty towards God; how often you have spoken words and committed actions in the presence of God which you never would do in the presence of a clergyman or other respectable person. Repent of it, beloved children, and make a firm resolution never to forget the presence of God; to look at Him constantly with the eyes of faith, and to behave in His presence as it becomes a believing Christian, who knows that God, his future judge, everywhere sees him, and hears all his words.

IV. The fourth principal duty of a Christian towards his God is, the duty of *Obedience*. We have strict duties of obedience even to certain persons in this world. Thus children are strictly obliged to be obedient to their parents; and servants are commanded by the word of God to be obedient to their masters in all things that are not against the law of God; and to be obedient even to wicked and peevish masters. But far greater is our duty of obedience towards God, who is our heavenly Father, and the best of Fathers, our Supreme Lord and Master, and the kindest of Masters.

To be obedient means, to fulfill the will of a superior. To be obedient to God means, then, to fulfill His holy will. When a master wants his servant to do something for him, he will tell him what he has to do, and the servant will know the will of his master. But how can we know what God, our heavenly Lord and Master, wants us to do? God has established several means by which we may understand what is His will, in order to fulfill it. The voice of conscience is one of these means by which God gives us to understand His will. The voice of your conscience is the voice of God. Pay attention to the voice of your conscience and you will understand that. When you propose to do wrong, or are in danger of committing sin, your conscience will immediately warn you not to do evil, to avoid it by all means. On the contrary, when you propose to do good, and find opportunity to do so, your conscience will encourage you to do all good you can. See here the plain will of God. To avoid evil and do good, this is for us invariably the will of God. So, then, beloved children, in order to fulfill the holy will of God Almighty, listen to your conscience and follow its dictates, avoiding what it forbids you, and doing what it commands you; and by so doing you will fulfill the sacred duty of obedience to God.

Another means by which God Almighty makes us know His holy will is the "*word of God*" which is written in the Holy Scriptures and other good religious books, and is announced to us by the pastors of His church. Their instructions have been called the "*word of God*" from the first times of Christendom, as we see in Holy Scripture (I Thes, ii, 13). And our Savior commands us expressly to listen to the pastors of His church with the same respect and submission as to Himself. He commands them to preach His doctrine to the whole world, and assures us that we hear Himself when we hear them. Dearly beloved children, in order to be obedient to God, your heavenly Father and Supreme Master, be faithful in the fulfilling of the precepts and instructions of your good pastors and confessors. Be thankful to God that He makes you know His holy will by these means and profit by them. Remember what an awful responsibility awaits you on the day of judgment if you do not profit by such means of salvation.

V. The fifth principal duty we have towards God, is the duty of *Love*; that we ought to love God above all. This is a most holy duty of every Christian; but, unfortunately, much neglected, and very rarely fulfilled as it ought to be. How strict and important this our duty is, we may understand by the express command of our Savior to love God, and by his minute description of the character of our love towards God. Not only did he say that we must love God, but he explained that we must love the Lord our God "with our whole heart and with our whole soul and with our whole mind and with our whole strength." The ancient Fathers of the church wondered that it was necessary to give to Christians an express commandment to love God. "Is it not natural," they say, "to the heart of a Christian, who is a child of God, to love his heavenly Father above all? Was it necessary to *command* it, to *prescribe* it?" Oh, certainly, it was! And notwithstanding this express commandment and the detailed description of it, very few Christians love God according to this description of our Savior.

Consider often, beloved children, these four marks of the true love of God, and examine yourselves whether your love has these marks. And do not think that only a few chosen and extraordinary souls are obliged to love God thus. No! we are all obliged so to love Him!

The first mark of the true love of God is, that we love Him with our *whole heart*; that is, that we do not divide our heart between God and the world, between the Creator and the creature. God is a jealous God, as we see in Holy Scripture; He suffers no other lover besides Him, much less above Him. He wants your whole heart, or nothing. If you love anything more than God, or as much as God, you have not the true love of God. And if you are not earnestly ready to part with anything in the world for the love of God, if He requires it of you through the mouth of a pastor of His church, you do not love Him with all your heart; your heart is divided, and consequently not accepted by God at all. But understand well, beloved children, when we are commanded to love God with our whole heart, this means not that we must not love anything but God. We may love, and we are commanded to love, our parents, our relatives, our benefactors, our friends, even our enemies. But we must love all in God, according to the will of God, and for God's sake; and God in all and above all. And so we will love Him with our whole heart.

The second mark of the true love of God is, that we love Him with our whole soul. This is a Scriptural expression. We often find in Holy Scripture the word "soul" instead of "life." So, for instance, our Savior says that whosoever shall lose his "soul" in this world for His sake, shall find it in the next; that is, whosoever shall lose his "life" for his Savior's sake in this world, shall find true life in the next. To love God with our whole soul, signifies that we ought to love Him more than our own life, and be firmly resolved to lose our life rather than to lose Him, through sin. It ought to be our firm and earnest resolution rather to die than to offend God. But, alas! how often will the Christian commit sin, even a mortal sin, not to save his life, but for a mere trifle, for the pleasure of a moment, for a small lucre, for the vapor of a worldly honor, for the sake of a worldly friend, and so forth. What would he not do if his life were at stake! And still we are called upon— all of us—to lose rather our life than to offend God with a single sin! This is the meaning of the solemn appeal of Christ: "Love the Lord thy God with thy whole soul!"

The third mark of the true love of God is, to love Him with our *whole mind*; that is, that we should occupy our mind and our thoughts continually, or at least frequently, with the presence of God. It is natural to a loving heart to remember often the object of its affection. Imagine a good loving child who lives at a distance from his kind and loving father. That child will almost continually think of his father, and will long after the happy moment of his reunion with the beloved object of his filial affections. So ought every Christian to do, because he has the happiness to be a child of the best of Fathers. And so he will do if he loves God with his whole mind. He will think continually of his heavenly Father, and never forget His holy presence. And happy, infinitely happy, is the Christian who never forgets the presence of his God and Father. He will behave decently, and will carefully avoid all that could offend his beloved Father, in thoughts and words and actions; and will lead a holy life in the love of God.

The fourth mark of the true love of God is, that we love Him with our *whole strength.* The true love of God is the greatest happiness and the most precious privilege of a Christian. It is that splendid wedding-garment in which he will be admitted to the happiness and eternal joy of the "Lamb's nuptials." Nothing in the world can be obtained without endeavors and labor; and the more precious the object and the greater the fortune aimed at, the more serious the efforts to obtain it. As the true love of God is decidedly the most precious treasure of a Christian, so also our efforts to obtain and possess it ought to be extreme. But when we consider Christians as they commonly are, we will see how earnestly and perseveringly they endeavor to obtain riches and honors and pleasures, and all the comforts of this perishable life. And the love of God? This is commonly crowded out entirely, or, sought after as a by-thing, not as the "*One Thing Necessary.*"

Dearly beloved in Christ Jesus! With all the eagerness and solicitude of a loving father's heart I entreat you, in the name of God, whose Holy Providence has now committed you to my spiritual care, be faithful in the fulfilling of these principal and most essential duties towards God our heavenly Father. Especially endeavor to have the true love of God, which is the very foundation of all Christianity, and the glorious mark of a happy predestination. If you love God sincerely and above all, you will easily fulfill all other duties towards Him. Nothing is difficult, nothing tedious, to a loving heart.

The grace of our Lord Jesus Christ, and the charity of God, and the communication of the Holy Ghost be with you all. Amen.

+FREDERIC,
Bishop and Vicar Apostolic of Upper Michigan.

Chapter XLV

Bishop Baraga's First Letter to the Leopoldine Society After His Elevation to the Episcopate.—He Goes to Europe to Secure Priests and Funds for His Infant Diocese.

Bishop Baraga being placed at the head of a new, extensive, but poor, diocese, naturally began to look about for means to provide for the spiritual wants of his people, of whom, perhaps, one-half, if not more, were Indian converts. Hence, under date of January 23d, 1854, he penned the following letter to the Leopoldine Society:

"Through the Providence of God, who protects and governs His holy church, I, although unworthy, have been made Bishop and Apostolic-Vicar of Upper Michigan, in North America, and have been consecrated in Cincinnati on the first of November of last year.

"Upper Michigan is as yet an entirely new country. It is but ten years ago since it was ceded by the Indians to the United States government. Soon after, however, important copper and iron mines were discovered there, and then the white population began to increase most marvelously. Germans, Irish, Canadians, poured in masses into Upper Michigan, which country soon put on another appearance. By far the greatest majority of these settlers are Catholics. It was now that the want of priests began to be painfully felt. I was the only priest, who for several years had to care for all the Catholics there—Germans, Irish, Canadian-French, and Indians, until at length Providence called me to care in a higher sphere for these so abandoned Catholics.

"Without having been there, a person can imagine that providing for a diocese in such a distant, extensive, and religiously so much neglected country must be accompanied with incredible difficulties and much unpleasantness, and that the first bishop, who has been entrusted with this task, may justly complain that a burden has been placed on his shoulders, which would be formidable for those of an angel, *vel angelicis humeris formidandum opus*.

"In such a country everything must be erected: churches, houses for priests and religious teachers, schools, houses for Brothers and Sisters of various useful religious orders, etc. However, I do not ask the generous Leopoldine Society to contribute anything towards these buildings. I shall endeavor to prevail upon the good people who inhabit Upper Michigan to erect these buildings at their own expense.

"The Catholics of Upper Michigan are, partly, converted Indians, of whom we have, thanks be to God, already five thousand; partly Germans, Irish and Canadians, who for the most part belong to the laboring classes and are obliged to earn, day after day, their living in the sweat of their brow. Still they have a good will and are ready to do all in their power to provide for the necessary buildings and for priests and teachers, if they can but obtain them. I hope to find on my European tour individuals of capacity, who will joyfully render them all spiritual assistance and likewise instruct their children in all useful branches of knowledge, unto the honor of God and the salvation of those abandoned souls.

"For one sole building do I wish to receive pecuniary assistance from the Leopoldine Society, namely, for my future cathedral. May I be permitted to apply this grand name to a building of moderate dimensions, to be constructed of brick, which is to be 90 feet long, 45 feet wide, and 30 feet high. The little city in which I intend to fix my Episcopal See is Sault Ste. Marie, at the entrance of the immense great Lake Superior. There is at present an old wooden church there, which for years has been too small on account of the rapidly increasing population. Another, larger church is absolutely necessary, and this will serve at the same time as cathedral for the bishop. This church, although comparatively small, will certainly cost from eight to nine thousand dollars, which is more than 20,000 florins C. M. I most urgently entreat the Rev. Directory to contribute as much as possible towards this sum. In case I obtain sufficient means, I will build this church somewhat larger, about 100 feet long and 50 feet wide, a thing much to be desired on account of the future.

"Another absolutely necessary outlay, for the defraying of which I humbly ask the Rev. Central Directory, is the procuring of all those things which my new priests, whom I intend to take along with me to America next spring, will need in their future dwelling houses, such as furniture, beds, stoves, etc., etc. All these things will have to be first procured (in America), as these Rev. Fathers are intended for places where hitherto no priest was ever yet stationed. I need ten new priests and I have good prospects of finding them. The traveling expenses of the bishop and of so many priests will also call for a considerable sum.

"Besides, everything that a priest needs in the exercise of his holy functions will have to be procured, such as vestments of five different colors, albs, altar linen, missals, chalices, ciboriums, monstrances, etc., etc. These holy objects can be procured nowhere as cheaply as in Vienna. Hence I pray the Rev. Central Directory to give me the means to procure these holy objects.

"These are my principal needs and unavoidable outlays for the erection of the diocese of Upper Michigan entrusted to me. Under such circumstances the beginning must necessarily be difficult and expensive; but it will not always remain so. When once provided with priests and other necessaries, the usual running expenses of the diocese will not be very great. Hence I beg the Rev. Central Directory to take the circumstance into consideration that I come but this one time with such a great petition; for a little assistance now would be but of little service to me, whereas hereafter a small annual contribution will be of great help to me."

Soon after his consecration Bishop Baraga set out for Europe to procure priests and necessary funds for his Vicariate-Apostolic, afterwards diocese of Sault Ste. Marie and Marquette. It was not an easy task to find suitable missionaries. Priests were needed who could speak English, German, and French. Such priests were exceedingly rare.

He went to Paris to see what they could do for him at St. Sulpice, the college for foreign missions. Two young priests offered their services at once, though they had been trained and ordained for the East India mission. Bishop Baraga hesitated to accept their generous offer. Perhaps he feared that by receiving them he would be taking the spiritual bread out of the mouths of many poor Catholics in India. "Call the students together," he said to the Superior of the house, "and perhaps I shall find someone that will suit." Seating himself in the prefect's chair in the study hall he scrutinized the uplifted faces of the many bright young men before him. Suddenly his eyes fell upon a young man of handsome, intellectual features. The bishop pointed him out and asked who he was. "That, my lord," said the Superior, "is Martin Fox (Fuchs), a young man from Berlin and a student of promise and rare abilities. A natural orator, he commands the French language almost as well as his native German. But he, too, has expressed a wish to go to India," "Send him to my room," said the bishop, "I wish to talk with him."

Martin had an interview with the bishop, the outcome of which was that he offered himself for the American mission. But there was one great drawback—Martin did not know a word of English. "You will have to go to Dublin for a year," said the bishop to him. "A year in Dublin with your ability ought to give you a fair knowledge of the English language, and they say that is the place to get the genuine article."

So Martin, after taking a tearful leave of the many friends he had made at St. Sulpice, set out for Ireland. The rest of the story will be told in his own words:

"I parted from Bishop Baraga as from the best and most indulgent of fathers. My own father died when I was very young, and I resolved to do my best to please a prelate, who inspired me with such a deep affection.

"I had no trouble in conversing in French or German till I got to Queenstown, or to the Cove, as they called it then. From there to Dublin I had to get along by signs. Arrived at the capital,

I pointed out my luggage to a cabman, pronounced the talismanic word, 'All Hallows,' and away we went at a brisk trot for the university. It was raining, and doubtless the heavy atmosphere increased still further the miserable homesick feeling which was fast growing on me. As the gate clanged behind me, I felt I was shut out forever from home and friends."

No doubt a young man of Martin's sunny disposition soon got over his homesickness, and his warm-hearted Irish colleagues made him soon at home at All Hallows. In due time Martin Fox was ordained by Bishop Baraga. He was the *second* priest ordained by Baraga, and Rev. E. Jacker the third.

February 1st, 1854, Bishop Baraga paid his second and last visit to Döbernig, where his cradle had stood. Again he knelt for almost a whole hour at the baptismal font, where he had received the sacrament of regeneration fifty-seven years before. With a heart overflowing with gratitude and amid tears and sobs he called to mind the many graces and favors he had received since that memorable day on which he had been made a child of God and an heir of an eternal kingdom. Then he arose from his knees, ascended the steps of the high-altar, and for an hour preached a touching, soul-stirring sermon on the greatness and sublimity of the grace of Baptism. Thousands of his hearers wept tears of emotion whilst listening to the burning words of the saintly bishop. In Treffen he administered the holy Sacrament of Confirmation to his grand-nephew, Joseph Gressel. He also preached in Laibach, in St. Martin, Bischoflack, Metlika and other places. He generally spoke on subjects not looked for by his audience. All hoped and wished to hear from his lips something about his experience in the Indian missionary field, but of that he spoke but seldom, and then very little.

Bishop Baraga returned with five priests, Rev. Lawrence Lautischar, a Slavonian, being one of them. The latter, after laboring for sometime in Arbre Croche and elsewhere, went to Minnesota and worked for the conversion of the Chippewas near Red Lake, on which he met his death by freezing, on December 3d, 1858. He was a very zealous and pious priest. Two brothers, by the name of Roesch, or Resch, also came over on this occasion. One of them, Joseph, remained in the diocese as a secular priest; the other, George, became a Redemptorist. Besides the above-named, there were two other priests, the one a Tyrolese, the other a Frenchman, whose names the writer has been unable to ascertain.

Chapter XLVI

B. Baraga Returns Home.—He Goes to La Pointe, Ontonagan, and L'Anse.— First Ordination in Sault Ste. Marie.

On the 21st of August, 1854, after a long and tedious voyage, B. Baraga arrived at his episcopal city, Sault Ste. Marie. But his stay was short. On the 25th of the same month he left for La Pointe, his first mission in the Lake Superior region. For almost a year the good people of that island had been without a pastor, Father Skolla, O.S.F., having left on the 9th of October, 1853, to take charge of the Menominee Indians residing then on the Oconto River. The Indians at La Pointe were highly rejoiced to see their Father again, after an absence of several years, especially as he had brought along a priest to reside permanently with them. This was Rev. Angelus Van Paemel, a Belgian. His stay, however, was very short, only two months. Then came Rev. Timothy Carrié, whose Baptismal entries extend from September 10th, 1854, to December 25th, 1855, when he was succeeded by Rev. A. Benoit and the above-named Father Van Paemel. Father Benoit's last Baptism was on the 25th of July, 1858, about which time he left for France, when Rev. Angelus Van Paemel took exclusive charge of the mission. He was a very zealous, mortified, and pious man. His successor was Rev. John Cebul (or, as some write the name, Chebul), who came in June, 1860, and remained in the mission for twelve years. The mission then included Superior, Fond du Lac, Bayfield, Bad River Reservation, and Courtes Oreilles.

Bishop Baraga remained eight days at La Pointe, during which time he labored with his customary zeal for the spiritual well-being of his former parishioners, by preaching and hearing confessions almost all day long. A majority of the people, Indians and whites, received the holy sacraments. He then gave Confirmation to the candidates for that holy sacrament, whom he had thoroughly prepared by frequent instructions.

By the way, the writer wishes to remark that Baraga, both as priest and as bishop, was greatly impressed with the importance of Confirmation, evidence of which we have in his Indian catechism, where the instruction for that holy sacrament takes up four and a half pages, and in his book of instruction, the "Nanagatawendamo-Masinaigan," twenty pages are devoted to this subject.

The time he spent at La Pointe was truly a season of grace for its people, a spiritual renovation, a revival in the best sense of the word. He remarks that this Confirmation at La Pointe was the first given by him in his own diocese.

From La Pointe he went to Ontonagan, which was then quite a stirring little town. He remained there twelve days, during which time he was occupied with regulating the affairs of this new congregation and hearing the confessions of the Germans and Indians. He appointed an Irish priest, who could speak French fluently, as resident pastor. During the absence of B. Baraga in Europe the Catholics had built a beautiful and spacious church, in hopes of thereby sooner getting a resident priest, which in fact they did. B. Baraga blessed this new church and also administered Confirmation.

From Ontonagan he returned to Sault Ste. Marie for only a short time, four days, during which he gave Tonsure and Four Minor Orders to Rev. Thiele. He then went to L'Anse, where he had labored for ten years prior to his elevation to the episcopal dignity. Speaking of this visit he says:

"The joy of my dear children was great, since their earnest desire to see me as bishop was fulfilled. I remained in L'Anse twelve days and had to perform all priestly functions alone, as in La Pointe. I had to instruct the candidates myself for Confirmation and hear the confessions, for the missionary, who is now there, was sent there but lately and cannot yet speak Indian. The former priest had asked to be removed to Arbre Croche. Also here in L'Anse all, or almost all, have come to confession. On the first of October I administered Confirmation in this my dear mission of the Holy Name of Jesus, at which all were filled with deep emotion, my dear children and I, too. I even wept with emotion. It was remarkable and consoling to behold the emotion and eagerness with which they saw standing before them their father and missionary with crozier and mitre, and to hear him speak in their own language words of the deepest consolation to them. The most of our Indians here have already seen bishops, but they have never heard one address them in their own tongue."

On the 7th of October Baraga returned home. On the 21st of the same month he ordained Rev. Thiele a priest. The latter said his first Mass the next day at St. Mary's church in Sault Ste. Marie, on which occasion the bishop preached a sermon proper for the occasion. This was the first ordination that ever took place in the diocese of Marquette, and Father Thiele had the honor of being the first priest ordained by saintly Bishop Baraga.

As to B. Baraga's personal appearance at this time, we will give Hon. Richard R. Elliott's recollection of him, as he saw him in 1855. He says (American Catholic Review, 1896, page 111):

"Our recollection of the personality of Bishop Baraga is quite distinct; but we will describe him as he appeared to us in 1855, when he was Vicar-Apostolic of Upper Michigan.

"He was then 57 years old. He had spent twenty-three years of his mature life in missionary work in the lake regions; he had compiled and had printed the most extensive series of Indian Philological works known in modern times, the last of which, a work of 334 pages, in the Chippewa language, had just then been published in Cincinnati.

"But he had not laid down the missionary cross, although, perhaps, it was heavier to carry than ever before.

"He was a man frail in appearance, whose weight, apparently, would not exceed one hundred pounds. He was short in stature, with regularly proportioned frame, small feet and hands; his features were classic, and mild in expression; his eyes were blue, but passive; while his face was tanned to the color of a half-breed, the general expression of which tended to abstraction. His hair, which he wore rather long, was a light brown; it was abundant, but apparently lifeless; it had probably become so from the necessity of keeping his head protected from the cold atmosphere in which he lived during ten months of the year.

"We were present at the second Plenary Council of Baltimore in October, 1866, and we saw the bishop after he had been stricken down by an apoplectic stroke, while his purple robe was stained with blood."

In the July number of the same magazine he says (American Catholic Review, 1896, page 609):

"No wonder, then, that when, after two decades of toil such as had been his, we saw Frederick Baraga in his episcopal robes in Detroit in 1855, we were overcome with the evidence his personality but too plainly indicated, of the exhaustive missionary work he had performed on the Lake Superior Peninsula and on the shores of its adjacent waters.

"Although at the time mentioned his slight form was unbent, the kindly gleam, which in former years had greeted his friends from his soft blue eyes, indicating the benevolence of his heart, was no longer bright, because those eyes had been partly seared by the snow-blasts and the sleet of Lake Superior storms, as hurtful to human sight as is the burning sand of an African simoon; while his face, from constant exposure, as we have stated, had become tanned to the color of a half-breed."

Chapter XLVII

Labors of B. Baraga in 1856; He Visits Fort William, Grand Portage, Superior, La Pointe, and Other Places.

We give here in full B. Baraga's letter of the 1st of October, 1856. He writes as follows:

"This year I began my episcopal visitation at Lake Superior on the 26th of June. On this day I set out from Sault Ste. Marie, and after a long and tedious voyage"—most probably in a batteau or canoe—"I arrived, on the 11th of July, at Fort William. I was most agreeably surprised when I saw the beautiful, though small, church, which, under the supervision of Father Choné, had been erected a few years ago in this mission. I preached to the Indians, who were highly delighted to hear a bishop preach in their own language, a thing they had never heard before. On the 13th of July I confirmed here seventy-seven Indians, large and small; for this was the first holy Confirmation that was ever given there.

"From Fort William I went, accompanied by Father Duranquet, to Grand Portage. Here I preached several times to the Indians and confirmed fifty-three of them, and this likewise was the first Confirmation ever conferred at Grand Portage.

"From here I went in a birch-bark canoe to the newly-started little city of Superior, at Fond du Lac Bay. There is no church here as yet, but the zealous missionary Van Paemel is working hard to have one soon. There was no Confirmation here because Rev. Van Paemel was absent. He was busy in La Pointe preparing people for Confirmation. I preached on the 27th of July five sermons at Superior, three in the morning and two in the afternoon, in English, French, and Indian. This is one of the greatest difficulties of our missionaries that they have such mixed congregations so that they cannot satisfy the people with one sermon, but are obliged to preach two or three sermons in different languages.

"From Fond du Lac (means Superior) I went to La Pointe, where my first mission at Lake Superior was located, which I opened in 1835. I preached here several times, and on the 3d of August confirmed forty-six persons. In La Pointe Confirmation has already been administered several times. Bishop Rese confirmed here in 1838, Bishop Henni in 1844, and I gave Confirmation here now for the third time.

"From La Pointe I went to Ontonagan. I was agreeably surprised when I saw the improvements which Rev. Father Dunne had made in the church as well as in the parsonage. On the 10th of August I preached three sermons and confirmed twelve persons. From here I went to the mines, where there are already two nice churches, which have been erected this year through the generous contributions of the miners and the zealous endeavors of Father Fox. On the 17th of August Confirmation was given for the first time at Minnesota mine and twenty-seven children and adults received this holy sacrament. On the same day the church at Minnesota mine was dedicated to Almighty God and named St. Mary's, to the great satisfaction and joy of the multitudes who had come there.

"Thence I went to another mine, called the Norwich, where also a small, neat chapel had been built this summer. On the 24th of August I dedicated this church to Almighty God under the name of St. Francis Xavier. On the same Sunday I confirmed thirty-three persons. After these visitations I returned to Sault Ste. Marie."

On the first of November of that year (1856) we find an entry in his journal, in which he complains of his weak stomach and poor digestion; and on the 30th of December he says that during the foregoing night he had been quite deaf. And this is not to be wondered at. It is almost certain that he made the whole voyage, over 500 miles by the way he traveled, from Sault Ste. Marie to

Superior, in a birch canoe, or at least made a part of the journey in an open boat.

Moreover, at times he suffered great mental depression or sadness from various reasons, especially the bad conduct of some in his diocese. Here is one of his entries:

"Nov. 1, 1856. This is the third anniversary of my consecration; a very sad day. I might almost say: 'Dies ille vertatur in tenebras… obscurent eum tenebrae et umbrae mortis; occupet eum caligo et involvatur amaritudine.'"

"Dec, 15. A very cold night. Today I put fresh relics in my Pectoral-Cross. Yesterday and today I have again thoughts of resigning. Could I but know the will of God in this regard, I would soon be at ease and *determined* for one or the other side."

Thus we see that his elevation to the episcopacy increased his burdens. He had trials from without and trials from within. His deep sense of the awful responsibility resting on the episcopal dignity was a source of continual anxiety to him. It was this that gave him no rest, but urged him on to do all he possibly could for his people and his own soul's salvation. He felt indeed that the burden of the episcopacy is an "onus vel angelicis humeris formidandum," "a burden formidable even to the shoulders of an angel."

When at home he labored zealously and untiringly, performing all the duties of a simple priest, hearing confessions, attending sick-calls, instructing the little ones, and so forth. Thus on November 30th he made the following entry:

"Sunday; preached today in English, French, and Indian. I began Indian catechism, which I mean to continue all winter on Sundays. In the evening I was called across the river to Francois Grant, to whom Father… had been lately. Old Marie has received the last sacraments.

"Dec. 1st. This morning Father… related to me that the brother of Francois Grant had come to conduct him or me to his very sick brother; but Father… had said to him: 'Do you believe that the bishop will go to your brother's place at midnight?' And so the young man went away without calling me. As soon as I learned this I immediately carried the Blessed Sacrament to the sick man and gave him also Extreme Unction."

"Dec. 18. I instruct daily two small Indian boys, Louis and Charley, whom I began to instruct the day before yesterday and whom I shall instruct all winter, if they but come."

We have here the model bishop, a true pastor of souls. To him all are alike. The poor Indian boy is as dear to him as the son of a white millionaire. Like his divine Master, he regards in the child, not riches, earthly greatness, and nobility, but the immortal soul redeemed with the Blood of Jesus.

Chapter XLVIII

Happenings During 1857.—B. Baraga Makes His Annual Visit to the Principal Missions of His Diocese.—Interesting Communication of Hon. C. D. O'Brien.

As things were not going well at Mackinac and St. Ignace, B. Baraga determined to go there, although it was in the dead of winter and dreadfully cold. As all old settlers of the Northwest will remember, the winter of 1857 was terribly long and cold and the snow unusually deep. But B. Baraga heeded not the hardships of this winter's journey. It meant a hard voyage on snowshoes in the bitter cold of January for six days going and returning. But duty called and in such a case Baraga always obeyed. After three days traveling he arrived at his destination, where troubles and affronts were his portion. On Sunday, the 18th of January, he preached at Mackinac a sermon of reconciliation, whereby peace, at least for a time, was restored. Having accomplished his task he started, on the 20th, on his homeward journey. One night he was obliged to camp in the woods, when the thermometer registered 40 degrees below zero, and when he was in danger, as he states in his journal, of freezing his face.

On the 7th of March we find the following entry in his journal: "How beautiful and true are these verses:

> "With peaceful mind thy race of duty run;
> God nothing does, or suffers to be done.

> But what thou wouldst thyself, if thou couldst see
> Through all events of things as well as He."

On the 23d of April, 1857, he received the Papal Bulls, in which his church is designated: "Ecclesia Marianopolitana," and he himself is styled: "Episcopus Marianopolitanus."

On the 26th of May he set out from Sault Ste, Marie to visit the missions of the southern part of his diocese. In Garden Island he preached against the degrading vice of drunkenness and prevailed upon all the men to sign the temperance pledge. One after another he visited the stations along the shores of Lake Michigan, everywhere performing all the duties of a zealous bishop.

He then went to Detroit to look after the interests of his Indian schools. While there he assisted at the solemn dedication of St. Philipp's German church and the blessing of its bell. At the request of Bishop Lefevre, B. Baraga preached on this occasion in German and English, and on the following Sunday he delivered a German sermon at St. Joseph's church. He then returned home, where he arrived on the 15th of July. As usual, his stay was short. On the 20th of the same month he left to visit the western mission stations of his diocese. On the 23d he arrived at La Pointe, where he stayed four days with Father Van Paemel, and on Sunday confirmed twenty-four persons. It was on this trip that he brought Hon. Dillon O'Brien and his family to La Pointe to take charge of the school on the island. The writer had the honor of once meeting with Mr. O'Brien at Hudson, when the latter was there selling his interesting work, "The Daleys of Daleystown." His sons, who are able and much respected lawyers, reside in St. Paul, Minn.

On the 23d of August the bishop ordained Rev. Fr. Louis Sifferath, who was afterwards, for several years, stationed at Little Traverse, now Harbor Springs. He is the author of an Ottawa catechism, a copy of which is in our possession. In the same year (1857), on the 31st of October, Baraga ordained Rev. Patrick Bernard Murray.

We insert here in full the following most interesting communication of Hon. C. D. O'Brien, of St. Paul, as it will prove agreeable reading for many of our readers at the west end of Lake Superior. He says:

"I remember very well our arrival at La Pointe, although I had forgotten the precise day of the month until reminded of it by an extract from Bishop Baraga's diary. It was the 23d day of July, 1857, and I had come with my father and mother and the other members of the family, from Detroit, on the steamer Illinois, then commanded by Captain Wilson, who afterwards was drowned on the occasion of the sinking of the Lady Elgin. We arrived some time during the night or early in the morning, and went directly from the dock to the old church, being accompanied by Bishop Baraga. I remember that we waited there until daylight, and afterwards took possession of a house in the immediate vicinity where we lived during our residence on the island.

"My recollection of Bishop Baraga is rather indistinct. I remember him as a rather small, slender man, exceedingly reserved in his demeanor, and with a very sweet low voice. He was idolized by the Indians, the half-breeds and the old voyageus, among whom he had spent so many years, and each seemed to have an intense and personal affection for him.

"At the time we came to La Pointe, it was a busy, hustling little place. The dock was a large structure, furnishing the safest possible landing for all boats. It had upon it a large warehouse, and on the shore adjoining it, there extended along the lake shore, towards Pointe De Fret, quite a little row of houses; some occupied as stores, some as warehouses and others as cooper shops. There was quite a large building which was used as a hotel on the left hand side as you passed up from the dock, and on the right, another large one, or at least large as I recollect it, which was used as a store by Julius Austrian. Behind this building was a grass plot, and fronting on that, a long row of one-story houses which had been the offices of the American Fur Company. Behind this row of buildings was quite a large garden, surrounded by a high stockade fence, and in my time, that garden produced apples, cherries and currants, besides all the ordinary vegetables.

"Behind the garden was the old church, standing in the church yard where, at that time, the dead were buried on the surface of the ground, the coffin being laid upon the ground and surrounded by a little frame-work of logs, which was filled with sand from the lake shore. At a subsequent period Bishop Baraga required all the bodies to be interred in the ground. The schoolhouse stood in the church yard, and there must have been an average attendance of from twenty to forty pupils of both sexes.

"The town proper consisted of clusters of houses built on each side of a road-way running east and west, close to the lake shore, terminating on the west Pointe De Fret, and on the east at Middle Fort, which was either an episcopalian or a presbyterian mission, but at which no missionary was stationed during my time. Still farther to the east was what was called Old Fort, consisting of a clearing on the eastern side of the island, from which all of the buildings had been removed, but which had grown up to grass and second growth timber.

"There were about three or four white families on the island; the people were mostly half-breeds, the descendants of intermarriage between the old voyageurs and the Indian woman, and nearly all the men of middle or beyond middle life were Canadian French and had been voyageurs or *coureurs des bois*, and had evidently settled upon the island to pass their old age there with their families. In addition to the groups of houses at La Pointe proper and Middle Fort, there was a settlement upon the western side of the island, at a distance of one or two miles.

"The people were a most innocent, affectionate and happy people. They made their own boats and nets, and the barrels, half-barrels and quarter-barrels in which they packed their fish. During the winter they went out trapping. They raised potatoes and other root crops, and one or two of the white men occasionally raised wheat and oats, but very little of it. There were only two or three horses in the entire settlement, and one or two cows. In winter nearly all the hauling was done with dog teams; nearly every family owning from three to four dogs. These animals were fed upon fish heads taken from the fish in the fall, filled frozen into barrels and kept during the winter for dog food. During the entire time of my residence on the island I never knew of a case of larceny but one, and that was committed by a negro who had been left there by some steamboat. I remember the thrill of horror that went through the entire community at the idea of such a crime being committed. Drunkenness was rare.

"The great events were the arrival of the first steam boat in the spring. Payment time in the fall, when everybody went to Bad River on the Reservation to attend the payment. Christmas day, when we had midnight Mass, and New Year's day, when visits were exchanged, and everybody who had a house kept it open.

"In the spring and fall great flights of migratory birds used to light upon the island and were killed for food; in June pigeons were particularly numerous. The berry season included strawberries, raspberries and blueberries, and altogether the life, while perhaps monotonous, was of great simplicity and singular beauty.

"From the time navigation ceased until it opened, we were an isolated community. Provisions were stored and provided for in the fall, precisely as if one were going on a voyage, and the first boats used to bring small packages of meat and sausages in their ice-chests, which were sold to such of the inhabitants as could pay for them, and were considered rare delicacies.

"A more simple, hospitable, honest community could not exist anywhere, and there was an element of cheerfulness and good nature that permeated the entire community which I have never seen since.

"The old voyageurs were a singularly interesting class of men; uneducated, perhaps, but of a singular dignity of manner and speech and of the utmost morality; scrupulous in the performance of their duties both to God and man. On Sundays, in the little old church, the head of the family always sat with stately dignity on the outside of the pew, and while they indulged in chewing tobacco during the service to a very large extent, yet the habit was conducted in such a simple and dignified way that it ceased to surprise or annoy anybody. The choir in the church included four or five of these old men who sat within the chancel and sung the responses and all of the hymns. I can almost see them now, clad in their white surplices and red shirts, intoning with the utmost dignity all of the responses.

"Father Van Paemel was a most devoted missionary; a man of rigid and austere demeanor, but who devoted himself to the care of his people with an utter disregard of his own comfort. No matter what the distance might be, the condition of the weather, or the difficulties to be overcome, he instantly departed on a sick call, whether with a dog-team, on snowshoes, or in a boat, to penetrate any part of the wilderness where his services might be required. With him was associated for a short time Father Benoit, a French missionary, who, unable to endure the rigors of the climate, returned to France within a year or two. These were succeeded by Father Chebul, who is, I believe and hope, still living. Without the austerity of Father Van Paemel, Father Chebul was an ideal missionary, besides which he was an accomplished linguist. Three months after his arrival at La Pointe, he preached in French, Chippewa and English, having learned the latter two during the ninety days previous to the sermon. I have often been told by the voyageurs how in the winter time they have tracked him going to or coming from a distant sick call by the blood oozing through his moccasins where the snow-shoe strings had pressed upon his too tender feet.

"There were many stories extant among the people of Bishop Baraga, and of the many wonderful things which they said had been effected by his prayers; of his calmness in dangers and of his devotion to his people in the arduous duties of his diocese, traveling in summer by boat and canoe, and in winter with dog-teams and on snowshoes. There was one particular story they were fond of telling. It was, that on one occasion towards spring, Bishop Baraga was traveling with a guide along the shore of Lake Superior, and in crossing a wide bay at some distance from the shore, the ice suddenly parted, and he and his guide were being rapidly blown out into the open lake, where, of course, certain death awaited them. The guide, in a panic, threw himself at the feet of the bishop and besought absolution, but the bishop said to him, calmly, that he should repress his fears, that God would not permit a missionary on duty to a sick member of his flock who needed his ministration, to be cut off, and calmly kneeling on the ice proceeded to pray. The man then told how the wind veered around, blew the ice back to the shore, thus enabling them to regain it, when they found that instead of being in danger or delayed they had actually been forwarded on their journey by the movement of the ice.

"C. D. O'Brien"

Chapter XLIX

B. Baraga Attends the II. Provincial Council of Cincinnati and Has Three of His Indian Works Printed.—His Hardships on the Way.—He Visits the Missions of Lake Michigan and Lake Superior.

On the 12th of February, 1858, Bishop Baraga departed from Sault Ste. Marie to go overland to Toronto and thence by rail to Cincinnati. He had a twofold object in view. The first and main object was to attend the II. Provincial Council of Cincinnati, which opened on Sunday, the 2d of May, and ended on the following Sunday, May 9th. Another very important matter he had in view was the printing of his prayer book in both the Ottawa and Chippewa dialects and also of his Chippewa "Gagikwe-Masinaigan."

On this winter journey he suffered great hardships. For the first three days he traveled tolerably well in a sleigh, but on the 16th he was obliged to use an Indian dog-train, a "carriole," as they were called, drawn by three dogs. Wherever he stayed overnight he said night and morning prayers, in common with the family and others present, preached, baptized and performed his other priestly functions as circumstances might call for. Baraga was every inch a priest, and that at all times and everywhere. He never lost sight of his priestly dignity and seized upon every occasion to exercise his holy ministry for the instruction, edification, and salvation of those with whom he came in contact. What a lesson for priests!

From Jibaonaning B. Baraga traveled with some mail carriers to Pinatangwishing. A little beyond French River he stopped overnight in a very small house belonging to an Indian. On the 18th of February he has the following entry in his journal:

"From here to the lodges (wigwams) of some Indians, where I fared *a little better* than if I had lodged outdoors.

"Feb. 19. From here to the empty house of a mail carrier, *without door or window*, where I spent the night miserably on the 'carriole.'"

He finally arrived at Toronto, where he took the train to Buffalo and Cincinnati, arriving at the last named city on the 25th of February. At Cincinnati he lodged with F. Hammer, "where I will stay until my works shall have been printed." While at Cincinnati he received the joyful news that the "Ludwig Mission Society" of Munich, Bavaria, had sent him six hundred dollars for his diocese.

On Sunday, the 11th of April, he celebrated Pontifical High Mass at St. Mary's church, on which occasion he gave first holy Communion to the children, and in the afternoon he confirmed seventy-five children and adults in the same church. During all this time he was occupied superintending the printing of his Indian works, reading and correcting proofs, a difficult task, as printers of Indian works do not understand a word of what they are printing, and therefore are very liable to make mistakes.

B. Baraga also attended the II. Provincial Council of Cincinnati from the 2d to the 9th of May. We regret being unable to give any particulars of the part he took in the deliberations of said council.

Finally, on the 25th of May, after a sojourn of three months, he left Cincinnati to return to his Episcopal See. With a heart full of gratitude to God and his generous benefactors, he remarks that during his stay in Cincinnati he had received over four hundred dollars, a great help for his poor diocese, the missions of which were for the greater part among Indians, who contributed little or nothing towards the support of their missionaries.

On the 29th of May he arrived at Sault Ste. Marie, where he rested but a week, and then set out to visit the Indian missions of Lower Michigan in the southern part of his diocese. On Sunday, the 13th of June, he blessed F. Weikamp's church and cemetery at

Cross Village, preached twice that day in Indian and confirmed twenty-seven persons. The 15th and 16th he spent at Garden Island "in amaritudine cordis mei" on account of the universal prevalence of drinking on the part of the Indians there. After confirming thirty persons on the island, he returned to Cross Village. The next place he visited was Middle Village, where he preached twice to the Indians and confirmed eleven.

On the 22d of June he went to Cheboygan, where he heard confessions for two days in spite of the heat, which was so oppressive that the very candles on the altar melted. He then returned to Little Traverse, where, on Saturday, he heard confessions until almost midnight. On Sunday he preached two most pathetic sermons to his former parishioners and then heard confessions in great numbers; the following day he was also confined to his confessional until midnight. Thus the good people of this place, the "Arbre Croche" of former days, appreciated and spiritually utilized the presence of their father and bishop. Father Sifferath was then stationed there, whose goodness and humility Baraga extols in his journal.

RT. REV. IGNATIUS MRAK, D.D.

From Little Traverse he went to Eagletown (Grand Traverse), where he confirmed twenty persons. This mission and several others were under the care of Father, afterwards Bishop, Mrak, who has devoted a long and most useful life to the care of the poor Indians of Michigan. He is still alive and resides at Marquette, where the writer had the honor of forming his acquaintance some two years ago. He was then eighty-five years of age, almost fifty of which he had spent on the Indian missionary field. Notwithstanding his great age he was comparatively healthy and active. From him we gleaned many items of interest in regard to his saintly countryman, Bishop Baraga. It was there, also, we enjoyed the kind hospitality of our former classmate of the Salesianum, Rt. Rev. Bishop Vertin, of Marquette, who kindly loaned us B. Baraga's journal, from the pages of which we gather most of our information in regard to B. Baraga's episcopal activity.

RT. REV. JOHN VERTIN, D.D.

Sunday, the 11th of July, B. Baraga spent at "Cathead," where he preached four times that day in French and Indian. He then went to Mackinac, where, on the following Sunday, he confirmed forty-five persons. After his return to Sault Ste. Marie, on the 24th of the same month, he ordained Rev. P. V. Moyce, who, however, did not remain long in the diocese.

As was his custom, B. Baraga did not stay long at the "Sault." He may justly be called the itinerant bishop, for he was "always on the go." He had been at home but a few days when he left again to visit the western portion of his diocese. Fortunately, the writer has a letter of Baraga, written to the "Wahrheits-Freund," under date of October 24th, 1858, in which we find an interesting account of his trip. We will give it in full:

"*Most Respected Editor*—Please publish the following account in your valuable, widely circulated and much read paper, the 'Wahrheits-Freund.' It may be of interest to some of your readers.

"My mission diocese is divided into two parts. A part of it borders on Lake Michigan, which is south of my dwelling place, Sault Ste. Marie. The other is northwest of here on Lake Superior. The first part of the diocese I visited in the fore part of last summer and sent an account of said visit to your paper. The northwestern part I visited later on, and three days ago I returned from this missionary visitation.

"On the first of August I arrived at La Pointe. This mission is ever dear to me, because it was the first I founded at Lake Superior. On the 29th of July, 1835, I landed there for the first time and was received with great spiritual joy by the few Catholics who resided there at that time. To my great consolation I found much to do in instructing the catechumens, who flocked hither in great numbers, and the baptisms of converts were very numerous. At my present visitation I remained there twelve days, preached, baptized, and gave holy Confirmation. Thirty Indians were confirmed here.

"From La Pointe I went with the zealous missionary, Rev. Van Paemel, to Fond du Lac, a mission station, which I had also visited for the first time and founded in 1835. At my first visit there I had many baptisms and the same in my subsequent visits. On the 15th of August of this year I administered the sacrament of Confirmation, forty of my dear Indians being confirmed. This was the first Confirmation that ever took place in Fond du Lac. A person can imagine the feeling of a bishop, who, surrounded by these simple-hearted, faithful Christians, confers holy Confirmation in a mission, in which this holy and strength-giving sacrament had never before been administered.

"The next station I visited was Portage Lake, a mining station, the inhabitants consisting of Irish, Canadians, and many Germans. Rev. Father Jacker, of L'Anse, usually attends this mission. After I had preached in English, French and German, and given confirmation on the Sunday I spent there, which confirmation was also the first in this place, I made arrangements for the building of a church on the lot which had been bought for that purpose. I opened a subscription or collection, and I myself subscribed a sum of money, and in a short time, I might say, in a few moments, one hundred and thirty dollars were collected. We have at present a large school house, in which the missionary says Mass and preaches whenever he comes, but it is too small for the many Catholics who are here. I hope that we shall soon have a suitable church.

"The next mission I visited was L'Anse. This mission I founded in 1843 and I was missionary there for ten years. It is now under the spiritual care of Rev. Edward Jacker, who works hard in order to preserve the Indians already converted in a truly Christian life and to instruct them more and more in the Catholic religion, as also to bring pagans over to the holy church of God. Father Jacker deserves great credit for what he does for the mission school, which he teaches every day for from five to six hours.

"Some of my most consoling reminiscences are connected with this mission. When I enter the small, unpretentious missionary room, which the very zealous missionary, Edward Jacker, now occupies, I remember the many consolations and spiritual joys I enjoyed here when I saw how a deeply sunken band of Indians, entirely demoralized through drunkenness, had been changed into a congregation of fervent Christians through the powerful and beneficent influence of the holy word of the Cross, which God in His unfathomable mercy caused to be preached to them in their own expressive language. In this little room, too, I have labored much for Indian literature. It was here I composed the Indian Grammar and Dictionary and a comprehensive work for our missions.

"On Sunday, the 12th of September, I preached to the Indians in the morning and afternoon and conferred Confirmation on thirty of them, who had been prepared for this sacrament.

"Another mission station which gives me much consolation and spiritual joy is the mining station Minnesota. Here and in the surrounding mines is the largest congregation of Catholics in the whole diocese, Irish, Canadians or French from Canada, and especially many Germans. Here Rev. Martin Fox, a Prussian, works and labors with untiring zeal and wonderful perseverance.

He is the builder of three churches, two of which are remarkably beautiful and spacious. They are, it is true, built of wood, but inside they are plastered in such a manner that they look as if they had been constructed of solid masonry and ceiled. And the architectural style of these churches is so beautiful and symmetrical that it is a pleasure to look at them. The persevering zeal with which Rev. Father Fox labors, not only in building churches, but also in attending his various missions, deserves great praise. Although he is German, he speaks and preaches very fluently in English and French, and he is loved as much by the French and Irish as he is by the Germans. Forty-five persons were confirmed here.

"I next visited another mining station, where another German priest, Rev. Louis Thiele, labors with unflagging zeal, in word and indeed. He has several missions to attend, of which the most important are called Cliff Mine and Eagle Harbor. He always preaches in three languages, English, French, and German, because the people of his mission belong to those three nationalities. Rev. Thiele is already busy building two churches. The first one at Eagle Harbor is large and very beautiful, and as an addition to the church there is built a large and beautiful house for the missionary. He had great trouble to build such a beautiful and large church with the scanty means at his disposal. May God reward him in eternity! Rev. Thiele also exerts himself very much in converting Protestants. When I was at his place he again baptized four Protestants, English-speaking persons, whom he had previously properly instructed, and received them solemnly into the Church of God.

"The mines hitherto spoken of are copper mines. But we have also very productive and really inexhaustible iron mines. At Marquette is such an iron mine, and we have there a church and congregation, which is attended by a French priest, Rev. Duroc. He, too, has built a small church and parsonage. But as the church had become too small, he enlarged it last summer."

Thus the good bishop labored with tireless zeal for the "flock, over which the Holy Ghost had placed him as bishop to rule the Church of God, which He had acquired by His Blood." But he was not spared the bitter cup of sorrow, sadness, and interior desolation of spirit, with which God in His inscrutable wisdom tries His faithful servants from time to time. He had ordained a priest, whose sole object in entering the priesthood seems to have been "a large congregation with a big salary." Of course, B. Baraga never knew the man's disposition; for he would never have "imposed hands on him" had he known his sordid love of money. He gave to the unhappy priest his dimissorials, thus ridding the diocese of this hireling. But such occurrences deeply saddened the noble and sensitive heart of Baraga. Hence we find, under date of Nov. 1st, the following entry:

"Nov. 1. Fifth anniversary of my consecration. Sad! The past saddens me; the present torments me; the future fills me with uneasiness. *I would infinitely prefer to be an Indian missionary.*"

But he consoles himself with the reflection:

> "Look not mournfully into the past, it cannot return;
> Wisely improve the present, it is thine;
> Go forth to meet the shadowy future, without fear and with a manly heart."

Chapter L

Death of Rev. Lautischar.—B. Baraga Visits His Mission Stations.—Arrival of Father Chebul. Baraga's Opinion in Regard to the Feasibility of Forming Indian Priests and Sisters.—Interesting Reminiscences of Rev. Father Chebul About B. Baraga.

On the 1st of February, 1859, B. Baraga made the following entry in his journal:

" Today I received a number of letters; amongst others one from Rev. Pierz, with the sad news that the remarkably zealous missionary, Father Lautischar, had frozen to death on the night of the 3d of December on Red Lake."

Under date of the 23d of June, 1859, B. Baraga wrote as follows to the Leopoldine Society:

"A few days ago I returned from a missionary visitation journey and I hasten to send a short account thereof. I came back from this journey half sick and exhausted, for it was a trip full of hardships through all our Ottawa missions. On these missions one has either to go on foot from station to station or travel in a small canoe on the stormy Lake Michigan, a thing often dangerous. Such canoe voyages would be still more dangerous were not the Indians so skillful in the management of their canoes. On such journeys a person must sometimes pass the night on the shore of the lake, and the nights this spring were very cold.

"This spring I departed at the earliest opportunity I could find for Mackinac and St. Ignace, in order to begin my visitation. This opportunity, however, did not present itself before the 15th of May, because the ice remained in our St. Mary's river very late. When I arrived at those two mission stations, the people there, who depend principally upon fishing for their living, were already gone to their spring fishing. These poor people are employed by the whites to fish for them. Their employers furnish them with empty fish-kegs, nets, and salt and pay them from four to five dollars for every keg of fish they fill and salt down. Among these fishermen are many adults, who have not yet been confirmed, because they are never at hand when the bishop comes. The missionaries, therefore, told me that I should come in winter in order to find them at home. Hence I will be obliged to make a journey on foot with snowshoes from Sault Ste. Marie to Mackinac and St. Ignace in the first days of February, 1860.

"These winter journeys I find somewhat difficult now, for in the first place I am become unaccustomed to them, and secondly on account of my age, for by next February, if I live, I shall be in my sixty-third year. At that age, especially if a person has in former years suffered hardships, he is already a little stiff and feels the cold. Walking during the day goes tolerably well, but when one is obliged to camp out in the open air at night in the woods in this northern climate it is unpleasant. By reason of the tiresome walking on snowshoes over hills and through valleys a person is sweating all day, notwithstanding the cold, so that one's underclothes become wet. Then when he stands still in the evening, he soon feels terribly cold and begins to tremble as if he had the fever. If I could arrive at some house every evening on these winter journeys, traveling would not be so hard, but in this desolate country a man has often to walk several days before seeing a single house. Such is the lot of a missionary bishop, although I do not find it so hard because I have been a missionary in this wild country for so many years. The only thing that weighs on me is my advanced age.

"From the mission St. Ignace I went in a birch-canoe to the Indian village, Cross Village, where a noble German missionary of the Third Order of St. Francis, Rev. Seraphin Zorn, labors zealously among the Indians for the honor of God and their salvation.

He has learned the Indian language in a comparatively short time. This is an exclusively Indian mission. Mackinac and St. Ignace are mixed missions. In these two places there are Indians, half-breeds, Canadian-French, and Irish, but in Cross Village all are Indians.

"As soon as they saw the canoe coming from afar, they rang the church bell and all assembled. The schoolmaster, who is a Brother of the Third Order, came at the head of his school children, who carried two banners, the Indians following behind. They came down to the beach to receive their bishop. Then they all knelt down to receive the episcopal blessing, whereupon they accompanied me amidst the firing of guns and ringing of bells to the mission church, where, after a short address, I again gave them my blessing. That is in general the way the Indians everywhere receive their bishop. I always have much consolation in this mission, for the poor Indians there are good and very assiduous in attending church and their missionary is exemplary and zealous.

"From there I sailed to the Beaver Islands, which are situated in the middle of Lake Michigan, between Upper and Lower Michigan. Two of these islands are inhabited, one by Indians, the other by whites, who are for the most part Irish. When I first came to these missions only Indians lived on the islands, but some years ago the whites began to settle on large Beaver Island, and the very worst kind of whites, namely, the Turkishly inclined Mormons with their countless wives. In a short time there were over three hundred families of these horrible people there, and they carried on things in such a high-handed manner all over the beautiful island that no others could settle there. Besides their Mohammedan polygamy, they were a kind of pirates and thieves. They committed so many bad deeds that the neighboring towns, especially the inhabitants of Mackinac, united, hired a large steamboat, and with arms in their hands drove the thievish Mormons from Beaver Island.

"Now this large and beautiful island is inhabited almost entirely by Catholics, mostly Irish and some Germans and French. They earnestly long to have a church and priest in their midst. On the 22d of May, the fourth Sunday after Easter, I said holy Mass there in a large, spacious school house, and preached in English for the first time on this island, and after Mass confirmed twenty-four persons. They were all adults, with the exception of one boy; some of them were old men and women who had never before had an opportunity to see a bishop in their neighborhood. After divine service the women and children went out and I held a meeting with the men to deliberate where and how a church might be built on this island.

"Then I sailed over to the smaller Beaver Island, called Garden Island, which is inhabited by Indians, who are visited from time to time by Rev. Father Zorn. All these Indians are now Catholics and hold fast to the faith, notwithstanding the bad examples around them when the Mormons were living in their neighborhood. Thus far they had their old chapel, built of bark, but they are now on the point of building a decent church. It will be constructed from the most beautiful cedar I have ever seen, which is already hewn and ready to be used. Such a building made of cedar can last more than a century, provided the roof be repaired from time to time.

"Accompanied by the zealous missionary, Rev. Zorn, I visited two other mission stations, and on the 3d of June I arrived at Little Traverse, the former Arbre Croche. This was my first mission amongst the Indians, which I opened on the 28th of May, 1831. Here the Indians have a beautiful, spacious church, which they have built themselves. In fact, these Indians are already pretty well advanced in civilization. They are almost all carpenters and make their own boats. When I first came here the Indians had but birch-bark canoes. Now we do not see them anymore.

"At this visitation a thing occurred to me that had not yet happened in our Indian missions. A young Indian maiden of about 18 or 19 years, who, according to the testimony of the missionary, has led for years a pious life and gone often to holy Communion, came to me and entreated me earnestly to receive her in the Ursuline Convent at Sault Ste. Marie. I wondered at such a request from an Indian, because this nation only wishes for and respects the matrimonial state as the Hebrews and other nations of ancient times. In order to act with certainty I sent for her parents and questioned them in regard to their daughter. They stated that several young men had asked her to marry, but that she had not accepted any such proposal and that she intended to live single all her life. I asked her then, repeatedly whether she really wanted to leave all and enter a convent, and she declared that such was her sole wish. So I took her along and she was received as a novice in our Ursuline Convent. I wonder whether she will persevere."

From Baraga's journal we learn that the name of this pious young Indian maiden was Margaret Sagima, The bishop brought her to the Ursulines at the "Sault" on the 17th of June, 1859. In a few days she grew homesick, and already on the 26th of that same month he was obliged to send her home on the "Lady Elgin." In this connection he makes the following reflection in his journal:

"N. B.—One should never try to form a priest of an Indian man, or a Sister from an Indian woman."

The writer fully concurs with B. Baraga's views in this matter. The Indian, although ever so pious and well-meaning, is naturally too fickle-minded, too destitute of spirituality (we mean, naturally too gross, too sensual), and too much attached to his kindred to be ever fit for so sublime a calling as the sacerdotal or religious state. That we honestly believe to be the *rule*; there may be *exceptions*, of course.*

The bishop continues: "At Little Traverse Rev. Louis Sifferath is stationed as missionary. He is a conscientious, zealous, and pious German priest, who in a short time has learned the Indian language tolerably well and daily perfects himself in it. After I had visited two small Indian mission stations with Rev. Sifferath and preached everywhere to the Indians, I arrived, on the 9th of June, at Grand Traverse. This is the mission of Rev. Father Mrak, who has worked for many years as a zealous and enlightened missionary among the Indians. I was very agreeably surprised there when I saw how beautifully Father Mrak had repaired and beautified his church, both interiorly and exteriorly.

"On our return from Grand Traverse we were obliged to go ashore at night, which was stormy and cold. We spent the night sleeping on the beach. I had no blanket with me, but, fortunately, had my cloak. *I lay down on the cold sand and passed the night*

---

* The writer has fortunately learned of the actual existence of an Indian priest named Rev. M. T. Vincent, a *Huron*, of Lorrette, near Quebec, who said the Requiem Mass at the funeral of his Chief, Maurice Sebastian Ahgniolen, on the 30th of December, 1896. Ahgniolen had been grandchief of his people at Lorrette and a man highly esteemed by all, hence some of the most notable men of the Canadian government honored his funeral by their presence.

shivering with cold. Next morning I could scarcely speak and could hardly stand up; I had caught a bad cold.

"On the 17th of June I again arrived at Sault Ste. Marie, to my great joy and that of others. I shall remain here a couple of weeks and then undertake a new missionary journey to Lake Superior, which will last two months."

As he had intended, B. Baraga started from the "Sault" on the 29th of June, 1859, his sixty-second birthday, to visit his western missions. He arrived at L'Anse on the 2d of July and was much consoled at the flourishing condition of that Indian mission, always so dear to his heart. It had grown to such an extent that the church was too small to hold all the people on Sundays. He was still more consoled when he was assured by some pagans from Lac Vieux Desert (Gete-Kitigan) that they themselves and many of their relatives and acquaintances would come next summer to L'Anse and embrace the Catholic religion. The good bishop in the joy of his heart promised to come next year at an earlier date. He said he would stay with them longer to instruct the pagans, and would enlarge the church by one-half. He therefore respectfully petitioned the Leopoldine Society to assist him, as he could expect little pecuniary help from the Indians.

He next visited Eagle Harbor and Clark's Mine. This mine was worked by a syndicate of French capitalists of Paris, and all the miners in their employ were Catholics. This mission was attended by Rev. Thiele, of Eagle Harbor. The people were partly French-Canadians and partly Irish. Bishop Baraga asked the directors of this mine to let him build a small church there for the miners that the priest might no longer be under the necessity of saying Mass in a private house.

Having spent the Sunday at Eagle Harbor with Rev. Thiele, preaching and hearing confessions, he went with him to the celebrated Cliff Mine, out of which millions of dollars' worth of copper had been taken, and which yielded from 150 to 180 tons of the most beautiful pure copper monthly. In 1859 a large and beautiful church was built and completed. It was called St. Mary's church. A house was likewise built for the priest, whom they hoped soon to get. Thus far it had been attended every third Sunday from Eagle Harbor. B. Baraga contributed three hundred dollars and a bell that cost him one hundred and sixteen dollars to this church. The directors of this mine, although not Catholics, contributed one hundred dollars. B. Baraga was highly pleased with the people of that mission on account of their piety and great assiduity in attending divine service and receiving the holy sacraments. Every time the priest came he had large crowds of penitents for confession, and all that could do so attended Mass.

B. Baraga next visited Marquette, near which, he says, are rich and inexhaustible iron mines of a superior quality. These mines are located about fifteen miles from Marquette. A church was being built at the mine, while at "Little Marquette," as he calls the city, there was a small church in 1859, attended by Father Duroc.

From Marquette Baraga went on the "North Star" to La Pointe, where he arrived on the 23d of August. He preached there on Sunday in Chippewa, English and French, and confirmed seventeen persons.

B. Baraga also visited Portage Lake (Houghton) on the 29th of July, where there were five productive copper mines in close proximity. A church had been built there in the fore part of 1859, which B. Baraga blessed on the 31st of July, naming it after St. Ignatius, founder of the grand Jesuit Order, whose feast occurs on that day, and "whose spiritual sons," says he, "were and still are the greatest missionaries." He dedicated it with extraordinary solemnity, singing Pontifical High Mass, assisted by Revs. Thiele, Jacker, and O'Neil. In his fervor he preached on this solemn occasion in English, German and French. He left Rev. O'Neil there as the first resident priest.

After visiting several smaller missions, B. Baraga went to Minnesota Mine, "where the distinguished missionary, Rev. Martin Fox, labors with holy and untiring zeal. Besides his large congregation at Minnesota, which consists of Irish, German, and French, he has three other congregations to attend, which he visits from time to time. Besides a great holy zeal, God has given him a strong and enduring bodily constitution, which triumphs victoriously over hardships that would exhaust two ordinary priests. May the good God yet keep him long and reward his untiring labors."

On the 4th of September he blessed Father Fox's church.—"the largest and most beautiful in the diocese"— in honor of the holy Name of Mary. On this occasion "the beautiful organ, which

F. Fox had ordered from Buffalo, was heard for the first time. This is the *first real organ* throughout my poor diocese; for here in my cathedral, as well as in other churches, we have but organ-like instruments, called melodeons."

Under date of the 21st of September, 1859, we find the following entry in his journal:

"The thirty-sixth anniversary of my ordination. Deo gratias! The eighteenth anniversary of my meditating morning prayer. Deo gratias infinitas!"

The above entry as to his meditative morning prayer shows that he had already begun that holy practice of meditating at least one, oftener two, hours, when stationed at La Pointe. B. Baraga did what the Apostles said: "Nos autem orationi et verbo Dei instantes erimus"—"But we will give ourselves continually to prayer and to the ministry of the word."

On the 13th of October he writes:

"Rev. John Cebul (Chebul), who is intended for Minnesota Mine, arrived today, on his twenty-seventh birthday. He left for his destination on the "Mineral Rock" the next day."

Last spring Father Chebul related an anecdote connected with his arrival in Sault Ste. Marie, which illustrates the simple kind-heartedness and humility of Bishop Baraga. He went along with young Father Chebul to the steamboat, on which the latter was to depart. He had two satchels. B. Baraga took both of them to carry. Chebul remonstrated with him and tried with kindly violence to get them out of his hands. "Bishop," says he, "it does not look well for you, a bishop, to carry my satchels." "Never mind," says the bishop, "you must spare yourself; I am old and used to these things. I am bishop; you must obey."

He tells of another incident in the life of B. Baraga, showing his humility and mortification. When Father Chebul had charge of La Pointe it happened that the bishop stopped with him overnight in a room in the rear of the church. There was but one bed in the room. Father Chebul wanted his bishop to sleep in the bed, whilst he would help himself some other way for that night. But the bishop would on no account sleep in the bed, saying, "No! You must spare yourself; you must mind; I am the bishop." And so the good bishop lay down on the bare, uncarpeted floor with only a mat under his body and a cloak for a covering. He would not even accept a pillow.

On another occasion Bishop Baraga and Father Chebul were to go on some business to the Indian village Odanah, in the Bad River Reservation, a short distance from Ashland. "Bishop," says Chebul, "let me take Mr. Remillard along to help row the boat." (Theophile Remillard is today an octogenarian still living at La Pointe, where he has now resided for almost sixty years.) "No!" says the bishop; "Remillard is a poor man and must work to support his family." So they started with only a young man to row the boat, namely, Charles Haskins, who now resides at Ashland. The wind was against them and young Haskins made but slow headway against the waves, so that Father Chebul was obliged to take a pair of oars to help him. "Don't do that, Father Chebul," says the bishop. "Well," says Chebul, "if I don't row, the wind will drive us back to La Pointe." Finally the bishop acquiesced. "Father Chebul," says he, "forgive me for not having followed your advice." After they got to Chequamegon Point — Shagawamikong in Indian—they could proceed no farther, when all of a sudden F. Chebul thought of a rope he had stowed away in the prow of the boat. He then told Haskins to land, and tying one end of the rope to the boat, the young man was made to take the other end and draw the boat along walking on the beach, while F. Chebul himself acted as pilot; and so they proceeded to Odanah via Bad River, instead of going by way of the Kakagan, which would have been considerably nearer.

Father Chebul also tells this incident showing the judgment of God against the enemies of B. Baraga: A certain priest, whom charity forbids us to name, was giving great scandal through drinking, and his parishioners petitioned B. Baraga to remove him. The latter came to investigate the matter and suspended the unhappy priest. The priest had a few men of the parish on his side who took his part against the bishop. One of them came to intercede for the unhappy priest and spoke very disrespectfully to B. Baraga. In his excitement the man raised his hand in a threatening manner as if intending to strike the bishop. The same day the unhappy man lost his arm.

Even Protestants and men of no religion had great respect for Baraga. A certain man used to keep a stopping place and often secretly sold whisky to the Indians. Baraga, who often stopped at this house on his travels, would gently reprove him for his conduct, when he generally made some lame excuse, saying he only gave it to the Indians when sick, to cut the camphor, and so forth. Finally, however, he tired of the unpleasant, though gentle rebukes, of B. Baraga and meditated revenge. He knew that the bishop was fond of cake, and so he told his wife, who was a Catholic, but a very poor one, to make liquor-cake, which she did. Baraga ate of it in his simple, child-like way, surmising no harm. Then he said to B. Baraga, "You always reprimand me for giving liquor to the Indians, and you have yourself taken a pint of brandy in that cake." Baraga mildly answered, "I am sorry for you. I always took you for a gentleman—I am sorry." This mild rejoinder, this simple appeal to his better nature, pierced him as if a dagger had been thrust through his heart. He at once realized the meanness of the petty trick and fell on his knees, Protestant though he was, before Baraga and humbly asked his pardon. He afterwards perished on the "Sunbeam," which foundered in Lake Superior with all on board except one Canadian-Frenchman named Frajeau, who resided at Superior for many years and died there.

Although a little out of the chronological order, the writer wishes to relate another anecdote showing the high esteem in which B. Baraga was held by all classes. They looked upon him as the beau-ideal of a Christian gentleman. When B. Baraga visited Bayfield and La Pointe for the last time he was very feeble, and his hands would tremble, being partly paralyzed. Father Chebul accompanied him on the boat on the return voyage to Marquette. McK. was captain of the boat. At dinner B. Baraga tried to eat a little soup, but his hand trembled so much that he spilt most of the soup before the spoon reached his mouth. Captain McK. saw this. "Father Chebul," says he, "take my place at the head of the table!" Reluctantly F. Chebul obeyed, not knowing what the captain meant to do. Presently the captain went down to B. Baraga and, seating himself at his side, he fed the bishop with the spoon, holding the bishop's head with his other hand. This sight moved the passengers, especially the ladies, to tears, as the captain was otherwise a "rough-spoken man." They followed him out after dinner and thanked him in the name of humanity and Christianity for his kind act to Bishop Baraga.

Chapter LI

Doings and Happenings of B. Baraga During the Year 1860.—Great Miseries on His Winter Trip to Mackinac and St. Ignace.—He Visits Superior, La Pointe and Bad River Reservation. Interesting Entries from His Journal.

When B. Baraga visited Mackinac and St. Ignace, in the spring of 1859, the fishermen, mostly French-Canadians and half-breeds, were already gone to their fishing grounds, some seventy to eighty miles distant. He was told that he could find them at home only during winter. So he promised the Fathers in charge of those missions to come again during the following winter. This winter journey from Sault Ste. Marie to Mackinac generally took two and a half days going and the same length of time returning, and made it necessary to sleep out in the open air four nights.

Trusting in God's help, the Bishop set out on his journey on the 6th of February, 1860. He was accompanied by two men, who carried the necessary provisions and the blankets to sleep on at night. The weather was very cold. The bishop got a ride of three miles on a carriole, and then having put on his snowshoes he traveled quite a distance. It would have moved any compassionate soul to tears to see this feeble old man, with heavy snowshoes on his feet, drag himself along slowly following his half-breed guides, who walked ahead to pack down the snow a little. Now and then, at short intervals, the good men would stand still and look back to see whether their Father was following them. The poor bishop perspired freely, notwithstanding the great cold. They kept walking on through the virginal forest until noon, the walking being very fatiguing to the good bishop. At noon they kindled a fire and cooked tea, and this tea and a piece of bread was their dinner. After dinner they resumed their journey and by evening reached the wigwam of an Indian chief, they having traveled twenty miles that day. B. Baraga "passed the night passably well, thanks to his double blanket and the care of his guides." The wigwam was an old, abandoned one, *which was totally open on top and had no door.* The reader may imagine what a comfortable night Baraga spent in such a place after his hard day's travel.

The next morning he arose at four o'clock to say a part of his office before daybreak. On those winter journeys the breviary could be said only early in the morning and in the evening before going to sleep.

The next morning his traveling companions prepared a frugal breakfast, consisting of bread and tea, and such were all his meals on this journey. He traveled all day again on snowshoes, doing tolerably well, but towards evening he felt greatly fatigued, so much so that he could scarcely stand on his feet.

They halted and made preparations for camping. The guides shoveled the snow away a little with their snowshoes, then brought spruce boughs and spread them on the snow, and that was the bishop's bed for the night. Then they chopped some wood and made a large fire, for it was very cold under the open sky, especially as his underclothes were all wet from perspiration after his tiresome walk. Having said his office and taken his tea, Baraga lay down in the name of God on his cold bed and slept a little from time to time, with no roof over-head but the starry canopy of heaven.

Finally, the third day of his journey dawned. He was in hopes of reaching the mission of St. Ignace by noon, for he felt very tired. He remarks: "How old age has affected me! Formerly, when I was as yet a missionary at Lake Superior, I could travel continuously for weeks without feeling fatigued. Now a journey of two or three days tires me out."

Early in the morning, as soon as they could see sufficiently to walk, they started, and by half-past ten they emerged out of the forest, in which they had been traveling since they left the Sault, and arrived at Lake Huron, which was entirely covered with ice. From this point they could see the country about the mission of St. Ignace, from which they were still fifteen miles away.

They had walked but a short distance on the ice when a most welcome sight greeted their eyes. Over twenty tastefully decorated sleighs came from Point St. Ignace and Mackinac traveling with great speed to meet the bishop. The good people had learned the time of his intended arrival and so they set out in season to meet their beloved bishop and escort him in triumph to St. Ignace.

When they drove up they alighted from their sleighs, and, kneeling down on the ice, implored the episcopal benediction, which the good bishop gave them with a heart full of emotion. And now followed mutual salutations and acts of kindness. Everyone wished him to partake of the refreshments they had brought along, which was done by the weary travelers. Then all got on their sleighs, and swiftly traveled over the smooth ice towards St. Ignace, where they soon arrived. Father Piret rang the church bell, at which the people assembled in the church and received the episcopal blessing.

B. Baraga remained in St. Ignace eight days. All, both priest and people, were glad that the bishop had come, for on Sunday he confirmed ninety persons, whom he would never have found there in summer. In large dioceses the confirming of ninety persons is nothing extraordinary, but at that time and in that sparsely settled diocese such a number was considerable. Among the confirmed were several adults and old people. The good bishop thanked God for having enabled him to make that winter journey on foot in order to confer the holy Sacrament of Confirmation on those good people.

He appointed the following Wednesday, February 15, as the day of his arrival in Mackinac, six miles from Point St. Ignace. On that day nineteen sleighs, tastefully decorated, from Mackinac and St Ignace, met and conveyed him in triumph to Mackinac, where the zealous pastor, Rev. Father Murray, awaited him at the door of the church. The people assembled and received the episcopal benediction. He remained in Mackinac seven days, and on Sunday confirmed eighty-two persons, whom he would very likely not have found at home during spring or summer. On these two Sundays he preached in English, French and Indian, so that no one might go away without hearing the word of God in his native tongue.

On the 23d of February he started on his return home. The good people conveyed him again on the ice as far as where the trail entered the forest. On his return trip he had the same hardships and miseries to undergo as he had undergone before and which we have already described. After two days and two very cold and unpleasant nights he reached home on the 25th of February.

On the 11th of March we find the following entry in his journal:

"Sunday, Dom. III Quadr. A well-spent day, dies plenus, thanks be to God! Preached four times, English, French, Indian, French, and I believe that they were useful, practical sermons. Deo gratias!"

"March 12. Great grace! *Three full hours!* (he means three hours of consoling conversation with God in his 'meditative prayer'). A beautiful, sunny day, but very cold and windy—a real March day—sunny, cold, and windy."

On the 15th of April we find this expressive entry:

"Sunday. Great spiritual misfortune this morning! *Instead of rising at 3 o'clock, rose at 5 — two little hours absolutely lost!* Preached two sermons to empty pews. I think the church was never so empty as today. The mail expected for three weeks arrived at last."

We must bear in mind that these entries were not made with a view to publication. They are written in three or four languages. Often an Indian or Italian or French word or sentence will occur in the same entry. This shows they were intended to be strictly private. We publish occasionally one or another to give our readers an insight into the inner life of B. Baraga. The above-given entry speaks volumes. It discloses B. Baraga as a man of interior life, a man of meditation, even on Sundays, when there is so much work.

On May 1st B. Baraga left Sault Ste. Marie on the "Lady Elgin" to go to Portage Lake. On the first day they proceeded without hindrance, but at White Fish Point they came upon immense fields of ice extending on all sides as far as the eye could reach. They were detained in this sea of ice for twenty hours. At length the wind shifted and drove the ice out into the open lake, thus opening a channel for the boat. Such immense fields of ice are seen occasionally on Lake Superior even late in May, at times even in June.

The first mission Baraga visited was Portage Lake, or Houghton. There was a pretty large church at this place, which, however, had become too small on account of the constant influx of miners, a large percentage of whom were Catholics. Father Jacker subsequently became pastor of Portage Lake mission, and labored there for many years. The writer met him for the first time at Hancock, opposite Houghton, in the fall of 1881, and with him visited Father Terhorst at the mission of L'Anse, in the town of Baraga. The modern town of L'Anse, at the head of Keweenaw Bay, is not the site of B. Baraga's ancient mission. The latter is about two miles from Baraga, the county seat of Baraga County, and the postoffice of the mission is called Assinins, from an old Indian chief, who used to reside there in Baraga's time and who was of great assistance to him in compiling his celebrated Indian works.

As the church at Houghton was altogether too small, the people resolved to build a second church. This second church was built at Hancock.

B. Baraga then went to the "little city of Superior." The people were exceedingly glad to again see "a servant of God," for the pious and zealous missionary, Rev. Van Paemel, who used to attend this mission from La Pointe, became so sick in the fall of 1859 that he was unable to do any more missionary work and was obliged to return to his native country, Belgium, to recover, if possible, from his illness. The people of Superior, who were very affectionately attached to him, felt very sad when they saw him leave, the more so as they were obliged to be without a priest during the long winter, for the sick missionary departed on the last steamer. After that there was no more chance for a priest to go to La Pointe and Superior before May, when navigation again opened up. B. Baraga remained in Superior ten days, performing all the functions of a parish priest. He frequently spent the whole day in the confessional. He also blessed their marriages, baptized, and instructed the children and adults.

Thence he went to La Pointe, where he stayed ten days and performed all the duties of a simple priest. He remarks: "I was just in my element there and very much satisfied, for Indian missions are exactly my element. I baptized sixty-four persons, partly children and partly adults, in Superior and La Pointe. Only a few had died since the departure of the sick missionary. Thus the mission congregations steadily increase, whilst, on the other hand, the wild, unconverted Indians are dying away more and more."

To give an idea of B. Baraga's modus operandi on these Confirmation visitations we will give the entries, day after day, in his journal during his stay at Superior and La Pointe. They may prove interesting to many Catholics at the west end of Lake Superior.

"May 25, 1860. Arrived at La Pointe at noon, stopping scarcely fifteen minutes. The same also at Bayfield. I had no time to view the new church. I promised to return to La Pointe in about twelve or fourteen days, and remain there a couple of weeks. *In the evening arrived at sad Superior.*

May 26. I was at home all day waiting for people who came to visit me. No Confessions yet; probably they will not come till late at night. Very few came; I hope they will come during the week and next Sunday.

May 27. Pentecost Sunday. This morning were very few confessions, and so but few communions at the first Mass, which I said at half-past seven. At the second Mass there were still less, and but few people. Three short sermons at Mass and three again after Vespers.

May 28. Today I visited poor Mrs. Damè and heard her confession. She has a terrible cancer around her nose and mouth. Mr. Anglois gave me the "Recipe" for curing cancer.

May 29. Last night it stormed and rained fearfully. *Terrible streets in Superior!* Fortunately there are sidewalks almost everywhere, otherwise there would be no getting through in this weather. Brought holy Communion to Mrs. Damè.

May 30. There were many confessions today and many communions in the morning, as also many candidates for Confirmation to be instructed. In the afternoon I heard the confession of sick Mrs. Ryan. Misera afflicta humanitas!

May 31. A very beautiful day. Old May wants to coax us a little before he leaves us. Brought holy Communion to Mrs. Ryan. Thus far I have baptized ten children, but perhaps there are yet more to be baptized. Baptized another today.

June 1. June, my birth-month, begins nicely; we will see how he will behave hereafter. Many confessions. The people of Fond du Lac are beginning to come, some are even coming from the Indian Reservation.

June 2. An extraordinary day of work. Continual confessions and instructions for Baptism and Confirmation, also for first Communion.

June 3. *Sunday.* Today there were more people in church than on Pentecost Sunday, because they came from different places. A great working day; but, alas! only till 4 P. M., for then I had to leave. The "North Star" came sooner than expected. Twenty-two confirmations. Confirmed *all alone.*

June 4. Arrived at La Pointe at 1 A. M. Read Mass at 7, and then heard confession of sick Tchetchigwais. Had many confessions in the evening.

June 5. Brought holy Communion to Tchetchigwais very early in the morning; then said Mass, and then I set out for Bad River and arrived there in five hours. Stopped at Nawadjiwans, where I found a neat chapel upstairs. Immediately after my arrival I went to visit sick Wabado. In the evening, prayers and sermon.

June 6. Last night I did not sleep much on account of the mosquitoes and crying of babies. After Mass I carried the Blessed Sacrament to sick Wabado, to whom I also gave Extreme Unction. It rains terribly from time to time.

June 7. *Corpus Christi.* At 10 A. M. I had Mass and sermon, afterwards baptized two adults and four children. In the afternoon Vespers and sermon. Towards evening I called Nawadjiwans and made an arrangement with him for the upper story of his house.

June 8. Sailed from Bad River at 9 A. M. and arrived in La Pointe about 2 P. M. Soon afterwards I went to a sick half-breed, the son of Michael Basinet, and heard his confession. Then I went to Bayfield to Colonel Drew, who paid me two hundred and seventy-five dollars for Dillon O'Brien. Many confessions in the evening.

June 9. Great day of work. Heard confessions all day long and had some baptisms. I paid Nawadjiwans forty dollars for the upper part of his house, for a chapel.

June 10. Sunday. Extraordinary day of work! *From 4 o'clock in the morning till 10 o'clock at night I had work uninterruptedly; remarkably many confessions, five sermons, twenty-three baptisms, and three confirmations; the church was filled to its utmost capacity.*

June 11. Today there is not so much to do. In the afternoon I went to visit sick Dufaut and sick Chalut and heard their confessions. In the evening there were some confessions."

"After having performed all that was to be done at La Pointe, I went to the mining town of Minnesota, where Rev. Martin Fox is pastor. He has now finished his large and beautiful church and has such a large congregation of Germans, Irish, and French, that his church, which is the largest in the diocese, can scarcely hold two-thirds of his congregation. Many have to stand outdoors during divine service on Sundays. Luckily his church has three doors, so that the people, who stand outdoors, can see the priest at the altar and hear the sermon.

"Last winter there were two priests at Minnesota Mine, namely, Rev. Martin Fox and Rev. John Chebul, from Carniola (Krain), Diocese of Laibach. I sent Rev. Chebul, immediately after his arrival, to Minnesota Mine, in order to learn English and French. He devoted himself with so much earnestness and with such success to these two languages that he preached and heard confessions in English and French for the last three months. In less than six months he has learned (and that well) those two languages, of which, previously, he knew scarcely anything, at which we are all astonished, for such a thing was never known to us before. I have now sent him to La Pointe (in 1860), from which place he will attend Superior and other smaller missions. At Minnesota Mine he does not need to know Indian, but in his present mission he cannot do without it. I hope that, being stationed there and being so highly gifted with the faculty of learning languages, he will be able, within one year, to preach in the Indian language without an interpreter.

"Having visited these missions and provided for them, I returned to Sault Ste. Marie to attend to my correspondence, some of which called for a speedy answer."

B. Baraga made a second trip to the western end of our lake in 1860 on business affairs connected with these western missions. On the 4th of August he arrived in La Pointe, and the next day, which was a Sunday, he preached four short sermons in three languages. He praises Mr. Perinier for his work in beautifying the church. Next day he went over to Bayfield with Father Chebul and saw Hon. Henry M. Rice (Indian name, Wabi-Manomin), who promised to have a house built without delay for the priest, provided the latter would come to reside in Bayfield. B. Baraga gave his consent, and that very same day work on the parsonage was begun.

While at La Pointe, he was called to Odanah, Bad River Reservation, to attend sick Charlotte Haskins, and stayed in the village overnight. The family of Haskins have done much in times past for the missionaries who attended Bad River church, as it was with them the priest generally stopped. Edward Haskins still resides at the old place on the reserve. His brothers, Charles and William Haskins, and their sister, Charlotte, now reside in Ashland. May God reward them for all they have done in years past for the Fathers attending the Bad River Indian mission.

B. Baraga then went to L'Anse, where he found everything in good order. He had Mass there on the Feast of the Assumption, the church being crowded with Indian worshippers. Soon after we find him in Houghton, where, on Sunday, the 19th of August, he preached at early Mass in English and French, and again in English at late Mass, which was said by Rev. E. Jacker. The next day he went to the other side of Portage Lake to secure lots for a church. Having visited several other missions on Keweenaw Point, he returned home.

One of the happiest events of the year for the diocese of Sault Ste. Marie and Marquette and for the Indian mission was the ordination of Rev. Gerhard Terhorst, which took place on Sunday, December 23, 1860. He said his first holy Mass on Christmas day. The bishop adds, in recording these facts: "God grant that he may become a good missionary!" The bishop's prayer has been heard. Again: "May 21, 1861, Father Terhorst is preparing for his departure to L'Anse." The good Father has thus been laboring in this Indian mission since 1861, which is now over thirty-nine years. May God prolong the life of this zealous Indian missionary for many a year to come!

Chapter LII

Bishop Baraga Attends the III. Provincial Council of Cincinnati.—Hardships Endured on the Way Thither.—His Visit to the Scattered Missions of His Diocese.

In the winter B. Baraga had no communication with the outside world except by traveling long distances on snowshoes. Hence he was obliged to make all his episcopal visitations during the season of navigation as far as possible. However, in the early part of 1861 he was obliged to deviate from the rule above mentioned, as he wished to attend the III Provincial Council of Cincinnati, which opened on the 28th of April. As navigation at the Sault did not open much before the first of May, Baraga was obliged to go on foot all the way from Sault Ste. Marie to Alpena, at which place he could take a steamer.

He set out from the Sault immediately after Easter, walking on snowshoes all the way to Mackinac—a two and a half days' journey. From Mackinac to Alpena he traveled, partly on foot and partly on a dog sleigh, covering the distance in five days.

As the hardships of this journey, most probably, were the cause of B. Baraga's subsequent poor health and premature death, we will give some of the particulars, as gleaned from his journal.

"April 1, 1861. Easter Monday. Day of departure, at 10 A. M. Rode as far as Sobrero, then walked about twelve miles, partly on snowshoes, partly without them; then camped; a good night, not very cold.

April 2. Broke camp at 6; walked all day till about 5 P. M., with great hardship and much fatigue, then camped for the night in Fridette's hunting lodge.

April 3. Started about 5:30 A. M., and walked with great fatigue, without snowshoes, which were hurting me, until 1 P. M., when we came to the ice at Pine River. When half way across, Bellanger met me with his horses. I stopped overnight with him.

April 4. Rode away from Bellanger's at 6 A. M., and arrived at Mackinac at 7:30 A. M.

April 5. Departed from Mackinac at 8 A. M. with Theodore Wendell, riding, and about 12 o'clock arrived at Cheboygan, where we stayed overnight at the home of Jos. Allair, whose wife is a Burke.

April 6. Rode fourteen miles from Cheboygan with Lavigne's team, who on the way back fell into a crack in the ice and lost his life. Camped very comfortably that night.

April 7. Sunday. Unfortunately we could not keep this Sunday, but walked many miles, partly on good, partly on bad roads, until we came to a bad, abandoned shanty in the evening where we camped and where it smoked much, and there I said the *whole long office* de Dominica in Albis.

April 8. Walked again, but more on bad, than on good roads, until we arrived at Grand Lake, where we camped pretty well, for the night.

April 9. We started early in order to arrive at Thunder Bay, by night, if possible. The roads were bad and much water everywhere. Still we reached Alpena at about 1 P. M. with the help of God.

April 10. Have been feeling unwell for several days on account of constipation. Laid down the larger part of the day. Partook of a light breakfast, but had neither dinner or supper. In the evening Mr. Lockwood came and we talked about a place to build a church. He donated one lot, and I paid him forty dollars for another. So we will have a church in Alpena.

April 11. Am worse today than I was yesterday and have much pain. Remained in bed all day, and ate no dinner.

April 12. Am feeling miserable today, suffering severely. Partook of neither breakfast nor dinner. Remained in bed until 4 P. M. when I felt better.

April 18. This was one of the saddest days of my life. May God preserve me from such days! It is a gloomy day, snowing and storming fearfully."

The Bishop continues in his letter: "After I had stayed there some days a steamboat came along on which I went to Detroit:—and from there per train—to Cincinnati, to the III. Provincial Council which lasted from April 28 until May 5. At the conclusion of the Council I returned home and again took up my usual visitations to the missions. I generally commence with the Southern part of my extensive, but little settled diocese, but this year peculiar circumstances induced to begin with the Northern part."

As to Baraga's part in the deliberations of said Provincial Council we know nothing. He mentions that the 2d of May "was the commemoration of the deceased prelates and other clergymen. At 9 o'clock was Requiem, at which I preached. Dined at the Seminary."

"May 3. Wrote to the Central Direction of the Ludwig Mission Society in Bavaria, in the name of the Council."

The first missions B. Baraga visited after his return were Marquette and Negaunee, both of which were under the care of Rev. Duroc. As there was a church at the last-named place and there were many Catholics, the people asked for a resident priest, but the bishop could not comply with their request, having no one to send them.

In the meantime the bishop bought a house, that stood some miles away, had it taken down and transported to town and put up again, thus saving considerable expense.

From there he went to the Cliff Mine, where Rev. Andrew Andolschek was stationed. This zealous Father also had charge of Eagle Harbor, which he attended every other Sunday.

"In La Pointe," B. Baraga writes, "Father John Chebul is very active. God grant that he may not exhaust himself prematurely. He has a very extensive and difficult mission. Last winter he was called to a sick man, who lived ninety miles from La Pointe.* There was no other way to make the journey thither and back again than on snowshoes. It took him six days to go and he was obliged to sleep in the woods every night. As he did not know beforehand how far it was to the sick man's village he took provisions along for only three days. He had to eat very sparingly therefore and suffer hunger, besides enduring the hardships of the journey. He stayed at the place several days, instructed the Indians and half-breeds and baptized about thirty persons, mostly adults. He can teach catechism and preach pretty well in Indian. A gentleman who wrote an article about this mission-trip for a German newspaper, says, among other things: "Rev. Father Chebul belongs to the diocese of Sault Ste. Marie and we can but congratulate Rt. Rev. Baraga for obtaining such priests, who offer to God all their poverty and hardships and labors with apostolic love for the salvation of their flock."

Under date of November 11, 1861, B. Baraga writes: "It is now three months since I made my last report to the Leopoldine Society. Since then many things pleasing to a Christian have occurred in this diocese. I visited the southern part of this diocese, where our most important Indian missions are located. The population keeps continually increasing. Especially has the mission of Cross Village increased rapidly, so that its church is much too small. We therefore resolved, the last time we were there, to enlarge it considerably. I encouraged the Indians to work at it themselves, in order not to be obliged to hire high-priced carpenters. The Indians of this mission, who were converted a long time ago, can work well. They build their own houses and make their own boats.

---

* The bishop does not mention the name of the Indian village to which F. Chebul was called. Judging from the length of time it took him to make the journey thither—six days—it is highly probable that the village was Lac du Flambeau (Indian, Wasswaganing). That village is eighty miles by rail from Ashland and about one hundred from Bayfield, where F. Chebul then resided. In fact, he told the writer, about a year and a half ago, that he had been in Lac du Flambeau about the year 1862. He was called on a similar errand to Lac Courtes Oreilles (Indian, Ottawa-Sagaiganing) about the year 1865. It took but three days to make the journey thither. He was accompanied by George Roussain, a half-breed Indian, still living at Courtes Oreilles.

"In the neighboring village, Middle Village, they are also under the pleasing and consoling necessity of enlarging their church. The Indians belonging to this mission have shown themselves willing to do so. This coming winter they will make all necessary preparation for the work."

On Sunday, August, 25, B. Baraga gave holy Confirmation at Harbor Springs to twenty-six persons and preached twice that day to the Indians. On the 28th of the same month he arrived at Grand Traverse (Eagletown) at 7 P. M. *sick*. The next two days he was obliged to remain in bed. On the 31st he got up but still felt very weak. On September 1 we find the following entry:

"Sunday XV p. T. I still feel weak; however, I read Mass at 6:30 and preached at 10 o'clock and confirmed six persons. Did not preach in the afternoon."

Baraga founded a new mission and built a mission chapel on the so-called Sugar-Island in Sault Ste. Marie River, twenty miles from Sault Ste. Marie. There was a small settlement of Indians on the Island, some of whom were already baptized; the others were still pagans. In order to give them a better opportunity to become converted and obtain their eternal salvation, B. Baraga caused a small chapel to be built, which he dedicated to St. Joseph, on the 27th of October. The chapel was crowded with Christians and pagans. All rejoiced that in this desolate out-of-the-way Indian place there now stood a church.

He remained with those Indians almost three weeks, said Mass every morning and instructed them morning, noon, and evening. He had the certain hope that all the Indians of this place would be converted, and that perhaps other Indians would come and settle there so as to live near the church. He promised to visit them every month and to stay with them five or six days each time. He also recommended them to meet every Sunday in their church before and after noon, to say the rosary and sing pious hymns in their language; which they did.

This church, although small and built of wood, as were all his churches, nevertheless cost much money because carpenter wages were very high.

And now let us view B. Baraga in a new role, namely, that of *a carpenter* for his Indian mission. There are some of his entries:

"October 3, 1861. Made a tabernacle for St. Joseph's Indian Reserve.

October 4, 1861. Still working on tabernacle and began steps (on altar).

October 5, 1861. Finished steps today.

October 7, 1861. Made frames for altar cards, for St. Joseph's church.

October 8, 9, 10, 1861. Worked for St. Joseph's church.

October 11, 12, 1861. Made a nice small Baptismal casket.

October 14, 1861. Worked the whole day on frames for Stations.

October 15, 1861. Finished the frames for the XIV Stations.

October 16, 1861. Worked all day for St. Joseph's church.

October 18, 1861. Worked all day again and finished everything for St. Joseph's church.

October 19, 1861. Made some little articles for the church and mission of St. Joseph.

October 21, 1861. Packing things for transportation, for the interior of St. Joseph's church.

October 22, 1861. Day of departure. It was beautiful in the morning; it rained in the afternoon before we arrived at Payment's place, but nothing was damaged, thanks be to God! I stayed at Payment's overnight.

October 23, 1861. Said Mass at Payment's and then went to St. Joseph's Mission, where we happily arrived at noon. In the afternoon we arranged the altar, etc.

October 24, 25, 1861. Working continually in the church of St. Joseph—put up wood-shed.

October 26, 1861. The people worked on the wood-shed and carried in the wood. I ought to have gone to all the houses, but I went only to the chief, who, however, had not yet arrived. In the afternoon and evening I had a considerable number of confessions.

October 27, 1861. Sunday Dom. XXIII p. T. Mass at 10 o'clock and sermon. In the afternoon Stations and sermon. In the evening a long instruction.

October 28, 1861. Instructions after Mass on the precepts of the church again today. In the evening instructions. Every morning after Mass and every evening instructions."

We might add many entries of Baraga's journal, did we not fear to tire our readers. The above are sufficient to give them an idea of the restless activity of this saintly man. Praying, working, instructing, filled up his time. He seems to have had no time for amusements or relaxations of any kind. He continues in his letter to the Leopoldine Society:

"Next year, when I get a little money again, I intend to build another small church in an Indian settlement on St. Martin's Island in Lake Michigan, in order that the Indians there may embrace Christianity. Some of them have already expressed their desire to become converted, if only a missionary would come to them. Now, that is what I intend to do this winter, in order to build there a small church.

"Another benefit also comes from having churches in Indian villages, namely, the Indians assemble there on Sundays when no priest is with them, and pray and sing there."

Chapter LIII

B. Baraga Writes on the Civil War.—Establishes a New Indian Mission at St. Martin's Bay.—Visits the Mission at the "Baye Des Goulais".

In his letter to the Leopoldine Society, dated August 30, 1862, B. Baraga thus expresses himself on the civil war then raging:

"This year untold misery and oppressive want as to the necessaries of life prevail everywhere on account of the terrible civil war, which rages horribly in the interior of this once so happy and peaceable country. Thousands and hundreds of thousands of useful individuals, who were the support of their families, are torn away from their feeble parents, their helpless wives and children, and thousands of families are plunged into the most direful poverty. It is sad to hear wherever we go, lamentations and cries of misery. However, I must admit that there is less to be seen and heard of this misery in my out-of-the-way diocese than in the southern part of this country, the actual theatre of this most sad war."

In consequence of the many hardships and miseries endured during his seven day's journey on foot in April, 1861, his health was greatly impaired. Whenever he walked but a short distance even during the following summer he felt pain in his breast. He thought that his journeys on foot were at an end.

But in the beginning of the next winter, 1861-1862, he felt an urgent desire to visit and convert a band of Indians who lived three days journey from Sault Ste. Marie at St. Martin's Bay. He had never been there before as it was an out-of-the-way place and very difficult to reach. Considering the poor state of his health he entertained but slight hopes of reaching the Indian village. Still he would not give up all hope without making at least an attempt.

So he put on his snowshoes, took a guide and set out on his journey. Scarcely had he walked a mile when he felt such an oppression in his left chest that he thought he would have to fall down. Recommending himself to God, he continued to walk on. He could not endure the thought of giving up this attempt at converting those poor Indians. Thanks to God, the feeling of oppression on his chest gradually decreased and finely disappeared altogether. Although traveling for several days on very hard roads with heavy snowshoes on his feet, the old, feeble, but zealous missioner felt no evil effect from his journey. God strengthened His servant.

On the third day he arrived at the Indian settlement. After taking a much needed rest, he visited the poor people. He found them without any knowledge of God and of His Son, "Jesus Christ, whom He had sent." At first his words fell upon very poor soil, as the following entries in his journal show:

February 7, 1862. This afternoon at 2 P. M. I arrived at the Indian settlement. I lodged in the house of the "trois filles," which is neat and in proper order. I went to the old chief and spoke to him about religion, but he answered that in no case would he become a Christian.

February 8. I spoke to three young Indian women today about religion, but these poor creatures declared very plainly that they would not embrace religion.

February 9. Sunday, Dom. V. p. Ep. At ten o'clock I called the chief and as many as were willing to come to the house of the "trois filles" and spoke to them about the necessity of the Christian religion, but the chief emphatically declared that neither he nor any of his people would take religion.

These extracts from B. Baraga's journal show that the Indians of that place were stiff-necked heathens and that at least then he did not make many converts, "Crediderunt quot quot praeordinati erant ad vitam aeternam." It is not unlikely that these unhappy pagans had come in contact with bad whites and bad Indians professing Christianity. If so, it is not hard to explain their outspoken aversion to religion. The scandalous lives of some so-called Christian Indians is a great barrier to the conversion of their pagan countrymen. It is a sad fact that contact with the white race has always been detrimental to Indian conversion and morality.

But his visit to St. Martin's Bay was not entirely fruitless. The word of God penetrated the hearts of those obdurate pagans, almost against their will as it were. Some of them were converted and baptized, and the zealous missionary was in hope of gradually converting the entire village.

He also resolved to build a small church there, in order to have a suitable place to offer up Holy Mass, preach the Word of God, and teach catechism.

Scarcely had Baraga returned from this new mission, when he made preparations to visit another, formerly attended by the Jesuit Fathers stationed at the Sault and which was but one day's journey distant. On the day appointed he departed early in the morning and courageously made his journey on foot to the Indian village, located at "Baye des Goulais." At first he feared that the dreadful oppression in his breast might again appear, but, thanks to God, it did not. He walked all day over hills and through valleys. The Indians wondered when they saw their aged bishop coming to visit them and were much rejoiced. He spent many days with them, said Mass every day and instructed them. Many of them made their first Communion on this occasion. They were particularly pleased when he promised to have a little church built for them the next spring.

This promise was fulfilled during the following summer. B. Baraga bought a large quantity of lumber and other building material and had it shipped by boat to the Indian village. He then engaged two French carpenters who erected a neat little church in a short time. The whole outlay was but $252, from which the reader will readily conclude that it was not quite as large as St. Peter's Church at Rome.

"During summer," B. Baraga writes, "I made my visitations, partly on water, partly by land, or riding. Last spring I visited the missionaries stationed at the copper mines, who are all very active in the service of God for the salvation of souls entrusted to them. There is a lack of priests at the mines of Lake Superior. The mining towns are steadily growing, new churches are being built, and one priest frequently has to attend two or three churches and congregations, a thing often connected with many hardships on account of the distance of one church from another. Thus Rev. Edward Jacker attends two churches and the number of Catholics of both churches is about four thousand. A second priest would be very desirable so that each of these churches would have its own resident priest. Rev. Henry Louis Thiele also has two churches at a large distance from each other, each having a large congregation. Another of my priests, Rev. Martin Fox, has four churches and congregations to attend, which are far apart from each other. Nevertheless he endeavors, as much as possible, to give divine services to these different congregations on Sundays and holydays. How much I desire to give him an assistant, if I had one.

"In like manner Rev. John Chebul has four churches and congregations to attend, which are several days' journey from each other. He tries assiduously, as much as at all possible, to attend them, but in so doing he is ruining his health. It is my greatest desire to send one more missionary into those regions, could I but find one. It is, however, difficult to find suitable priests for this diocese; for in every mission-station of this diocese the knowledge of three or four languages is necessary, namely, English, French, German, and in some places, Indian. There are few priests who can speak so many languages well and fluently. Several missionaries, who could preach in different languages, were obliged to leave this diocese because the state of their health did not allow them to perform such arduous missionary duties any longer."

The good bishop's letter gives us but a very imperfect idea of his daily labors as bishop and Indian missionary. During the winter of 1860 and 1861 he was alone most of the time, without an assistant priest. During all that time he was obliged to perform the duties of an ordinary priest, attending not only to the people of the Sault, but also visit in outside missions. Every Sunday he said two Masses, generally preached two, often three, sermons in as many different languages, instructed the children in catechism, held Vespers or said the Stations. He was assiduous in visiting the sick and relieving the poor, in one word, become "all to all" to gain all unto Christ. He was as attentive to the spiritual wants of the poorest Indian child as he would be to those of any grown person, whether white or Indian. With him color or nationality or social position counted for nothing—the soul was all—everything else, nothing.

Chapter LIV

Bishop Baraga's Labors During the Year 1863.—Anecdotes About Bishops Baraga and Marty.

As our sources of information in regard to the latter years of B. Baraga are meagre, we prefer to give the letters, which he wrote to the Leopoldine Society, in full. Under date of August 4, 1863, he wrote from Cincinnati:

"Not earlier than yesterday did I receive the kind letter of the director of the Leopoldine Society dated June 11, 1863. I thank you for the charitable help of 1,000 florins for my diocese. As I am informed, the income of the Leopoldine Society is not very great and many applications for assistance had to remain unfilled. I return my sincerest thanks to all benefactors of our missions.

"I am at present in Cincinnati in order to attend to the printing of an Indian work. As everything is dear here, so also printing. The printing of an Indian book is particularly dear, as the printer does not understand a single word of it and hence asks more than for the printing of an English work.

"We now have sad times here, a horrible, all-destroying and desolating war. Things look very warlike and desolate in Cincinnati; everywhere are to be seen soldiers, cannons, etc. They are here to protect the city, because a hostile invasion is feared. I wish very much to be through with my work, so as to return to my distant and quiet diocese. There we see nothing of the war, except what we read about it in our daily papers.

In my diocese everything continues in its usual, quiet way. Churches and congregations keep on increasing, but unfortunately the number of my priests increases but slowly. We suffer much from the want of priests. Unless a priest have a little of the missionary spirit, he will not like to go so far north; such priests prefer to remain in the more civilized states. But the few that are in my diocese, *fifteen in number*, are, thanks be to God, good priests, faithful and zealous laborers in the vineyard of the Lord, and each of them has several stations to attend. Five of them are Indian missionaries and preach twice every Sunday in the Indian language, once in the morning and once in the afternoon. Poor Indian missionaries! It requires much patience and heroic self-sacrifice to spend one's life with the poor, simple, and naughty Indians.* May God reward them forever! I know the Indians. I have spent twenty-three years with them and I would be with them still, had not Providence called me elsewhere. However, I am not yet entirely free of the Indian and never will be as long as I live. In the Sault I have many Indians, who all come to me to confession, and whenever I go on my visitations I have Indian confessions to hear.

"In the northwestern part of these states the Indians have taken a great part in the disturbances which prevail here. Our Indians, however, were and are always quiet and peaceable."

"Since my last report," writes B. Baraga, December 29, 1863, "which I made from Cincinnati, where I was having a new edition of our Indian prayer book printed, I have traveled over almost all my diocese. Everything goes well, thanks be to God, and the number of Catholics is constantly increasing in our congregations and missions.

"My first visit was to Ontonagan, at Lake Superior, where Rev. Martin Fox is untiringly laboring. He is alone without any assistant priest and has four churches to attend, which are far distant from each other. Ontonagan is now renowned on account of its Ursuline Convent, which was built last year (1862) and which

---

* This is the first time B. Baraga speaks in a disparaging manner of his Indians, calling them "naughty." No doubt a great change had gradually come over many of his once fervent converts. The influx of whites, the numerous saloons in the mining towns and elsewhere were exercising a baneful influence upon the Indian converts and pagans. Whisky and money are the two great enemies of the red man.

is in good condition. It is the only convent in this poor diocese. Some years ago I had a convent of the same Order in Sault Ste. Marie, which unfortunately could not support itself, as the place is too poor. The Sisters could not obtain pupils enough and hence the Ven. Mother Superior determined to remove to Canada, where they received as many pupils as they can accommodate. Canada is almost entirely Catholic—not now anymore—especially in country places and small towns.

"The above-named convent in Ontonagan flourishes visibly under the blessing of God. It contains many Sisters within its walls, has thirty-two boarding scholars and a considerable day school. The Superioress of the convent is Ven. Mother Magdalen Stehlen, an experienced, prudent, and energetic woman of an undertaking spirit, who has introduced and arranged many useful things. Last summer she undertook a journey to Canada and obtained an increased number of members and other assistance. Next summer she intends going there again to promote thus the good and noble object she has in view.

"In the other congregations and stations everything continues in the usual way. The poor missionaries have indeed much to do, for their congregations are large and they are often obliged to travel long distances and that on bad roads, when they are called to the sick. They are always under the necessity of hearing confessions and preaching in three languages, English, French and German. They have an almost continual war to wage against the vice of drunkenness, which causes the greatest disorder and plunges whole families into misery.

"Our now Disunited States exhibit a very sad spectacle. It is now already the third year that this most pernicious civil war is raging. The North wants to subdue the South, which, however, does not allow itself to be subjugated, for it is too brave and fights with great enthusiasm for its cause. The whole country is being desolated and ruined. Already 700,000 men and youths, who were the support and bread-earners of their families, have been slaughtered in this horrible war by their brethren and fellow citizens, and countless useful citizens have become miserable cripples for life. Many of them had both legs or arms shot away, so that they are in the most helpless condition and cannot even take their own food. How many thousands of families have been reduced through this unhappy war to extreme poverty! How many have been reduced to beggary! How many poor orphans have lost their protectors and supporters, wander about without anyone to care for them and go, perhaps, to meet their eternal ruin! And what vandalic desolation has not come upon those States, which are the immediate theatre of this terrible war! Whole towns and cities have been burnt down, farms and plantations ruined and large fertile tracts of land entirely desolated! This unhappy land now owes many thousand millions of dollars and this debt increases two million every day during this war. This our country's debt will probably never be paid. We will hardly be able to pay the annual interest of these debts.

"The saddest thing is that no one can tell the end of this terrible war and that we have no prospect of an early peace.

"The South declares stubbornly and enthusiastically that it will accept no other conditions than the acknowledgment of its independence, and the North declares just as stubbornly that it will never acknowledge the independence of the South. What will come of this God alone knows.

Here in the distant North we do not feel exactly the immediate evils of this desolating civil war; only a great dearth of everything. Everything has risen in price terribly. For many things we must pay twice or three times as much as we used to formerly, and it is to be feared that these high prices will continue to rise."

We give the following anecdote of F. Terhorst, as it gives an insight into the kind-heartedness of B. Baraga:

One time B. Baraga visited Father Terhorst at L'Anse. An Indian, hearing that the bishop was there, came to see him. In the course of the conversation he said to the Bishop: "You spoilt the Indians; you gave them too much." The good bishop seemed to pay no great attention to what the Indian had said to him. When the latter had departed, B. Baraga said with much emotion betrayed in his voice: "Did you hear what he said to me? See, I have done everything for them, and now they tell me that I spoilt them." Then assuming a air of authority he said to F. Terhorst: "Don't you give them anything!" "Well, Your Grace," said the Father, "but sometimes it may be impossible to refuse them; they may be in great need of help." But the bishop insisted on his prohibition. While the two were thus conversing in the room, B.

Baraga looked out through the window and saw a poor Indian woman coming towards the house. "Oh, there comes that old begging woman again," he exclaimed, mentioning her name. She was admitted, of course, to see the bishop and F. Terhorst withdrew. In a few minutes the good bishop came into F. Terhorst's room and said: "Father, can you lend me three dollars to give to that poor woman? I will return the money." The Father gave the desired amount to his bishop, remarking: "You see, Bishop, that we cannot always carry out your instructions about not giving alms to the Indians. Sometimes it may be necessary to help them a little."

It seems that poor Indian women have the custom of going to their spiritual Father when in corporal need. This reminds the writer of a little incident that happened, we believe, to Bishop Marty some years ago. One day he was giving Confirmation in a Sioux mission where some Sisters had charge of the school. While the good bishop was preaching and praying and working in the church, one of the Sisters was preparing the dinner. A good old Indian woman was sitting in the kitchen eyeing eagerly the preparations for the grand episcopal dinner. The Sister took the pot of beans from the stove and put a nice roast into the oven. She had occasion to go out for a moment. When she came in again, what was her horror at seeing a hungry Indian dog running away with the roast whilst the poor old squaw was helping herself to the beans and digging her fist into the pot, at the same time innocently exclaiming: "How good the beans are which the good God gives to our Father!" When, after divine service, the bishop came in and was told by the disconsolate Sister how dreadfully his dinner had fared, he could not help laughing heartily at the ludicrous misfortune, and he dined minus roast and beans.

Chapter LV

Labors of B. Baraga in 1864.—Two Letters Dated Sept. 18 and Nov. 29, 1864.

Instead of giving mere abstracts from Bishop Baraga's few remaining letters to the Leopoldine Society, we prefer giving them in full.

"Since my last report many things have happened in these unhappy States (written Sept. 18, 1864). Our most destructive civil war continues raging more violently than ever. Our president does not want to hear of any proposals of peace and has lately ordered a conscription of half a million of soldiers. The whole country suffers in consequence; everything is twice and three times as dear as formerly and the whole country is being deprived of its most active and useful citizens. Our missionaries suffer very much as a matter of course. Everywhere they complain that many members of their congregations are being taken away, others fly to Canada for fear that they will be compelled to serve in the war.

This year a Provincial Council was to have been held at Cincinnati, but on account of the war disturbances the Archbishop of Cincinnati considered it advisable not to have it this year. I had gone as far as Detroit to attend the Council, when I was informed that there would be none this year.

"My first missionary visit this year I made to an entirely new place called Alpena, where not long ago a nice country town was started and where there are many Catholics. I spent six days in this place and said holy Mass on Sunday in a large school house. It was the first holy Mass ever said in this place and the people assisted at it with much devotion and feeling. After Mass I preached, and said among other things, that it would be desirable to have a church built there. In the afternoon we met again in order to deliberate about building a church. I bought a lot in the middle of the growing village for one hundred and fifty dollars and opened a subscription list to animate the people to contribute towards the new church. I subscribed one hundred dollars as my contribution, after which some subscribed ten dollars, others twenty dollars, forty dollars and fifty dollars. Even the Protestant population contributed liberally and now a nice church will built here, which, with God's assistance, will be completed next year.

"From Alpena I went to Beaver Island in Lake Michigan, on a small steamer, where I had established a mission thirty-two years before. Here the zealous missionary Father Murray labors. With great labor and much exertion he has built a pretty large church and a house for any priest that may be stationed there. He has accomplished much good since he came there. His principal care and endeavor is to combat the vice of intemperance amongst his people. For this purpose he established a temperance society, which many have joined. The Sunday I spent on Beaver Island I confirmed sixty persons and gave Holy Communion to one hundred and ten. Amongst the confirmed were some old people, who heretofore had had no opportunity to receive the Holy Sacrament of Confirmation. The first chance I had I left the island and returned home. I stayed there but a short time as I still had much traveling to do in this extensive and laborious diocese.

"I visited La Pointe, where I founded a mission thirty years ago and in which Rev. John Chebul labors with undaunted, praiseworthy zeal, at present. He has several missions to attend. The principal place is Bayfield, where the missionary generally resides. His mission is very laborious. He has four churches to attend, which are far distant from each other. I spent ten days in his mission and confirmed fifty-three persons, mostly Indians and half-breeds.

"From Bayfield I went to Ontonagan, where we have an Ursuline Convent, the only one in this poor diocese. It is in a flourishing condition, has fifteen Sisters and novices and about thirty boarding scholars; they have also a day school for outside pupils. Rev. Martin Fox, a German priest, is the confessor and director of this convent, whose active and prudent directorship gives assurance that the convent will be kept in good order. In addition to this convent and church to attend at Ontonagan, Rev. Father Fox has three other churches to attend far distant from each other. At present an assistant has been given to him, who relieves him considerably in the care of his extensive mission. I confirmed forty-two persons at Ontonagan this year. On the Sunday which I spent there I had a real missionary joy. There are, namely, in the neighborhood still some pagan Indians. As soon as they heard that I had arrived, some of them came to me and asked for Holy Baptism. I commenced at once to instruct them and on Sunday I baptized nine of them, mostly adults, for which I returned heartfelt thanks to God, for it is a long time since I baptized so many.

"I received much consolation and joy at Marquette, where Rev. Henry L. Thiele is now stationed. The church there is altogether too small to hold all the congregation. The wish to have a large new church had long ago become loudly manifested, but the former priest being advanced in years was lacking the necessary energy and determination for undertaking anything. But since Rev. Thiele, who has built already many churches, arrived there, and is actively developing his energies, everything is rapidly advancing and in a short time a beautiful, durable, and large church will stand there unto the great joy of his faithful congregation. The members of the congregation have contributed to the building of this new church, some fifty dollars, others one hundred dollars, others again one hundred and fifty dollars, and one gave even six hundred dollars."

In his letter of November 29, 1864, B. Baraga writes: "I have just returned from a two months' visitation amongst the Indian missions. First I visited the mission of Cross Village. I was very much pleased at the good progress this mission has made since my last visit. As the church was too small, the Indians determined to build an addition and fit it up. What they had resolved to do that they really did. They executed the work so beautifully and durably that no white carpenter could have done it better. It is true, the zealous missionary, Rev. Louis Sifferat, helped them at it considerably. In order to animate the Indians, who are naturally slothful, to work, he himself put his hands to the work and encouraged them more by example than by word to labor assiduously at enlarging their church. I remained until the following Sunday, on which I preached twice to the Indians and gave Confirmation.

"From there I went to Middle Village, another Indian mission, which is attended from Cross Village. There also the mission church is too small. Preparations are being made to build a larger one. I hope the work will soon be taken in hand. It is a pleasure to see how the Indian missions are growing, whereas the pagan Indians in the woods, who will not hear about conversion, are remarkably decreasing in numbers. I have often heard from my Indian guides on my former missionary journeys, when passing by places: "Here was once a large Indian village; now not a single Indian lives there, or only a couple of families, who eke out a miserable existence." On the other hand the Indians in the mission stations increase more and more and live happy and are satisfied.

"From Middle Village I went to the mission of Arbre Croche, which was my first Indian mission. Thirty-four years ago I began my missionary life here, which I have ever since continued, for I always consider myself a missionary. The Indians of this mission, especially the aged, are always happy to see their former missionary in their midst and I myself always feel very happy when I remember the many consolations I had in this mission, for then conversions were still very frequent and numerous. Whole families became converted and were baptized together, father, mother, and all their children. The missionary stationed at this mission, Rev. Seraphin Zorn, is incredibly zealous and active, so that I admonished him to moderate his zeal a little because he is in danger of prematurely sacrificing his health and precious life. He preaches every morning after Mass and often makes long journeys to visit and instruct the Indians that live at a distance. I conferred the Holy Sacrament of Confirmation here also and preached to the Indians, who likewise feel happy, when hearing their old missionary preach.

"From this mission I went to Grand Traverse, the mission of the aged missionary, Rev. Ignatius Mrak. He has been laboring in the Indian mission field for a long time and his ministerial labors are very hard, for besides Grand Traverse he has ten other smaller missions to attend, which he visits from time to time, and he has to preach in four different languages, Indian, English, French and German. To some of these stations he is obliged to go on foot and carry all things necessary for holding divine service in his satchel, to others he goes on horseback or in a boat. I went with him to some of these missions to administer holy Confirmation, but was often obliged to dismount from my horse and go on foot because I was afraid that the horse might fall down and injure me as the roads were uncommonly bad. I spent two weeks with this excellent missionary and conferred holy Confirmation at different stations on Sundays. I went with him to Carp River, where the good people built a small church, so that when the missionary comes he may there read Holy Mass and preach. I have blessed this little church to the joy of that Christian congregation. In like manner I blessed the spacious grave-yard, which the good people have fenced in. I would gladly have fulfilled the earnest wish of this good congregation to give them a resident priest, but unfortunately I am in want of priests. The Catholics of my diocese are increasing in numbers, but seldom do priests offer themselves to come to this distant and difficult diocese.

"From Carp River my way led me to Mackinac. This mission is very old, for Jesuit Fathers labored here as missionaries over two hundred years ago. At present this mission is without a priest, but the missionary at Point St. Ignace, Rev. Andrew Piret, comes here every other Sunday and attends the mission. I confirmed one hundred and twenty-three persons in these two missions, partly children, partly adults. From Mackinac I set out to return home, where I arrived on the 26th of November.

"Notwithstanding my advanced age I always feel very well, thanks be to God. I hope to serve the Lord in these missions for a long time. I am very well satisfied with my priests. They serve God zealously and uprightly and they willingly bear privations and hardships. I assist them as much as possible and I thank the Rev. Directors of the Leopoldine Society for the charitable help they annually give me. In regard to pecuniary matters I depend upon Europe; whatever I have, I receive from there. My diocese has no income whatever, not a farthing!"

Chapter LVI

Interesting Account of the Founding of the Sisters' School at L'Anse Mission.—B. Baraga's First and Last Dying Gift to the School.

We give the following account as we have it from the lips of Father Terhorst, the venerable pastor of the above named mission, a most zealous missionary who has devoted thirty-nine years to the religious, moral and social elevation of the Chippewa Indians of his mission. We hope that the Rev. Father will not be offended at the liberty we take of giving his most interesting narrative to the public for the honor of God and the edification of the reader.

Father Gerhard Terhorst, an Hanoverian by birth, was ordained by Bishop Baraga in 1860, and in the following year was appointed to succeed Rev. Edward Jacker as pastor of the L'Anse mission. The bishop told him to go there remarking that he had spent ten of the most pleasant years of his life there. At first F. Terhorst felt lonesome in his Indian mission and wished to leave. But B. Baraga encouraged him to stay and advised him to busy himself with manual work. Being entirely isolated from the society of the whites and confined exclusively to his Indians, the young Father soon learned to talk Chippewa fluently.

The government had appointed a certain Mr. D. as Indian teacher for the L'Anse Reservation. He was the father of seven children, but totally unfit to teach Indian children. F. Terhorst soon saw this and was determined to secure Sisters for his school. Mr. D. was, of course, highly displeased and in a letter complained of the father to B. Baraga. B. Baraga wrote to Terhorst not to molest Mr. D., advising him, at the same time, of the impracticability of having Sisters in L'Anse, as there were no means of supporting them. But F. Terhorst did not relinquish his idea. Mr. D. then tried to turn the Indians against him and made up a petition to have him removed. He endeavored to get the Indians to sign the petition, who, however, politely but firmly refused. So it was sent to Sault Ste. Marie without their signatures. The good bishop felt somewhat aggrieved at F. Terhorst and wrote to him: "I forbid you in virtue of holy obedience to speak against D. to have him removed." Next Sunday the Father told his Indians what the bishop had written to him, assuring them, however, that his sentiments in regard to this matter remained unchanged. "We are not allowed to *speak*," he told them, "but we can *think* about this matter."

Mr. D. finally realized that it was useless for him to stay. His school was a failure and but few children attended it, and he saw it would be the best thing for him to go. So, one day, he came to F. Terhorst and offered to leave, if the latter would buy his furniture, which he agreed to do. This left the school without a teacher, at least for the present.

Unexpectedly Sister Agatha, now Provincial of the St. Joseph Sisters of St. Louis, and Sister Julia came in a boat with Father Jacker from Hancock, Mich., to the L'Anse mission. Ven. Sister Agatha was well pleased with the place and said that they were willing to take charge of an Indian school. F. Terhorst was highly delighted at this hopeful prospect of securing good Sisters for his school. He told the Ven. Sister Agatha and her companion, Sister Julia, that he would inform them within two weeks of his decision in the matter, which of course, depended on the consent of Bishop Baraga. The bishop happened, soon after, to be at Hancock and the subject was broached to him. He answered, as usual, that he would be glad and willing to have the Sisters take charge of the L'Anse Indian school, but that he did not know how they were to be supported. F. Terhorst told the bishop that he had never asked him for a contribution nor did he expect any from him now; that all he wanted was his consent. This the bishop gave.

As Father Terhorst was about leaving the room, B. Baraga told him to wait a moment, when he forced upon him his silver watch as an offering for the school. At first the Father declined to take the poor bishop's watch, but the latter insisted, saying he had another at home. So Father Terhorst reluctantly accepted the gift. Going into another room where Fathers Jacker, Dwyer, and Sweeny were, he held up the watch saying: "What will you give me for the watch?" Father Sweeny offered $25.00 and the watch was his. This aid came very opportunely, as there was a freight charge of $23.00 due on the Sisters' baggage, which Father Terhorst would not have been able to pay had it not been for this providential donation of the good bishop. So the Sisters began their labors among the poor Indian children of L'Anse. F. Terhorst surrendered to them his own house and went to live in a room in the rear of the church.

Shortly after the Indian agent, Mr. S., arrived and was highly displeased at what he considered the Father's encroachment on his rights. "It is not the priest's business, but the agent's," said he, "to appoint a teacher for the school. I will send a teacher for the school."

The next day a great Indian council was convened across the bay at the Protestant mission. Father Terhorst instructed the headmen to stand by him firmly in this most important matter, and he gave them plainly to understand that unless they did so he would resign and leave at once. There were two theologians stopping with him at the time.

They went to the council out of curiosity, but Father Terhorst stayed at home.

When the council was opened the agent unfolded his plan, which was to remove the Sisters and appoint a teacher. At this the Indians grew fearfully excited, and shouting and brandishing their tomahawks, they told him it was their doings and their will that the Sisters were there and that they did not want to have them removed. The agent became greatly alarmed and his face grew pale as a sheet. He thought his last moment was come and that his scalp would be lifted off his head. Luckily, a good thought struck him, and he said: "We will let this matter about the school pass for the present. I will see Father Terhorst and we will arrange all things satisfactorily." The next day I called on Father Terhorst and said he was highly pleased to see the Sisters have charge of the school. And so no further attempts were made to disturb the school. The school was opened in 1866 and has been held ever since and has done incalculable good. At present (1895) it has sixty to seventy white orphans and forty-eight Indian boarding scholars and forty day scholars. All the buildings are large and solidly built of stone. Father Terhorst, although now an old man, enjoys comparative good health and superintends the school and mission with watchful care and fatherly kindness. He is every inch an Indian missionary, and woe to the man that dares to run down the Indian in his presence! God grant that his useful and self-sacrificing life may be prolonged for many a year!

From the lips of Father Terhorst we also have the following interesting anecdote. When B. Baraga was in his last sickness, only a few days before his death, F. Terhorst called on him. He inquired of the good Father how he was getting on with his school. F. Terhorst told him it was doing well. The bishop then pointed to a tin box on a library shelf and requested him to hand him the box, which was done. Then he asked him to take the key of the box from under his pillow and give it to him. With his weak, trembling hand the bishop opened the box and told Father Terhorst to take the money in it, which was twenty dollars. Upon F. Terhorst's remark that it was all the money he (the bishop) had, and that it was not right to take it, the sick prelate answered: "I don't need any more money— take it!" So to the last he showed his great esteem for Father Terhorst and his Indian school. He gave him the last money he had and died absolutely penniless.

Sister Julia, who is now at the Mother-House in St. Louis, Mo., gave the writer the following interesting statement as to the founding of the Indian boarding and day school at the L'Anse mission (Assinins P. O., Mich.):

"When in June, 1866, two Sisters of St. Joseph, Sister Agatha and Sister Julia, from the Mother-House of St. Louis, were sent by Rev. Mother St. John to see and negotiate with Bishop Baraga concerning the establishment of two Houses in his diocese, he could not sufficiently express his joy and satisfaction at the prospect of having good schools, wherein the little ones of his flock could be trained up in the fear and love of God; and when they told him that, if he so desired, they thought their Rev. Mother would also send a little colony to L'Anse to open a school for the numerous Indians, among whom he had labored for ten years, he could no longer contain himself, but wept tears of joy and gratitude.

"Three colonies subsequently left St. Louis for the following places and arrived there in the month of August of the same year, viz: St. Mary's at Sault Ste. Marie, St. Joseph's at Hancock, and St. Xavier's at L'Anse, and probably no one experienced greater joy than the saintly bishop, when told of the assured success of these three establishments. As long as he lived he proved himself their friend and benefactor."

Chapter LVII

Removal of the Episcopal See from Sault Ste. Marie to Marquette.

In the early part of 1865 B. Baraga was asked by some of his priests residing in the Upper Peninsula of Michigan to remove his episcopal see to a more central point of the diocese. One of these was Father Jacker, who was very intimate with his bishop, as their mutual correspondence discloses, and who was also very much beloved and respected by him. Under date of February 23, 1865, B. Baraga writes him as follows:

"I wrote to you lately that I would speak to you orally regarding the removal of my episcopal see. But I can tell you now very briefly my opinion in the matter...

"You say that my see in the Sault is out of the centre of the diocese. But that is not correct. You are thinking only on my northwestern missions at Lake Superior; but I have almost as many missions, though not so populous, in the southern part of my diocese at Lake Michigan: Alpena (where a large church is now being built), Point St. Ignace, Mackinac, Beaver Harbor, Cross Village, Little Traverse, Grand Traverse, with five or six missions. All these would complain and feel bad were I to remove my episcopal see to Lake Superior. An old Latin proverb says:

> "Si in qua sede sedes,
> Et tibi commoda sit ista sedes,
> In ista sede sede,
> Neque ab ea recede."

"We shall therefore continue sitting on our old seat until death takes us off from it.

"Your innermost loving Father in Christ,
                              "+Frederic."

It seems, however, that Father Jacker did not despair of being able to induce the bishop to change his mind. This appears from a letter of reply written to him from the Sault and dated October 26, 1865. B. Baraga writes him as follows:

"Your worthy letter of the 7th inst. unfortunately did not come to hand until today. Dear F. Jacker, your St. Scholastica Remedy has worked wonderfully! All of a sudden it came before the eyes of my mind that I am bound in conscience to remove the episcopal see to Lake Superior. I choose Marquette, first because of the name; 'Marquettensis' is more proper than 'Hancockensis.' Hancock was a heretic or perhaps an infidel; Pere Marquette was a saintly missionary 'cujus memoria in benedictione est.' Secondly, Marquette is a pleasant, quiet, and central place, with many means of communication... (My God, what is this? I can scarcely write any more; my right hand is lamed. O, do use the St. Scholastica Remedy for my right hand; otherwise I will soon be unable to write.")

A change of mind came over the good bishop later, as we see from his letter to Father Jacker, dated December 22, 1865:

"I know not whether your prayer continues to work or what. I had no peace of mind until I resolved to remove to Hancock. For a long time I was reluctant to do so; but it did not help. In Hancock I am in the midst of my missionaries and can have a Pontifical High Mass, a thing I could not have in Marquette, where I have but one assistant priest. And, moreover, all bishops, as we see, reside in the principal city of their respective diocese—Baltimore, New York, Boston, Philadelphia, Cincinnati, Chicago, Milwaukee, Detroit, etc. Now, Hancock is at least three times as large as Marquette, with Houghton nearby. My successor would blame me for having removed my episcopal see to a small place in preference to a larger one. In May, God willing, I will come and live in the house, which you have bought prophetically (?) in my name, and I shall build an addition to it. Is the long side or gable end towards the street? You may speak of it; it is no secret."

Still Hancock did not become the episcopal see, as B. Baraga had at last intended. "Man proposes, but God disposes." Rome spoke and that ended the matter. We have before us B. Baraga's letter to F. Jacker, dated Sault Ste. Marie, Mich., December 11, 1865:

"Rev. F. Jacker—The answer from Rome has arrived. The Holy Father allows me to remove my episcopal see to Marquette (not to Hancock), but I am to retain the former title, 'Marianopolitanus,' besides the new one 'Marquettensis.' Very curious. Such an answer I had not expected. I shall therefore remove to Marquette, but I will never use the two titles, except when writing to Rome. On all other occasions I will always write: Bishop of Upper Michigan."

In his two letters to the Leopoldine Society, dated Sault Ste. Marie, March 24, 1866, and Marquette, August 4, 1866, he speaks at greater length of the reasons impelling him to remove his See to Marquette. We will give both letters in full, *for they are the last letters he himself wrote to said society*. His two letters of 1867 to that society were written by Rev. F. Jacker, in his name, and over his signature, as he was then unable to write himself, his right hand being paralyzed.

"This time I have to inform the Leopoldine Society of an affair very important—at least to us here—namely, the transferring of my episcopal see from Sault Ste. Marie to Marquette, at Lake Superior. For several years my missionaries at Lake Superior asked me to come and live nearer to them, but I kept on postponing it. Finally, last fall I resolved to fulfill their wish and petitioned the Roman See for permission to do so, which request was granted without any difficulty. So, in the month of May, as soon as navigation opens, I shall remove to Marquette. "The reason of this removal is the greater facility of communicating with my missionaries. This place, Sault Ste. Marie, is an out-of-the-way place, with which during five months—from the end of November till the beginning of May—there is no communication possible except by traveling on foot with snowshoes. Navigation is impossible on account of the ice, and roads there are none here for horses. The letters we write during winter have to be carried by mail carriers, who are obliged to travel on snowshoes hundreds of miles through frightful forests before they come to a station whence a person can travel with a horse. When I write in winter to a missionary at Lake Superior I cannot expect an answer in less than two months. It takes one month for the letter to get to the missionary, and another month for the answer to come to me. And this will never get better here. They will never build wagon roads here on account of the horrible desolateness and poorness of the land and on account of the great distance from settled places.

"It is quite different now at Lake Superior. I say now, for ten or twelve years ago the Lake Superior country was as yet but little settled. At present public roads have been built everywhere, on which a person can travel and ride in summer as well as in winter. There are railroads there which are in operation, and others are being constructed. Hence I remove my episcopal see from this lonesome Sault Ste. Marie to Marquette, which is far more favored. I, therefore, request the Reverend Directors of the Leopoldine Society to direct hereafter their letters to me to Marquette, Lake Superior, Michigan.

"I do not know how the winter is in Europe; with us here it is extremely cold. The thermometer of Fahrenheit, which we use here, is generally 10, 20, 30 degrees below zero, and twice it sank even to 40 degrees. The French priest who is stationed here, and who in his youth was in Russia, says that even in Russia the thermometer does not sink to 40 degrees below zero.

"Our mission affairs go on prosperously, thanks be to God. The number of my missionaries increases and new churches are being built from time to time because the population in the country keeps on continually increasing. Our churches, it is true, are but of wood and small in comparison with churches of old countries, still they are houses of God and serve the same purpose for which large and magnificently built churches are constructed."

In his second letter of that same year, dated Marquette, Mich., August 4, B. Baraga writes:

"In my last report I mentioned that with the approbation of the Holy Roman See I had transferred my episcopal see from Sault Ste. Marie to Marquette, because communication is far more easy with Marquette than with Sault Ste. Marie, especially during winter. Marquette is named after one of the first and most zealous Jesuit missionaries of this country. It is a beautiful small city situated at Lake Superior; it is small as yet, but growing rapidly. This summer about forty houses are being built.

"The church in Marquette is a beautiful large building. It is the largest and most beautiful church in Upper Michigan, a veritable cathedral, which was begun last year and was completed this year. It has cost over twelve thousand dollars, which is very much for us in Upper Michigan. Unfortunately, it is not all paid for yet and there is still a heavy debt on it.

"From here I make my canonical visitations to the different mission stations at Lake Superior. This summer I have been almost continually traveling. Only from time to time do I return home for a few days to answer letters, of which I always find a great number on hand.

"Everything goes its usual way in the different missions. Things are everywhere arranged as in regular parishes, with the only difference that priests are obliged to preach and hear confessions in three or four different languages—English, German, French, and Indian—in order thus to satisfy all the hearers, who are people of different countries. In this very thing consists the greatest trouble of the priests of this diocese and it is with very great difficulty that the bishop can find priests who can speak these different languages.

"Thus far I have visited the white missions, but in a few days I will start on a journey to the Indian missions, which are still more interesting than those of the whites."

Chapter LVIII

Bishop Baraga's Last Sickness and Death.

Father Jacker, writing in the bishop's name to the Leopoldine Society, under date of January 28, 1867, says:

"Hitherto I enjoyed continually good health, but at the beginning of the Plenary Council of Baltimore a great sickness befell me, which still continues and renders me unfit for all business. A German paper has published the following account of my sickness:

"The Apostolic Delegate, Archbishop Spaulding, then took his seat on the platform before the altar and the Council was opened with the prescribed prayers and hymns, after which Rev. Dr. Keough, one of the secretaries, read the decrees of the Council. The archbishop then requested the people to pray for Rt. Rev. Bishop Baraga, who was lying very sick at St. Agnes' Hospital. Divine service concluded with giving the Apostolic Benediction. We regret to be obliged to state that Rt. Rev. Bishop Baraga, whose diocese embraces the Northern Peninsula of Michigan, besides the adjacent islands, was struck with apoplexy in the archiepiscopal residence and now lies in a critical condition at St. Agnes' Hospital. As we were informed, the Rt. Rev. Prelate was found unconscious in the corridor near the steps, and it is believed that he fell down some steps when he was struck with apoplexy. The episcopal cross has somewhat injured his breast. Several eminent physicians treat the Rev. Prelate. As he is a German (?) bishop and a reader and friend of our paper, we consider ourselves doubly obliged to ask the prayers of our readers for this pious man.'

"I feel continually yet the effects of the above-mentioned apoplectic stroke. I am not only unfit to write—it is only with great difficulty and after long exertion that I can scarcely sign my name—but I also feel myself unfit for all business. I hope, however, that it will be better next spring. At the Plenary Council a Coadjutor was given me, but it is yet undecided who it will be. Three names were sent to Rome, as usual, but the decision will not arrive before next summer.

"One of the most pleasing things I have to report in regard to the progress of religion at Lake Superior is this: that well-attended convent schools exist in five different places, namely, that of the Ursulines here in Marquette and Ontonagan, and those of St. Joseph Sisters at Sault Ste. Marie, Hancock, and L'Anse. The last-named Sisters have the advantage of instructing also boys to the age of twelve years. The introduction of Sisters at L'Anse contributed much towards promoting school attendance on the part of the Indian children. If the poor missionary residing there succeeds in keeping up this school for the mission, the greatest blessings are to be hoped therefrom. The number of Sisters at all the above-named places is about twenty-five. In three places the schools are supported by the respective congregation itself. For the Sisters at poor Sault Ste. Marie I have to contribute annually four hundred dollars. In addition to this I have considerable outlays for building repairs. The three Sisters at L'Anse receive a little from the government; the other expenses have to be paid by the poor missionary, who is supported by me."

In his letter of April 3, 1867, he writes: "The state of my health for the last six months remains unchanged unfortunately. I am so weak that I can scarcely speak so as to be understood, or move. I rise every morning and walk from time to time up and down in my room in order to lie easier in bed. When a person sees or hears me he would think that I could scarcely live a week longer. Yet I continue living and waiting for my successor, who is to come this summer.

"For the last four months I have been unable to say Mass; but I will use all my strength to read Mass on Holy Thursday and consecrate the Holy Oils.

"As to my diocese, all places are supplied with priests. There are now *twenty-one priests* in the diocese, and only then when new settlements spring up will there be need of more priests. What a difference between the present and the past, when the holy sacrifice had to be offered up for the most part in private houses. In the beginning of the diocese there were but two priests in the whole diocese, now there are twenty-one, and there are churches in all the larger settlements. Only in case new mines are discovered (and operated) will it be necessary to build more churches. Our churches are built at the expense of the respective congregations, nevertheless the bishop has to contribute the most of any. We are well supplied with schools, every congregation having one, which is kept either by Sisters or by secular teachers. Moreover, the missionaries have far less fatigues and hardships to endure than formerly, when the few priests that were here had to travel large distances on bad roads, now they do not need to travel so far; the roads are mostly good and almost everywhere there is an opportunity to travel by water and land…"

On the 28th of June, 1867, he wrote from Marquette:

"About two months ago I wrote last and spoke, among other things, about the state of my health. I mentioned that I needed some assistance, especially this year, because my moving from Sault Ste. Marie, my former episcopal see, was accompanied with many expenses, and because here in Marquette a heavy debt remains on the newly built cathedral, so that instead of drawing a revenue from it, as most bishops do from theirs, I am obliged to make considerable contributions towards paying the debts and procuring such things as are yet necessary… Moreover, my sickness has cost me much and does still every day. I have been so sick for nine months that I can neither read Mass nor say my breviary, nor scarcely speak, through weakness.

"The priest who has charge of this congregation labors hard, especially in instructing the children. Last Sunday was first communion of the children. The number of first communicants was about fifty. In order to prepare them well for so holy an act, the missionary not only instructed the children here—the boys and girls separately—but also visited once every week three settlements five miles from here, in order to gather together and instruct the children there. At the same time he had evening devotions every evening during Lent, at which he preached in different languages. Scarcely were the Lenten devotions ended, when he had May devotions and also daily devotions with sermon during the Octave of Corpus Christi.

"The church we have here is the most beautiful and the largest of the diocese; but it has cost much. The contract was made for eight thousand dollars; but, with the stone foundation, which was not included in the contract, and other additions and improvements, the whole amounts to fourteen thousand dollars... The creditors hold me liable (for the debt) and are pressing me for payment. I am thus in a very painful situation and ask most urgently for abundant assistance. This petition is very urgent, for I have never been in such a predicament before. Sick as I am, and to be continually pressed by creditors, whom I am unable to satisfy, this is sad indeed. I beg of you, therefore, most earnestly to help me in my need."

The same touching appeal for help resounds in Baraga's last letter (written for him by Father Jacker) of July 26:

"Last year about this time I received a check from you (the Leopoldine Society directors) through Messrs. Brauns & Co. This year I have as yet received nothing from Vienna. I entreat you most urgently not to abandon me in my need. I was never so much in need of help as just now. My sickness of ten months, of which I still suffer, and my old debts, which I cannot pay, make me truly unhappy. If I do not receive help this year from Vienna I do not know how it will go with me. I have still to govern the diocese; my successor will not come this year. He who was recommended *primo loco* has declined. Hence other names will have to be sent to Rome, in order that the Holy Father may choose among them.

"I beg of you once more very urgently not to abandon me this year."

We will give here the particulars of the death and burial of B. Baraga as we have them from the pen of Father Jacker:

"When I wrote the last time to the directors of the Leopoldine Society, at the request of Rt. Rev. Bishop Baraga, he was still able to sign the letter with a trembling hand. Now this hand rests in the grave!

"The long sickness of the beloved prelate, or rather the gradual decline of his vital force, which began to manifest itself very much some years ago, and which slowly brought him nearer and nearer to his blessed end, ended with a couple of weeks of great pain. Since New Year the pious sufferer spent most of his nights sleepless. In the night before Epiphany severe pains and difficulty of breathing came upon him, so that it was considered necessary to administer to him the Sacraments of the dying. This condition lasted several days. An apparent improvement of health followed, but it was only the forerunner of the gradual extinguishing of the vital force. Still the dying bishop retained the use of his mental faculties to his last moments, and even when his tongue was unable to articulate, he tried to make known his wishes and orders partly by writing, partly by signs, in which he succeeded in most instances, though only after great efforts.

"At two o'clock in the morning of the 19th of January, 1868, on which day the feast of the Holy Name of Jesus fell in that year, he exhaled his pure soul after an agony of only a few moments.

"The cold season of the year made it possible to postpone his solemn obsequies so long that at least some priests of the diocese were able to arrive in time to attend. On the 31st of January we buried our good Father in a vault constructed for that purpose in the basement of the cathedral. Only six priests were present. But the large church could not hold the crowds of people of Marquette and the surrounding country. Not only Catholics of different nationalities were present, but also the majority of the Protestant population, who by common agreement stopped all works on that day and vied with the flock of the deceased bishop in manifesting their appreciation of his great virtues and merits.*

"Thus ended a man whose purity of soul and singleness of purpose, whose mortified life and burning zeal, joined to uncommon talents and acquirements, faithfully and successfully employed in the service of God and of the most abandoned of his creatures; a man whose extraordinary achievements as a pioneer of Christianity will not allow his memory to pass away as long as

---

* The following Fathers attended Bishop Baraga's funeral: Jacker, Terhorst, Bourion, Duroc, Burns, and Vertin, now bishop of Marquette.

souls capable of appreciating so much virtue and excellence will live in this upper country, which has been the principal field of his labors, and where his body now rests to await the summons for resurrection."

The following inscription is engraved on the slab enclosing his grave:

I. H. S.

Hic Jacet Corpus III   ac Revd
Frederic Baraga D. D. Ottawa et
Chippewa Indianorum Apostoli I
Episcopi Marianopolitani et Marquettensis.
Natus die 29   Junii, 1797, in
Carniolia, Austria.   Ordinatus Presbyter
Labaci die 21   7   1823, Consecratus
Episcopus die 1 9 1853; Obiit die
19   Jannarii, 1868.

R. I. P.

Chapter LIX

Short Resume of the Life and Labors of Bishop Baraga; His Many Virtues and Accomplishments; A Model Student, Priest, Indian Missionary, and Bishop.

In the preceding pages we have endeavored to give a faithful, reliable account of the life and labors of saintly Bishop Baraga. We are informed by Bishop Vertin, of Marquette, a countryman of Baraga and the last ordained by him, that the inhabitants of Dobernik, B. Baraga's native place, intend to erect a monument this year, the centenary of his birth, to their distinguished countryman in the parish church, where he was baptized just one hundred years ago. We hope that this little work of ours will also serve as a centenary monument to this saintly missionary and bishop of the Northwest, a monument which will help to perpetuate the memory of his noble deeds and great virtues unto future generations.

B. Baraga had the unspeakable blessing of having had pious, God-fearing, thoroughly Catholic parents. Although he lost them at an early age, his mother dying when he was scarcely eleven years old, and his father four years later, still the lessons of piety, charity and other virtues they had taught him never became effaced from his mind.

At the University of Vienna and at the gymnasium and seminary of Laibach he was a model student, diligent, conscientious, faithful, and persevering. He was gifted with extraordinary talents, had a clear, logical mind, remarkable memory and great love for linguistic studies.

His progress in all branches of study was astonishing. At the same time he was a pure-minded, innocent, God-fearing youth, of whom we are morally certain that he retained the white garment of Baptismal innocence untarnished by any mortal sin to the day of his death.

As priest in Europe we find him a model of all sacerdotal virtues, laboring with all the zeal and energy of a true pastor of souls for the spiritual welfare of his people. He never knew what it was to be idle, lukewarm, or careless in the service of his divine Master. Old and young, sinners and just, all felt the effect of his burning zeal for the salvation of souls, all were attracted by his soul-stirring discourses and instructions, by his kind, sympathetic, winning ways to God and the practice of religion and virtue. Even at this early stage of his sacerdotal career we find him composing works of devotion and instruction for his Slavonian countrymen, which even to this day have retained their hold on the popular mind and heart.

As Indian missionary he was second to none in self-sacrificing labor and success as converter of Indians. He justly deserves to be called "The Indian Apostle of the Northwest." His converts are numbered by the thousands, not to speak of innumerable sinners, whom he won to God by his instructions in the pulpit and confessional, and by his books of piety. Only on the great day of judgment will all the good be known which he effected during his long and fruitful priestly and episcopal career.

As bishop we find him indefatigable in promoting the cause of religion and virtue in the extensive territory committed to his care, which for many years embraced not only the Upper Peninsula of Michigan, but also a great part of Lower Michigan, northern Wisconsin, eastern Minnesota, and parts of Ontario. Every year he visited almost all the missionary stations and congregations of this extensive territory, often suffering untold hardships and miseries, traveling in winter on snowshoes, sleeping under the open air or in some wretched Indian wigwam, shivering with cold, living on a little bread, cheese and tea. He never used stimulants of any kind, although often in sad need of them when exhausted by cold and long walks. He was a teetotaler of the strictest kind and preached temperance, teetotalism in his Indian works of instruction, knowing but too well that liquor is the Indian's greatest enemy.

B. Baraga was deeply humble. Of this we have abundant proofs in his life as described by us and in the unanimous testimony of all who were personally acquainted with him. Not long ago, we heard from Mr. Charles Belle Isle, a venerable octogenarian of Bellil Falls, Wis., the following touching incident, of which he himself was an eye witness. One day he and Mr. Charpentier, father of Alexie Charpentier, of Odanah, Wis., were walking in the streets of La Pointe with Father Baraga. This was in 1841. They met a pagan Indian, most probably accompanied by others of the same stamp. Without the least provocation, this man went up to Father Baraga and spat in his face. He then walked away, laughing derisively. Charpentier, fired with indignation at the insult offered to his beloved pastor, raised his hand to strike the impudent wretch and give him a well-merited beating; but Father Baraga restrained him, quietly saying: "Let him be; he doesn't know any better!" We are here forcibly reminded of the words of Jesus on the cross: "Father, forgive them, for they know not what they do." This Indian must have been one of the very worst sort, a fanatical pagan; for, as a rule, all Indians, even pagans, respect the Catholic priest. We would, therefore, not believe what was related to us were it not vouched for by Mr. Belle Isle, who was an eye witness of the deed.

Another proof of B. Baraga's great humility is found in the following letter of his to Father Jacker:

"SAULT STE. MARIE, Mich., May 16, 1863.
"*Rev. and Most Beloved Father Jacker*:

"Your most valuable letter of the 11th and 12th inst., in reply to my five letters, I have just now received. My much beloved Son in Christ, you are my greatest, almost my only, consolation in my multifarious sorrows and humiliations. Especially do I rejoice in the innermost of my heart at the heroic word, which I find today in your letter: 'Should I not live to see the time' (when, namely, your place can be supplied with other good priests) 'I must be satisfied even then.' Yes, truly, be perfectly satisfied with the arrangements of your bishop, which you can receive with all certainty as God's doings and you will work out your eternal salvation with the greatest certainty.

"Now I leave all to you; do as you like; you have my approbation and my weak blessing upon all (you may do). O, that I were a saint in order to give you a powerful blessing! I have never felt so much as now my poorness, unfitness, and insufficiency. However, I thank God for all these humiliations which He permits to befall me. 'Bonum mihi, Domine, quia humiliasti me!'

"It will please me exceedingly, dear Father Jacker, to see you here; but come soon, for later on I must go to Cincinnati to have some Indian books printed, of which there is everywhere a very great want...

"Your loving Father in Christ,
"+Frederic,
"Bishop."

No wonder that a man so humble and so deeply convinced of his weakness should feel so merciful and patient towards others, especially to poor sinners. His heart was like the Heart of Jesus, full of compassion for the weak and fallen. Witness his instructions to F. Jacker in regard to some unhappy members of his flock:

"Treat old M. as strictly as possible, but to expel him from the mission village would mean to deliver him to certain eternal ruin. Be glad in heart if he is willing to remain in the mission village, where a person can speak to him exhortingly from time to time."

Again: "In the meanwhile I advise you, in general, not readily, or never, to employ the means of expulsion from the church. On the contrary, one should invite just those, who live sinfully, to be sure to come always to church, when they are in the village, that they may hear religious instruction and be brought to a change of heart. Treat sinners with meekness (but not with laxity in confession). Thereby you will accomplish more than with down-casting banishment of the sinner. Yes, for the lion it may do to throw down and destroy all that is before him. Not so for the pastor under the good Upper-pastor, who went kindly after the lost sheep and did not cast it off."

As to B. Baraga's love of prayer and meditation we have spoken of it repeatedly in the foregoing pages. He was preeminently a man of prayer, spending every morning two or three hours in that holy exercise, and who rose long before daybreak to devote the silent hours of the early morning to communion with God. Even when walking all day through snow, ice, and cold, he would say his breviary before daylight and again after dark, by the light of a camp fire, though shivering with cold.

He was grave and dignified in his whole exterior, as all acquainted with him testify; the very picture of a refined, dignified, Christian gentleman. He was unobtrusive, kind, sympathetic and gentlemanly in his whole deportment and bearing. Although a man of vast learning and keen observation, he never paraded his knowledge in company or sought public applause. He loved to conduct divine service with all possible decorum and solemnity as it justly deserves and in order to make a salutary impression on the people.

He was very active, being always busy with some useful occupation. This is evidenced by his multitudinous correspondence and his literary works. His life might justly be described as sanctity in action.

He was highly mortified, never using stimulants or liquor of any kind, seldom, if ever, partaking of meat, and living on poor, plain food, bread, cheese, tea and the like. He was unmindful of ease and comfort and satisfied with poor lodging and food.

But it may be asked, Did not Bishop Baraga have any failings whatever? We answer, He had one; but that was rather a failing of the head than of the heart. It had its origin in his zeal and noble-heartedness. A close study of his diary or journal, which he kept for ten years of his episcopal life, shows that at times he acted rather hastily in ordaining, respectively, receiving priests into his diocese. Facts and names might be given, but it is unnecessary. Those very mistakes, however, are an evidence of his pastoral zeal, solicitude, and noble-heartedness. As the mines in Upper Michigan were rapidly being opened and worked, a strong tide of Catholic immigration set in, and in a few years there were thousands of Catholics, where, before, there had been but few. To provide his people with good priests was his great endeavor. For that reason he went to Europe shortly after his consecration; but of the five priests he brought along, perhaps not a single one remained long in his diocese. One of them, Father Lautischar, came in 1854, and left in 1858 for the Indian missions of Minnesota. Of the other four, one became a Redemptorist and one, it seems, apostatized. What became of the other two is not known to the writer.

As B. Baraga needed priests very urgently for the rapidly increasing population of his diocese, he gladly received priests, and ordained candidates for the priesthood without being sometimes sufficiently acquainted with them and their fitness for the pastoral charge. He meant well and always tried to do what was right, but at times his eagerness to provide for the spiritual wants of his people caused him to act rather precipitately. It was a mistake of the head, not of the heart; a lack of judgment and discretion. Such mistakes may and do happen to the holiest and best of men, for "to err is human."

Moreover, his noble-hearted disposition made him naturally inclined to form a good opinion of those with whom he came in contact. Hence it is not to be wondered at that sometimes he was cruelly deceived. This explains his occasional attacks of great sadness. Being imbued with a deep sense of his awful responsibility as bishop of a large diocese, and noticing the unpriestly conduct of one or another of his clergy, he felt keenly the great injury that such were doing to the cause of religion, and saw his own mistake in receiving or ordaining them. Hence his lamentable complaint: "Would that I could be an Indian missionary again! I would far sooner be an Indian missionary than a bishop." Hence the occasional remarks in his journal that he would like to resign, if he but knew that such was the will of God.

We are of the deepest conviction that Bishop Baraga was a man of uncommon holiness of life. His very shortcomings show that, although human and therefore liable to err, he was a most zealous pastor of souls, noble-hearted, but at times too confiding. If they are faults, they are those of a noble man and saint.

Bishop Baraga was a man of God, a priest according to the Heart of Jesus, a bishop of Apostolic virtue, a man full of the purest and strongest love of God and his neighbor. He lived but for one object, and that was to make God known and loved and served by all men as far as it could be effected by his influence and example. He deserves a foremost place in the ranks of our deceased prelates. His memory is held in benediction by the people of the Northwest, especially by those who had the happiness to be acquainted with him. This was shown particularly at his funeral, at which Protestants and Catholics vied with each other to show their respect, love and veneration for him. Michigan has perpetuated his memory by naming a county, town, and post office after him.

In the foregoing pages we have given but a mere outline of his life and deeds. Who can tell his many acts of charity and kindness to the poor and suffering? Who can relate the numberless hardships and miseries he endured in endeavoring to bring the light of faith to so many poor, despised, abandoned creatures, the pagan Indians of the Northwest, in order to save their immortal souls? Only on the day of judgment, when all things shall be brought to light, will it be known what this saintly man did and suffered for the love of God and the salvation of souls.

Let us hope that the day will come when his name will be enrolled in the catalogue of the Saints. Reports of wonderful cures circulate among the people. It is desirable that those upon whom such cures have been wrought, or who have certain knowledge of them, report the same to the proper ecclesiastical authority for investigation as to their truth and supernatural character.

We shall now give two such accounts as we have them from the lips of Ven. Mother Julia, of the Mother House of St. Joseph's Sisters in Carondelet, St. Louis, Mo.

A man working in the mines injured his knee so badly that it was thought his leg would have to be amputated. A priest told him to apply to his sore knee a piece of the candle which B. Baraga had held in his hand when dying, and to invoke him with great confidence, as he had always been so good and kind to the sick. The man did so and tied the piece of candle to his bandaged knee. The next day he was perfectly well.

A certain Mrs. W. had a dairy farm between Marquette and Negaunee. For a long time this woman had suffered from sore knees; the evil seemed incurable. One day she went to B. Baraga and asked the person who was doing the housework to let her have his old stockings. The latter told Mrs. W. that she could not give them without his permission. So she went to the bishop and told him about the woman's request. "Let her have the stockings," said the sick bishop. The afflicted woman put on the bishop's stockings and her ailment left her. About ten years after this occurrence, long after B. Baraga's death, someone stole from her, it seems, at night, a certain quantity of butter, which she had intended to sell in Marquette. In her anger and excitement she went to a fortune teller to ascertain from her who it was that had stolen her butter. No sooner had she done so than her old ailment returned as a just punishment for her sin.

With this we finish our life of saintly Bishop Baraga. May the many examples of virtue, which occur so abundantly in his holy and self-sacrificing life, animate us all to walk in his footsteps and to serve God in singleness of heart and purity of intention in that state of life in which Divine Providence has placed us.

To the Holy Catholic Church we unreservedly submit all and everything written on these pages, declaring that in applying the words, holy and saint, to Bishop Baraga, we do not wish to forestall any decision of the Church in this matter, nor do we ascribe any but human credence to any of the wonderful facts and cures narrated above.

FINIS

Bishop Baraga toward the end of his life.

Short Biographical Sketches

Of Missionaries Who Have Labored Amongst the Indians of the Northwest.

REV. FRANCIS PIERZ

REV. FRANCIS X. PIERZ

Rev. Francis Pierz (Slov. Pirec) was born near Kamnik, Carniola, Austria, of Slavonian parents, on the 21st of November, A. D. 1785. Little is known of his early years. He attended the town school of Kamnik conducted by Franciscans. After having attended school there for two or three years, he went to Laibach and entered the Gymnasium. Here he devoted himself to the study of his native tongue and French, besides the other branches of learning taught at said celebrated seat of learning. At the end of his classical course he graduated with special honors and entered the ecclesiastical seminary of Laibach, in which his celebrated countrymen and fellow laborers in the Indian missionary field, Rt. Rev. Fr. Baraga and Rt. Rev. Ig. Mrak, made their studies. By earnest study and fervent prayer Pierz prepared himself for the sublime dignity of the priesthood. Knowing the great utility of linguistic knowledge, he studied a great number of European languages, becoming very proficient in all of them. It is a notable fact that Slavonians and Poles, as a rule, possess linguistic talent in a remarkable degree.

In 1813 he was ordained by Bishop Kovacic and that same year assigned to the parish of Kranjska Gora as assistant priest. In this place he labored for seven years, at the end of which time he was made parish priest of Pecah, where he labored zealously and with much fruit for ten years.

Father Pierz took great interest in promoting not only the spiritual, but also the temporal well-being of his poor but pious people, who were mostly farmers. He was a great expert in gardening. Wherever he was stationed he cultivated a large garden full of the choicest vegetables, flowers, and fruits. He also published a work in Slavonian, entitled, "Kranjski Votnar," in which he explains the best method of successful gardening.

From Pecah he was removed to Podbrezje, where he labored most zealously for five years. Here he published two additional works on gardening. It was while here that the thought occurred to him of going to the Indian country. This resolution was awakened, or at least strengthened, in him by a letter he received about this time from his zealous and beloved countryman, Father Baraga, who was then stationed at St. Claire, Mich. Father Pierz was told, in words dictated by burning zeal, all the good he could accomplish in the wilderness of America, and how few there were to labor in that part of the Lord's vineyard. Baraga's words met with a sympathetic response on the part of his countryman. F. Pierz at once resigned his parish in order to devote the remainder of his days to the salvation of the poor, abandoned Indians.

Although fifty years of age, he set out on his journey to Vienna on the 16th of June, 1835. Thence he went to Havre de Grace, France, whence he took ship to America, and on the 18th of September of the above named year, he arrived at Detroit, where he was most cordially received by Bishop Rese. Being endowed with a poetic vein, F. Pierz composed a poem describing the many incidents of his long voyage on land and sea. Describing his first impressions and experience as Indian missionary, he wrote as follows:

"On the 16th of June (1835) I left my dear country, Carniola (Krain). After many dangers and sufferings I arrived, well-preserved and happy, in Detroit. The bishop received me in a fatherly manner. He told me to go to Lake Superior in order to act as assistant to Baraga in the place where that indefatigable missionary is stationed. The place was full of Indians. The season being too far advanced, and no traveling being done on the lake (Superior), I was obliged to stay at La Croix (Cross Village), where I have been working in the vineyard of the Lord for the last four months."

As we learn from a letter of Baraga, written about this time, F. Pierz was intended for Nagadjiwanang (Fond du Lac, Minn.). At a later period he visited that Indian mission and even began the erection of a church there, which, however, was never completed.

F. Pierz continues: "I soon became aware of the truth of all that had been written about this diocese (Detroit). All the priests I have met so far are real treasures of the holy church. This is especially true of F. Baraga, whom all, without exception, esteem most highly. These missionaries live in poverty, as the Apostles also did in the beginning of Christianity. The mission churches are built of logs; they are very plain, but neat. You can see in them only a poor altar, but pious Christians; only candlesticks of wood, but priests of gold. Nowhere in these churches can you notice outward ornaments or treasures, but exemplary Christianity, the spirit of the first Christians manifested in the manners and piety of the people.

"In La Croix I found about two hundred Catholics. With God's help I soon increased this number, through the conversion of Indian pagans. I hope to increase it so much in a short time that this place will become a missionary station. All the converts gained through the fruitful labors of our illustrious Dejean,

Baraga, and Senderl still live in their baptismal innocence. They were exceedingly glad to see me as their missionary and this the more so as they are but seldom visited by a priest. They were not idle, but made the best possible use of my visit to them.

"On the first Sunday of Advent I blessed their new little church. I preached in French and was in the confessional every day. Their pious eagerness for hearing the word of God and receiving the sacraments is untiring. Their esteem for the church, for their holy faith and its priests is beyond expression. I often admire their humility, purity, and love of their neighbor. They evince laudable eagerness for acquiring social customs and civilization. Many of my (Indian) pupils learned to read their Indian prayer book in four months. They all show great joy in attending divine service and they go to Mass regularly, even those who live far away from church. Mothers bring their little ones to be blessed. It is a great pleasure to live and labor among such Christians and a great joy to preach the Gospel to such hearers. The blessing of God is evidently to be seen. Tears of joy come to my eyes when at the daily Mass I give the Bread of the Angels to these devout Christians, or when, during instruction, I read in their red faces what the divine mercy is operating in their innocent hearts; above all, when through the Sacrament of Baptism I bring many a poor, lost sheep to the fold of Christ, and when I perceive how the kingdom of God is gaining ground amongst these inhabitants of the forest.

"Palm Sunday and Easter Sunday were days of great joy. I explained to them the blessing of the palms and what it meant. They all came to church with evergreen boughs of cedar, singing the antiphon: "Hosanna to the Son of David!" I thought these branches were indeed a most becoming sign of heartfelt piety, which alone is dear to the Lord.

"On Easter Sunday I wished to bless, as is customary, meat, bread, and other eatables, that they might have a joyful meal after so long a fast. They answered that they could not fulfill my wish, as they had neither meat nor bread, but only some potatoes and corn and a few fishes. 'But we wish,' they said, 'to receive the True Lamb of God and enjoy so much the more the Food of the soul.' In fact, on Easter Sunday nearly all received their Redeemer. The hopeful young men sang very beautifully during divine service. Those who had not received Holy Communion on Easter Sunday, did so on Easter Monday. Thus I live among the red-colored people very much satisfied. Indeed, I often enjoy more heartfelt pleasure and consolation than in all my twenty years' work in the old country.

"For this reason I praise Divine Providence and thank God that in His holy and fatherly keeping he brought me to the New World. I am often fatigued when performing the many onerous duties which are necessarily connected with my labors, still I am perfectly well and highly satisfied in this flourishing mission. I can exhibit it as a living example (of true Christianity) to my countrymen and other Christians in Europe. Indeed, at the last judgment, these children of the wilderness will put to shame many Christians who are tired of the teachings and consolations of our holy Church. On that account they neglect the supernatural helps of religion and desire only such things as satisfy their natural inclinations. They desecrate with gluttony, intemperance, and very often with impure pleasures, those holy days which remind us of the great mysteries."

By the end of 1836 La Croix (Cross Village) had grown so much that it was made a regular mission station and put in charge of F. Pierz. As the Indians of this place were obliged to leave their village and go to their hunting grounds to follow the chase, F. Pierz went to Sault Ste. Marie. This place was inhabited by pagan Indians and French-Canadians, many of whom were but nominal Catholics. They had not seen a priest for almost a year. The devoted missionary experienced much opposition from some non-Catholics, who disliked the presence of a Catholic clergyman in their midst. In the year 1838 F. Pierz founded two Catholic missions not far from Sault Ste. Marie on the northern shore of Lake Superior, namely, one at Michipicoton and the other at Okwamikissing.

About this time Bishop Rese appointed Very Rev. Frederic Baraga Vicar-General for that portion of his diocese situated in Wisconsin. The chief of the Indians at Kitchi Onigaming (Grand Portage, Minn.) asked F. Baraga to send a priest to his place, as all his people were desirous of Baptism. This was most joyful news to that saintly man. He at once wrote to F. Pierz, and the latter left Sault Ste. Marie and went to La Pointe, Wis., where Baraga was then stationed. After a few days' rest in La Pointe, Father Pierz embarked for Grand Portage, where he had the happiness of founding a flourishing Indian mission. Besides imparting to his good Indians oral instruction on the saving truths of religion, he devoted a great deal of time in trying to teach them how to read and write their own language, using for this purpose Baraga's Chippewa prayer book, the "Anamie-Masinaigan." In the fall of the same year, 1838, he established another Indian mission at Fort William, in the Province of Ontario, Canada. Then Vicar-General Baraga commissioned him to take charge of Arbre Croche and its dependencies left vacant by the departure of the Redemptorist, Father Sanderl, under whose able and zealous management the mission had been in a very flourishing condition. Speaking of the Indians of the North Shore and elsewhere under his care, he (F. Pierz) wrote, in 1838, to the Leopoldine Society as follows:

"During the three years I have spent among the Indians I have had many occasions in various places to notice the conduct and moral standing of both baptized and pagan Indians. I must say that they are good-natured, humble, and docile. They are always open to good and salutary influences. Even in their wild state, when not perverted by others, they live an innocent and pure life. When a missionary comes to them they listen to him with great attention and become good Christians. It is more difficult to convert those who have been victims of deception on the part of white people. By selling them whisky and other intoxicating liquors they make them most abominable wretches. Among no nation on the face of the earth will you find so few instances of theft, injustice, or infidelity as among Indians. Murders are very rare."

Though engrossed with the care of an extensive Indian mission, comprising many stations, F. Pierz did not forget his dear Slavonian countrymen in Europe. He continued to write articles for the "Agricultural Association" on all interesting topics relating to farming, gardening, inventions, etc. The society showed its appreciation of his services in the cause of agriculture by presenting him with a silver medal.

Another incident made him happy. At his request, and especially that of F. Baraga, another Slavonian priest left his country to devote himself to the Indian missions, namely, Father—afterwards

Bishop—Mrak, the worthy fellow laborer and successor of Bishop Baraga in the Episcopal See of Marquette. Bishop Mrak was born in Poljane, Carniola, Austria, on the 16th of October, 1810, and is thus at present 90 years of age. In the year 1859 B. Baraga made him Vicar-General for the Indian missions located in the Lower Peninsula of Michigan. Ten years later he became his successor in the See of Marquette. Like his illustrious countrymen, Baraga and Pierz, he has spent about forty or more years in the Indian mission field, and at present (1900) is chaplain at the Sisters' hospital in Marquette. We now have two Slavonian bishops in the United States, namely, Rt. Rev. Ig. Mrak and Rt. Rev. James Trobec, besides a great number of zealous Slavonian priests. All honor to their country!

In 1845 several government agents from Washington came to Michigan to examine the state of affairs amongst the Indians of the Northwest. They were most agreeably surprised at the progress made by the Catholic Indians in the arts and customs of civilized life. Many of these Indians were living in neat, comfortable houses and were skillful workmen. F. Pierz took the inspectors around in the Indian village and showed them everything of note. The latter were so well pleased with what they saw and noticed, that they made presents to the good, gray-haired priest for his Indians.

Like Baraga, F. Pierz was a strong advocate of temperance. The following incident will illustrate his success. On a certain occasion some fur-traders had brought a great many barrels of whisky into his mission. So strong, however, were the new converts in their dread and hatred of drunkenness that none of them would even touch a drop of liquor. Speaking of B. Baraga and F. Pierz, Hon. Maximilian Oertel, for many years editor of a German Catholic paper, says:

"If our president and his counselors would listen to the good advice which Father Pierz, Bishop Baraga, and other missionaries gave them, there would never be anything heard about Modocs and other Indians." By this he means that if our government had followed the advice of our Catholic missionaries, the Indians would never have risen in their savage fury and committed such outrages and horrible cruelties on the whites as they have done from time to time, especially in 1862, in Minnesota.

From 1838 to 1842 F. Pierz labored most zealously among the Indians, especially those of the North Shore, at Fort William, Grand Portage, and other places. From 1840 to 1852 he seems to have spent most of his time at Arbre Croche and its dependent missions. In 1848 the last named place had a population of 1,842 Catholic Indians. Besides this place, F. Pierz had charge of ten other missions. This was, however, too much for an old man of sixty years. Hence he requested his bishop to divide the missions between him and F. Mrak, which was done. In the twelve years which he had spent among the Ottawas he had established six flourishing missions and built as many churches.

In 1852 F. Pierz, at the earnest invitation of Bishop Cretin, of St. Paul, went to Minnesota to work at the conversion of the numerous Chippewas of that state. From time immemorial the Sioux and Chippewas have been inveterate enemies. Frequent encounters occurred between them, especially at the headwaters of the St. Croix and Mississippi rivers. For an interesting account of these Indian wars we refer the reader to the work of William Whipple Warren (a Chippewa half-breed born in La Pointe, Wis.), bearing the title, "History of the Odjibways," which forms volume five of the Minnesota Historical Society's collection. The work is well worth reading. It is much to be regretted that the gifted author died at the early age of twenty-eight.

Two great Indian missionaries devoted their lives to the conversion of these two powerful Indian nations, Father Ravoux, now of St. Paul, Minn., among the Sioux, and Father Pierz among the Chippewas. Under such circumstances their labors must naturally have been attended with many dangers and hardships.

The Council of Baltimore, in 1849, decreed that the large state of Minnesota be made a bishopric, with its episcopal see at St. Paul. In 1850 Very Rev. Joseph Cretin was appointed first bishop and consecrated January 26, 1851. He died February 22, 1857. At the end of 1852 there were but seven churches and ten priests in his extensive diocese. At present, 1900, there is one archbishop, three bishops, 430 priests, and 471 churches in Minnesota. What a change!

In 1852 five of the ten priests in the diocese of St. Paul were laboring among the whites and the other five among the Indians. There were then but 2,500 Catholics in the whole diocese. The number of Indians in the state at that time is put down at 50,000, which we are inclined to think is an exaggeration. These Indians were in every respect inferior to the Ottawas, being mostly all uncivilized pagans and addicted to intemperance and war.

When B. Cretin invited F. Pierz to labor in his diocese amongst his poor Indians, the latter, although weighed down with the load of sixty-seven years, accepted the good bishop's proposal and without delay betook himself to his new field of labor. In a very interesting Slavonian poem he describes the customs, habits, and peculiarities of the Chippewa Indians. This poem he sent to his friends in the old country. His mission took in a great part of Minnesota. He resided at Crow Wing and attended Mille Lacs, Leach Lake, Red Lake, Long Prairie, Belle Prairie, etc. The inhabitants were chiefly Indians, half-breeds, and French-Canadians; later on, Germans. It was in Belle Prairie that the present bishop of St. Cloud, Monsgr. James Trobec, first labored. F. Pierz worked with great zeal and success amongst his Indians. He also visited Nagadjiwanang (Fond du Lac, Minn.), where Fathers Baraga and Skolla had preached the Gospel and made many converts. Speaking of his labors at Crow Wing, Belle Prairie, and elsewhere, he writes:

"Last winter I gave daily instruction in the Christian doctrine to the Indians at Crow Wing. In the spring I attended the missions of the whites which belong to my district on the eastern shores of the Mississippi. French, Irish, and Germans are the predominant nationalities."

In the early part of June F. Pierz went to Methi (?) Sagaigan. He was obliged to travel through swamps and traverse lakes and rivers going thither. He declares that he never was so tired in all his life as on this journey. His cook and teacher were his sole companions. All three of them were obliged to carry heavy packs, containing their provisions, church utensils, etc., notwithstanding which they made twenty miles in eight hours. When they arrived at Lake Kegonoganika they found a canoe and with it traversed the lake. Towards the evening of the second day they arrived at their destination. This will give the reader some idea of the hardships this aged, Apostolic missionary had to endure in attending his many missions.

In a letter written in 1857 to his friend, Rev. M. Kristan, in Vace, Carniola, he says that, although being seventy years of age, he felt well and healthy. He had founded *ten new missions* during the last three years and built two Indian, two French, and six German churches near Sauk River. He gave the German missions to the Fathers of the Benedictine Order and the others to a French missionary. He was determined to devote the remainder of his life to the Indian mission. The next spring he intended to go north, from 400 to 600 miles, to the Chippewas at Red Lake. He went thither with F. Lautischar, and the latter was left there to continue the good work. He froze to death on Red Lake in 1858, and was buried at Crow Wing by F. Pierz Dec. 26th of that year. About four or five years ago his remains were brought to Duluth and buried there. Father—now Bishop—Trobec preached an eloquent sermon on this occasion. F. Pierz composed a beautiful poem on the virtues and noble qualities of his departed friend and assistant.

In January, 1864, Father Pierz went to Europe to procure pecuniary assistance and zealous priests for his many missions. He visited the principal cities of his native land, preaching in many places two and three times a day. He succeeded in securing a goodly number of priests and theologians for the American mission. We mention the following names: Very Rev. Jos. Buh, of Tower, Minn., Vicar-General of the diocese of Duluth, who has labored long and well among the Indians at Sandy Lake, Cass Lake, and Upper Mississippi; Rev. John Zuzek, Ignatius Tomazin, and Jas. Trobec, now bishop of St. Cloud. They came from the diocese of Laibach, Austria. From the diocese of Gorica were Rev. A. Plut, John Tomazevic, and Jas. Erlah. It was also on this occasion that the present occupant of the archiepiscopal see of Milwaukee, Most Rev. Frederic Xaver Katzer, came from Europe. The theologians, Stern, Spath, and Erlach came with him. In 1865 Fathers Buh and Zuzek aided Pierz in the missionary field. F. Buh labored at Winnibigoshish among the Chippewas, and Zuzek at Crow Wing. In June, 1865, Rev. Ig. Tomazin joined the ranks of the Indian missionaries of Minnesota.

They all went to St. Paul together to make their retreat, at the end of which Father Pierz celebrated his golden jubilee in the cathedral of St. Paul, and made a Latin address to the assembled Fathers.

In a letter to the bishop of Laibach he writes that on the 16th of August they saw a luminous cross in the sky of indescribable beauty. F. Tomazin was the first to notice it and pointed it out to Pierz. This wonderful cross shone for fully thirty minutes. "These signs," remarks F. Pierz, "are certainly not meteors or other fantastic phenomena. They are undoubtedly signs of divine mercy for the conversion of the Indians. Seeing these signs, mothers brought their little ones to be baptized. Even the adults willingly received the consolations of the Church."

As his health was beginning to fail, his many friends advised him to resign his mission, and an accident occurring at this time injured his health very much. On a journey to Sauk Centre the good old missionary, then eighty-four years old, fell out of the vehicle in which he was riding. He but slowly recovered from the effects of this accident, but, being gifted with a strong, good constitution, he gradually regained his former health. In 1870 we find him in Otter Tail still attending the neighboring missions. But now his sight began to fail. In a letter dated Rich Prairie, Jan. 20th, 1870, he complains that he had lost his sight to such an extent that he could not see to read newspapers. "In the eighty-seventh year of my age I fail visibly. The year before last I could still easily attend twelve missions and preach in French, German, and Indian."

In 1873 Father Pierz left for Europe to spend the remainder of his days with his dear friends in Carniola. For thirty-eight years he had labored amidst a thousand hardships and privations amongst the Ottawas and Chippewas of the Northwest. Considering that all this amazing labor was done by a man fifty years of age when entering upon his Apostolic career in the Indian missionary field, and that he continued therein uninterruptedly until his eighty-eighth year, we must say that his case can scarcely find a parallel in the missionary records of ancient or modern times.* The nearest

---

* Since writing the above we learn that Father Du Ranquet, S. J., came from France in the thirties, and has been among the Indians ever since—that is, for a period of over sixty years! All honor to this noble Indian missionary, of whom Bishop Baraga always speaks in terms of great respect in his journal. He is now stationed at Wickwemikong, Manitoulin Island.

approach to it is that of his worthy and zealous fellow missionary and countryman, Bishop Mrak, of Marquette, who is now (1900) ninety years old. Father Pierz's missions were given to Fathers Buh and Tomazin. At present almost all the Indian missions of Minnesota are in charge of the Benedictine Fathers.

On the third of September, 1873, F. Pierz left for Europe. Father Tomazin accompanied him. After a month's voyage they arrived at Laibach on the third of October. While sailing on the broad Atlantic, in his 88th year, F. Pierz composed a most interesting and touching poem, entitled, "Song on Bishop Baraga." The fact, as well as his many letters, reveal his deep love and veneration for saintly Baraga, whose many virtues he had learned to prize and imitate.

He made Kaninik, near which he had been born, his home for some time, staying there with the Franciscan Fathers. The year following he went to Laibach, where he died on the 22d of January, 1880, in his 94th year.

His funeral was conducted with great solemnity. The Bishop of Laibach, Msgr. J. K. Pogacar, with a great number of the clergy, the various societies and delegates from all parts of the country, came to pay their last tribute of respect to the man and priest, the pride and glory of Slavonia, and one of the greatest Indian missionaries of modern times. His dear friend, Canon Zupan, preached an eloquent funeral sermon on the labor and virtues of the deceased. Canon Zamejec made it his duty to collect voluntary contributions for erecting a suitable monument on the grave of the great missionary priest. However, Father Pierz has erected a monument more enduring than brass in the grateful hearts of thousands of devoted Catholics on both sides of the Atlantic.

On May 20, 1885, the Catholics of Stearns County, Minnesota, celebrated the centenary of Father Pierz's birth and the thirtieth year since his first holy Mass in that country. "What an astonishing difference between now and then," writes F. Bull. "In those days nothing was to be seen but roving bands of Indians, roaming from place to place without any fixed habitation. Now we behold beautiful churches and magnificent buildings on all sides where F. Pierz first planted the Cross."

But F. Pierz has another claim on the grateful remembrance of the people of Minnesota. He was not only a pioneer of religion, but also of civilization. He was an organizer and promoter of immigration. In his numerous letters published by the press he directed attention to the agricultural and other resources of Minnesota and thus induced many to make it their home. The German settlers of Minnesota have added millions to the national wealth by their industry and thrift.

REV. OTTO SKOLLA, O. S. F., St. Obs.

A Short Sketch of His Labors in the Missionary Field.

As Father Skolla succeeded Baraga in La Pointe, it seems but right that we should give a short account of his missionary labors. It is much to be regretted that nothing can be found about his parents, birthplace, or early years. In obedience to an order of Very Rev. Bernadine de Montefranco, Minister-General of the Franciscans from 1856 to 1862, he wrote a Latin account of his labors at Mackinac, La Pointe, Fond du Lac, Oconto River and Keshena, which was published in the Franciscan monthly, "La Palestina," in 1891. We have followed this account and his letters published in the "Berichte der Leopoldinen-Stiftung," Vienna.

Father Skolla was born in Dalmatia, Austria. He entered the Franciscan Order and belonged to that branch of it which was called "Of the Strict Observance." For some time he resided in a monastery of his order near the very place where the holy house of Nazareth had been deposited by angelic hands prior to its transportation to Loretto, Italy.

Even in his youth Skolla felt a great desire to labor at the salvation of souls as missionary. This desire increased by the frequent reading of mission accounts, especially of those written by F. Baraga. So, finally, he wrote to him to be admitted to labor with him at the conversion of the Indians. In the month of August, 1840, he received a letter from Baraga, in which the latter stated that the bishop of Detroit would receive him into his diocese to work among the Indians. This was happy news for F. Skolla.

He immediately asked his Provincial, Very Rev. Felician Rant, to grant him permission to devote himself to the Indian mission. After a due trial of his vocation the permission was given in writing. He then wrote to the Leopoldine Society of Vienna to kindly furnish him with the necessary traveling money. The directors of the society gave him 400 florins through the hands of the bishop of Laibach. Then he wrote to the Apostolic Nuntius in Vienna to obtain through his mediation the necessary dispensation from those points of his vows and rule, which were incompatible with Indian missionary life. The Nuntius sent this letter of F. Skolla, accompanied with his recommendation, to the Sacred Congregation de Propaganda Fide at Rome, which granted the dispensation.

After all these necessary preliminaries had been duly settled, F. Skolla took leave of his Franciscan brethren and went to Tergestum. After a few days he embarked on a merchant ship, called "Fallmouth," on the 24th of September, 1841. The ship soon encountered fearful storms. She sprang a leak and was often in great danger of foundering, as she was small and altogether unseaworthy. The sea voyage lasted three long months, during which time they encountered more than twenty severe storms. What made the voyage still more tedious was the circumstance that he had no countryman on board except a Pole, who was very unruly and once came near being killed by the captain of the vessel. Their food was very salty, and the water scarce, impure, and full of worms. Provisions also became low, as the voyage lasted unusually long on account of the many storms and contrary winds. Finally, on the 25th of December, 1841, Father Skolla landed at New York.

As soon as he had got ashore he inquired for the bishop's house, and, arriving there, presented his letters to the bishop. The latter directed him to F. Ivo Levitz, a countryman and a Franciscan of the same province to which Skolla had belonged. He stayed with him until spring, assisting him in the care of his large flock. F. Skolla preached his first sermon in the New World on New Year's day, 1842.

In the beginning of May he left New York, traveling for almost two weeks on the Erie Canal. About the 15th of May he arrived at Detroit, and was kindly received by Bishop Lefevre, who had but lately succeeded B. Rese, resigned. The kind-hearted bishop questioned Skolla as to the particulars of his journey, country, and plans for the future. He asked the bishop to let him go to F. Baraga, to act as his assistant, as had been agreed on between B. Rese, Baraga, and himself. The bishop, however, told him that he could not let him go there at present, as he had too few German priests in his diocese, but that he would allow him to go the next year.

Father Skolla, therefore, took charge of the German congregation of Detroit, which then numbered some 6,000 souls. He resided with the bishop. Besides the German, there were also an Irish and a French congregation in Detroit. The latter was in charge of Rev. Francis Vincent Badin, Vicar-General. The Cathedral congregation consisted then of French and Germans. The Germans had high Mass with sermon at 8 A.M., and the French at 10 A. M. Strict order was observed in the bishop's house. No one was allowed to go out without permission. Spiritual reading was held at table and prayers said in common every evening. The religious instruction of the German children at the parochial school devolved on F. Skolla, and we may be sure he did his duty well. He had, moreover, to attend some German and French missions, Cotrelville, Lake Plaisante, and Pontiac.

In June, 1843, F. Skolla was sent to Mackinac, whither he went, accompanied by his countryman, Father Pierz. From Mackinac they went in a birch canoe to Arbre Croche (Harbor Springs). The following Sunday Skolla preached in French, and his sermon was interpreted into Ottawa by an interpreter. Towards the end of July he returned to Mackinac, where he was most joyfully received by the people of the island. He estimates the population, most of whom were French-Canadians and half-breeds, at two thousand souls. The Catholic soldiers at the fort used to attend holy Mass regularly and F. Skolla would preach to them a short English sermon, as his knowledge of the English language must have been very limited as yet. In 1845 the soldiers left to take part in the Mexican war. During his stay of two years at Mackinac he baptized more than forty pagan Indians.

In the beginning of autumn, 1845, B. Lefevre came to Mackinac and gave confirmation to a great number of adults and children. On this occasion he gave permission to Father Skolla to go to L'Anse to labor with F. Baraga in the Indian missions of the Lake Superior country. Father Skolla left Mackinac in September, 1845, and went by steamer to Sault Ste. Marie, which then had scarcely twenty houses. Next day he embarked on a merchant vessel, which in twelve days brought him to L'Anse. After staying three days with Baraga they went together in a birch canoe to La Pointe. At first F. Skolla was naturally very much afraid to ride in such a frail boat—a mere nutshell, so to say—but seeing how unconcerned his Indian companions were, how they were laughing and singing all the time, he soon conquered his unnecessary fear and got used to this new mode of traveling. In fact, the writer can say from experience that it is safer to travel on water in a birch canoe than in many of our dug-outs and small boats—that is, if you have Indians to paddle and steer the canoe. On the 3d of October, the Vigil of St. Francis day, the Founder of his Order, Father Skolla arrived at La Pointe, and the next day said Mass on the island for the first time.

The good people of La Pointe received the missionaries with great joy. Baraga introduced the new pastor and spent a few days with his dear former parishioners and then departed for L'Anse. F. Skolla said high Mass every Sunday at ten o'clock, and after the first Gospel would preach in French. The Mass being ended, he would preach for the Chippewa portion of his flock, Antoine Gaudin (Gordon) acting as interpreter. The writer is personally acquainted with Mr. Gaudin, who now resides at Gordon, Wis., and has a hotel and store there. He is a practical Catholic and the mainstay of religion in his town. He has likewise contributed very liberally towards the erection of the neat little church in Gordon, and on Sunday he acts as quasi-pastor to his Chippewa countrymen, reading to them the prayers of Mass and the Gospel.

At La Pointe, on Sunday afternoons, Vespers were sung in Chippewa, followed by Benediction with the Blessed Sacrament. Then F. Skolla would give a catechetical instruction to his Chippewa flock, Antoine Gaudin again acting as interpreter. Every Wednesday and Saturday he used to hear confessions by means of an interpreter until he had become sufficiently proficient in Chippewa to be able to dispense with his services. The people were innocent and simple; they were accustomed to confess even their slight faults with great sorrow and contrition, and oftentimes they would weep bitterly when accusing themselves of more grievous sins. After holy Communion the whole congregation devoutly said the holy rosary.

In May, 1846, F. Skolla went to Fond du Lac, Minn., with the above named interpreter and some half-breeds, where he was welcomed with signs of unfeigned joy by the newly converted Indians. The pagans were engaged in their great medicine dance, which generally lasted several days, at times even two weeks or a month, if they had plenty of provisions. Before beginning the dance one of their orators made a speech. He spoke as follows:

"Our forefathers have faithfully kept the great medicine dance until this day because it prevents sickness and keeps our children healthy. You know there is a manitou (god) in the earth, who makes the plants and herbs to grow, who gives us fishes out of the waters and wood and fire with which to cook our victuals and warm ourselves. This manitou below in the earth gives us food and drink. But there is another manitou above, who rules the winds, the air, and the seasons. Know that if you observe the great medicine dance you will go, after death, to a place of happiness, where you will always beat the drum and dance the great medicine dance. But those who despise the great medicine dance shall have to pass, after death, over a long bridge, under which two large serpents are lurking. When such a soul gets to the middle of the bridge she is seized and devoured by those two serpents!"

Another orator spoke as follows:

"My children, I think that your fathers, some of whom have died long ago, told you what a great famine they suffered in this place and how they hunted through all the forests in this vicinity; but they did not bring home from their chase neither bear, nor rabbit, nor wolf; neither did they have anything else wherewith to sustain life, so that many of them died of hunger. You know that some of your brothers received letters of acknowledgment and large medals from the English government for having helped the English in their war with the French-Canadians, because they had fought bravely; many, however, fell in said war. This fact is a subject of great praise to our nation, but also a cause of great ruin to our people on account of your brothers who perished. You know, likewise, that our forefathers, many centuries ago, came from very distant countries through a narrow strait of the sea to our shores.* They used to worship the sun, the moon, the stars, fire, water, statues of stone, crabs, beavers, owls, and serpents. They built shrines in shady places, and temples, in which oracles were to be given. Behold, this same worship of the manitous (gods) continues with us to the present day. Therefore, my children, do not join the religion of those people who are dressed in black (priests), who preach about the Cross; but keep faithfully your domestic gods, as your forefathers have done, in order that our nation may not be scattered amongst other nations, lest it be entirely dissolved and eradicated. I therefore enjoin upon my sons, the medicine men, to watch that none of our people join the religion of the black robes, so that our name may continue. Hence, my sons, I shall give you a feast today, but tomorrow and the following days of this festival every family is to contribute. Should any one of them be unable to furnish all necessaries for the feast, their neighbors are to help them. People are to bring from the chase deer and rabbits and that will suffice for the entire time of the great medicine dance. Beat the drum, young men! Begin the dance!" Then all, both young and old, shouted: "Taia! Ataiia! Well! Very Well!"

Then with folded arms and great reverence they walked in procession around a wooden owl placed upon a post in the middle of a medicine lodge. At the entrance a linen cloth was spread on the ground, on which lay all kinds of roots and herbs supposed to possess medical powers or held in superstitious veneration, to which they offered a kind of sacrifice in the shape of tobacco. The medicine men, or jugglers, would often touch these plants and roots with their hands and add some herbs of their own. Then they mixed the roots and flowers with tobacco and certain paints, made from a decoction of roots or some other substance, and formed magical signs over them. This ceremony ended, they sat down with their wives and children to eat.

As the pagans at Fond du Lac were then too much occupied with their superstitious performance, F. Skolla did not accomplish much at this, his first, visit; he baptized but six persons. On a subsequent visit to the same place he went to see the pagans

---

* The speaker seems to allude to an old tradition that they came from Asia to America via Behring's Strait.

in their wigwams and quietly and kindly spoke to them about religion, but in vain. On his way back to Francis Roussain he said sadly to himself: Why did you come here? You will accomplish nothing. Suddenly he met a very old Indian of dark complexion, who could scarcely move along from want and sickness. Skolla asked him, "Are you sick?" "Yes," say he, "I am very sick." "Friend," said the missionary, "what a happiness would be yours if you would but believe in the Lord Jesus Christ, the Son of God, whom I am preaching! See, you are sick and suffer hunger, but if you receive Baptism you will be happy forever in heaven and you will never again be hungry or sick." The old, hitherto obstinate, pagan answered: "Just now, at this very moment, I was thinking in my mind whether I could be baptized, for my last hour is near at hand. Come, therefore, and baptize me now." The good Father, overjoyed, instructed him immediately and then baptized him. The next day the old man died. He had always been a medicine man and very strongly attached to paganism. "Spiritus spirat ubi vult"—"The Spirit breatheth where he will." On this occasion Father Skolla remained a whole month in Fond du Lac and baptized fifteen Indians, adults and children.

In 1853 he made his last visit to Fond du Lac, in company with John Bell and family. When disembarking he noticed a particular joy depicted on the faces of his good neophytes. He asked his host, Francis Roussain, for the reason. The latter replied: "It was the will of God that you came to us today, for while you were still a great distance away we already knew that you were coming. A young pagan boy of scarcely eight years, and very sick, nearby, whilst lying in bed, said this morning to his parents, joyfully: "Behold, I see a man with a black garment at such a point—naming the place—who is coming to baptize me. I see him sitting in a boat and holding a book in his hand. John Bell and his family are coming with him." What the boy said was exactly true. For at that very place and at that very time F. Skolla had in his hand "The Imitation of Christ" and was reading some chapters in that book. He was then some six miles or thereabouts from Fond du Lac.

When Mr. Roussain related this incident to Skolla, the latter went immediately to the boy's house. The whole family was silent, but full of consolation. Finally the pagan mother stooped down to her sick child and said to him: "See, my son, the priest is here whom you have desired so earnestly to see in order to be baptized by him. Come, my son, tell now in his presence, that he may hear it himself, what you have seen this morning." The sick boy having regarded the Father with an expression of much inner contentment, said, with a weak voice: "Today before noon, from my bed here, when you were at the entrance of the lake (where the St. Louis River enters St. Louis Bay, an arm of Lake Superior), I saw you sitting in the boat and holding a book in your hand. Bell was also with you and his wife and three children. And I said to my mother, 'Behold, the black gown (priest) is coming here to baptize me.'" The mother then said: "I, too, and my whole family want to be baptized by you." The boy was then duly instructed and baptized, and died not long afterwards. At his funeral F. Skolla held a funeral sermon, very appropriate for the occasion. He spoke as follows:

"Dearest friends! Take good notice of my words.

The Great Spirit says: "Happy are the dead who die in the Lord." Now you are living on earth and after a few years your life will come to an end and then none of you will be left any more on the face of the earth. The same thing will happen to your children and the whole human race. You frequently see your brethren taken away out of this world and you don't see them any longer. Their souls enter another world, but their bodies putrefy in the ground. But those same bodies shall rise again on the last day, when all men who are on earth shall have died. But some shall rise unto eternal life and others unto eternal death. Eternal life is the happiness of heaven and eternal death is the torment of hell. Those go to heaven who are baptized and during all their life do good, who believe in one God and in the Son of God, Jesus Christ, who died on the Cross to destroy the sins of the whole world. Finally, they go to heaven who devoutly worship God. But those will be cast into hell who refuse to be baptized and will not believe in the one God, Creator of all things, namely, idolators, who worship wood, stones, animals, and all those who live wickedly and die in sin.

Dear friends! How can you escape eternal death unless you believe and live rightly? You have seen manifestly with your eyes and heard with your ears what great grace the Great Spirit has shown to this deceased little boy; and why? Because he desired

Baptism so ardently. Endeavor, therefore, to accept the light of faith as he did, that you may be numbered amongst the children of God, as he is now inscribed in heaven amongst the choirs of the blessed. Have pity on your one, only soul, created by the Great Spirit, and renounce your darkness and blindness, all of you, who are the slaves of senseless idolatry which is nothing else than diabolical deception and deceit. Throw the drum into the fire, the drum by whose sound you do not cease day and night to summon the devil, for he willingly comes to those who invoke him.* But woe! because after death he will throw their souls into hell to burn in the fire forever.

"But you, who have been baptized in Jesus Christ, persevere until death in doing good works that you may obtain from the hand of God an eternal crown. For know this, that he alone is truly happy who, being baptized, believes firmly in God, loves Him and serves Him faithfully until death, and endeavors in all his actions to fulfill the holy will of God. Certainly he that lives thus and does what is good until the end of his life will die in the Lord and be clothed by Him in heaven with a golden garment and rejoice forever in His kingdom."

This sermon was listened to most attentively by all present and left a deep impression on their minds. A few days later the parents and relatives of the deceased boy, with several others, asked to be baptized. During his three weeks' stay in Fond du Lac Father Skolla baptized seventeen pagans. During all this time he stopped with Francis Roussain, who treated him with great kindness. The latter died many years ago, but his wife and two sons

---

* Very Rev. Father Jacker, deceased, gives in one of his written lectures a specimen of an Indian incantation song:

"Nin wawenabamigog ehe! ehe!

Nind igog ehe! ehe!

Ogimag ehe! ehe!"

These same words are repeated for a quarter of an hour, or even for an hour, if deemed necessary. The meaning is:

"They choose me ehe! ehe

They tell me ehe! ehe!

The chiefs ehe! ehe!"

When F. Jacker asked the Indian, whom he heard singing the above words, what kind of chiefs he meant, his answer was: "I do not know, perhaps the wicked manitous" (devils!)

and daughter still reside at Fond du Lac. A brother of his, George Roussain, lives at Courtes Oreilles, and is an exemplary Christian. As Skolla noticed that provisions were becoming scarce with his kind-hearted host, he set out to return to La Pointe. Although the pagan Indians on the island of La Pointe were strongly attached to paganism, still many were converted, besides others who came from Courtes Oreilles, Lac du Flambeau, Grand Portage, and Pigeon River. The total number of baptisms in all his missions at La Pointe (1845 to 1853) was about 440.

During all the eight years F. Skolla labored at La Pointe he had but three visits of brother clergymen. It was an unusual sight to the good people of La Pointe. In 1847 he was visited by Fathers Baraga, Pierz, and Choné, with Skolla a whole month. One Sunday they had a solemn high Mass with deacon and sub-deacon, at which F. Choné preached an eloquent sermon.

In 1849 F. Skolla was twice visited by Very Rev. Boulanger, S. J., Provincial of his Order. The first time he remained but a short time, as he was on his way to visit the various missionary stations of his Order on the North Shore. On returning from this official visit to his brethren in Canada he stayed with Father Skolla three weeks and preached a most eloquent sermon, which made a deep and lasting impression on all present.

In 1853 many of the inhabitants of La Pointe left their beloved island and moved to Sand Lake and other parts of Minnesota, in obedience to instructions from the Indian Department at Washington. At last there were but ten families left. Subsequently many of them returned. Seeing his Indians thus moving away, F. Skolla wrote to Bishop Henni, of Milwaukee, to give him some other Indian mission in his diocese. This was done. He was removed to the Keshena Reservation, where many Menominee Indians resided at that time.

On October 9, 1853,* he left La Pointe, amidst the sad cries and lamentation of his poor people, who tried very hard to detain him. He gave them his parting blessing and embarked. His poor Indians were never again to see him in this world. He first went to Milwaukee, via Sault Ste. Marie. The very day he arrived at the Sault, Bishop Baraga had left for Europe, and so F. Skolla did not

---

* The parish record says: September 19th, 1853.

have the pleasure of meeting his beloved countryman. He continued his journey and arrived at Milwaukee, where he stayed two weeks with Bishop Henni.

By way of Detroit and Mackinac he went to Green Bay, where he remained a few days with F. Parodin. He walked to Oconto River, which took him two days. His predecessor in the Menominee mission, Rev. Florimund Bonduel, had left on account of some trouble between the Indians. They were very much pleased to have another priest so soon and secured a deserted house, repairing it and fitting it up for a temporary church; they likewise built a small house for the missionary.

Here F. Skolla labored with his customary zeal and during his six months' stay near Stiles he baptized 150 pagans. With the help of some of his people he translated the Pater, Ave, Credo, Confiteor, and act of contrition into the Menominee tongue. On Sundays the Indians used to sing during holy Mass the pious hymns they had learned in Chippewa. At first F. Skolla preached to them in Chippewa, and although their knowledge of that language was somewhat imperfect, they listened to him with great attention, striving to understand what was being preached to them. They would spend a great part of the evenings singing pious hymns, in which exercise they took special delight. Happiness was depicted on every face, the happiness which had its origin in the conscious possession of interior peace and the grace of God. Brotherly love, unfeigned kindness, and great joy reigned amongst those simple-hearted children of the forest. In reading Skolla's account of them we are reminded of the primitive Christians, "who were one heart and one soul."

Speaking of his Indians, he writes: "'The Menominees are very quiet and good-natured. There are good, fervent Christians amongst them. They hate intoxicating liquors, and it is the virtue of temperance which most powerfully impels them to embrace the Catholic faith. They dislike forbidden pleasures and feastings. When they have an entertainment they observe the rules of sobriety, modesty and edification. My Catholic Indians have only one great banquet during the year, and that is on Three King's day, or Epiphany. The chiefs are called "Ogimag"—kings—in Indian, and so in their simple way they want to celebrate the feast of their patron saints, the Three Kings, and show themselves a little.

Every year a chief gives an entertainment, to which his relatives contribute. Everything passes off most innocently in mutual love and kindness, and Indian religious songs are sung whilst the guests are eating."

"On the 10th of May, 1854, the government superintendent, Dr. Hubschmann, came to Wolf River Falls. He wrote to me to come to that place immediately with my Indians in order to deliberate on important affairs concerning the Menominees. I went thither immediately with my forest children and we were received by him very friendly. He began immediately to speak to the people about their affairs and asked me to interpret in Chippewa what he had told them in English, which I did. The government superintendent—most likely a government commissioner —stayed two days and spoke to them three times in order to explain to them what had been decided on concerning them in Washington. The United States agreed to give them for fifteen years a saw and grist mill, a black smith and carpenter, and two schools were to be erected. The agent of the Menominees will soon come to Wolf River Falls and give to each Menominee family a piece of land for cultivation. The chiefs have signed their names and the whole matter has been forwarded to Washington to be ratified by congress."

In a letter dated August 22, 1856, F. Skolla mentions that he went to Milwaukee to see B. Henni about certain affairs concerning his mission. He stayed with him a week, during which he paid a visit to the Salesianum. Fathers Heiss and Salzmann received the Indian missionary very kindly and showed him the Seminary, which then had but thirty students. Having transacted his business with his bishop, Father Skolla returned to Keshena.

The first church, "the bark church," was built in 1854, near Lake Keshena, about three-fourths of a mile east of the village of Keshena. The site selected by Skolla for his mission was on the south side of the lake, where the shore is high and steep and commands a full view of the lake and the surrounding country. He induced the Indians to build a small church and parsonage at once. Both buildings were very primitive; no floor but the bare ground and the roof covered with bark; his house consisted of one room. Near the church was the cemetery (now no longer used), where about one hundred lie buried. In 1856 the second church was to be built in the village of Keshena. From November, 1853, until August, 1856, Father Skolla baptized 302 Indians, one of whom was an old chief far over 100 years of age. The neophytes were full of fervor; every Sunday from twenty to thirty received holy Communion.

To promote temperance amongst his Indians, Father Skolla had a picture hung up, depicting the evils of drinking and the beneficial effects of temperance. On the left, a drunken man with ragged clothes is seen striking his poor wife with a poker, whilst she is clasping to her breast her poor infant child. A devil with a diabolical laugh on his ugly face reaches to him a glass of brandy taken out of a jug labeled, "Fourth proof brandy." The poor children crowd around their mother, crying. On the right side is seen a fine gentleman instructing his little son. A young daughter sits at a table full of nice things to eat. The happy mother holds a smiling baby on her lap whom she is lovingly caressing. The Indians used to look a great deal at this picture, which made a deep impression on their minds and induced 260 of them to take the temperance pledge; eighty took it for life and kept it faithfully.

Although a man of great sanctity, Father Skolla, nevertheless, became the victim of vile slanders. Some malevolent, superstitious Indians used to lurk about his poor, little shanty, watching through the holes and cracks in the walls everything he was doing inside. He kept a cat and would, for a pastime, play with it, as he was staying all alone and had no one with whom to converse. He would then talk to the cat, and the Indian spies outside hearing him, but seeing nobody with him in the room, were convinced that he was talking to ghosts. In a similar manner, when they saw him play chess alone, as it is said he did at times, they imagined, perhaps, that the figures on the chessboard were bad spirits with whom the Father had intercourse, or that the white figures represented the whites and the dark colored ones the Indians; and their mutual struggle on the board typified the struggle of the two races for the mastery of the land. Moreover, they saw him sometimes in the evening walking in the graveyard or entering the church to pray. It is said that he spent much of his leisure time praying in the church. This pious custom gave rise to a most horrible calumny. He was charged with opening the graves at night and taking out the hearts of newly buried corpses to make out of them "bad medicine" for injuring people.

This charge was supported by an old pagan Chippewa, who was on a visit with the Menominees. This Indian knew Father Skolla and came one day to see him. Skolla had a box in which he used to put his things. The Chippewa sat on the box, and, tapping on it with his hand, said to his companions: "This box contains a piece of dry flesh which the priest has taken from the body of a dead person to use it as bad medicine." This calumnious and stupid story was repeated all over the reservation and believed by many Indians, especially pagans. One day a young person was buried and the miserable charge was made again. So strong was the sentiment against the priest that some demanded that the corpse be exhumed and examined. F. Skolla was informed of this. He mildly said: "You can do as you please, but by doing so you will only hurt yourselves." The disinterment was then omitted, but at some other occasion it was actually done to satisfy curiosity. It is easy to be seen that such calumnies must have been a great hindrance to his missionary work, as they created feelings of distrust and aversion against the priest, the more so as many Indians were very ignorant and superstitious. At first a small sum out of the annuities was reserved for the missionary's support. This was subsequently withheld, most likely on account of those base, lying reports circulated about him. As he had no other means of support, he was obliged to leave in 1857. It seems he, shortly after, returned to his monastery in Carniola. His missionary account was published in the Franciscan monthly, "La Palestina," in 1891. From a foot-note in the February number it appears he was then still alive and residing at the monastery.

VERY REV. EDWARD JACKER

Of the Diocese of Marquette, Mich. A Short Sketch of His Life and Labors.

VERY REV. EDWARD JACKER. V.G.

Very Rev. E. Jacker was born September 2, 1827, in Ellwangen, Wurtemberg. His parents were staunch, devout Catholics. His father, a pious and most conscientious man, was professor at the Gymnasium of Ellwangen. He was a very learned man and author of some works.

Young Jacker began his studies at the gymnasium of his native town. A classmate of his and his most intimate friend was Dr. F. J. Holzwarth, subsequently a prominent German writer and author of a history of the world.

About the year 1846 Jacker entered the University of Tubingen as candidate of theology, later that of Munich, where he took a course in philosophy. Uncertain as to his vocation, he accepted the position of tutor with the family of Count Grime at Liege, Belgium, with whom he remained three years, improving his French and gaining the love of his pupils. Arthur, one of the Grime family, subsequently became an attaché to the Austrian Court. He always remembered his tutor with filial affection. Either previous to or after his stay in Belgium, Jacker temporarily filled the vacancy of professorship at the gymnasium of his birthplace and here also won the love and admiration of the students attending his class.

At last he came to a decision regarding his vocation and resolved to enter the Benedictine Order. He, therefore went to St. Vincent's Abbey, Westmoreland Co., Pa., in the spring of 1854, and at his admission received the name of Frater Beda, He did not remain there long, however. The newly consecrated Bishop

Baraga was then looking for laborers among the Indians of his diocese, and Jacker at once and enthusiastically followed this call.

He was ordained in 1855 at Sault Ste. Marie and sent to the Indian mission of L'Anse. He was the third successor to F. Baraga in said mission, the immediate successor being Rev. Angelus Van Paemel, whose name appears in the Baptismal Record of said mission from August 7, 1853, until August 1, 1854. The next priest in L'Anse was Father Limagie, with whom the writer was personally acquainted, for he was the writer's successor in New London, Wis., in 1868 and 1869. Father Limagie, who was a Belgian by birth, was stationed at L'Anse from August 4, 1854, until August 12, 1855. Then came Father Jacker from September 20, 1855, to April 3, 1861. He stayed at L'Anse for five years and then moved to Houghton, from which place he visited the mission from time to time until 1861.

Father Gerhard Terhorst arrived in L'Anse the day before Corpus Christi, 1861, and has ever since been in charge of said mission. About this persevering and energetic Indian missionary the writer might say much did he not know his dislike of public notice and fear to wound his well-known modesty.

At L'Anse F. Jacker soon became master of the Chippewa language, the rudiments of which he had acquired under B. Baraga's guidance. From this place he also attended the new mining towns about Portage Lake, where a mixed population of Irish, French, and Germans began to form congregations. Every alternate week he visited the mines thirty miles distant, proceeding thither, according to the season, either on snowshoes or in a frail bark canoe. He would then preach in the three languages and attend to the many and various calls of his holy office.

In 1861 Father Jacker was removed to Hancock. During his long stay in that town, especially during the first years, when he had no assistant, he was overburdened with work, and the strain, both physical and mental, was such that it gradually undermined his health and was the cause of his premature death. In a letter to the writer, his brother, Hon. Fr. Jacker, says:

"I was often with him during that period and thus had occasion to witness some of the trials of a missionary's life. After hearing confessions up to a late hour on Saturday nights, again in the confessional Sunday mornings, first low, then high Mass. Hardly having put aside his vestments, he was waylaid at every door by crowds of parishioners, who solicited his attention in behalf of their various concerns, and but few minutes were left him to partake of his belated dinner. Neither was there rest for him in the afternoon. The door bell was kept ringing all day and sometimes in the middle of the night there came a call demanding his immediate presence at the bed of a person dying miles away.

"Besides these pastoral duties, he had other difficulties to contend with. He was a poor money collector and a still poorer financier. His too confiding and trusting nature was at times abused by unscrupulous persons. Though his parishioners generously contributed to his support, he never accumulated any money. *He lived and died poor!*

"When, during the latter part of his life, and upon his special request, he was again permitted to go among his dearly beloved Indians, it was a happy change for him. While coasting along the western shore of Lake Michigan in a small boat, or penetrating the interior to visit the scattered domiciles of the "red man" in out of the way places, he found time to write up something for a magazine or to collect materials for his "hobby" in comparative philology (if the attempt to find proof for the common origin of man by tracing and comparing the roots of words in diverse languages deserves this appellation), thereby making good use of the talent given him by his Maker.

"Besides being master of several languages, he possessed a general knowledge of the grammatical construction of many others, perhaps of all languages, of which even an analysis in print has been attempted. His frequent marginal notes on the pages of linguistic works, which he succeeded to accumulate in time, seem to indicate this; and his critical remarks in this respect were not superficial, but deep and of fine discrimination.

"Of his death—he never took to bed in his sickness and breathed his last in a chair—died literally in his boots.

He wrote letters to his friends and relatives up to the last hours, using a lead pencil with his trembling hand."

The writer was personally acquainted with Father Jacker and corresponded with him a great deal between 1885 and the time of his death. These letters he treasures with jealous care as tokens of friendship from a dearly beloved friend. F. Jacker assisted the writer very much when, in 1886, the latter was writing his little work, "Missionary Labors of Fathers Marquette, Allouez, and Menard in the Lake Superior Region."

Under date of August 16, 1886, he writes as follows:

"DETOUR, Mich., Aug. 16, 1866.
Rev. Father Chrysostom Verwyst O. S. F., Bayfield, Wis.

REV. DEAR FATHER —I believe I was the last to write —some time in May. Possibly a missive of yours went astray; our postal arrangements are not the best; people complain that letters are sometimes lost. We have a double mail, one over land from St. Ignace, one by boat from Cheboygan, and both are irregular.

Should it be possible that your work has not yet come out? I am anxiously waiting for a copy. I want one from your hand; as many more as I may need, I shall order from the publishers.

There is a bare possibility that I may run up to see you sometime in September, when I hope to get as far as Hancock. It will depend on the amount of money as well as of time that may be at my disposal.

Father Atfield, of Menominee, invited me to visit the Indians in that neighborhood. As most of them are Menominees and some know but little Otchipwe, I advised him to apply for one of your Fathers in Keshena. If he insists on my coming, I think I shall go in September, as I have to go as far as Escanaba, anyhow. For that purpose I am studying the works of your *Wamanominewenesit*. By the way, where is he at present?

Detour is the quietest mission I have ever had. Still, I would rather be in a little Indian settlement, so as to learn the language again. If the collection ordered by the Plenary Council amounts to something handsome, Bp. Vertin may yet come to the resolution of giving me such a place. Here I have to work for my living—that is, I have to give the greater part of the year to those that support me, and to the Indians a few weeks now and then.

My best respects to Father John. I hope he will yet believe in your studies.

In unione precum,
Yours most sincerely,
E. JACKER."

The reader will pardon us for inserting the following testimonials of Father Jacker's worth as a self-sacrificing priest and Indian missionary. They come from all directions and are from parties who were well acquainted with this saintly man. They were published in the "Ohio Waisenfreund," of Columbus, Ohio, under date of December 14, 1892.

"Thirty-seven years ago."

The editor says:

"Under this heading we published the letter of a German-American priest of Michigan, in order to rescue it from oblivion, but we did not know the name of the writer. But now we can give that, too, for in regard to this pious priest the saying is truly verified, 'His memory shall be in benediction' as we see from the notices which we have received concerning him. The name of this long ago deceased priest is Edward Jacker, from Ellwangen, Wurtemberg. According to the unanimous testimony of our correspondents this priest led a saintly life and closed a career on earth for which God will have given him the crown of life."

A correspondent from Minnesota writes:

"The name of the priest was Edward Jacker. I was well acquainted with him, for I served his Mass for about four years on Sundays and week days, and I received from him my first holy Communion, and I can testify of him that he was the most pious priest I ever knew. That was in Hancock, Mich., to which place he came some years before us. He came to Hancock like a beggar, his clothes all ragged and torn, after having lived many years amongst the Indians. Also in Hancock he always had Indians in his house. He was beloved by Catholics and Protestants, for he was goodness itself. About five years ago I received a letter from him, and, if I am not mistaken, it is about three years ago that I read in a newspaper that he had departed this world to obtain, no doubt, a good reward from God. Whether he was from Wurtemberg I do not know, but I am sure he was a Suabian.   J. W."

From Michigan one writes:

"We were well acquainted with the writer of said letter since the early part of the sixties, and his memory is held in the highest respect by all those who were ever acquainted with him on our peninsula, regardless of creed. The writer was Rev. Father Edward

Jacker, who died five years ago, born in Ellwangen, Wurtemberg, on September 2, 1827, and deceased at Marquette, Mich., on September 1, 1887. Three days later he was consigned to eternal rest in Hancock, according to his wish, in the cemetery which he himself had blessed twenty-five years before.

"P. J. W."

Another writes: "That priest is undoubtedly the celebrated Father Jacker, who not long ago discovered the grave of the Frenchman Marquette. He died some years ago. He was a man whose self-sacrificing labors remained unknown, but who in reality was a remarkable man and priest. It is certain that too much good cannot be said of him, for only few are his equals. It is to be regretted that such an able man did not have a larger field for his capabilities, where he could have done infinitely more good. It is to be regretted that men like Jacker disappear without being known. Could his deeds and life be written, they would be a source of consolation to many and an incitement to perseverance when in sorrow and want, both of which he had superabundantly.

L. H."

Another speaks of him thus: "I knew him personally and have called him to a dying person thirty miles away. I do not believe that there will ever come a priest to this part of the country and do what he did, and every Catholic speaks most highly of him. It is not to be described what he suffered among the Indians, and money he could never keep, *for he gave every cent to the poor, and when he was buried not a cent of money was found with him.*"

REV. LAURENCE LAUTISCHAR

His Short Missionary Career and Sad Death.

The subject of this sketch, Rev. Laurence Lautischar (Slav. Lautizar), was born on the 11th of December, 1820, in Srednjivrh, near Kranjska Gora, Carniola, Austria. His parents were pious country people, who brought him up in the fear of God and in the practice of every Christian virtue. Being a child of great promise, very talented and pious, his parents had him study for the priesthood. At the Gymnasium and Seminary of Laibach, where he studied, he was respected and beloved by his professors and fellow students. He received the Sacrament of Holy Orders August 3, 1845.

After his ordination he was sent to Treffen, B. Baraga's birthplace, where he labored in the capacity of assistant priest from 1846 to 1851. He was then transferred to Dobrova, near Laibach, in which town there is a very celebrated shrine of the Blessed Virgin Mary much frequented by pilgrims from far and near. F. Lautischar labored here likewise as assistant priest from 1851 to 1854. In both places he worked zealously in the confessional and pulpit for the salvation of souls.

Rt. Rev. Frederic Baraga having been consecrated on November 1, 1853, Bishop of Amyzonia and Vicar-Apostolic of Upper Michigan, went, soon after his consecration, to Europe in quest of priests and funds for his diocese. He came to Carniola and was everywhere received with great respect by his countrymen, who from all sides flocked together to see and hear the beloved bishop, whose fame as a great Indian missionary had preceded him. Several Slavonian and German priests offered themselves for the American mission, and one of them was F. Lautischar.

On the 10th of May, 1854, he bid a tearful farewell to his dear mother and relatives and set out for America. After a stormy voyage he arrived in New York on the 14th of July, 1854. He remained at Sault Ste. Marie a short time with B. Baraga and then was sent to La Croix to act as assistant priest to Rev. Father Mrak. In June, 1856, he was put in charge of Arbre Croche, where he labored humbly, unostentatiously and zealously until the early part of 1858.

As the Indian missions of Michigan were in a good, flourishing condition, F. Lautischar thought he might do more good if he went to labor amongst the pagan Indians, who were in greater need of a missionary than the good people of Arbre Croche. So he began to correspoFnd about the matter with his countryman, Rev. Father Pierz, who was then stationed at Crow Wing, Minnesota. The latter rejoiced at the prospect of getting a good assistant to help him in his large missionary field. Bishop Baraga consented to give F. Lautischar the "exeat" from his diocese and he was received by the Very Rev. Administrator of St. Paul diocese, the Episcopal

See having become vacant by the death of Rt. Rev. Joseph Cretin on February 22,

1857. Traveling by way of Milwaukee, Prairie du Chien, and St. Paul, from St. Paul to Crow Wing, a distance of 160 miles, he traveled by stage. He was welcomed with open arms by good Father Pierz. The latter was as poor "as a church mouse;" he had not a cent of money, but, fortunately, Father Lautischar had eighty dollars left after paying his traveling expenses. This sum of money was truly a God-send for the intended missionary trip to Red Lake, where F. Lautischar was to be stationed in the very heart of paganism.

With the money brought by Lautischar the necessary outfit for the intended journey was procured. This outfit consisted of a couple of large tents for the missionaries and their Indian guides and carriers, cooking utensils, flour, pork, and tea, besides the necessary church vestments, missal, chalice, etc. Moreover, some of the money was used for paying the Indians and half-breeds who were to act as guides and carriers. All being duly prepared, the missionaries and their Indian companions set out from Crow Wing on foot. We do not know the exact distance from Crow Wing to Red Lake, but looking at the map of Minnesota we should judge it to be about 250 miles, perhaps more, by the way the missionaries had to travel on a zig-zag Indian trail, around swamps and lakes and hills.

They arrived at Red Lake on the 14th of August, after many hardships and sufferings, of which not the least was the torment endured day and night from clouds of mosquitoes which infest the woods and swamps and drive the poor traveler almost mad. Well does the writer remember his trip of seven miles through a Minnesota forest, or rather swamp, on his way to an Indian village. To walk was out of question; had he done so the hungry, blood thirsty mosquitoes would have eaten him alive. So he had to run, as fast as his legs could carry him, through thick and thin, through mud and slush, knocking incessantly right and left with a large handful of leaves and branches to keep the pests from flying into his eyes and mouth and nose. Even then, after all his exertions, after battling with the foe for almost two hours, his neck and wrists were all red and swollen from mosquito bites. We can then imagine what the poor missionaries must have endured on their long trip to the Indian country. We verily believe there are more mosquitoes in one township of Northern Minnesota than in the whole state of Missouri.

On the 15th of August, the feast of the Assumption of the Blessed Virgin Mary, the missionaries offered up the holy Sacrifice of the Mass on the shores of Red Lake. After a stay of six weeks, F. Pierz returned to Crow Wing, leaving Lautischar to work at Red Lake. The latter stopped with a French half-breed by the name of Pierrish, which in the Chippewa language is the word for Peter, and would mean: Bad Peter. He was very kind to Father Lautischar, who made his home with him and used his house as a chapel. The good missionary was assiduous in giving instructions to both Catholics and pagans. At his arrival he found but ten half-breed Catholic families on the reservation. They had been baptized many years ago by B. Baraga at Lake Superior, but had forgotten almost everything about religion. The Indians liked the young, warm-hearted, zealous missionary and listened eagerly to his instructions. In a short time he had converted several Indians and half-breeds.

But his missionary labors came to a short and sad end. At the invitation of some Indians living on the other side of the lake, he went to see and instruct them on December 3, 1858. When he got through, he started to return, although it was towards evening and a fearful blizzard was raging. The poor Father became blinded by the flying snow and sleet, so that he could not see whither he was going. Moreover, he was too thinly clad for the rigorous cold of a Minnesota winter. After wandering about on the open lake in the dark night and blinding storm he finally succumbed to the cold. His legs froze and so he could no longer walk. After crawling around for some time on the ice he finally lay down and died. Like St. Francis Xavier, whose death occurred on the 3d of December, in the greatest poverty, misery and abandonment, so Father Lautischar likewise died in darkness, misery and cold, without the consolations of religion in his last hour. We can imagine the sufferings and agony of the poor Father dying all alone in that dark night out on the lake. But we may be sure that he made good use of his last moments to prepare for death, offering the sacrifice of his young life to God for the salvation of the poor Indians, for whose sake he had left Fatherland and parents to perish in trying to bring them to God.

There was great lamentation and sadness when, next morning, they found their dear Father dead, frozen, out on the lake, not far from the place on the shore where the mission house stood. After some days the good Indians decided to take the corpse to Crow Wing for burial. The only conveyance they had was a dog-train, on which they tied the box or coffin containing the Father's mortal remains.

When they arrived at Crow Wing it was about Christmas—a sad Christmas indeed for poor F. Pierz, who had thus suddenly lost his dear reverend assistant and friend. His only consolation was that, the deceased having ended his pious and self-sacrificing life in the service of God, and working for the poor Indians, his soul was happy in heaven, praying for the conversion of his poor people. He was buried at Crow Wing on December 26, 1858, in the cemetery adjoining the church. A wooden Cross was put on his grave.

Writing to his reverend friend, Dean S. Vilfau, at Novomesto, Carniola, about Father Lautischar's untimely death, F. Pierz says:

"I have to inform you, most sorrowfully, that the learned and pious Laurence Lautischar is no more. He entered a better life because the world was not worthy of him. On the day of St. Stephen I solemnly buried him in Crow Wing. He froze to death while coming from his mission. Undoubtedly he is one of the many saints in heaven. He offered to God the great gift of self-denial in choosing to leave Bishop Baraga in order to go into the wilderness after poor Indians. He left his dear mother, relatives, and many friends to increase his merit before God. In Arbre Croche he did much good during his three years' stay there. All praised him for his great piety and many virtues which adorned him so abundantly. That mission was too small for his Apostolic zeal and for this reason he wrote to me. I was very glad to get him. Being one in mind and soul with me, strong and always ready to work, we started on foot from Crow Wing for the upper country along the Mississippi. After a journey of three days, amid great hardships, we came to Leech Lake, Ga-Sagaskwadjimekag, where 1,400 Indians awaited us. We remained eight days with them, preached to them, and cured the sick with my homeopathic medicines. They listened with great attention to us and many assured us that they would become converts. Their chiefs promised to do all they could for us, if we would but stay with them.

"We walked four days more and finally reached my last station—Red Lake. Here we found ten families of half-breeds; some of them had been converted by Bishop Baraga. We gave instructions to the Indians for six weeks and baptized many of them. Our dear Laurence understood my way of acting with the Indians admirably and he preached in the Indian language in such an humble and endearing tone that I could not help admiring him. He was dear to all.

"The holy season (of Advent and Christmas) was approaching and duty called me to the whites to give them an opportunity to receive the holy sacraments. I gave to my assistant the choice either to stay at Red Lake, or go to some other mission during winter, or go with me to Crow Wing and stay with me there. He preferred to stay at Red Lake that he might do more good. I did not oppose him. At the same time I gave him the good advice not to leave home and go to some far-off mission during winter.

"At last we sadly parted and I went to Crow Wing. I was just with the French at Belle Prairie when I received the dispatch with the sad news that my dear assistant had been found frozen on Red Lake. Immediately I took the proper steps to have his precious remains brought to Crow Wing for burial. His sudden death has brought the deepest sorrow to my heart and I have shed many tears. The thought that he is certainly of the number of those who pray before the throne of God for the poor Indian missionaries and their flocks has consoled me for a moment.

"He had been told that on the other side of the frozen lake there were a large number of natives who wanted to see him. He started on foot, alone, and never thinking of any impending danger. As he was returning home, towards the evening, the bitter north wind was blowing hard; the messenger of Christ was to be the victim. Thus his pure soul went amid prayer and suffering to heaven. Not only in Red Lake, but also in Crow Wing, the

Christians and savages mourned the death of their beloved priest for many days.

"As to me, nothing can replace the loss of him and my soul is in the greatest sorrow, though he died a happy death. I have planted on the grave of my dear friend a white Cross, which, though wooden, is blessed and moistened with my tears. It will stand till I will be able to procure a more respectable monument for the eternal remembrance of my dear missionary companion."

The venerable missionary composed a poem in the Slavonian language, in which he describes the great virtues and noble qualities of the lamented Father. Some years ago his remains were taken to Duluth and buried in the cemetery lot reserved for deceased priests.

THEODORE J. VAN DEN BROEK, O. P.

One of the Pioneer Indian Missionaries of Wisconsin. Short Sketches of His Life and Labors.

REV. FATHER VAN DEN BROEK, O.P.

Father Theodore J. Van den Broek, O. P., was a Hollander by birth and stationed for some time in Alkmaar, Holland. He left his native land in 1832, and having landed at Baltimore, he went, via Wheeling, Cincinnati, and Louisville, to St. Rose, near Springfield, Washington County, Kentucky, where there was a house of the Dominican Order, to which he belonged. The whole journey from Antwerp, Belgium, to St. Rose, took nine weeks. Here he prepared himself for missionary work, studying the language and customs of the country. After a short stay at St. Rose, he was removed to Somerset, Perry County, Ohio, where there was another house of his Order.

On the 4th of July, 1834, he arrived in Green Bay to labor in the Indian missionary field. Here he found only ten Catholic white families, although more were living in the interior of the state at Little Chute, Butte des Morts, etc. He completed the priest's house, begun by F. Mazzuchelli, and labored zealously among the whites and Indians of his flock. The Catholic church and parsonage were then located at Menomineeville (Shanteetown), half way between Green Bay and De Pere. Scarcely a year after his arrival the towns of Navarino and Astor, now Green Bay, were built, and as the Catholics of these places formed one congregation with those of Menomineeville, we will call the mission Green Bay.

The first building in Green Bay, used as school house and chapel, was built of logs in 1823, during or shortly after Father Gabriel Richards' visit to that town. The Catholics of that place had not seen a Catholic priest for fifty years. Father Richard did an immense amount of good during the week he spent with them, baptizing 128 persons and marrying twenty-six couples. The church, begun in 1823, was finished under the care and supervision of Father Badin and blessed by him on June 26, 1825. This log church was destroyed by fire that very same year. In 1831 Bishop Fenwick, of Cincinnati, selected a site for a new church, which was begun by Rev. S. Mazzuchelli, and finished by the Redemptorist Fathers Sanderl and Hatscher in November, 1832, at a cost of $3,000. This church was also destroyed by fire in 1846. Another church, bought of the Methodists, shared the same fate in 1871.

Father Van den Broek labored at Green Bay, sometimes alone and sometimes with Father Mazzuchelli, from 1834 till the winter of 1836. It seems he left Green Bay in December of the last named year and went to reside at Little Chute. As the Redemptorist Fathers, Sanderl, Hatscher, and Prost, remained in Green Bay but a short time—Father Sanderl succeeding F. Baraga in Arbre Croche in 1833—the care of the Green Bay mission again devolved upon Father Van den Broek for the next two years,

1836 to 1838. He was accustomed to have Mass there every other Sunday. While residing in Green Bay, he sometimes said two Masses on Sundays, the first one at Green Bay and the second at Little Chute, walking the entire distance (twenty to twenty-four miles). Once his feet bled profusely from the pegs in his boots, whence he was obliged to stop on his way to have them extracted. Another time he lost his boots in the deep mud. Besides the hardships endured in his travels, he had often to suffer hunger, as his Indians were rather negligent in providing for his wants.

When he first came to Little Chute, he lived for half a year in a wigwam, fifteen feet long and six feet high, which served as church, dwelling, and school. As soon as he had baptized some Indians he began to teach them to read Bishop Baraga's prayer and catechetical books. Here in his wigwam he was visited by snakes, wolves, and those worst of all nuisances, starving Indian dogs, who would often steal the poor Father's dinner, stowed away, in the shape of meat or fish, in some old Indian kettle.

His mission for some years embraced a very large part of Wisconsin. He attended Green Bay, Little Chute, Hollandtown, Butte des Morts, Fort Winnebago, Fond du Lac, Prairie du Chien, Poygan, Calumet, and other places. He visited the more distant missions generally in winter. Oftentimes he was obliged to sleep, during bitter cold winter nights, in the snow, with no other roof overhead than the starry canopy of heaven. Once, when called to attend a sick person, about 240 miles distant, he got lost in the woods, his guide having got drunk at a fort, where the Father had stopped over Sunday to give the Catholic soldiers a chance to attend to their religious duties. After riding about for several hours in the dark through the woods, having lost his way, he finally tied his horse to a tree, took off the saddle and used it for a pillow on which to rest his aching head. Rain fell in torrents and howling wolves were in close proximity. Next morning he said his prayers and made a vow that he would offer up a holy Mass in thanksgiving should he find his way out of the woods. In those days Wisconsin was almost one unbroken forest and to get lost in such a wilderness was a most dangerous predicament. After having prayed most fervently to Almighty God for deliverance from the great danger to which his life was exposed, he mounted his horse, let the reins loose and allowed the animal to go whithersoever Divine Providence might direct it. In less than five minutes he was on the road and soon arrived at the sick person's house. Incidents like these give the reader some idea of the hardships this Apostolic man endured.

Father Van den Broek was not only a missionary; he was also, like his illustrious fellow laborer in the Lake Superior country, F. Baraga, a civilizer of his Indian people, who were mostly Menominees. He worked most industriously himself, and digging his garden with hoe and spade, raised, the first year he came to Little Chute, plenty of corn and potatoes. The second year he cultivated a sufficient quantity of breadstuffs besides vegetables, his Indians helping him with a good will to till the ground. He also trained them to handle carpenter tools, made them masons, plasterers, etc. With their help he erected a neat church, seventy feet long, with a nice little steeple, which he completed in 1839 and dedicated to St. John Nepomuc, the glorious martyr who gave his blood for the inviolability of the seal of Confession. The writer has been in this church more than once and within its hallowed walls he received the holy Sacrament of Confirmation from Bishop Henni in 1857. If his memory serves him right, the following inscription was to be seen over the church door:

"In this solitary wilderness, an unexplored region,
Father Van den Broek came to establish religion."

Between 1834 and 1842 F. Van den Broek converted and baptized more than six hundred Indians, not to speak of those he converted between the last named year and that of his death, 1851.

But Father Van den Broek has not only a claim to the grateful remembrance of the Catholics of Wisconsin as a zealous Indian missionary, but also as an originator of Catholic colonization. On the 29th of May, 1847, he left Little Chute, and crossing the broad Atlantic, visited his native land, Holland. The same year he published, at Amsterdam, a pamphlet, describing some of the many advantages Wisconsin held out to the industrious immigrant, and induced many of his countrymen to settle in our state. Three ships with Hollanders sailed for America in 1848, in two of which were Catholic priests to attend to the spiritual wants of their countrymen, namely, Fathers Godhard, O. S. F., and Van den Broek, O. P. The latter sailed from Rotterdam, March 18, 1848, in the "Maria Magdalena." He landed at New York May 7, and arrived at Little Chute June 7, with a large number of Hollandish immigrants.* Among those who left their country on that occasion was Hon. Mr. Wigman, for many years president of the Catholic Knights of Wisconsin, a lawyer of great reputation and a practical and devout Catholic, who resides at Green Bay; William A. Verboort—afterwards Father Verboort—first resident priest of De Pere (died in Oregon), and the writer, then a boy of six and a half years, came over that same time. These immigrants from Holland settled at Little Chute, Hollandtown, Green Bay, De Pere, Freedom, and other localities. They were soon followed by others, and at present form quite a large percentage of the Catholic population of the Green Bay diocese. They are second to none in strong, practical Catholicity, zeal for their church, religion, and schools, and command the respect of all classes of our people by their industry, thrift, and orderly conduct. The tree that Father Van den Broek planted at Little Chute, in 1848, has spread its branches over a large part of Northeastern Wisconsin, and offshoots of it are found in Minnesota, Nebraska, South Dakota, Oregon, and other states.

Father Van den Broek continued to labor with his customary zeal after his return to Little Chute, in 1848, until his death in that town, November 5, 1851, at the age of sixty-eight years. He was succeeded by the Fathers of the Holy Cross, who for many years continued the work of their worthy predecessor, laboring zealously among the Hollanders, French, Irish, and Indian half-breeds of Little Chute and vicinity.

In those days "Franciscus Busch"—now Hollandtown —was in a very primitive state. The writer's home was a log building with a wooden chimney and no floor but the bare ground. The

---

* Rev. Father Godhart, O. S. F., arrived in Hollandtown on the 8th of June, 1848. The following were the first settlers of said town: Henry Gerrits, Albert van den Berg, Jan Verboord, Johannes Tielemans, Martinus Verkuilen. The writer is personally acquainted with all of them. Some of them, perhaps all, came over from Holland with him on the same ship. As Father Godhart was a Franciscan, he made St. Francis of Assisium the Patron-Saint of the church and congregation he was organizing; hence the name, "Franciscus Busch," by which the settlement was known amongst the Hollandish Catholics of that part of the country.

parish church was constructed of hewn logs, and was about 25x45 feet. The men sat on one side and the women on the other. Many came to church in their wooden shoes, and some of the women had their quaint, Hollandish bonnets or caps on, and wore heavy gold earrings hanging down their ears.

The place was attended from Little Chute about one Sunday every month, but, priest or no priest, all the Hollanders would go to church every Sunday and holy day of the year. The venerable Patriarch of the settlement, Van der H., acted as quasi-pastor on all Sundays when there was no Mass. The first thing would be the Stations or the holy Way of the Cross, then the prayers of the Mass in Hollandish. At the Gospel he would read a short, practical sermon from some book, adding occasionally a remark or two of his own, sometimes, too, gravely announcing to the congregation the fact that his sons had shot a deer, that the people might know where to get a good piece of venison for a reasonable consideration.

A sturdy farmer acted as usher and passed round the collection box during service, and every time a copper fell rattling into the box he would say, with his stentorian voice: "God zal't loonen! God zal't loonen! God will reward it! God will reward it!"

Every fourth or fifth Sunday the priest would come from Little Chute to say holy Mass in "Franciscus Busch." There would be a double or triple row of penitents reaching from the door to the altar railing. When a penitent would leave the confessional, sometimes two or three would start on a run, trying to get to the priest first. Had a Protestant seen this performance he would have come to the conclusion that confessing one's sins must not, after all, be such a hard or disagreeable thing, for the people raced, so to say, with each other to get to the priest first.

There were occasional seasons of jollification, for instance, during the Carnival days before Ash Wednesday, and when the "St. Francis Guild" had their shooting day. A bird made of the wood of some tough pine root or some other material would be placed on a high flagstaff or liberty pole and then the aspirants for kingly honors would shoot at the bird until, riddled with dozens of bullets, it would tumble down. The victor would be declared king for the next year and then there would be a good time all around, though we think the king had to pay pretty dearly for his royal dignity, as he would have to get a large silver heart or plate made to wear on grand occasions and was expected to be liberal to the "boys."

Dances were indulged in occasionally, but at rare intervals and only during the daytime. Before dark every young lady was supposed to be at home. Those were days never to be forgotten! Alas, for the simple, innocent pleasures of those bygone days! Our young people of the present day know them not. They are too eager for night dances, theaters, and similar body and soul-destroying amusements.

APPENDIX

UNUM EST NECESSARIUM

(One Thing Is Necessary)

Frederic Baraga,
Bishop

[Translated from Chippewa]

My children, whom I love, I salute you well.
 Our Lord God made all things and he owns all things. As he wills, so all things happen. But especially does he take good care of prayer, his religion, on earth. He, our Lord, brought religion, when he came on earth, when he came to have mercy on us, and he first preached it, when he taught man. But when he wanted to leave the earth, he appointed twelve men, that is, his Apostles, to go about and preach everywhere on earth, and at the same time he told them to appoint everywhere men to preach in their place. And that is what they did, so there were always priests and bishops until this day, and until the end of the world there will always be such everywhere on earth. But he, Jesus, takes good care of religion; for he said that he would take care of it always. He also appoints bishops; it is his will that there shall always be such in his church.
 And so he willed also me to be bishop, although I am unworthy, and he gave me all the Christian Indians here, and he wants me to take good care of them, to exhort them well to always practice their religion, to pray well, to behave well until death. And that is now what I shall do as long as I live.
 But now I begin, now for the first time, as bishop I address you all together, my children, whom I love! Listen to me, obey me, you whom I love! I want to tell you various good things now. Read well this my letter; not only once are you to read it, read it often, and do all things as you are now exhorted (to do). But if one cannot read the letter, do you, who can read it, have compassion on him, read all of it to him, tell him all that is in my letter.

My children, whom I love, keep always well your religion as long as you shall live on earth. You are happy in having taken the true religion. For man lives not only here on earth, he will live forever after his life on earth is at an end, his soul will live forever. But, our souls will be there forever well off if we are Christians, and if at the same time we live a good life. Therefore keep well your religion that you may be happy forever in heaven, after you have been poor on earth. Never mind another religion; it is not the right one. Be thankful to God that you were given the true religion, and always keep it well. And pay no attention to Indian-religion (Indian paganism). It is very foolish, God our Lord hates it (Indian religion). A Christian acts very wrong and offends God much if he still minds or resumes what he renounced when he was baptized.

Keep well your religion, my children; strive after eternal happiness in heaven; for the Lord wants you to be happy forever. All that God did in making heaven and earth and sending his Son on earth, he did all, that thereby his name might be sanctified and men thereby be happy. If man living on earth obeys God, he will receive from Him eternal happiness in heaven, but if he disobeys Him he will not see eternal happiness, but on the contrary, he will suffer, he will suffer greatly, and he will suffer greatly forever.

But this is what you should do, my children, whom I love; always obey well Our Lord God, do as you are exhorted; thereby you will sanctify the name of God and you will make happy your souls. Jesus said: "But one thing is necessary." But what is that? It is that we love and serve God well, and so make happy our souls. No occupation (work) on earth is so important as that, that we serve Our Lord God and so go one day to heaven. That is just for what we are on earth.

Remember, my children, what God has done to give us eternal life in heaven. Namely first, he wants us to live on earth; he gives us religion, the holy sacraments and his grace; he has given even his Son, whom he loves, to die on the cross in order that we may be happy in heaven forever. Truly, God desires much that we be happy, he prizes highly our happiness. He sacrifices his Son to make our souls happy! My children, may you well understand this, so that you too may prize your happiness as God himself prizes it.

This also remember, my children. If you obtain everlasting happiness in heaven, you yourselves shall be happy, you yourselves have all you shall have gained. God will not be more happy, if you are in heaven, and he will not be less happy if you burn in hell. You alone will have what you have gained. May you well understand this.

Understand also this. If you live justly and so gain everlasting happiness in heaven, you have gained all; you are very happy. But if you are bad, and so do not gain everlasting happiness in heaven, you have lost all, you have ruined all, for nothing else will you be happy (i. e. nothing else will make you happy), you will be very miserable forever in hell. Real happiness is not anywhere here on earth, it is only in heaven. But if you do not gain the happiness that is in heaven, you will suffer forever. It is truly sad. Although a person knows that he is to be only a short time here on earth, he knows that real happiness is not on earth, it is only in heaven; he really knows all that; but he does not mind it, and he lives so as if he had to live only here on earth and as if he would entirely cease to exist, when he died on earth. You, my children, do you not act so. Understand how it is; understand for what you are on earth. Only for this are you on earth, to gain eternal happiness in heaven. If you really gain it, you will be very happy, even if you are poor on earth. But if you do not gain it, you will be very miserable, even if you are honored on earth, rich, and well. If one is well off on earth but does not mind eternal life and does not strive after it, he will be there the more sad on that account; for he will think: Truly I have been foolish whilst I lived on earth. I loved only what is on earth, only it I minded. But now I have lost it, but in place of it I have gained everlasting suffering! May you well understand this, my children, may you heed it!

Always truly serve God, whilst you are living a short time on earth; act well as the Lord likes; from your whole heart believe all that Jesus taught us when he came to be a short time on earth; do not reject even one single word. Some things, that Jesus has taught us, are indeed hard (to be comprehended); we would be unable to comprehend them, if we were to employ our reason only; our reason is too weak. But let us use faith; let us strongly believe here on earth all that Jesus said; there in heaven we shall plainly see how all things are. If something is too difficult for you to understand, think immediately: I indeed do not understand this, I do not know how it is, but God, he knows it. Because he said it, therefore I believe. Afterwards in heaven I shall know all.

Keep well, my children, your faith as long as you live, that God may love you, for St Paul says: No one will be loved by God, if he does not believe. And Jesus says: "He who will not believe, shall suffer forever in hell." But do not think that faith alone is sufficient for you to gain eternal life in heaven. Protestants believe that; but it is not so. It is written in God's book (holy Bible): if one believes only, but does not do good at the same time, his faith is dead; it is of no use. Endeavor with all your heart to keep well your faith, your religion, and at the same time do as your religion teaches you. We are told: "Let your faith be living." If we truly try to live so as our religion teaches us then our faith is living. And a living faith will give us everlasting life in heaven.

I exhort you, my children, keep well your faith, your religion; live according as you hear religious preaching; and you will be very happy in the kingdom of God.

And especially do I exhort you to pray every day, for Our Lord Jesus says: "Pray always, never give up." Always pray well every day, morning and evening, occasionally remember God during the day, do never forget him. If a person does not pray in the morning, he will not be very strong to fight the devil. For he, the devil, wants to give us a bad thought, that we first think evil and so also then do evil. If a person prays well, he will strongly resolve, he will really fight the devil, he will not take bad thoughts from him, and he will not be bad. But if he does not pray, he will not make strong resolutions, but soon fall into sin. Do not be slothful in praying, my children; always pray every day, and at the same time reflect on what you are saying when praying. Instruct well your children in religion. A Christian parent does very bad, if he is slothful in teaching religion to his children. Be not slothful; you will suffer for it on judgment-day.

Pray well especially on Sundays; do not work then; and enter the church as often as people enter. Love very much the church, for it is God's house on earth. If a person usually enters well God's house on earth, he will enter God's house in heaven after he has ended his life on earth.

My children, whom I love, respect God well and always, and glorify him from your whole heart. Never show greater respect to any person on earth than you show to God. Respect and glorify Our Lord God more than all people on earth. But it often happens that a person shows greater respect to people on earth than to God. Reflect that you may understand. If a person converses with a priest, he will not speak ill; he will not speak immodestly; he will not say anything bad; for he respects the priest, who is listening to him. But if he converses with another, who is his comrade in impurity, he will talk various foolish, immodest things. Understand! Does he not respect more highly the priest than God? If he is heard by the priest, he does not talk bad, but if he is not heard by him, although he is heard of God, he talks all kinds of bad things. And so he really respects more a person on earth than God. Truly, he acts very wickedly, it is very bad. Hence you are told, my children, respect God more than all the people living on earth. What you would not say, what you would not do before the priest, never say it anywhere else, for Our Lord God is everywhere; he is always looking at you, he is always listening to you.

If a Christian is told: As you respect the priest so should you also respect God, he should immediately think: too little would I respect God; is God not more to be prized than all priests and bishops? Truly, he is more to be prized, yet he is not respected as much as the priest is respected. A person would not talk bad before a priest, but before God he talks bad very much. It is really sad! Do not act so, my children. Respect well and glorify very much Our Lord God. Always remember him; he is everywhere; he sees you always, he hears you always. Do not act wickedly, for the Lord sees you; do not talk wickedly, for the Most-High hears you.

Always obey God well, my children. He is highly worthy; he has created all things and to him belong all things. Obey him well. Christians are told to obey even those who are living on earth, namely, children to obey their parents, and servants to obey their masters. Far more are we exhorted to obey God, for to him we all belong entirely.

God always speaks to us in our hearts; he always tells us that we should hate and shun all that is bad, and on the contrary should do only what is good. If a Christian is inclined to do bad, immediately he is told by God in his heart: don't do that, it is bad, thus he will be told by Him. But if a Christian is inclined to do good, immediately he will be requested by God to do the good. It is thus that God always speaks to us in our hearts. Very happy is the Christian who always listens to God speaking to him.

Again, the Lord speaks to us in sermons. When a Christian listens to a sermon, he really listens to God. Although really the priest preaches, yet he preaches so as Our Lord Jesus preached. And Jesus says: "If one listens to him that preaches, he listens to me myself."

My children, whom I love, obey well the priest's preaching; God you will obey. And as often as you confess, receive well all you are told then, do all well, God speaks to you then.

But especially, my children, love God. If a person loves God well, he will do everything right, he will not do anything bad purposely. We are very justly told that we should love Our Lord God, and Jesus teaches us how we should love him; for he says: "The Lord, thy God, thou shalt love with thy whole heart, and with thy whole soul, and with thy whole mind, and with all thy strength," thus says Jesus. Endeavor, my children, to love him so as Jesus teaches us.

With thy whole heart shalt thou love God, says Jesus. If a person loves God more than all that is on earth, and gives his whole heart to God, such a one loves God with all his heart. If one strongly resolves to avoid sin, and if he would rather wish to be killed than do evil purposely, such a one loves God with his whole soul. And if he always remembers God, just as if he saw him, and so at the same time thinks: I will not speak ill and I will not do evil, for the Lord hears and sees me, such a one loves God with his whole mind. If a Christian very strongly resolves to live well, if he always thinks: May I live well, and at the same time really avoids what is bad as much as he can, such a one loves God with all his strength.

He indeed is happy who really loves God! Well now, my children, always endeavor to love God well. But since you love him, hate on the other hand all sins. Especially reject and hate bad drinking; truly, it is very bad. When a person is drunk, he talks and does various bad things. Hate also adultery and impurity. Fear God, for he always sees us.

My children, whom I love, hate all that is bad, as Our Lord God hates it, but accept, love everything that is good, as God likes; and you will be happy forever in the kingdom of God in heaven.

Amen.

+ FREDERIC,
    Bishop (Great Black-gown).

UNUM EST NECESSARIUM

(One Thing Is Necessary)

FREDERIC BARAGA,
KITCHI-MEKATEWIKWANAIE.

Ninidjanissidog Saiagiinagog, Weweni kid anamikoninim.
Debeniminang Kije-Manito kakina gego o gi-gijiton, kakina gego gaie win o dibendan. Win onendang, mi kakina gego ejiwebadinig. Memindago dash anamiewin, win od ijitwawin o mino ganawendan aking. Win debeniminang o gi-bidon anamiewin gi-bi-ijad aking gi-bi-jaweniminang, win gaie nitam gi-bi-gagikwe, gi-kikinoamawad anishinaben. Api dash jaigwa wi-nagadang aki, o gi-assan midasswi ashi nij ininiwan, mi sa o kikinoamaganan tchi baba-gagikwenid misi aking; bekish gaie o gi-inan tchi assawad misiwe ininiwan meshkwat ge-gagikwenidjin. Mi dash ga-ijitchigewad, mojag dash gi-aiawag mekatewikwanaieg, kitchi-mekatewikwanaieg gaie, binish nongom gijigak; binish dash tchi ishkwa-akiwang mojag ta-aiawag misiwe aking. Win dash Jesus weweni o ganawendan anamiewin; gi-ikito sa tchi ganawendang kaginig. Win gaie od assan kitchi-mekatewikwanaien; win od ineniman tchi aianid od anamiewigamigong.

Mi dash gaie nin gi-inenimid tchi kitchi-mekatewikwanaiewiiân, aiano-apitendagosissiwân; kakina dash nin minig oma anishinaben enamianidjin, nind inenimig dash tchi mino ganawenimagwa, weweni tchi anamiawad, weweni gaie tchi ijiwebisiwad binish tchi ishkwa-bimadisiwad aking. Mi dash iw nongom ge-dodamân ged-ako-bimadisiiân.

Nongom dash nin madjita, nongom nitam, eji-Kitchimekatewikwanaiewiiân, kakina mamawi ki ganoninim, ninidjanissidog saiagiinagog! Pisindawishig, babamitawishig, saiagiinagog! Anotch gego wenijishing ki wi-windamoninim nongom. Weweni wabandamog mandan nin masinaigan, kawin eta abiding ki da-wabandansinawa, sasagwana sa wabandamog; kakina dash dodamog eji-gagikimigoieg nongom. Kishpin dash awiia nissitawinansig masinaigan, mano kinawa nessitawinameg jawenimig, kakina dash agindamawig, kakina windamawig minik eteg oma nin masinaiganing.

Ninidjanissidog saiagiinagog, weweni mojag ganawendamog kid anamiewiniwa ged-ako-bimadisiieg aking. Ki jawendagosim gi-odapinameg gweiakossing anamiewin. Kawin sa oma aking eta bimadisissi anishinabe, kaginig win ta-bimadisi gi-ishkwa-aiad aking, kaginig o tchitchagwan ta-bimadisiwan. Ta-mino-aiawag dash ki tchitchagonanig wedi kagigekamig, kishpin anamiaiang, bekish gaie weweni ijiwebisiiang. Mi dash iw ge-ondji-ganawendameg weweni kid anamiewiniwa, tchi jawendagosiieg kagigekamig gijigong gi-ishkwa-kitimagisiieg aking. Kego wika babamendangegon bakan ijitwawin; kawin gwaiakossesinon. Migwetch inenimig Kije-Manito gi-minigoieg gweiakossing anamiewin, weweni dash ganawendamog kaginig. Kego gaie wika babamendangegon anishinabe-ijitwawin. Memindage gagibadad iw, apitchi dash Kije-Manito Debeniminang o jingendan. Kitchi matchi dodam enamiad, o kitchi-nishkian gaie Kije-Maniton, kishpin keiabi babamendang, gonima gaie neiab gego odapinang minik ga-webinang gi-sigaandasod.

Mino ganawendamog kid anamiewiniwa, ninidjanissidog; kagige jawendagosiwin gijigong wikwatchitog; kid inenimigowa sa Debendjiged tchi jawendagosiieg kagigekamig. Minik ga-dodang Kije-Manito gi-ojitod gi-jig aki gaie, gi-bi-ininajaowad gaie Ogwissan aking, kakina gi-ijitchige tchi ondji kitchitwawendaming od ijinikasowin, anishinabeg dash tchi ondji jawendagosiwad. Kishpin anishinabe bemadisid aking babamitawad Kije-Maniton, o ga-minigon kagige minawanigosiwin gijigong; kishpin dash agonwetawad, kawin o ga-wabandansin kagige minawanigosiwin, meshkwat dash ta-kitimagisi, ta-kithi-kitimagisi, kaginig gaie ta-kitchi-kitimagisi.

Mi dash iw ge-dodameg, ninidjanissidog saiagiinagog; mojag weweni babamitawig Debeniminang Kije-Manito, dodamog eji-gagikimigoieg, mi ima ge-ondji-kitchitwawendameg Kije-Manito od ijinikasowin gaie dash ki tchitchagowag ki ga-jawendagosiawag. Jesus gi-ikito: "Bejigwan iw aiapitchi-kitchi-inabadjitong." Wegonen dash iw? Mi sa tchi sagiang weweni gaie tchi anokitawang Kije-Manito, mi dash tchi jawendagosiangwa ki tchitchagonanig. Kakina anokiwin minik endagog aking kawin apitendagwassinon epitendagwak iw tchi anokitawang Debeniminang Kije-Manito, mi dash ningoting gijigong tchi ijaiang. Mi sa iw gwaiak wendji-aiaiang aking.

Mikwendamog, ninidjanissidog, ga-dodang Kije-Manito tchi mininang kagige bimadisiwin gijigong. Nakawe sa oma aking tchi bimadisiiang kid inenimigonan; ki minigonan anamiewin, kitchi Jawendagosiwinan, o jawendjigewin gaie; tibinawe Ogwissan saiagiadjin o gi-migiwenan tchi nibonid tchibaiatigong, mi sa tchi jawendagosiiang gijigong kagigekamig—Geget Kije-Manito kitchi inendam tchi jawendagosiiang, o kitchi apitendan ki jawendagosiwininan. Ogwissan o pagidinan tchi jawendagosiad ki tchitchagonanin! Apegish, ninidjanissidog, weweni nissitotameg, mi dash gaie kinawa tibishko tchi apitendameg ki jawendagosiwiniwa, win Kije-Manito epitendang.

Ow gaie mikwendamog, ninidjanissidog. Kishpin gashkitamasoieg kagige jawendagosiwin gijigong, kinawa ki ga-jawendagosim, kinawa ki gad-aianawa minik ge-gashkitamasoieg. Kawin Kije-Manito nawatch ta-ondji-jawendagosissi, kishpin kinawa gijigong aiaieg; kawin gaie win awashime pangi ta-jawendagossiessi kishpin kinawa anamakamig danakisoieg. Kinawa sa eta ki gad-aianawa ga-gashkitamasoieg. Apegish weweni nissitotameg.

Ow dash gaie nissitotamog. Kishpin gwaiak bimadisiieg, mi dash gashkitoieg kagige jawendagosiwin gijigong, kakina gego ki gi-gashkitonawa; kid apitchi jawendagosim. Kishpin dash matchi ijiwebisiieg, mi dash gashkitossiweg kagige minawanigosiwin gijigong, kakina gego ki gi-wanitonawa, kakina ki gi-banadjitonawa; kawin bakan gego ki gad-ondji-jawendagosissim, ki ga-kitchi-kitimagisim kagigekamig anamakamig. Kawin oma aking gwaiak jawendagosiwin ningotchi dagossinon, gijigong eta dagomagad. Kishpin dash iw jawendagosiwin gijigong endagog gashkitamasossiweg, mi tchi animisiieg kagigekamig. Geget kashkendagwad! Anawi o kikendan bemadisid wenibik eta tchi aiad oma aking, o kikendan gaie dagossinog aking gwaiak jawendagosiwin, gijigong eta dagomagad. Gwaiak o kikendan kakina iw; kawin dash o babamendansin, mi dash iji bimadisid tibishko enendagosid oma eta aking tchi bimadisid, tchi apitchi ishkwa-aiad dash api nebod aking. Kego kinawa, ninidjanissidog, ijiwebisikegon. Nissitotamog ejiwebak; nissitotamog wendjiaiaieg aking. Mi eta wendji-aiaieg tchi gashkitamasoieg kagige bimadisiwin gijigong. Kishpin geget gashkitimasoieg, ki gad-apitchi-jawendagosim, missawa kitimagisiieg aking. Kishpin dash gashkitamasossiweg, ki ga-kitchi-kitimagisim, missawa kitchiwawisiieg aking, kitchi daniieg, kitchi mino aiaieg gaie. Kishpin awiia mino aiad aking, babamendansig dash kagige bimadisiwin, wikwatchitamasossig gaie, awashime win wedi ta-ondji-kashkendam; ta-inendam sa: Geget nin gi-gagibadis megwa gi-bimadisiiân aking. Mi eta aking endagog nin gi-sagiton, nin gi-babamendan. Nongom dash nin gi-waniton iw, meshkwat dash kagige kotagitowin nin gi-wikwatchitamason! Apegish, ninidjanissidog, weweni nissitotameg, apegish babamendameg!

Gwaiak mojag anokitawig Kije-Manito, wenibik bimadisiieg aking; weweni dodamog eji-minwendang Debendjijed; kakina debwetamog enigokodecieg minik ga-iji-kikinoamonang Jesus, gi-bi-aiad wenibik aking; kego ganage bejig ikitowin webinangegon. Geget anind gagikwewinan sanagadon, ga-iji-kikinoamonang Jesus; kawin ki da-gashkitossimin tchi nissitotamang, kishpin kid inendamowininan eta aioiang; osam jagwadad kid inendamowininan. Debweiendamowin dash aioda; songan kakina debwetanda oma aking minik ga-ikitod Jesus, wedi dash gijigong kakina mijisha ki ga-wabandamin ejiwebak. Kishpin gego osam sanagak tchi nissitotameg, pabige inendamog: Kawin nin nin nissitotansin iw, kawin nin kikendansin ejiwebak, win dash Kije-Manito o kikendan. Win gi-ikitod, mi wendji-debwetamân Panima dash gijigong nin ga-kikendan kakina gego.

Weweni, nissidjanissidog, ganawendamog ki debweiendamowiniwa ged-ako-bimadisiieg, Kije-Manito tchi sagiineg; ikito sa kitchitwa Paul: Kawin awiia o ga-sagiigossin Kije-Maniton, kishpin debweiendansig. Jesus gaie ikito: "Aw ge-debwetansig ta-kagige-kotagendam anamakamig." Kego dash inendaugegon, pijishig debweiendamowin tchi debisseg, ge-ondji-gashkitamassoieg kagige bimadisiwin gijigong. Bakan ejitwadjig o debwetanawa iw; kawin dash awansinon. Ojibiigade Kije-Manito o masinaiganing: Kishpin debweiendang eta awiia, mino dodansig dash bekish, nibomagadini o debweiendamowin, kawin ningot inabadassinini. Enigokodecieg wikwatchitog tchi mino ganawendameg ki debweiendamowiniwa, kid anamiewiniwa; bekish gaie dodamog mojag eji-kikinoamagoieg anamiewin. "Ta-bimadad ki debweiendamowiniwa," kid igomin. Kishpin sa gwaiak wikwatchitoiang tchi iji bimadisiiang eji-kikinoamagoiang anamiewin, mi tchi bimadak ki debweiendamowininan. Bemadak dash debweiendamowin ki ga-minigomin kagige bimadisiwin gijigong.

Kid iji gagikimininim dash, ninidjanissidog, weweni

ganawendamog ki debwciendamowiniwa, kid anamiewiniwa; ijiwebisig eji-nondameg anamic-gagikwewin; ki gakitchi-jawendagosim dash Kije-Manito od ogimawiwining.

Menindage dash gaie kid iji gagikimininim tchi anamiaieg endasso-gijigak; ikito sa Debeniminang Jesus: "Mojag anamiag, kego wika anijitangegon." Mojag sa, endasso-gijigak, kigijeb onagoshig gaie weweni anamiag; nonda-gijig dash aiapi mikwenimig Kije-Manito, kego wika wanenimakegon. Kishpin awiia anamiassig kigijeb, kawin gwetch ta-mashkawisissi tchi miganad matchi maniton. Mojag sa win matchi manito ki wi-minigonan matchi inendamowin, tchi matchi inendamang nitam, mi dash gaie tchi matchi dodamang. Kishpin awiia weweni anamiad, ta-mashkawendam, gwaiak o ga-miganan matchi maniton, kawin o gad-odapinamawassin matchi inendamowin, kawin gaie ta-matchi-dodansi. Kishpin dash anamiassig, kawin gwetch ta-mashkawendansi, waiba dash ta-pagishin batadowining. Kego kitimikegon tchi anamiaieg, ninidjanissidog; mojag endasso-gijigak anamiag, bekish gaie nanagatawendamog ekitoicg anamiaieg. Kinidjanissiwag gaie weweni kikinoamawig anamiewin. Kitchi matchi dodam enamiad wenidjanissid, kishpin kitimid tchi kikinoamawad onidjanissan anamiewin. Kego kitimikegon, ki gad-animisim dibakonige-gijigak.

Memindage dash enamiegijigakin weweni anamiag; kego anokikegon iwapi; anamiewigamigong gaie pindigeg dassing-pandigengin. Sagitog apitchi anamiewigamig, mi sa Kije-Manito o wigiwam aking. Kishpin awiia weweni paiapindigedjin Kije-Manito o wigiwaming aking, ta-pindigana Kije-Manito o wigiwaming gijigong gi-ishkwabimadisid ogidakamig.

Ninidjanissidog saiagiinagog, weweni gaie mojag manadjiig Kije-Manito, kitchitwawenimig gaie enigokodeeieg. Kego wika awiia bemadisid aking awashime manadjiakegon eji-manadjieg Kije-Manito. Awashime manadjiig, awashime kitchitwawenimig Debeniminang Kije-Manito, kakina dash bemadisidjig aking. Sasagwana dash iw ijiwebad, awiia awashime manadjiad bemadisinidjin aking, Kije-Maniton dash. Nanagatawendamog mi dash tchi nissitotameg. Kishkin sa gaganonad mekatewikwanaien kawin ta-matchi-gigitossi, kawin gaie ta-winitagosissi, kawin sa gego maianadadinig ta-ikitossi; o manadjian sa mekatewikwanaien pesindagodjin. Kishpin dash bekanisinidjin wadji-gagibadisinidjin gaganonad, anotch gego gegibadadinig, beshigwadadinig ta-ikito. Nissitotamog! Kawin na win awashime o manadjiassin mekatewikwanaien, ejimanadjiad Kije-Maniton? Kishpin mekatewikwanaien nondagod, kawin matchi gijwessi; kishpin dash nondagossig anawi dash Kije-Maniton nondagod, anotch gego matchi ikito. Mi dash geget bemadisinidjin aking awashime o manadjian, Kije-Maniton dash. Geget kitchi matchi dodam, kitchi bata-ijiwebad iw. Mi dash wendji-igoieg, ninidjanissidog, awashime manadjiig Kije-Manito, kakina dash bemadisidjig aking. Minik ge-wi-ikitossiweg, ge-widodansiweg gaie enassamid mekatewikwanaie, kego iw wika ningotchi ikitokegon; misi sa aia Debeniminang Kije-Manito; kaginig ki ganawabamigowa, ki pisindagowa gaie.

 Kishpin enamiad enind: Eji-manadjiad mekatewikwanaie, ki da-iji-manadjia Kije-Manito; pabige da-inendam: Osam pangi nin da-manadjia; kawin na Kije-Manito awashime apitendagosissi, kakina mekatewikwanaieg, Kitchi-mekatewikwanaieg gaie? Geget awashime apitendagosi, kawin dash ganage iw minik manadjiassi, mekatewikwanaie eji-manadjiind Enassaminid mekatewikwanaien kawin ta-matchi-ikitossi, enassaminid dash Kije-Maniton kitchi nibiwa ta-matchi-ikito. Geget kashkendagwad! Kego ijiwebisikegon, ninidjanissidog. Weweni manadjiig, apitchi kitchitwawenimig Debeniminang Kije-Manito. Mojag mikwenimig, misi sa aia; kaginig ki wabamigowa, apine ki nondagowa. Kego matchi dodangegon, ki wabamigowa sa Debendjiged; kego matchi ikitokegon, ki nondagowa sa Maiamawi-Ishpendagosid.

Weweni gaie mojag, nindjanissidog, babamitawig Kije-Manito. Apitchi win apitendagosi; kakina gego win o gigijiton, kakina gego gaie od apitchi dibendan. Weweni babamitawig. Potch bemadisinidjin aking tchi babamitawawad, inawag enamiadjig, mi sa abinodjiiag tchi babamitawawad onigiigowan, enonindjig dash tchi babamitawawad debenimigowadjin. Awashime dash kid iji gagikimigomin tchi babamitawang Kije-Manito, win sa kakina kid apitchi dibenimigonan.

Kije-Manito mojag ki gaganonigonan kideinang, mojag ki gaganonigonan tchi jingendamang tchi ojindamang gaie kakina maianadak, meshkwat dash wenijishing eta tchi dodamang. Kishpin enamiad wi-matchi-dodang, pabige Kije-Maniton o ga-ganonigon odeing: Kego dodangen, manadad, o gad-igon. Kishpin dash wi-mino-dodang enamiad, pabige Kije-Maniton o ga-gagansomigon tchi mino dodang. Mi sa eji-ganoninang mojag Kije-Manito kideinang. Kitchi jawendagosi dash enamiad pesindawad mojag Kije-Maniton, eji-ganonigodjin.

Minawa dash ki gaganonigonan Debendjiged gagikwewining. Api enamiad pesindang anamie-gagikwewin, gwaiak Kije-Maniton o pisindawan. Anawi geget mekatewikwanaie gagikwe; tibishko dash gagikwe, Jesus Debeniminang ga-iji-gagikwed. Ikito gaie Jesus: "Kishpin awiia pisindawad gegikwenidjin, nin igo nin pisindog."

Ninidjanissidog saiagiinagog, weweni babamitawig mekatewikwanaieg gegikwedjig; Kije-Manito ki ga-babamitawawa. Dassing gaie waiebinigeiegon, weweni odapinamog minik egoieg iwapi, weweni kakina dodamog, Kije-Manito iwapi ki ganonigowa.

Memindage dash, ninidjanissidog, sagiig Kije-Manito. Kishpin awiia weweni sagiad Kije-Maniton kakina gego gwaiak dodam, kawin gego ondjita matchi dodansi. Apitchi dash gwaiak kid igomin tchi sagiang Debeniminang Kije-Manito, ki kikinoamagonan gaie Jesus ged-iji-sagiang; ikito sa: "Debendjiged ki Kije-Manitom ki ga-sagia kakina kideing, kakina gaie ki tchitchagong, kakina gaie kid inendamowining, kakina gaie ki mashkawisiwining;" mi ekitod Jesus. Wikwatchitog dash, ninidjanissidog, gwaiak tchi sagieg, eji-kikinoamonang Jesus.

Kakina kideing ki ga-sagia Kije-Manito, ikito Jesus. Kishpin sa awiia awashime sagiad Kije-Maniton kakina dash aking endagog, kakina gaie ode minad Kije-Maniton, mi aw saiagiad kakina odeing. Kishpin awiia apitchi songendang tchi ojindang batadowin, awashime gaie minwendang tchi nissind, iw dash tchi bata-dodang ondjita, mi aw saiagiad Kije-Maniton kakina o tchitchagwang. Kishpin gaie mikwenimad mojag Kije-Maniton, tibishko sa go wabamâd, mi dash bekish inendang: Kawin nin wi-matchi-ikitossi, kawin gaie nin wi-matchi-dodansi, nin nondag sa Debendjiged, nin wabamig gaie, mi aw saiagiad Kije-Maniton kakina od inendamowining. Kishpin dash enamiad apitchi mashkawendang tchi mino ijiwebisid; apegish mino ijiwebisiiân, mojag inendang, bekish gaie geget ojindang maianadak minik eji-gashkitod, mi aw saiagiad Kije-Maniton kakina o mashkawisiwining.

Geget jawendagosi gwaiak saiagiad Kije-Maniton! Mano sa, ninidjanissidog, mojag wikwatchitog weweni tchi sagieg. Epitch dash sagieg, meshkwat jingendamog kakina batadowinan. Memindage webinamog, jingendamog gaie matchi nimikwewin; apitchi geget manadad. Anotch bata-ikito, bata-dodam gaie awiia ga-giwashkwebidjin. Ojindamog gaie kakina bishigwadisiwin, gagibadisiwin. Gossig Kije-Manito, ki wabamigonan sa mojag.

Ninidjamissidog saiagiinagog, kakina sa go maianadak jingendamog, eji-jingendang Debeniminang Kije-Manito; kakina dash meno-ijiwebak odapinamog, minwendamog, eji-minwendang Kije-Manito; ki ga-jawendagosim dash kagigekamig Kije-Manito od ogimawiwining gijigong.

Mi ge-ing.

+ Frederic,
Kitchi-Mekatewikwanaie.

A FEW PECULIARITIES OF THE CHIPPEWA LANGUAGE.

Long words, *e. g.*—
    Mitchikanakobidjigan—fence.
    Kijabikisigan—stove.
    Debeniminang—Our Lord.

No gender; win means he, she, it; this explains the frequent mistakes made by Indians when speaking English, using the pronoun he promiscuously for all genders, *e. g., he* is a good woman.

All nouns are classed under two heads, animate, and inanimate; the former embrace all objects living, or grammatically animate, *e. g.*—
    Inini—man.
    Ikwe—woman.
    Kwiwisens—boy.
    Ikwesens—girl.
    Akik—kettle (gram. animate).
    Tashkibodjigan—sawmill (gram. animate).

Inanimate are all lifeless objects, either naturally or grammatically so considered, *e. g.*—
    Kitigan—a field.
    Kijewadisiwin—kindness.
    Wiiawima—body (gram. inanimate).
    Nishkinjig—my eye (gram. inanimate).

Few real adjectives; mostly adjective-verbs, *e. g.*—
    Kitchi—great, much.
    Pangi—small, little.
    Mino—good.

Matchi—bad.
Onijishin—it is good.
Manadad—it is bad.

Two-fold form for expressing first person plural: we, us, our, *e. g.*—

Ninawind—we, our (person addressed *not* included).
Kinawind—we, our (person addressed included).

This dual form of "we" is observed in all nouns with the possessive pronoun "our;" also in all moods and tenses of active verbs.

Verbs have (a) a positive and a negative form; (b) a dubitative or historical form, *e. g.*—

Giwe—he goes home.
Kawin giwessi—he does not go home.
Giwedog—perhaps he goes home.
Kawin giwessidog—perhaps he does not go home.

There are nine conjugations. Each conjugation has a positive and a dubitative form, which each have again an affirmative and a negative form, making thus, we might say, thirty-six conjugations, *e. g.*—

a, e, i, o—wab*i*—he sees (1st conjugation),
am—inend*am*—he thinks (2d conjugation),
in, on—dagwish*in*—he arrives (3d conjugation),
a—wabam*a*—he is seen (4th conjugation),
enan—od atage*nan*—he gambles for it (5th conjugation),
an—o waband*an*—he sees it (6th conjugation),
a, e, i, o—wabandjigad*e*—it is seen (7th conjugation),
ad—manad*ad*—it is bad (8th conjugation),
an, in—onijish*in*—it is good (9th conjugation).

Each of these verbs have a negative form; that makes eighteen conjugational forms. Then each of them has an affirmative dubitative form; that makes twenty-seven conjugational forms, besides we have a negative dubitative form, which makes nine additional forms; in all thirty-six conjugational forms. Now, each of these thirty-six forms have their moods, tenses, etc., making it necessary to learn by heart, perhaps about 3,000 or 4,000 different terminations; truly, an herculean task.

The Chippewa language is infinitely rich in verbs, is a language of verbs, everything almost is drawn within the magical circle of the verb. Nouns are transformed into verbs, e. g.—

 Inini—man; ininiwi—he is a man.
 Ikwe—woman; ikwewi—she is a woman.

Adjectives are made into verbs, e. g.—
 Kijewadisi—he is kind.
 Sassagisi—he is stingy.

Numerals are changed into verbs, e. g.—
 Bejig—one; bejigo—he is one.
 Nij—two; nijiwag—they are two.

Adverbs are changed into verbs, e. g.—
 Mamandadodam—he acts wonderfully.
 Minotchige—he does well.

Prepositions are expressed mostly verbially, e. g.—
 Nin ganona—I speak *to* him.
 Nin ganodamawa—I speak *for* him.

The Chippewa language is the most regular, systematic language the writer knows of—all goes by rule—scarcely any exceptions, and all terminations follow certain systematic rules. It is more regular or systematic than either Greek or Latin.

DIFFERENT CLASSES OF VERBS.

1. Reciprocal verbs. They show a reaction of the subject on itself; *e. g.,* nin nondas=I hear myself.

2. Communicative verbs. They show a mutual action of two or more subjects upon each other, or simply mutual action; *e. g.*, nin wabandimin=we see each other;—nimiidiwag=they dance together.
3. Personifying verbs. They represent inanimate things as doing actions of an animate being; *e. g.*, o nissigon ishkotewabo=fire-water kills him.
4. Reproaching verbs. They show that their subjects have some reproachful habit or quality; *e. g.*, niba= he sleeps;—nibashki=he sleeps too much.
5. Substantive verbs. They are derived from substantives; *e. g.*, inini=man;—ininiwi=he is a man.
6. Adjective verbs. They describe the quality, etc., of their subjects; *e. g.*, John songisi=John is strong.
7. Numeral verbs. They indicate the number of their subjects, *e. g.*, nissiwan aw ikwe ogwissan=the sons of that woman are three=she has three sons.
8. Adverbial verbs. They indicate how their subjects act; *e. g.*, winigijwe=he speaks immodestly.
9. Abundance verbs. They signify an abundance of what they express; *e. g.*, sagime=a mosquito;—sagimeka=there are many mosquitos.
10. Possessive verbs. They indicate ownership or possession; *e. g.*, mokoman=a knife;—omokomani=he has a knife.
11. Working verbs. They signify the doing of a work or making something; *e. g.*, mikana=a road;—mikanake=he makes a road.
12. Feigning verbs. They designate feigning or dissimulation; *e. g.*, mawi=he weeps;—mawikaso=he feigns weeping.
13. Causing verbs. They indicate that the subject of such a verb causes some animate being to do something; *e. g.*, anoki=he works;—nind anokia=I make him work.
14. Frequentative verbs. They indicate a repetition or

frequent doing of a certain act; *e. g.*, nin pakiteowa= I strike him;—nin papakiteowa=I strike him repeatedly.
15. Pitying verbs. They are used to manifest pity; *e. g.*, bakade=he is hungry;—bakadeshi=he is worthy of pity, being so hungry.
16. Compound verbs. They are formed of two or more radical syllables, to which a verbal termination is annexed; *e. g.*, minwadjimo=he tells, relates, something good, from;—min=good; and adjim refers to relating news, stories; "o" is the verbal termination.

From one and the same root can be formed several classes of verbs; *e. g.*, wab, refers to seeing:
 nin wab=I see.
 " wabama=I see him, her.
 " wabandan=I see it.
 " wabandis=I see myself.
 " wabandimin=we see each other.
 " wabandamawa=I see his, *e. g.*, book.
 " wabange=I look on.
 " wabangen=I gaze at it.

Formation of verbs from one or more root-syllables; *e. g.*, misk, refers to red.
 miskobag=red leaf.
 miskobaga=there are red leaves on a tree.
 miskokinje=red-hot coals.
 miskonigade=it is painted red.
 miskosi=it is red (some animate object).
 miskotchiss=red turnip; *i. e.*, beet-root.
 miskondibe=his head is red.
 miskwa=it is red (some inanimate object).
 miskwabigan=red clay.
 miskwabigin=red flannel.
 miskwabik=red metal; *i. e.*, copper.
 miskwabo=red fluid; *i. e.*, chocolate.
 miskwadissige=he dyes red.

In Baraga's dictionary seventy-five words are given, compounded with the radical syllable, misk=red. Many more might be added. The same is true of countless other radical syllables, referring to color, warmth, coldness, goodness, badness, etc. Hence, the Chippewa language has a superabundance of words to express every kind of action and condition of being. It contains thousands of words not found in our modern languages and which we must give in a circumlocutory form. It is highly expressive and euphonic. As a rule, after every consonant follows a vowel. Only such consonants are combined in a syllable as are easily pronounced together. It is very plastic and new words could be coined from existing rootsyllables. In one word, it is a beautiful, regular, expressive language, rich in words.

HISTORICAL AND BIOGRAPHICAL NOTES

An Interesting Article on the Life and Labors of Bishop Baraga, Copied by "The L'Anse Sentinel" from the "Gladstone Delta"

The editor of the "L'Anse Sentinel" remarks:
"The following, pertaining to Father Baraga, is taken from the 'Gladstone Delta' of the 18th ult., but the name of the writer was not given.

"Baraga county, next door to Houghton, was named after Bishop Baraga, of recent missionary memory. This reverend name is most intimately connected with the present mining epoch of our peninsula. It is, in fact, the chief link that connects our present with our past in the annals of the missions, and in the story, yet untold, of the steps taken by the pioneers of this period to ascertain and make known the wonderful mineral and forest resources of this strip of 'Superior.'

"The Rt. Rev. Father Baraga was born in Austria in 1797. His family was an old and highly respected one, and relatives of Marquette's first bishop still reside in Treffen Castle, the place of his birth. He studied at the University of Vienna, and soon showed that unusual combination of a great love of study and meditation and a decided penchant for action. His sole aim at college was to direct all the energies of a strong mind and an ardent zeal to the struggle against error, doubt, and ignorance. One whose sole passions were thus to instruct, to alleviate misery, and to bestow blessings to the full extent of his abilities and his means, could be nothing but a missionary, and this zeal for the conversion of souls, together with a great linguistic gift, and an iron constitution, drew the student naturally to the field where the obstacles were the greatest and where his uncommon powers would be afforded full scope.

"With the departure from the peninsula of the Jesuit Fathers and their Indian neophytes, fleeing before the conquering

Iroquois, and the destruction by fire of the mission-buildings to save them from desecration, the first chapter in the story of the conversion of the Indian was closed. Young Father Baraga determined to open another chapter in this story and he came to America for the purpose of fitting himself for the Indian missions, leaving his bright prospects of advancement and success in his own land. He remained at the Cincinnati seminary long enough to become acquainted with 'the lay of the land' and the rudiments of the languages he must perforce use in his new field, and there began the work of bringing the savages under the influence of the Gospel—a work carried on by Marquette's successors up to sixty years before the 'disruption.'

"He began his labors at Arbre Croche (now Harbor Springs) in the lower peninsula. The mission became the rallying point of the Ottawas for many miles around. In thirty months he had mastered the language, published prayer and hymn books, and established the mission on a solid footing, and, securing a successor, he proceeded to the Grand, where he found the Ottawas fast becoming 'good' Indians, owing to the demoralizing influence exercised over them by bad whites in their neighborhood. Here he had hard work and still wonderful success. Having established this mission also on a permanent footing, he left it to other hands, and started on a long and toilsome journey to the Ojibways, who had settled near La Pointe or Ashland. It took Father Baraga three weeks to make the trip from the 'Soo' to Ashland. Eight years were spent here, during which his extraordinary capacity for learning languages—he spoke seven or eight modern tongues fluently—enabled him to compile and print a Biblical history and books of prayer for his flock. Again having settled his charge, he accepted an invitation of the Keweenaw band and founded his large mission near L'Anse. Here his task was to reform the Ojibwa, ruined by traders' fire-water, and to induce them to learn tillage and farming. His own lack of the knowledge of farming impeded this part of his work, and it was only after a successor came to him, who knew farming, that the settlement really became stable. Father Baraga bought this land himself and gave each Indian a tract and a good log house. He still worked at his prayer books and Biblical history, and here completed his magnum opus, the great Otchipwe grammar and dictionary, the first ever published, and the standard work to this day.

"In all his missions, Father Baraga was the instructor of his flock in the three 'R's as well as in the religious sphere. His two trips to Europe were made to collect for his missions, and he never returned empty-handed.

"The founding of the L'Anse mission was almost contemporary with the opening of the copper mines and this meant more work for the Father, as he was the only priest near. For eight years he visited the copper-country from L'Anse, traveling by canoe or on snowshoes, through trackless forests, carrying his altar-furniture with him. S. B. Ely, son of the iron country pioneer, speaks of the welcome extended the missionary by everybody on his arrival at a mining camp, and of the pleasure of listening to his incisive addresses in the three languages spoken by his followers.

"Father Baraga's hope was to die amongst his Indians; but when the peninsula became a diocese he naturally became its first bishop, over flocks mostly gathered by himself.

"Four years before his lamented death, he was exposed to rain and cold during an eight days' boat journey, and from the effects of this exposure he never fully recovered. During his last illness, his condition was, of course, an object of great concern to all who knew and admired the man for his self-denial and self-sacrifice. The Mr. Ely already quoted called and tried to insist on the bishop's taking some comfort during his illness; but the bishop simply replied that he was better housed than his Master was, and he would have no improvement. A big-hearted Irish woman, to whom Mr. Ely complained, stormed her way into the presence of her beloved pastor, and insisted on leaving a sum of money for some decent nourishment. The bishop, fast failing, tried to make his attendant understand he wanted something, and at length Father Terhorst, his successor at the mission, asked if it was the money, and the bishop nodded. The money was brought, and the dying apostle signed to the Father to take it for the mission, and thus satisfied, he died absolutely penniless, his large patrimony and revenues all having gone to charitable and religious purposes.

"Among the pioneer men of renown of the peninsula, the name of Baraga deserves special remembrance. A truly apostolic man, who counted neither ease nor life itself dear, so that he might faithfully follow his Divine Master in the care of souls. His work and his memory will remain with us forever."

A LAKE SUPERIOR HISTORICAL SKETCH

Massacre of a Dacota Peace Delegation at Sault Ste. Marie, Upper Michigan, in the Spring of 1674.

The present year must not be allowed to pass without one of our periodicals offering to the friends of domestic history the details of an event which, just two hundred years ago, caused considerable emotion among the savage inhabitants of Upper Michigan, and proved a turning point in their progress toward civilization.

Under the heading, "Massacre of Ten Nadouessi Ambassadors and Twenty Other Indians at the House of Ste. Marie du Sault," Father Dablon, then superior of the Jesuit missions in "New France" relates as follows (the words between crotchets being our own):

"The Nadouessi (Xadowessi, Dacota or Sioux), an extremely numerous and eminently warlike tribe, were the common enemies of all those Indians comprised under the name of Outaoucas (Ottawas) or Upper Algonquins. They carried their arms even far to the north, and waging war against the Killistinons (Kinoshtino or Cree Indians) who inhabited those parts, made themselves everywhere formidable by their boldness, their numbers, and their skill in combat, in which, besides other weapons, they make use of stone knives. They always carry two of them, one sticking in the belt, the other suspended from their hairs. However, a war party from Ste. Marie du Sault having surprised them in their own country, and captured eighty of them, obliged them to sue for peace. Consequently they sent ten of their bravest men to the Sault to negotiate. They were received with joy as soon as the object of their mission became known. Only the Killistinons, who had lately arrived, and others called Missisaquis (from the north shore of Lake Huron, near the mouth of the Missisaguing), not only showed dissatisfaction, but also resolved to prevent the conclusion of the peace, and even to murder those ten envoys.

This necessitated their being admitted to the French house built for the use of the missionaries.

Father Gabriel Druillettes profited of this opportunity to instruct them in the mysteries of our faith. They listened with so much docility that, at the end of the instruction, they went on their knees, and, folding their hands, called upon Jesus, the master of life, just now made known to them.

In the meantime the Indians flocked to the French house, one party to make peace with the Nadouessi, the other to hinder its conclusion. Every possible precaution was taken to prevent those that entered from bringing along arms; but, as the crowd was extremely large, five or six slipped in without being deprived of their knives. It was one of the latter, a Killistinon, who gave rise to the ensuing broil; for approaching a Nadouessi, knife in hand, he said, "Thou art afraid," and threatened to strike him. The Nadouessi, without being startled, replied, in a haughty tone and with undaunted mien, "If thou believest that I tremble, strike straight at the heart;" and, feeling himself stricken, cried out to those of his nation, "Brethren, they kill us." At these words those men, fired with the desire of revenge, and withal very vigorous and tall, rose up and struck with their knives at every Indian present, without discriminating between Killistinons and Sauteux (Ojibwas), in the belief that they had all equally conspired to murder them. It was not very difficult for them to make, in a short time, a great carnage, considering that they found the crowd, who expected nothing less than such an attack, unprovided with arms.

The Kilistinon who had begun the quarrel was one of the first that was pierced, and, with several others, thrown dead on the place (inside the house). Then the Nadouessi placed themselves at the door to guard it, and to stab those that would fly; but as they remarked that several had already escaped and gone in search of arms, they shut the door, determined to defend themselves until the last breath. In fact, they posted themselves at the windows, and having by chance found some guns and ammunition, they used them to keep at bay their enemies, who attempted to burn them by burning the house in which they were locked up. They killed some who went too near; but, in spite of all their efforts, some others approached the house and having piled up against it straw and birch bark canoes, set fire to them, and thus soon placed the Nadouessi in danger of being consumed by the flames. This obliged them to give a last proof of their courage; for all ten of them came forth with the arms in their hands, and, with incredible promptness, threw themselves into a neighboring palisade hut, from which they kept up the defense, and continued to kill as long as their ammunition lasted; but this failing, they were overwhelmed by the great numbers of Indians, who fired at them, and all were killed on the spot, together with two women who had accompanied them. A third one was spared, having been discovered to be only their slave, and an Algonquin by nation.

During all that tumult and massacre, the fire which the Indians had set to the house of the missionaries grew rapidly, and in spite of all that could be done, it soon consumed the building, which was only of wood, and placed the new chapel, which stood not far from it, in great danger. However, it was saved by great exertions. It was a frightful sight to see so many dead and so much blood running within so narrow a space, and to hear the shrieks of those who excited each other to the combat, and the groans of the wounded, amidst the confusion of an incensed rabble that hardly knew what they were doing.

Our Indians bewailed forty of their own, partly dead, partly wounded, among whom were some of their chiefs and foremost men. The missionaries on their part had great cause for grief, losing so soon the hope which the peace just about to be concluded had made them conceive, of going to preach the gospel to the Nadouessi. Besides, they saw themselves abandoned by the Indians of the country, who, fearing lest the Nadouessi, on seeing their men loiter, might suspect their fate and come to revenge their dead, dispersed and left the missionaries exposed to the fury of their enemies. Moreover, besides the daily danger in which they were of being massacred, not only at the Sault, but also in all other places where they were on mission, the progress which the gospel began to make through them was greatly checked for some time.

God has not failed to derive glory from those misfortunes, and to make use of them, both for the salvation of some souls, and for the showing forth of the extraordinary efforts of His omnipotence; for several of those that had been dangerously wounded asked for baptism, and having received it, were healed.

At a meeting of the Ottawas of Arbre Croche, held at Mackinac on January 14, 1829, to consult with their Representative in Congress, one of their head-chiefs spoke as follows:

"My Father! The headmen of the people, who are here assembled around you, want to open their hearts to you. They have seen here and in Arbre Croche their bishop (Rt. Rev. Edward Fenwick, of Cincinnati). He has given them a Catholic priest to reside with them. The chief men here before your eyes request you to help them in this important undertaking. My Father! We let you know that pious women are with us under the supervision of our priest, to teach our women and children to write and work, as also to do the will of the Great Spirit. My Father! We have at present a chapel and a school in bad condition and we would thank you very much if you would help us to fix them up better. Father! We hope that the President of the United States will help us. Moreover, the here assembled headmen of our nation request me to tell you that they are firmly resolved to sell no more land to the government of the United States. My Father! If any of our red brethren be foolish enough to be willing to sell their lands, we on our part will never sell ours.

Should, however, any of us make such an offering to you to cede their lands, we pray you to pay no attention to them and to drive them away from your door."

NOTES.

In his work, "History of the Ottawa and Chippewa Indians of Michigan," by A. J. Blackbird, the author asserts on page 42 that his brother, William Macatebinessi —Blackbird—was assassinated at Rome whilst studying at college. As this assertion seemed to be entirely groundless, as the young man was universally beloved and respected by his fellow students, the writer wrote to the Propaganda at Rome inquiring for particulars of the death of said Wm. Macatebinessi. Under date of February 18, 1896, the following answer was sent to him:

"Rev. Father —I received your letter of the 25th of last month, in which you ask for particulars in regard to the death of young William Macatebinessi, of Arbre Croche (Michigan), United States of America, who died at Rome June 25, 1833, whilst he was a student of the Urban College. After opportune inquiries it was ascertained that there is only a letter extant by which the notification of his death was communicated to Rt. Rev. Frederic Rese, Bishop of Detroit.

"Herewith I send you an abstract of said letter, which is conformable to the original.

"A. ARCHB. SARISSERN, Secrt."

The following is a true copy of the letter sent to Bishop Rese:

ROME July 13, 1833.

"*Most Illustrious and Most Rev. Lord*—I am sorry to notify Your Lordship of the loss sustained a few days ago of the good young man, William Macatebinessi of the Ottawa tribe, native of Arbre Croche, who was sent by you to Rome, was received among the alumni of this Urban College. Some time ago he complained of an internal pain, as a consequence, as he said, of an accident that happened to him in America, when a wheel passed over his breast. On the morning of the 25th of last June the rupture of an artery just in the aforesaid part of the body reduced him within a short time to the extreme and took him from this life. I give this notice to Your Lordship for your information, and that with due circumspection you may communicate it to the young man's parents.

"In the meantime I pray God that He may long preserve and prosper you.

"To Mons. Frederic Rese, Bishop of Detroit."

Total contributed by Leopoldine Society towards American dioceses from 1829 to 1846:

Baltimore	43,000 fl.
Philadelphia	23,500 fl.
Richmond	12,000 fl.
Charleston	61,000 fl.
Pittsburg	13,000 fl.
Cincinnati	115,495 fl.
Louisville	20,000 fl.
St. Louis	44,000 fl.
Little Rock	20,000 fl.
Chicago	9,000 fl.
Vincennes	57,800 fl.
Detroit	46,000 fl.
Milwaukee	8,500 fl.
Boston	16,000 fl.
Hartford	9,000 fl.
New York	28,500 fl.
Mobile	32,000 fl.
New Orleans	10,000 fl.
Natchez	12,000 fl.
Nashville	18,000 fl.
Dubuque	23,000 fl.
Kingston (Upper Canada)	6,000 fl.
Vicariate of Texas	7,000 fl.
Trinidad (Antilles)	4,000 fl.
	638,795 fl.
For Jesuit and Redemptionist Missions and individual Missionaries	48,418 fl.
	687,213 fl.

Pamphlet 19—1846.

Amounts of money contributed by the Leopoldine Society of Vienna, Austria, for the Catholic missions and dioceses of the United States and Canada:

1830,	"	"	"	34,420 fl.
1831,	"	"	"	15,786 fl.
1832,	"	"	"	47,000 fl.
1833,	"	"	"	53,276 fl.
1834,	"	"	"	32,000 fl.
1835,	"	"	"	30,620 fl.
1836,	"	"	"	34,200 fl.
1837,	"	"	"	40,840 fl.
1838,	"	"	"	48,071 fl.
1839,	"	"	"	36,400 fl.
1840,	"	"	"	37,264 fl.
1841,	"	"	"	47,720 fl.
1842,	"	"	"	39,061 fl.
1843,	"	"	"	37,523 fl.
1844,	"	"	"	41,233 fl.
1845,	"	"	"	44,696 fl.
1846,	"	"	"	43,970 fl.
1850,	"	"	"	43,301 fl.
1850,	(no contributions during 1847-'48-'49)			35,523 fl.
1851,	"	"	"	38,291 fl.
1852,	"	"	"	36,314 fl.
1853,	"	"	"	31,906 fl.
1854,	"	"	"	14,704 fl.
1855,	"	"	"	47,250 fl.
1856,	"	"	"	51,755 fl.
1857,	"	"	"	12,457 fl.
1858,	"	"	"	47,773 fl.
1859,	"	"	"	2,445 fl.
1860,	"	"	"	56,531 fl.
1861,	"	"	"	36,400 fl.
1862,	"	"	"	19,000 fl.
1863,	"	"	"	19,000 fl.
1864,	"	"	"	26,070 fl.
1865,	"	"	"	21,990 fl.
1866,	"	"	"	18,156 fl.
1867,	"	"	"	21,139 fl.

1,244,085 fl.

Notes taken from the Baptismal Register of Harbor Springs, formerly called Arbre Croche, by Bishop Baraga.

"On the 28th day of May, in the year 1831, the Most Illustrious and Reverend Edward Dominic Fenwick, Bishop of Cincinnati, brought me, the undersigned, a secular priest born in Illyria, a province of the Austrian Empire, here to perform the office of a missionary among the Indians of this region. He himself, the Most Illustrious and Rev. Bishop, remained here from the above-named day until the 3d of June, in which time he baptized two adults and twenty-six children.

"My predecessor, Rev. Peter John Dejean, a French secular priest, whom Very Bishop Fenwick sent here in the year 1829, baptized very many adults and children, being the first missionary staying and residing here, but he had no Baptismal Register; for which reason this begins only from the 29th day of May, 1831,

"Note. By the name: Arbre Croche is meant in this book the village here, where the Indians built the parochial church of St. Peter and the dwelling-house of the missionary. By the name Old Arbre Croche are meant, however, all the dwelling-places of the Indians from the place of the parochial church to the chapel of St. Paul, which dwelling-places are comprehended in the Indian name: Wagana-kisi."

"Frederic Baraga,
Priest."

"The church of Arbre Croche, lately built by the Indians alone, was lawfully blessed by me, the undersigned, missionary of this place, on the 25th of May, 1851, in virtue of episcopal delegation, in honor of Our Lord Jesus Christ as youth in the temple."

"Francis Pierz,
Roman Catholic Missionary."

Wherefore this mission shall be called hereafter 'Missio S. S. Adolescentiae Jesu."

+ Frederic,
Bishop."

Notes in regard to the origin of the La Pointe Mission, by Rev. Frederic Baraga, copied from the Baptismal Register of said mission.

"The undersigned missionary laid the first foundation of the church of this mission immediately after his arrival, i. e., on the 3d day of August, in the year 1835, and on the 9th day of the same month he celebrated Mass in this church for the first time, although it was still in an imperfect state. However, in order to finish this church and to firmly establish the whole mission, he left on the 29th of September, in the year 1836, and went to Europe, where through the contributions of pious benefactors he received funds to finish the church and pastoral residence of this mission. On the 8th of October, 1837, he returned from his journey to this mission, and after many labors and tribulations he completed this church and the annexed parsonage in the month of August, 1838.

"On the 2d of September of the same year, which was the first Sunday of September, this church was dedicated to God under the name of St. Joseph. On the 7th of the same month, our bishop, Rt. Rev. Frederic Rese, came to this mission for the first time, and on the 9th he confirmed one hundred and twelve neophytes and Canadians.

"This mission began on the 28th day of July, in the year 1835. For on that day the undersigned missionary, born in Illyria, a province of Austria, landed at this island, which they call St. Magdalen Island, sometimes also St Michael's Island, which prior to that day the 'beautiful feet of those evangelizing peace, evangelizing good things' had never yet trodden.

"The undersigned missionary found here some Canadian Catholics in the employ of the traders and a few Catholic half-Indians, who had been baptized in the Mackinac mission; all the rest 'sat yet in the darkness and shadow of death.'

"The missionary was received with great joy on the island. Some immediately offered him their children to be baptized and themselves to be instructed in the Catholic religion, which was done and daily was increased 'the multitude of those who believed in the Lord' who after the necessary instruction were regenerated by Baptism unto life eternal.

"In the year 1841 the undersigned missionary caused a new church to be constructed (the old one being demolished, which had been too badly constructed), and at the same time he built it there where it was nearer to the greater part of the Catholic congregation. In the month of July of the same year this church was finished, and on the first Sunday of August the undersigned missionary dedicated it to God under the name of the same saint, St. Joseph.

"On the 4th of October, 1843, the undersigned missionary departed from this mission in order to found, with the help of God, a new mission at L'Anse with the approbation of the Most Illustrious and Rev. Bishop Peter Paul Lefevre. On the 27th of July, in the year 1844, he again returned to this mission, not, indeed, to reside there permanently, but to announce during some weeks the word of God to this congregation and to administer to them the holy sacraments. On the 14th of August of the same year the Most Illustrious and Rev. John Martin Henni, first bishop of Milwaukee, canonically visited this church, and on the 16th day of the same month he confirmed one hundred and twenty-two Indians and Canadians. On the 3d of September of the same year the undersigned missionary returned again to his new mission, and only on the 28th of June, of the year 1845, did he visit this mission of St. Joseph again to exercise the care of souls for some time."

"FREDERIC BARAGA,
Missionary."

Baraga's youngest sister, Antonia, was born in the castle of Treffen February 4, 1803. On May 31, 1824, she married Felix von Hoeffern, son of Heribert Hoeffern von Salfeld, Knight of the Holy Roman Empire. F. Baraga himself performed the marriage-ceremony. His address to the married couple is still preserved by Rev. Joseph Benkovic. The writer is under great obligations to him for many interesting particulars concerning Baraga's parentage, early life, and labors in St. Martin and Metlika.

Felix von Hoeffern died childless. After Baraga's departure for the Indian mission, Antonia entered a convent in Paris to prepare herself, especially by the study of the French language, to be of service to her Rev. brother in the Indian missionary field. When Baraga was on his way returning to America in 1837 she joined him at Havre de Grace and came with him to La Pointe.

In a letter which she wrote in Mackinac on the 8th of September, 1837, to her sister Amalia, she, says that it was her intention to serve the Indians as teacher for their children and to instruct the Indian women in washing, cooking, and general housework. Speaking of her Reverend brother, she says:

"Our dear Frederic is so universally known that every one speaks of him and knows something to tell about him. I have heard that supernatural things are ascribed to him, things which only a special favorite of God can perform. Every Indian is acquainted with him. In Mackinac were a great many Indians, when they sold their land; they came from five different provinces (states); and everyone wished to speak with him and to see him. I have visited many of them in their cabins. When they heard that I was a sister of Baraga, they all shook hands with me, laughed, and gazed at me as long as I was in the hut, which I always left with tears in my eyes."

Some of the old Indians still remember Baraga's sister and how she kept house for her saintly brother. The climate of Lake Superior being too severe for her frail constitution, she was obliged to leave La Pointe. As to her subsequent career and the time, place and manner of her death, the writer could find nothing reliable.

The following acrosticon was composed by Father Baraga at his sister Antonia's departure from La Pointe, where she had kept house for him two years after his return from Europe in 1837. It was given us by Rev. Ant. J. Rezek, of Houghton, Mich., to whom we are very thankful for this proof of kind interest in our work.

>Angel Boshji naj te vedno spremlja,
>Nie verlasse Dich des Himmels Schutz,
>Tuta sis et salva in aeternum,
>Observez toujours la loi de Dieu
>Nuovo sempre sia il Vostro zelo
>Imitate the Saviour's holy life,
>Angwamisin, mino bimadisin.

Mission zum hl. Joseph in N. Amerika, im Juli, 1839.
>Dein Dich ewig liebender Bruder,
>>FRIEDRICH BARAGA, m. pr.

In the parish records of L'Anse we find the following entries:

"The undersigned missionary laid the foundation of this mission, with the help of God, on the 24th of May, in the year 1843, on which day he arrived here and remained twenty days among the Indians of this place. Some believed the word immediately and were baptized after the necessary instruction. But others said: 'If that missionary comes again, not to remain only for a few days, but to stay constantly with us, then we, too, will receive the doctrine, which he preaches, and Baptism. Wherefore he came again on the 24th of October of the same year and immediately began to prepare whatever things were deemed necessary for the firm establishment of the mission. With the special help of God the poor missionary was enabled to erect the church with adjoining parsonage, also fifteen small houses for the Indian people. Afterwards he built seven others. On the 16th day of June, 1844, which was the third (Sunday) after Pentecost, the Most Holy Sacrifice of the Mass was offered up for the first time in this church. But, of course, the church was then not finished. But when it was completed to some degree of perfection, the undersigned missionary solemnly dedicated it on the first Sunday of the same year to God Almighty under the Name of His Beloved Son, Jesus, who with the Father and the Holy Ghost is God forever, and at the same time he beseeched Him that He might mercifully deign to grant that whosoever should enter this church, asking benefits from Him in the Name of Jesus, might receive what he faithfully asked, so that he might experience how truly the Truth itself spoke, saying: 'If you ask anything of the Father in My name He will grant it to you.'

"On the 16th of July, 1846, the Rt. Rev. and Most Illustrious Peter Paul Lefevre, bishop of Zela and administrator of the diocese of Detroit, visited this mission canonically and on the following Sunday confirmed eighty-six Indians in this church of the Holy Name of Jesus."

"Frederic Baraga,
Missionary."

"On the 25th of September, 1854, the Most Illustrious and Rt. Rev. Baraga, bishop of Amyzonia, and vicar-apostolic of Upper Michigan, canonically visited for the first time this mission, founded by him, and on the following Sunday, which was the first Sunday of October, he confirmed forty-three Indians and half-breeds."

PRIESTS STATIONED AT DETROIT, MICH.

P. Constantin de la Halle	1703-1706
P. Dominicus de la Marche	1706-1707
Cherubin Denieau	1707-1714
Hiacynth Pelifresne	1715-1718
Calvarin, vicar-general of the mission of Tamaruas	1718-1719
Jean Mercier	1718-1719
D. Thaumur	1718-1719
Pantoin Delins	1719-1723
P. Bonaventura	1722-1735
P. Daniel	1735-1738
P. de la Richardin, on Bois-Blanc Island	1738-1754
P. Bonaventura, again, in Detroit	1738-1754
Simple Boquet	1754-1782
Payet	1782-1786
Pierre Frichette	1786-1796
Michael Levadon	1796-1802
Gabriel Richard	1789-1832

For a list of the priests who have officiated at Mackinac since 1671-1850, see "Annals of Mackinac."

Inscription on the tombstone of an Indian half-breed, found near the church of La Pointe, Wis.:

To the Memory
of
Abraham Beaulieu,
Born 15th of September, 1822,
Accidentally Shot
4th April, 1844.
As a Mark of Affection
From His Brother.

Short biographical sketch of Vincent Roy, lately of Superior, Wis.

HON. VINCENT ROY

Before ending this work on Bishop Baraga, we wish to add a short biography of the best Indian of the Northwest, Vincent Roy. He was born in or about the year 1824, below Fort Francis, on the banks of Rainy Lake river, on the American side, at the junction of Rainy Lake and Little Forks rivers. His grandfather came to that place about the year 1810 and opened a farm. He had about fifty acres under cultivation and raised a great deal of wheat, barley, potatoes, rootabagas, and other vegetables. He used to trade with the Bois Fort band of Chippewa Indians, going to Mackinac every year to dispose of his furs and to buy goods for next year's trade.

In 1839 he took his sons, Vincent and Peter, to La Pointe, Wis., where Father Baraga was laboring at that time. After his sister, Antonia de Hoeffern, had left in July, 1830, Father Baraga was accustomed to take his meals at Mrs. Lacomb's house. She was an aunt of Vincent Roy, being his father's sister. It was but natural that young Vincent should feel drawn to the great missionary and become very intimate with him. During all his life Mr. Roy entertained a boundless love and veneration for Bishop Baraga.

Vincent Roy engaged in the fur-trade to within a few years before his death. He had a trading-post at Vermillion Lake, Minn., and a store at Superior. It took almost two weeks to convey his goods and supplies to his trading-post. His Indian and half-breed packers were obliged to go up the St. Louis river, which is full of rapids, at which portages had to be made, that is, canoes and goods had to be carried past the rapids to smooth water, or overland from river to river.

The first priest that ever preached the Gospel to the Bois Fort Indians at Vermillion Lake, was P. Odoric Derenthal, O. F. M., about the year 1883. He was then stationed at Superior, whence he attended the Indian missions of Fond du Lac, Papashkominitigong near Cloquet, Barnum, Kettle River, Sand Lake—all in Minnesota; besides Bashaw, Spirit Lake, Yellow Lake, Mouth of Yellow River, Trade Lake, and other places in Wisconsin.

Some twenty years ago large deposits of iron ore were discovered near Vermillion Lake, and soon rich iron mines were opened on the Mesaba Range. This caused an influx of whites into that country and Tower, Virginia City, and other mining towns were started. A large number of Catholics, many of them Slavonians, work in those mines; they are under the pastoral care of Very Rev. Joseph Buh, vicar-general of the diocese of Duluth.

Vincent Roy married a daughter of Antoine Cournoyer, a French-Canadian, a good man and a fervent Catholic. We think his wife's name was Elizabeth. She resided at Superior, Wis., with Mary, her sister, the widow of Charles Roy, deceased, a brother of Vincent Roy. Vincent and his wife lived in true conjugal love, peace, and happiness. He was a model husband, kind, affectionate, industrious and saving. The writer was acquainted with him for many years and he can bear testimony to Mr. Roy's noble, Christian, gentlemanly behavior. He never drank a drop of intoxicating liquor, neither did he smoke, chew, or snuff. He was most scrupulously clean, neat and well-clad at all times. *He was a perfect gentleman.*

Mr. Roy's house was a model home. Although he had but little white blood in his veins, his father being a half-breed, partly French, partly Indian, and his mother, to the best of our belief, a full-blood Chippewa, Vincent Roy had adopted in his home life and general deportment the manners and refinement of modern civilization.

The writer does not know the exact time of Vincent Roy's coming to Superior; he was, no doubt, one of the oldest settlers there, probably arriving there prior to 1854. His fur-trade and other business, especially the rise of real estate values following the founding of West Superior, brought him considerable wealth, which he used very largely for the benefit of his less fortunate countrymen and the good of religion. Liberality is a characteristic virtue of the Chippewas and Vincent Roy possessed and exercised this virtue in a very remarkable degree. "A friend in need, a friend indeed." Many a poor Indian found in Mr. Roy such a friend. No other Chippewa in the Lake Superior country was as liberal and generous towards the needy and suffering as Mr. Roy. When Ireland was suffering a dreadful famine about the year 1880, little Superior, with its forty-five Catholic families, of whom scarcely a dozen were whites, contributed about Three Hundred and Seventy-five Dollars towards alleviating the poor people of said island and of the above-given amount Mr. Roy contributed a large sum.

Vincent Roy was a born leader among his people. His words and examples exercised an ennobling, elevating, Christianizing influence. His worthy wife nobly seconded her husband in all his works of charity and zeal. Their house was the home of priests and missionaries, where they always received a cordial welcome and were treated with the greatest kindness and respect. For four years the writer was an almost daily visitor at Mr. Roy's house, which he frequented so often in order to study the Chippewa language under so able a master, for Mr. Roy spoke and wrote Chippewa, English, and French fluently.

Mr. Roy's marriage was not blessed with children, but this very circumstance was made use of by Divine Providence to make him the father and friend of his poor countrymen. He was the mainstay of the small congregation of Superior, which for many years consisted chiefly of Indians and half-breeds. Mr. Roy contributed most liberally for church purposes and the support of the pastor. In fact, in every good work he was a leader, sparing neither time nor money.

Vincent Roy was also a practical Catholic, assisting at holy Mass every Sunday, and often on week-day. Every day, summer and winter, sunshine or rain, someone of his house would attend Mass, most generally his worthy wife, her sister Mary, and their pious mother, Mrs. Cournoyer. Mr. Roy was a frequent receiver of the holy Sacraments and during the latter years of his life he would go to holy Communion every week. He prayed a great deal at home and read spiritual books, of which he had quite a number, with great relish.

Vincent Roy was a model citizen, taking a lively interest in all political and social questions, especially those that regarded his state and city. He was pure and modest in his deportment, and the tongue of scandal never blackened his fair name. He was frank and outspoken in his opinions, but without being haughty or overbearing. He was of a joyful, pleasant disposition, and keenly relished a good joke.

To sum up, Mr. Roy was nature's nobleman, a true Christian, a patriotic citizen, "the uncrowned king" of the Lake Superior Chippewas. His memory is held in benediction by all who knew him. He died about three or four years ago in Superior, leaving his affectionate wife and a host of friends to mourn his loss.

Novena in Honor of Bishop Baraga

Bishop Baraga's cause for canonization was opened in 1952. He was declared Venerable by Pope Benedict XVI in 2012. To help further Bishop Baraga's cause, please report any graces or favors received through his intercession to: Bishop Baraga Association, 347 Rock St., Marquette, MI 49855, (906) 227-9117, bishopbaraga@dioceseofmarquette.org dioceseofmarquette.org/bishopbaragaassociation

For a free ebook and novena visit caritaspublishing.com

Novena for private devotion.

Nihil Obstat:
Rev. Timothy Ferguson, JCL, STL
Censor Librorum

Imprimatur:
✠ Most Rev. John F. Doerfler, STD, JCL
Bishop of Marquette
June 22, 2016

Opening Prayer
To be recited each day.

O God, I adore you with all my heart. I thank you for the life and holiness of your servant, Bishop Baraga. In imitation of your Son he poured himself out in your service, bringing your merciful love and saving Gospel to the peoples of the Great Lakes. Through his union with you in powerful intercession, please grant the favor I beseech you, (name intention) so that your glory may be manifested and we shall praise you forever, through Christ Our Lord. Amen.

First Day

Jesus said, "Whatever you ask in my name, I will do, so that the Father may be glorified in the Son. If you ask anything of me in my name, I will do it." John 14:13-14

"Prayer is the principal channel through which the grace of God flows into our hearts." -Bishop Frederic Baraga

Our Father... Hail Mary... Glory be...
Jesus, I trust in you. For love of you I forgive everyone who has ever harmed me.
Bishop Baraga, please pray for my intention.

Closing prayer on last page...

Second Day

Jesus said, "Ask and it will be given to you; seek and you will find; knock and the door will be opened to you. For everyone who asks, receives; and the one who seeks, finds; and to the one who knocks, the door will be opened. Which one of you would hand his son a stone when he asks for a loaf of bread, or a snake when he asks for a fish? If you then, who are wicked, know how to give good gifts to your children, how much more will your heavenly Father give good things to those who ask him." Matthew 7:7-11

"Truly, God desires much that we be happy, he prizes highly our happiness. He sacrifices his Son to make our souls happy! My children, may you well understand this, so that you too may prize your happiness as God himself prizes it." -Bishop Frederic Baraga

Our Father... Hail Mary... Glory be...
Jesus, I trust in you. For love of you I forgive everyone who has ever harmed me.
Bishop Baraga, please pray for my intention.

Closing prayer...

Third Day

Jesus said, "Heaven and earth will pass away, but my words will not pass away." Luke 21:33

"Keep well your religion, my children; strive after eternal happiness in heaven; for the Lord wants you to be happy forever. All that God did in making heaven and earth and sending his Son on earth, he did all, that thereby his name might be sanctified and men thereby be happy." -Bishop Frederic Baraga

Our Father... Hail Mary... Glory be...
Jesus, I trust in you. For love of you I forgive everyone who has ever harmed me.
Bishop Baraga, please pray for my intention.

Closing prayer ...

Fourth Day

"Since we have 'a great priest over the house of God,' let us approach with a sincere heart and in absolute trust, with our hearts sprinkled clean from an evil conscience and our bodies washed in pure water. Let us hold unwaveringly to our confession that gives us hope, for he who made the promise is trustworthy." Hebrews 10:21-23

"Jesus said: 'But one thing is necessary.' But what is that? It is that we love and serve God well, and so make happy our souls." -Bishop Frederic Baraga

Our Father... Hail Mary... Glory be...
Jesus, I trust in you. For love of you I forgive everyone who has ever harmed me.
Bishop Baraga, please pray for my intention.

Closing prayer ...

Fifth Day

"A woman suffering hemorrhages for twelve years came up behind Jesus and touched the tassel on his cloak. She said to herself, 'If only I can touch his cloak, I shall be cured.' Jesus turned around and saw her, and said, 'Courage, daughter! Your faith has saved you.' And from that hour the woman was cured." Matthew 9:20-22

"Always truly serve God, whilst you are living a short time on earth; act well as the Lord likes; from your whole heart believe all that Jesus taught us when he came to be a short time on earth; do not reject even one single word." -Bishop Frederic Baraga

Our Father... Hail Mary... Glory be...
Jesus, I trust in you. For love of you I forgive everyone who has ever harmed me.
Bishop Baraga, please pray for my intention.

Closing prayer ...

Sixth Day

"Now as Jesus approached Jericho a blind man was sitting by the roadside begging, and hearing a crowd going by, he inquired what was happening. They told him, 'Jesus of Nazareth is passing by.' He shouted, 'Jesus, Son of David, have pity on me!' The people walking in front rebuked him, telling him to be silent, but he kept calling out all the more, 'Son of David, have pity on me!' Then Jesus stopped and ordered that he be brought to him; and when he came near, Jesus asked him, 'What do you want me to do for you?' He replied, 'Lord, please let me see.' Jesus told him, 'Have sight; your faith has saved you.' He immediately received his sight and followed him, giving glory to God." Luke 18:35-43

"No occupation (work) on earth is so important as that we serve Our Lord God and so go one day to heaven. That is just for what we are on earth." -Bishop Frederic Baraga

Our Father... Hail Mary... Glory be...
Jesus, I trust in you. For love of you I forgive everyone who has ever harmed me.
Bishop Baraga, please pray for my intention.

Closing prayer ...

Seventh Day

Jesus said, "Suppose one of you has a friend to whom he goes at midnight and says, 'Friend, lend me three loaves of bread, for a friend of mine has arrived at my house from a journey and I have nothing to offer him,' and he says in reply from within, 'Do not bother me; the door has already been locked and my children and I are already in bed. I cannot get up to give you anything.' I tell you, if he does not get up to give him the loaves because of their friendship, he will get up to give him whatever he needs because of his persistence." Luke 11:5-8

"Do not be slothful in praying, my children; always pray every day, and at the same time reflect on what you are saying when praying." -Bishop Frederic Baraga

Our Father... Hail Mary... Glory be...
Jesus, I trust in you. For love of you I forgive everyone who has ever harmed me.
Bishop Baraga, please pray for my intention.

Closing prayer ...

Eighth Day

"Jesus withdrew to the region of Tyre and Sidon. And behold, a Canaanite woman of that district came and called out, 'Have pity on me, Lord, Son of David! My daughter is tormented by a demon.' But he did not say a word in answer to her. His disciples came and asked him, 'Send her away, for she keeps calling out after us.' He said in reply, 'I was sent only to the lost sheep of the house of Israel.' But the woman came and did him homage, saying, 'Lord, help me.' He said in reply, 'It is not right to take the food of the children and throw it to the dogs.' She said, 'Please, Lord, for even the dogs eat the scraps that fall from the table of their masters.' Then Jesus said to her in reply, 'O woman, great is your faith! Let it be done for you as you wish.' And her daughter was healed from that hour." Matthew 15:21-28

"My children, whom I love, respect God well and always, and glorify him from your whole heart... Make a firm resolution never to forget the presence of God: to look at Him constantly with eyes of faith and to behave in His presence." -Bishop Frederic Baraga

Our Father... Hail Mary... Glory be...
Jesus, I trust in you. For love of you I forgive everyone who has ever harmed me.
Bishop Baraga, please pray for my intention.

Closing prayer ...

Ninth Day

"As Jesus passed by he saw a man blind from birth. His disciples asked him, 'Rabbi, who sinned, this man or his parents, that he was born blind?' Jesus answered, 'Neither he nor his parents sinned; it is so that the works of God might be made visible through him. We have to do the works of the one who sent me while it is day. Night is coming when no one can work. While I am in the world, I am the light of the world.' When he had said this, he spat on the ground and made clay with the saliva, and smeared the clay on his eyes, and said to him, 'Go wash in the Pool of Siloam' (which means Sent). So he went and washed, and came back able to see.'" John 9:1-7

"Our Lord God made all things and he owns all things. As he wills, so all things happen." -Bishop Frederic Baraga

Our Father... Hail Mary... Glory be...
Jesus, I trust in you. For love of you I forgive everyone who has ever harmed me.
Bishop Baraga, please pray for my intention.
Closing prayer ...

Closing Prayer

To be recited each day.

Lord, I thank you for all the graces received through the intercession of Bishop Baraga by this novena. You are the Almighty Lord, who knows all things and who 'does whatever he wills, in heaven, on earth, in the seas' (Ps 135:6). I trust in your care, ever solicitous and full of loving-kindness, and so I commend my petition and myself to you, body, soul, and spirit, without reserve and with boundless confidence, to do with as you will. Amen.

Caritas Publishing brings you spiritual
riches of the Holy Roman Catholic Tradition
at the most affordable prices possible.
caritaspublishing.com

Made in United States
Cleveland, OH
14 July 2025